WHEN
ETERNITIES
MET

WHEN ETERNITIES MET

A True Story of Terror, Mutiny, Loss, and Love
in a Disremembered Second World War

MATT ROHDE

Publisher's Cataloging-in-Publication Data

Names: Rohde, Matt.
Title: When eternities met : a true story of terror, mutiny, loss and love
in a disremembered Second World War / Matt Rohde.
Description: First edition. | [Union Bridge, Maryland] : Pencil and Barn, [2017] |
Includes bibliographical references and index.
Identifiers: LCCN 2016956758 | ISBN 978-0-9980626-0-0 |
ISBN978-0-9980626-1-7 (ebook)
Subjects: LCSH: World War, 1939-1945--Personal narratives, Ukrainian. |
World War, 1939-1945--Personal narratives, American. | World War, 1939-1945--History. |
Mutiny--Ukraine--History--20th century. | Massacres--Poland--Świnoujście.
Classification: LCC D811.A2 R64 2016 (print) | LCC D811.A2 (ebook) |
DDC 940.54/81--dc23

First Edition published in the United States by Pencil and Barn
Copy Editing: Erin Cusick
Indexing: Connie Binder
Proofreading: Barbie Halaby
Cover photograph: personal wartime collection of Boyd Rohde
Images of newspaper front pages: courtesy of the *Wisconsin State Journal* and
Beaver Dam Daily Citizen
Image of Simon Doillon: collection of Pierre Bertin
Image of Simon Doillon mourning card: courtesy of Jean-Claude Grandhay
Other illustrations: images from author's family collection, US Army, and
US National Archives and Records Administration

For C

AML

Two paths meet here; no one has yet followed either to its end. This long lane stretches back for an eternity. And the long lane out there, that is another eternity. They contradict each other, these paths; they offend each other face to face; and it is here at this gateway that they come together.

The name of the gateway is inscribed above: 'Moment.'
—— Nietzsche, *Thus Spoke Zarathustra*

We ask for long life, but 'tis deep life, or grand moments that signify.
—— Emerson, *Society and Solitude*

This is a work of nonfiction. Anything presented as a quotation, including conversation, is taken verbatim from either a document or a personal interview. A reference to something seen, heard, or thought by a character either has a document behind it or a personal interview, as do references to weather conditions.

CONTENTS

1939

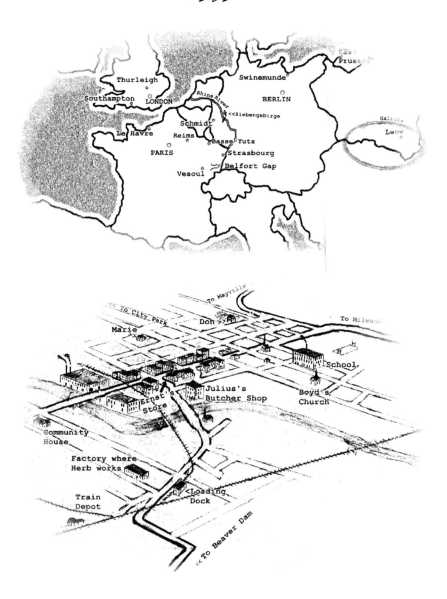

1944

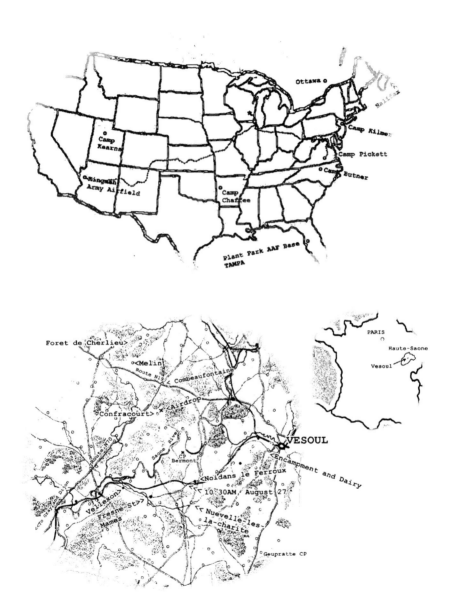

Death and the Strong Force of Fate Are Waiting

For all its voracious reach, it was a short war.

Living through it, the normal human continuum of experience and time was warped. Each year was an era unto itself. A few weeks could stand alone as an entire age. The stretch of a day carried its own full history. Any duration of time pointing forward was beyond calculation.

From afar, a grand sweep of the Second World War can be conjured. An obvious unfolding appears with clarity, particularly for those confident in their learned vision and received responsibility for determinations of proper apportionment.

From within, life during the war was little more than a rolling series of passages and spasms, each often absurdly disjointed from the next.

Physics tells us, as the philosophers once did, that the past, though fixed, and the future, though yet to be, are inextricably implicit in the present as equals. We reside in the arrogance of the now, in an age where moments are collected rather than occupied. Forgotten is that the immediate is always weighted down with conceit, disguising its own burdens and needs through a satisfying elevation that allows for incautious scribes of heroes, strategies, and lessons.

The arc of narrative can deceive. An individual life careens from one switchback to another, a trek of fits and starts, through shadows and fog, quite unlike the grand and determined themes we prefer our histories to expound.

For each, and for all, it is the largest moments on the path that provide breadth and direction, a deep-water steering unknowable in the disorientation of the instant, as the forces of chance and necessity surge all around.

Such moments are innermost, and can never be left behind. They remain as a powerful directional force even when willfully kept out of one's own internal reach for many years, if not a lifetime.

Especially so, in the wake of a war that remains beyond comprehension.

Part One

DESCENT

1939–1943

CHAPTER ONE

Julius

Sunday, February 16, 1997

BOYD OFTEN HAD himself a good laugh after the new funeral home was built on the western edge of town, where it shared a large parking lot with a liquor store and doctor's office. One-stop shopping, he liked to say.

His death earlier in the week had been neither sudden nor unexpected, a welcome end to a slow slide after the lung cancer diagnosis the previous June, just after his seventy-fourth birthday. There were few signs of grief among those gathered that afternoon. Some of those arriving were smiling as they stamped the snow off their feet, offering suggestions of the choice words Boyd would have used about the bitter cold.

A fresh overnight snowfall combined with blinding sunshine and a sharp north wind to induce immediate tears and a headache for anyone venturing out. For those already inside, each visitor entering through the front door was announced by a dazzling shroud of light and a rude blast of frigid air that caused heads to automatically turn and look.

So it was that almost everyone in the room found themselves squinting at the bent-over figure as he struggled through the doorway, shooing away assistance. Conversations came to a halt with the recognition that it was Julius Brown, who had turned one hundred years old the previous November.

All eyes watched him maneuver two canes as he started to make his way toward Marie, standing with her adult children in front of her late husband's coffin. With both trembling hands in a tight grip, skin stretched shiny and pale, one cane would jerk ahead, then the other. Then a small shuffle forward of each leg.

* * *

Julius was sobbing. Few things deliver a jolt as the sight of such anguish in one so ancient.

He paid no attention to the large drop of water teetering off the end of his nose. Straining and wobbling, he inched his way toward Marie. Each step was a separate drama.

Julius was saying something. He repeated it over and over. Only as he drew near to her did the words become clear.

"The boys are together now."

"Boyd's with Don now. The boys are together."

* * *

He ignored more offers of assistance as he stood in front of Marie, thin strands of dark hair slicked back and his thick black rectangular glasses not quite straight. Julius then continued down the receiving line and was hugged by Marie's daughter. She was the child of his son, Don. Boyd had raised her as his own.

Julius lurched on and came to the youngest son of Marie and Boyd. He was the one they had given the middle name Brown, standing there next to the youngest daughter of Myroslaw, another boy of the war no longer among the living. She greeted Julius.

* * *

There is no word in the English language for the sensation of being in the presence of the last few ripples against the shore, the unseen impact far away and long before. Transfixed at the sight of Julius, most in the room did not know they were witness to the final juncture of five lifetime paths. Each improbable course toward that very moment had been set decades before, by a few singular wartime events.

CHAPTER TWO

A Place Far Away

Friday, September 1, 1939

To consider life in the final days of the summer of 1939 is to look upon a distant and alien age, its waning operatic soul belonging to the previous century.

Time and distance were still laced together as a force of nature that framed human consciousness to a depth that today can barely be imagined, their gradual surrender to technology having only begun.

Europe was still the colossal presence in the world. America's slightly upward-looking gaze was not much different than a hundred years before. The great empire of Victoria lumbered on, continuing to bind its sons to exile, while plainly a relic that belonged to the days of wooden sailing ships.

The Great War had done nothing to resolve seething tensions surrounding notions of collective identity and the zero-sum nationalism that had broken through the surface, a gift from the Romantic period. It blended all too well with a peculiar alchemy devoted to ethnography and something vague called "race." More recently, a plague of well-bred fecklessness had further stirred old Continental hatreds that, though gilded in polite and civilized ways, had no bottom.

As for daily life, on both sides of the Atlantic it was formalities and prescribed rites that governed, providing millions with a predetermined direction in life while justifying hierarchies that not only sustained all manner of differentiation but allowed for a civil turn of the head away from any resulting inconvenience, or worse.

* * *

Boyd's mother was always up before first light. Since the move into town a few years before, there were no more chickens to let out or cows to milk. But Lylle would be forever synchronized to the hours of the farm.

Not Boyd. He had never minded doing farm chores as a younger boy, and he would always love working outdoors. Getting up early was another matter.

On Friday morning he came downstairs with a purpose. Only one thing was on his mind: getting to football practice on time.

The early-morning air was already sultry, the temperature heading toward ninety degrees. His mother was in the kitchen. Lylle was a tiny woman, her frail appearance contradicted by an unrestrained gumption and irrepressible energy. That summer she had been working odd hours at the canning factory to pick up some extra money. It would end soon, as the corn pack was about done.

Boyd knew his mother was quite attached to the social aspect of canning factory work. Sitting alongside a few other ladies as the cobs of corn went by, she could talk away an entire shift. It bothered him that his mother worked, and that it was manual labor. His parents were doing everything they could to send his sister, Blossom, to the Wisconsin Conservatory of Music in Milwaukee. She was two years older than Boyd, a gifted piano player and musician with a song-filled personality to match. By her early teenage years she was giving piano lessons around town.

* * *

Boyd would ride his bicycle the five blocks to school, although some days he would get a ride from his best friend, Don. He and Brownie had been pals since grade school, and they shared an intense love of baseball and football—the only two sports that counted for anything.

Both boys were the only sons of straight-ahead men of limited formal education who had a penchant for taking things apart and fixing them, and who had been raised in German-speaking homes by hard-driving immigrant fathers. Don's father, Julius, a foreman at the same small factory where Boyd's father, Herb, worked, had begun making plans to open up a meat locker and retail shop in the old three-story stone building that stood next to the river, a block from Main Street.

Don never seemed to be too far away from another classmate, Marie, although it had been more flirting than anything else. When she was younger, Marie had loved playing baseball with all the boys, and had been a friend of Boyd's since grade school. A few of their high school classmates suspected that Boyd carried a silent crush on Marie, making that judgment from the way he sometimes looked at her. Nothing ever came of it.

Marie's childhood was well dressed, her family insulated from the devastation of the Depression, which had battered the families of both Don and Boyd. Her father, Ernst, ran a dry goods store, a Main Street fixture since the early years of the century. Like Julius and Herb, he was the son of a headstrong German immigrant. Ernst had recently been following the news out of the Pacific, and had begun to buy as many pairs of galoshes and other rubber footwear as he could get his hands on. He would put most of them into the store's basement for storage. Some people thought he was crazy.

As teenagers, the lives of Boyd, Don, and Marie were already well defined by a generational exuberance over modernity as an unquestionable force of good. In their formative years they had been firsthand witnesses to technology removing many hardships of day-to-day life, forever tipping the scale considerably away from negative aspects of such advancements.

They were four years old when their town's Main Street was paved for the first time. During their preteen years, life introduced, for them and for families they knew, the new everyday presence of miracles like electrical lights and appliances, flush toilets, and the magical thrill of news, sports, and music coming from the big cities right through the air into their own homes.

All three grew up in households where, juxtaposed among such sweeping changes, an array of irksome cultural rites and strictures had lingered after coming from the old country. They were ready, if not eager, to cast such things aside. A quiet but deep social chasm would always exist between them and their parents, the cultural separation far more fundamental than any so-called generation gap of decades later.

* * *

The town was all.

Boyd, Don, and Marie grew up in a once-common self-contained American village existence now extinct. At the time, their town was one of more than four hundred in the state with a population of less than three thousand, most of them drawing a full-blooded identity from a high school, a few policemen, a newspaper, a range of independent local businesses, some surrounding small farms, and a factory or two. They were places with names like Hustisford, Fox Lake, Waupun, and Mayville. In some ways the latter was almost a twin of their town. Mayville was barely five miles away and with a few hundred more people. But it was a much different community, including a brawniness that reflected the particular mix of its local ingredients. Twelve miles to the west was Beaver Dam, considered a small city with just over ten thousand people, along with fifteen factories, two hospitals, a daily newspaper, and a radio station.

Their town's dense social fabric was bound together in large part by its newspaper, one of more than three hundred rural weeklies then in operation throughout the state. That week's edition included items about local events ("31 Gridders Start Drills!" according to the front page), some syndicated analysis of world news ("New Crisis Looms as Germany and Poland Mobilize Troops"), a novel serialization (*The Dim Lantern*, by Temple Bailey), several recipes, and some seasonal tips for the household and farm. Inside there was news of Marie's attendance, along with Boyd's sister, Blossom, at a bridal shower where there had been a "treasure hunt for the bride to be culminated with the finding of the gift of a breakfast set of dishes." The weekly listing of social activities as submitted by local residents featured fifty-eight brief items, including news that Mrs. Roy Kuhn of Waupun had spent Tuesday in town at the home of her parents, Mr. and Mrs. Erdman who lived on Walnut Street, and that Miss Esther Simon had visited her relatives in Milwaukee the previous weekend.

Across the river from the newspaper office was the maroon brick Catholic church. Ernst's father had come from the Catholic south of Germany, and his mother's family from the Protestant north. Their marriage had caused a temporary falling-out between Ernst's father and a priest, which resulted in the children being raised Lutheran. Ernst considered it an early stroke of luck, at least from his perspective of comparative weekly demands upon body and soul.

The home of the county's largest Lutheran congregation stood watch on the east end of Main Street, its brick steeple topped by a four-sided clock that tolled each hour and half hour, a background pulse that supported the town's daily rhythms. There were two services every Sunday, one in English and one in German. Both were conducted by Reverend Schwertfeger, who had confirmed Marie and Don in their Lutheran faith as eighth graders in 1936, when Don was still a full head shorter than Marie. A block and a half to the south of the Lutheran church was the Evangelical church that Boyd's family attended, its front entrance across the street from the large H-shaped brick building that housed the town's entire school system.

* * *

The street through the center of town was officially named Lake Street, although there was no lake. Before the Civil War, an earthen dam constructed for a mill had created an artificial lake, at that time thought to be the largest in the world, with steamship service to other towns along its perimeter. After complaints by farmers, and some lawsuits, the water was allowed to draw down and the lake disappeared, transformed into a large wetlands area. On the south edge of town there was a street officially named Main, a brief stretch of lonely road heading out toward the cemetery, but no matter what the map said, Lake Street was called Main Street.

It was lined, on both sides, with a bakery, dairy, furniture store, two drugstores, a bowling alley, two hardware stores, two jewelers, a hotel, a movie theater, and several clothing and general merchandise stores. Scattered in between were a few taverns and barber shops. Upstairs in many of the brick storefront buildings were a number of insurance dealers, lawyers, dentists, and doctors. There were several car dealerships in town, a lumber and coal yard, and two factories, one large and one small.

All this within walking distance for two thousand and two hundred souls.

* * *

Boyd's dad, Herb, was a sheet metal worker at the town's smaller factory. In 1939 he would earn eight hundred dollars, on the low side of what most basic laborers and foundry workers in town made. The owner and chief executive officer of the factory where Herb worked was paid four times as much as Herb. At the larger factory the men earned as much as sixty-seven cents an hour.

As foreman, Julius made twice what Herb earned, as did the town's police chief and the minister of Herb's church, Reverend Zellmer, as well as Reverend Schwertfeger. The local schoolteachers earned something in between, married male teachers paid more than single men or single female teachers. Married female teachers were rare, in their town and everywhere, often the result of school hiring policies.

The school superintendent, Walter Bussewitz, had arrived shortly after the Great War and was the source of widespread affection and genial amusement over his eccentric and polymath ways. Buzzy's wife had passed away in May. Throughout that summer, he had taken to spending time next to her grave writing poetry, some of which he submitted to the local newspaper for publication. Townspeople would soon begin chipping in to buy an engraved marble bench for him to sit on at the cemetery. To the wounded wonder of some, the installation of the bench would coincide with the end of his graveside poetry writing.

Buzzy's salary that year was thirty-one hundred dollars, the same as Gus Dieklemann, the chief operating officer of the bank, and Al Hyland, a church friend of Herb and Lylle's who was the chief engineer at the big factory in town where grain drills were made.

* * *

The town was a complicated enterprise. Its intricacy in operation ran far deeper than common descriptions, snooty or sentimental, about simpleminded boosterism and unsophistication. From the perspective of a later age, with its own ostentatious bent toward global tastes and outsourcing in all forms by individuals and institutions, the town's self-sufficiency astonishes.

In the early 1920s the school had burned down, a complete loss that was uninsured. During the two years it took to construct the new building, half the cost paid for by two large donations from the family that had started the larger factory, all of the school's grades were dispersed throughout the town. Space was offered up at four of the churches, the bank, the city hall, the post office, and the jail.

When Ernst was a boy, a group in the community sought the introduction of telephone service in town. They discovered that the Wisconsin Telephone Company would agree only to install its own limited version of operation, which did not include connection for the local farmers. The town went ahead and set up its own telephone company. In the summer of 1939 the operations were still housed in the same room on the second floor above the furniture store.

It had been only six years before—in 1933—when the US financial system had collapsed on a weekend in early March. Marie was eleven years old when, on a Friday, all the banks in Wisconsin were ordered by the state government to close for two weeks. On Saturday a new president was inaugurated, and he would soon announce the closing of all banks in the entire country. On the following day, a frigid gray Sunday afternoon that was spitting out the occasional snow flurries and icy rain, her dad headed downtown to city hall. The grim weather was a perfect setting for all of the town's merchants and others local business owners to gather themselves and discuss what they were now facing.

It was agreed that there would likely be a currency shortage. There was also agreement that it would bring paralysis to the community. A plan emerged to circulate scrip in denominations ranging from twenty-five cents to twenty dollars, which the two Wilcox brothers, Russell and Howard, offered to personally guarantee. Everyone present said that they would accept the scrip, that it could be used throughout the town as cash. The only exceptions were the two businesses owned by out-of-towners, the Power & Light Company and the Wisconsin Telephone Company, the latter having bought the local exchange a few years back. The plan would allow for food and other necessities to be bought and sold during the mandated bank holiday, however long it would last.

Such a scene was repeated that weekend across small towns everywhere, frightened men and women trying to hold things around them together in the third year of a relentless economic unraveling.

The Great Depression pushed many in the area to the very edge of survival, and a few beyond. For farmers, including Boyd's dad, the devastation had come earlier, an agriculture depression arriving in the 1920s when, after the end of the Great War, foreign markets were abruptly closed to American exports. Herb lost four farms in succession, and for a time the family had to move in with one of his brothers. Employment at the larger factory in town went from six hundred down to forty, and at one point in 1932 there were only nine men working at the plant. Throughout the 1930s, the size of the high school graduating classes kept shrinking, boys leaving school before completing their freshman or sophomore year in order to find some sort of work that would help make ends meet for their families.

Only during the last twelve months did it feel like the awful grip was loosening.

Some outside help had arrived, starting in 1936 and for each year that followed, when the city council was able to secure WPA projects, mainly for construction of sewer and storm lines on a number of streets in town. The work brought some jobs and money into the community, and the improvements would make for a better place for everyone to live in the years to come.

Long whispered about, decades later it would be confirmed that Frank Bodden's lumber and coal yard had carried the coal bills of many customers who did not have the thirty or forty dollars it cost to heat a home through the winter. Only when Frank was long gone was it revealed that his books in those years showed as much as thirty-five thousand dollars in outstanding accounts, representing hundreds of homes around town being heated through several cold Wisconsin winters.

* * *

The town had a small upper class, a vaguely defined and almost sheepish aristocracy (rightly so, others in town would say). In a handful of families, mainly connected to the founding and ownership of the two factories and the bank, their daughters were deemed by someone unknown to be worthy of the occasional photo in the society pages of one of the Milwaukee newspapers. But there were no gates around houses or neighborhoods. Their children played all around town, got dirty, and got in trouble alongside everyone else's children.

The great eveners were school and church, an arrangement that was a knowing and deliberate contradiction to the long ago experiences in a homeland. Athletics and outdoor activities served a similar role, as did the large number of civic organizations.

Leadership in the community came from all strands of life in town, without sharp lines of demarcation. All were needed to make things go. It was only a few years after his move to town that Julius had gotten himself elected an alderman of the third ward.

Ernst was active in the Advancement Association. The Rotary met on a Monday noon once a month over a starch-filled home-style dinner at the Community House, a large brick dwelling donated years before to the town for civic use. There was the American Legion, Legion Auxiliary, Junior Legion Auxiliary, a recently organized Lions Club, a Masonic Lodge, the Odd Fellows, the Order of the Eastern Star, the Garden Club, Rod and Gun Club, the City Band, a drum and bugle corps, a city baseball team, and the cemetery association. Each church had numerous organizations that were similarly aimed.

All thrived, people drawn from all parts of the community. Lylle shared the leadership of the Ladies Aid at church with a farmer's wife and another woman whose husband owned an oil company. Ernst went to ball games with his neighbor, a self-employed carpenter with little formal education, and they were sometimes joined by "the ol' professor," the nickname Ernst preferred over Buzzy when referring to the school superintendent.

The local Women's Club was a force to reckon with; during the upcoming autumn of 1939 they would take up the cause of better police enforcement at five intersections in town they identified as dangerous, while inviting educational speakers to their meetings that also featured fine arts programs. During the social part of the meetings, a teacher's wife would sit next to the doctor's mother, who poured the tea for Marie's grandmother, the widow of a machinist.

As a local marketplace, the town had the vibrancy of multiple providers and competition. Also embedded was a certain measure of restraint. The latter was neither formal nor quantifiable, but it was real and operated as an effective vaccine against the toxicity inevitably delivered to a society by a winner-take-all business model. More with deed than with speech, there was a natural wariness of concentrated power. It had been rooted well before the Depression, not as a political view or economic dogma but as a practical watchfulness to ensure a healthy circulatory flow through the town.

Being the wife of a Main Street merchant, Marie's mother was careful to divide up her grocery shopping each month among the five local stores: Oberdiek's, Darber's, Voss's, Simon's, and the Kroger. Ernst did the same with his haircuts. He even alternated between plumbers, which sometimes made for uncomfortable moments when an emergency required immediate service on someone else's installation.

* * *

The great waves of immigration into the area had been German, although scattered around the county and in town were Hungarians, Irish, and Poles, along with a handful of descendants of some original Yankee settlers, whose roots were English. Habits and rituals brought over still lingered, as did pieces of language, especially exclamations. The town's identifying culture was not about ethnicity, nor had it ever been such. The primary identifier, shared across the social and economic spectrum in that town, was an immutable stir toward making things, not only in a physical or commercial sense but as an overriding impulsion to make better the local setting of their lives.

Left behind in the old country had been the primitive and stagnant notion of a homeland, a full generation, almost two, having passed since so many had come over. And yet the American nationality that quickened their patriotism was understood not as a homeland but as a construct, a place of perpetual creation and inclusion. Most had been taught by their elders that being an American transcended any mystic rootedness or cabalistic identity in need of the salve provided by myths about a native soil.

One particular verity was central to the town's cultural essence of those days: no greater threat was presented to their lives than by deprivation and ignorance, a truth originally received from those pushed out of a homeland filled with hatreds and hardship. It was a doctrine that drove the community as a society. It was openly spoken about in such terms, by men and women, and to their children, whatever their economic status or other beliefs.

Nothing came closer to a sacred common faith. The meaning was in the doing, the learning, and the building, an embracing of betterment and the need to stretch one's self, no matter how difficult the effort or how imperfect the outcome. In that milieu, cleverness was a suspect quality, as was glibness, loutish conduct not to be encouraged in the young.

* * *

Most of the decade that was about to end had brought much to fear, a stomach-gnawing dread nothing like the cheap, giddy version of anxieties shamelessly peddled by twenty-first-century politicians. On that frigid March Sunday afternoon in 1933, what had brought Ernst and the others to the rickety old city hall building was not their concerns about market share or a good consumer experience, but a real and immediate threat to the very functioning of the society that surrounded them.

It was not a time of moral clarity. Nor was it a simple life. Openly acknowledged, with a mix of both humility and self-confidence, was that human beings do most things wrong and only a few things right, no matter one's station in life. Widely understood was that a logic in life could never be found in a sphere of certainty, but existed only within the varying deep rhythms of life's cycles and the confounding interplay of contradictions that always managed to coexist.

As with life itself, the town was filled with ambiguity and paradox. All the interconnectedness was a breeding ground for narrowness. Sometimes the atmosphere could be just plain suffocating. There was a rough and crude edge to things, along with the usual human displays of hypocrisy. On any street there was a house or two with troubled lives, difficult marriages, and damaged families. There were no people of color in the community. There were no non-Christian beliefs or heritage, at least none admitted to. Few surnames ended with vowels.

But within the town the notion of hierarchy could never hold a sharp edge. By numerical necessity, the basic patterns of life for individuals and for groups were unavoidably entangled and shared, not only economically but socially and culturally.

Strength was seen in a local citizenry that was well assorted. Sameness was not considered a virtue, and nonconformity was more than tolerated, to perhaps a surprising extent. All manner of oddities and misbehaviors in some of the town characters were accepted and even appreciated for what they delivered to life in the community. Expressions of allegiance were always on open display, believed to be a lofty element of one's character. But it was a pride that was an arm over the shoulder, a lean toward broader advancement and expansion, not a tool for giving focus to tribal distinction or separation from others thought to be lesser.

The town unassumingly steered toward inclusion, an ecumenical society fiercely intolerant of disrespect. People who lived there were imperfect and they knew it. The local culture and the town itself could only operate with a natural antagonism toward absolutism and, in particular, people who got up on their hind legs. Such qualities were understood as impediments to the organic functioning of the community.

Unrefined, as it surely was, and falling short of perfect, as it surely did, the small town's culture nurtured a primal notion of equity and decency not dependent on homogeny, something desperately sought for centuries across the European continent and theorized about by its intellectuals. As it would be many years later within America, after its self-contained small-town culture had been extinguished.

* * *

The cycles of the town were marked by rituals that carried everyone from one season to the next. By the end of the summer of 1939, attention had already turned to the high school football team. Joining Boyd and Don in the backfield would be another classmate, whose father owned the factory where Herb and Julius worked. Also on the team would be sons of farmers, sheet metal workers, a florist, a mechanic, and some of the proprietors on Main Street.

During the summer, Boyd had studied up on the football team's offense, the Notre Dame Box, with all its deceptive shifting and motion. He was pegged to be the starting halfback. Boyd carried a silent belief that he had been good enough the year before to have been a starter. But he had been a junior, and Lester had been a senior and a good athlete in his own right. That was just how things worked. Now it was his turn.

Boyd was two inches shy of six feet tall, which in those days was not short. A deep bass voice had recently emerged to join his dark complexion and relaxed curly hair. His appearance was a contrast to Don's smaller build and olive coloring. Both were still somewhat callow. But they already displayed what in those years was written about as the signature American male look, a leanness, pronounced in the jaw, and continuing down to a trim waist.

Few boys were more popular than Don. Gregarious and an unashamed mama's boy, he had the same forward lean and pigeon-toed stance as his father, which gave the correct impression of someone at the ready to mix things up. His voice had some overtones, more viola than violin. Brownie was as openhearted and as friendly as a boy could be, but a temper was always lying somewhere in wait. He liked to joke with Marie about whether hers was worse than his.

The town's culture included a longstanding practice of assigning nicknames to most males. Some were obvious, like "Brownie," or that of another classmate, Albert "Snuff" Senneff. Other nicknames, like "Cuts" and "Kicker," were from incidents long ago and already on their second generation. It was also popular to call boys by the name of their father. Henry Bodden's son, Bill, was "Hank." And all the way through high school, Boyd would also answer to "Herb."

Boyd had been given a lot of Herb's easygoing temperament. More than most, he never minded being alone. Even when he was in a group he had the ability to maintain a bit of space for himself. His quiet and deliberate manner was sometimes wrongly taken as a shy tentativeness, effectively hiding a farmhand-tough resilience and a constant silent chafing at the limitations he felt living in that small-town world.

* * *

Boyd, Don, and Marie knew as a given truth that the school year about to commence was intended to be nothing less than a pinnacle in their lives.

The nine months as a senior in high school were arranged to be an ordination, an elevated span of time that would never come again. In June it would be over and then they would start their lives.

For the class of 1940, it would be a senior year like none before and none since, bookended by cataclysmic heaves and shudders of a world spinning awry. In between, during the months of "phony war," their carefree top-of-the-heap life went forward as usual, but there was an off-key descant always in the background. It was faint at times, but the tones were no less ominous.

Three of the town's class of 1940 were planning to head off to college. At one time there had been a project in Don's family to sell raspberries from their huge garden laid out on several acres behind their house, earmarking the proceeds to send him to the university in Madison. But things had not worked out. Julius now had his eye on the butcher shop and retail venture, something for Don to step into and work alongside him.

For Boyd, and for Marie, college was not part of the future, not even thought about.

* * *

It had not taken long on that Friday morning of Labor Day weekend for Boyd to realize something was different.

On most normal mornings, Lylle was in constant motion in the kitchen. As in most households, the day was meant to begin with a substantial breakfast. Preparations would soon begin for dinner at noon, the big meal of the day. The evening meal was supper. Much to Boyd's perpetual chagrin, his mother was anything but a good cook. And she had no shortage of food-related quirks, such as insisting on warming up his orange juice on cold winter mornings, claiming it was healthier for him. Her skills were far more aligned to her passions of cleanliness, the church social calendar, and anything green and leafy. Lylle was also not given to extended periods of silence.

When Boyd came downstairs that morning, she was sitting at the kitchen table, drinking coffee with a serious look on her face. The radio was near her, and as was her annoying habit, the volume was turned up just a little too loud.

She said nothing to Boyd when he came into the kitchen, none of her usual reminders he called "morning sermons." There was not even the automatic mention of making sure to wash up in the "good soapy water" she frugally kept throughout the day in a small nearby basin, another habit from the farm.

Coming from the radio were bulletins, one after the other, switching between various locations in Europe and New York. There were other mornings that summer when Hitler could be heard barking out a speech to an audience that always sounded to Boyd like screaming animals. Newscasters were interrupting each other. There was a lot of talk coming out of the radio about a place called Danzig. Bulletins were announced from other places in Europe. A special session of Parliament was being called in London, scheduled to begin in a few hours. Another report said that evacuations from Paris had begun.

Lylle just sat with her coffee, staring at nothing in particular. Europe was going to war.

It was not a good day for mothers of sons.

CHAPTER THREE

Season's Turn

Friday, September 1, 1939

A VISITOR TO Central Europe during the late summer of 1939 would have come upon the teenager Myroslaw out in a field, likely with a scythe or a sickle in his hand. Most striking to any observer would have been the primitive tools in use and the absence of machinery, only a horse or an ox grudgingly assisting the work. There was no livestock to be seen. Water was moved by the pailful, not by plumbing. Paving was nowhere to be seen, nor were lampposts. The sun dictated the start and finish of each day.

Fifty miles to the south, the Carpathian Mountains lay, positioned at an angle running northwest to southeast. From there the land sloped gradually downward across fifty miles of monotonous plains and marshlands to the field where Myroslaw stood. With no elevated terrain to impede the weather barreling down from the north, the climate was an oversized presence in Myroslaw's life. It made few compromises and imbued a natural pugnacity to all those who labored outside from dawn to dusk, through the late-arriving spring, the short summer, and severe winter.

* * *

Myroslaw was a peasant. There was little to distinguish his work or his life from that of his father or his grandfather's father. His formal education had ended before his teenage years had begun. Already a third of his existence on earth had been spent doing tough manual labor.

His was a strenuous, blunted life from an earlier century, a predetermined role on earth that both required and yielded a sturdy frame and rugged soul. He had to be good with his hands, and he was, including his fists.

As with all men and women who work close to the soil, the surrounding landscape was part of his being, a stern and lonely sameness that stretched out in all directions under a large imposing sky. The rolling terrain with its occasional patches of thick forest and dark tilled soil made for a deceptively bucolic scene, a land of small tracts and scattered pale-white stucco homes with thatched roofs. Most were not much more elaborate than a good-sized shed, a few windows on the front and a smaller one or two as an afterthought on the side. Within steps was a garden that showed a modesty in inverse proportion to its importance.

Claims to holiness were not far away. A wooden building, much larger than any of the dwellings in the area, stood alone on its own territorial grounds defined by some trees grouped in a way that vaguely suggested human design. Rising above the boxy wooden structure were three unpretentious spires, something between a rounded steeple and a dome, one higher than the other two.

The tempo of Myroslaw's life was guided by the seasons, all activities ordained and dominated by the most ancient circular rhythms. The everyday drudgery was broken up only by saints' days and other ritual celebrations directed under the very strict baton of his church.

* * *

Less than twenty miles away, to the west and south, lived a girl of fifteen, Maria. Like Myroslaw, her teenage life also did not include indoor plumbing, kitchen appliances, electric lights, or the radio. Her clothes were made, not bought. Like most women, her responsibilities included tending to the animals and the garden area.

One day in the future Myroslaw will meet Maria and marry her. But not for another nine years, and an ocean away.

On the other side of the abyss that was about to open.

* * *

Myroslaw lived with his parents. He was the youngest behind two older brothers, Dmytro and Ivan, and a sister, Hanka. Quiet, but not shy, he tended to hold himself back and leave the boisterousness to others. When standing upright he was a solid five feet and eight inches, a weather-hardened presentation led by a stout nose and a strong jaw set underneath extremely thick and wavy dark hair.

He was still a boy, but he gave off a typical display of poverty's artwork of sinewy youth clothed in adult weariness. Perhaps it explained his lifelong way of moving in a mincing walk, something close to a tired waddle.

Like many in that area, his eyes and the rest of his rough-worn appearance showed tantalizing hints of genetic threads that probably reached back more than seven hundred years, when Batu Khan, the grandson of Genghis, invaded the area with his Golden Horde and laid terrible waste to what was then a principality of the medieval kingdom of Kievan Rus'. The epic storms of violence sweeping from the east across the Great Steppe would continue for centuries, until 1783, when Catherine II pronounced the absorption of the Crimean Khanate into the Russian empire.

* * *

Myroslaw knew the land around him as Halychyna. In other tongues it was Galicia. It was once a crownland under the Habsburgs, acquired in 1772 by an Austrian empress during a dismemberment of Poland. In the summer of 1939, Galicia was no longer the name of a political entity, only an informal reference still used for an imprecisely defined area in the easternmost part of the Polish state that had been resurrected in the aftermath of the Great War.

His father, Mykhailo, had once worn the military uniform of the Austro-Hungarian empire. An uncle had been in the Polish cavalry. Like his forebears, a national identity was not a part of Myroslaw's life. He was technically a citizen of Poland, whatever that meant, which was not much. Later in his life, after the Polish state had once again been extinguished, it would mean a lot.

Myroslaw was aware of being Ukrainian, or Ruthenian as his parents would have called it in earlier days. But more prominent as primary self-identifiers were his everlasting low economic and social status, and his church. The absence of a national consciousness or ethnic "national" identity was something close to a medieval mind-set, a lingering remnant of a feudal past never far removed from the impoverished rural life of Galicia.

Being a teenager mattered little. His young life had been devoid of the New World's protective celebrations of the freshness of youth, along with its staged entry into adulthood. The course of his wearisome life had been set before he was born. He was already well established on a familiar and certain path.

* * *

Escape was not easy.

In 1929 his brother Dmytro had managed to maneuver through the full playing field of bureaucracy and hucksters that awaited those from rural Galicia attempting to seek a new life elsewhere. Emigrants had to pass through Oświęcim, what the once-ruling Austrians in their language had called Auschwitz, 250 miles to the north. Dmytro had been a teenager when he had run the gauntlet and made it through, crossing the Atlantic and settling for a few years on the prairies of western Canada before moving eastward, to Ottawa. His timing was superb. The arrival of the Depression during the same year put an end to immigration opportunities once offered to those within Poland's borders by other countries, including the United States. Leaving Galicia was no longer an option.

* * *

As for Myroslaw's rough-edged soul, it was the property of what was known as the Greek Catholic Church. With its notable mix of Byzantine rite and allegiance to Rome, it had been brought forth into the world during the sixteenth century as the Unia, when Galicia was part of a Polish-Lithuanian Commonwealth. Two centuries later, the early reign of the Habsburgs included a venture into the arena of the divine, directing an official name change of the Uniate faith to the Greek Catholic Church.

In 1596, as in the summer of 1939, the hand of God was in the clenches of men of the earthly city who had their own political needs. The bishops of the Metropolia of Kievan Rus' had come forward with their desire for a sacred concord with the Holy See, with a readiness to turn away from the Patriarchate of Constantinople. Their action of faith was legally confirmed through the official grace of Sigismund III Vasa, Polish King and Grand Duke of Lithuania. As monarch of the Polish-Lithuanian Commonwealth, he had his own desires, mainly for diminished loyalties toward Moscow among Orthodox believers within his realm, important to his aim toward a greater "Polishness" among the people. The irony of the latter would be lost in later years.

The Union of Brest served to enshrine several great divides. Millions of other ethnic Ukrainians in the lands east of Galicia would remain within the Eastern Orthodox faith, where their steadfastness would continue. And there would be no neighborly joinder with the Polish Latin-rite Catholic Church. Whatever the exalted solemnity of the undertaking, *Ruthenis Receptis* would mainly serve the sinfulness of man, inflaming an already profane separateness of a most unecumenical society.

* * *

Galicia is often referred to as one of Europe's borderlands, a lazy sobriquet of place used to misdescribe one of the most grievous and repeated failures of human civilization. Myroslaw's Halychyna was a society of multiple cultures, each living astride the others and each deeply entrenched within itself while resentfully dependent on the others. The overall arrangement was a hardened knot of economic and ethnic echelons, traceable back through centuries to the days when Europe was first emerging from the upheaval left behind after the Black Death swept across the Continent.

The region was anything but a quaint mosaic of diversity. Its Poles, Ukrainians, and Jews, and a few other smaller ethnic groups blended only in the most reluctant and transactional sense, a profound and often officially sanctioned disrespect going across cultural lines. Among the intelligentsia, there was a swollen sense of cultural uniqueness and an intolerant absolutism that deliberately looked away from any inconvenient ambiguities or complexities of sect, status, and bloodlines that existed within the contrived boundaries around each group.

In rural areas of Galicia there was a commonality of poverty and grim cynicism. It brought no unity. The countryside had few industrial sights or sounds, an almost primeval quiet probably not much changed since the Middle Ages. The land was fertile ground for elaborate religious ritual and a fondness for mysticism. Life offered very little to believe in. Tenacious piety was abundant across all faiths. There was heavy consumption of alcohol.

The human sameness of it all was unadmitted at the time. In the twenty-first century it remains unacknowledged among those jostling over the proper collective memory.

* * *

Only a small portion of Galicia's population lived in towns and cities. The censuses of the day were tainted by agendas that directed counting techniques. In general, it was Ukrainians who lived in the rural areas. The landholdings of peasants in eastern Galicia were small, almost all fewer than four acres, and across Poland, half of the holdings by peasants were estimated as being incapable of yielding a level of subsistence for a family. The Great Depression had dealt the area a heavy blow, lowering historically pitiful net returns on agriculture by another 70 to 80 percent.

Larger estates drew laborers like Myroslaw and his family. Such lands were owned and administered by Poles, considered the local gentry. Their population in Galicia was scattered, greatly outnumbered by the Ukrainians except for pockets in certain urban areas.

The region had a significant population of Jews, almost a million residing in eastern Galicia when the Great War ended. Mostly Hasidic, they operated many of the shops, inns, and other businesses. In some small towns they made up the majority of the population, often in enclaves with a marketplace at its center, communities unto themselves and an inward world that kept itself separate, except for business transactions.

The Jews had arrived in Galicia during the thirteenth and fourteenth centuries. Five hundred or so years in the area limited them to newcomer status, ineligible as outsiders to enter the endless unchristian fray between Poles and Ukrainians over ethnic primacy and exclusive claims to the area as a homeland.

The Jews were permanent foreigners. Their dominant role in local commerce attracted resentment. They displayed an urban pallor instead of a peasant ruddiness. They wore black, covering themselves differently than those in Galicia who were not Jewish. The wearing of certain apparel would be taken up by some in the middle of the twentieth century (as it also would be in the twenty-first) as not only a matter of group identification but also as a somehow deliberate and actionable provocation.

The Jews were the ones with the most otherness, the most alien. To the Ukrainians, *chuzhi*. The word was not said politely.

* * *

To the north of Myroslaw's village was the great city of Lwów, forty miles as the crow would fly. Known as Lemberg during the days of the Austrian empire when it was the provincial capital of Galicia, Lwów remained one of the most beautiful and intellectually fervent cities in all of Europe. It was as distant from Myroslaw's life as a far-off galaxy, providing the same amount of cold and faint illumination.

Lwów was a place where three different alphabets actively intermingled: Roman, Hebrew, and Cyrillic. It was home to three different archbishops who reported to Rome, each with their own grand cathedral: Armenian, Greek Catholic, and Latin-rite Catholic. Polish and Yiddish were the main languages, business in the city conducted in German and Yiddish or a meld of those with Polish and other languages. The city had more Poles and Jews than Ukrainians, and was the only urban area in Galicia where Poles were a majority.

* * *

Around the time Myroslaw's parents were coming of age, the moniker

"Ruthenian" had been abandoned for "Ukrainian." The old term "Rusyn" (Ruthenian) was deemed too similar to "Russkyi" (Russian), the acceptance and use of the new term arriving from east to west. Perhaps for some in Galicia, adoption of the new name was a matter of solidarity, but the Ukrainian culture of Galicia, which had emerged in a side-by-side existence with Poles under centuries of Austrian rule, was quite different from the Ukrainian culture that had emerged to the east, under the rule and influence of the Russian empire. This was as unacknowledged by the radical and antagonistic nationalism that took root in Galicia as was the inconvenient blurring of cultural lines between those others who were so despised as foreign occupiers.

In the countryside where Myroslaw lived, there were Polish tints and more in the spoken language. In his house, the ubiquitous starch-filled half-circle dumplings made from unleavened dough and stuffed with potato or cabbage might be called *pirogi* instead of the Ukrainian *varenyky*. A visiting aunt was just as likely to be referred to by the Polish term *ciotka* as the Ukrainian *teta*. The lines between Poles and Ukrainians melded for certain customs, such as proper dietary restrictions on church festival days. For some in Galicia, there was a strict household rule of no dairy or meat on Christmas Eve. For others, the rule was if they had it, they ate it.

Such dietary and lingual veering was not without peril, potentially a sign to some of an impurity. In the circles of Myroslaw's family, "acting too Polish," meant one was putting on airs, an accusation worth avoiding.

And yet one in five marriages during that time united a Ukrainian with a Pole. The result of such sacred vows was considered a mixed marriage, despite more than three centuries of a shared spiritual faithfulness to the Holy See of Peter. The two Catholic churches were consumed with keeping children from being lost to either Polonization or Ukrainization, "soul-snatching" done in accordance with one's respective rites before God.

The earthly authorities offered by the Habsburgs had installed a practice aimed at balance, whereby the offspring of what God had joined together would be put asunder: boys were to be baptized in the rite of their fathers and girls would follow that of their mothers. With the demise of Austrian governance, the practice had faded, and an unhappy disorder followed.

There were Poles who were Greek Catholics, and there were

Ukrainians who were Latin-rite Catholics, both situations presenting unsuitable ambiguities to church leaders, who had taken on roles pertaining to national identity along with their other functions related to sin and salvation. A further complication was in the form of Galicia's "Old Ruthenians," Russophiles who did not have aspirations of a national Ukrainian identity. Happily, at least for those within the Greek Catholic Church, by the late 1930s they were fading away.

A few years after Myroslaw was born, the government of Poland had ratified a concordat with the Holy See. It included a specific commitment that at each Sunday mass the officiating priests would recite a liturgical prayer, in Latin, for the prosperity of Poland and its president, including on the Polish national holiday. Throughout the 1930s the relevant Polish governmental ministries were kept busy with reports of violations of the concordat's provisions by priests of the Greek Catholic Church.

As the Great War was ending, throughout Europe nationalities and subnationalities were astir in the wake of the near simultaneous demise of four great empires. Ten days before the armistice, fighting had broken out in Lwów between Poles and independence-minded Ukrainians, the conflict lasting until May of 1919. In Paris at the Peace Conference there was befuddlement on what to do with eastern Galicia and its mix of peoples. A border was drawn, which the Polish government ignored, carrying on with broader aims to the east, fighting against the Bolsheviks into Russian territory. No decision came from Paris on the fate of eastern Galicia until 1923, when the Polish annexation of the land was formally recognized.

* * *

The brief life of the Second Polish Republic, born in 1918, is a tired story, a part of every type of governance where the soul of the state is given over to fear. The curious notion of insider threats and the reflexive belligerence aimed at those deemed to be outsiders because of their otherness were as divisive and counterproductive as in the days of a fading Roman empire or the turbid waters of a later-age democracy in the early part of its third century.

The reach of the Polish government into Myroslaw's life in the countryside was limited. But throughout Galicia, its actions operated to ensure that the only welcoming entrance into the body politic was through the dark hallways of extremism. From a brutal "pacification" in the earlier years of the decade to matters such as land distribution, education, and the use of languages, the government's actions repeatedly gave nourishment to those whose threats it most feared, demeaning any non-Pole citizen otherwise perhaps inclined to work through a civic process toward social goals.

As for the most "other," whatever thin thread to a *res publica* Jewish elites had once felt under the Habsburgs was gone. The Polish state openly fretted about what it perceived to be a problem in the form of an unwanted group of people within its borders. Pogroms had increased and a new descent had begun.

* * *

Like much of urban Europe, over the previous few decades Lwów had moved from being an intellectual hothouse to a cauldron of incompatible and uncompromising brands of socialism, fascism, communism, nationalism, and Zionism. What had once been intelligentsia-driven agendas to advance a consciousness had mutated into extremist ideologies, right and left, thriving as always where there is detachment from the polity that set the conditions of one's own society. The contagion of group exceptionalism, its foundation framed in terms of the perceived difference from others, festered and spread as a handy means for legitimating identity and righteousness of cause. Then as now, whether in alignment or condemnation, intellectuals were inevitably prone to overstate the reach of a particular ideology while understating its per se ruinous corrosion on the function of a society.

In 1939 the Greek Catholic Church was a full-throated clarion voice of a Ukrainian national identity. But the loudest homilies were in the form of arson, bombs, and assassinations delivered by a tawdry band of factions who themselves were in deadly competition with one another and quite willing to murder other Ukrainians viewed as collaborators. One of the most famed groups spewing a violent and bizarrely spiritual intolerance was the Orhanizatsiia Ukrains'kylkh Natsionalistiv (Organization of Ukrainian Nationalists, or OUN), organized ten years before on a founding principle that called for "complete expulsion of occupying forces from our lands in a national revolution."

The ideology under the OUN stewardship was one of attention-grabbing provocation, with precious few specifics about the purified Ukrainian state that was envisioned, other than some vague totalitarian bromides then so much in vogue throughout Europe. Its founding manifesto stated that the OUN "places itself in categorical opposition to all those powers, domestic and alien, which oppose actively or passively this stand of Ukrainian nationalists," and that the future "Ukrainian State will also strive to root out the detrimental influences of alien domination in the cultural and psychological life of the nation."

The ill-fated Polish government's treatment of so many citizens of Galicia as foreigners delivered the precise standing sought by the most radical. At the same time, the OUN's hatred of the Polish government as a foreign enemy that was an occupying force usefully diverted attention away from the complications presented to their strain of national identity by the already created greater Ukrainian state directly to the east, along with its well-known collectivism, purges, and terror aimed at the Ukrainian intelligentsia, and state-directed famine.

* * *

One is left only to ponder the sense of humor of an Almighty watching over so many competing upward prayers about the consecration of national identity, the advancement of national prosperity, and the blessings for being exceptional. A divine gaze during those years would have observed both the Second Polish Republic and the OUN each separately beseeching the German chancellor, as though he were a man of *credenda*.

They sought assistance toward a solution to their respective problems, both of which came down to the challenge presented by the existence of other groups of human beings.

* * *

Little of the fervor of extremist Ukrainian nationalism and its mutually reinforcing entanglement of violence with the Polish state managed to ooze into Myroslaw's world of sweat, root vegetables, and ornery large animals. But the toxin that it fed on throughout Galicia was also in the countryside. The ground on which Myroslaw walked was contaminated, no less than the streets of Lwów. Inescapable was the oily slime of fear and hostility aimed against those who were not the same, the timeless human failing to resist cravings from a Paleolithic age toward righteousness and identity built on the divide from another group.

* * *

Thus Galicia.

A miserable relic of another age. What it could have been it most certainly was not.

Whether it was doomed by its own tightening noose of violent absolutism, inwardness, and exclusion will never be known. At the end of the summer of 1939 the state of Poland ceased to exist, a quick demise brought about by two outside forces joined together in conquest, one from the east and one from the west.

* * *

The Second World War began on the day Myroslaw turned nineteen. The launch was not presented to him with the well-dressed trumpeting Boyd heard that same morning. Myroslaw's war came in silence. In a few weeks, it would become a physical presence in his life, a new regime all but slithering in from the east as the Soviets entered the area under the arrangement with their German allies.

For the first time, he could be thankful for his poverty. He and his family were too poor to be considered *kulaks*, the initial designation of bourgeois enemies of the classless society that was to be formed. The Poles were targeted first, landlords and those seemingly an elite.

Collectivization began, the transformation that had already taken place for Ukrainians living in the already established republic to the east. Private businesses were done away with. While the new regime deemed a few Ukrainians and Jews as more equal than others, all of life in Galicia was made worse for everyone, from peasants to merchants and everything in between. Myroslaw's life of bare subsistence gradually turned into one of deprivation.

* * *

As the autumn progressed into the usual gray-toned gloom of winter, the blight of surveillance and paranoia took its place as a pillar of the new society. Even a casual conversation about the Russian conquest could not be had outside of the family. It was not safe. And nothing could ever be said around children.

The new regime made clear that enemies of the people had to be found in order to bring security to the people. Watchfulness and reporting suspicious activity were encouraged. An ever-present threat was posed by enemies inside and outside the local community, and no job of the state was more important than meeting those threats. The new authorities made it clear: if something was seen, something should be said.

There was no doubt that lists were being developed of people considered to be threats. Early on, some were tempted to believe that such lists would be limited to only obvious types of people identifiable by their elite status or group they belonged to. As was soon learned, though, anyone could be on such a list: Pole, Jew, or Ukrainian.

There was no comfort provided by a belief that one had nothing to hide. It was up to the state to determine who was a threat and to deal with it.

Just as the lists were secret, so was the process for determining such threats. One would find out only after it was too late. There was no explanation as to why someone was on a list, and no way to be removed from such a list. The process, the names, and the reasoning were all secret. The nature of ensuring security against threats to the homeland demanded such secrecy.

* * *

The days turned shorter and much colder. People began to disappear. Initially it was the elites, but through the winter and the long cheerless thaw into the cold mud of spring, the reach began to extend. It became obvious that no one was immune. Entire families vanished, often in the middle of the night.

Within only twenty-five miles of the sparsely populated area where Myroslaw lived, the People's Commissariat for Internal Affairs, also known as the Narodnyi Komissariat Vnutrennikh Del, or NKVD, would establish six prisons for placing people who were considered threats. There were tales of those being sent to places far away. And there were whispers of quick executions.

By the time the chill let go toward the summer of 1940, the terror was constant.

CHAPTER FOUR

The Distant Thunder of Ruin

Friday, November 3, 1939

THE STRAIGHT-FORWARD HANDWRITING was rarely called upon.

Dear Blossom,

<u>We won</u> and boy what a game. Berlin sure played dirty, just like Hartford. Silver ball & helmuts only worse than Hartford and the reffs were awful and how that Berlin team did slug. And the reffs could stand right in there and not call it. Even coach Dil ran out on the field and protested but no use, I guess they were trying to see if they couldn't get Boyd down and out at least that's what the fans said. Cause every time Boyd carried the ball and made good gain they would slug when down.

Boyd sure played a bang up game last nite the best I have ever seen him play. Oh yes I forget he was captain last nite. He sure was outstanding last nite on his end runs and dives through center. At the half it was tied at 12 all. Dilly protested against the ball and helmets so the referee made them use the tan ball and then did the boys go to town and how. Boyd made two more touch in the last half and made the score 25– 12 and now Mom will continue. Love, Dad. This is braging about Boyd I only do in the family circle.

Firm pencil strokes gave way to a lighter Spencerian hand. Lylle had once been a schoolteacher. Herb's formal education ended with the sixth grade.

Well, I got Dad to write about the game. The whole town is talking about it so I thought he could tell more than I could. Dad said the crowd from town was far bigger than Berlins, and Mr. Zellmer said Berlin always has played dirty like that. The Journal has just has a few lines in to-night's paper about it. Boyd said that Berlin sends it in to them when the game is there and . . .

* * *

The giant black headlines of early September had shrunk and faded. First frost had come early, and October finished much colder than normal, the days hovering around the freezing mark. The usual rituals to prepare for winter were almost complete, much of it devoted to frame of mind. Autumn was still hanging on, though, because of one thing. The boys had played seven football games and had yet to lose. There was high excitement all around town.

Boyd and Don were a backfield tandem, scoring touchdowns and playing a tough-tackling defense. After beating Berlin, the team headed into its final game, hosting the traditional Armistice Day encounter with their archrivals from Mayville. This year the conference championship would be at stake.

Armistice Day 1939 fell on a Saturday. A few days before, Mayor Yorgey issued an unusual dual-purpose proclamation, officially signed and sealed. It urged that "all our citizens give proper observance" to the twentieth anniversary of the Armistice, adding a further official request that "our places of business would be closed from 1:30 p.m. to 4:30 p.m. of that day," when the championship game was scheduled to be played.

And so Main Street was deserted on that Saturday afternoon. The air was crisp and fresh, a temperature of forty degrees that felt just right for football. The mid-November sun was bright and low in the southern sky, and the shadows were long.

More than a thousand people stood several deep around the playing field across the street to the east of the school. They watched the boys battle through a hard-fought physical struggle only to come up on the short end of a 6–0 loss. The game would be talked about for years.

* * *

Through the fall the faraway European tumult gave off a low buzz, always in the background. A "waiting war" it was called by some. Russia was taking aim at Finland. King Leopold of Belgium and Queen Wilhelmina of the Netherlands offered to mediate among the warring parties, and received a telegram expressing "high appreciation" from Pope Pius XII.

Basketball followed, and there were dances, club meetings, and an all-school operetta. Not a small amount of time was spent just driving around town or sitting in a booth eating a hot dog at Tom's while listening to the jukebox. In December, Don, Marie, and five others were in a one-act comedy by Booth Tarkington, *The Trysting Place*, their performance winning first place in the competition among schools in southern Wisconsin. At Christmas, and again later in the winter, the band performed in well-received concerts, Marie on clarinet and Boyd playing the tuba.

* * *

What passed for spring in 1940 came late. Like most years it was more of an escort for a departing winter than something that followed as a separate season. It was barely above freezing on election day in early April, when Brownie's dad lost his bid to remain as alderman of the third ward. He had an election day confrontation with Walter Erdman, his victorious opponent, and it had gotten out of hand. Julius paid a two-dollar fine (plus court costs) to the justice of the peace, having been found guilty on charges of assault and battery.

COURT FINDS BROWN GUILTY; FINED SATURDAY

An altercation between Julius H. Brown and Walter P. Erdman, opponents in the third ward race for alderman, resulted in charges

A snowstorm in mid-April left drifts a foot deep. The baseball season did not open until the final day of the month, when Boyd pitched a four-hit shutout to beat Hartford 13–0. The following Saturday he and Marie were off to Columbus, twenty-eight miles away, for the annual music festival. Twenty-four high schools from two counties participated, nine of which were from towns with a population of less than a thousand. Much was made of the school's musicians receiving twenty-nine firsts, even one for the band's marching. The whole event, including the Saturday afternoon parade and the evening grand concert of massed bands, was broadcast over WIBU, the radio station out of Beaver Dam.

* * *

The following week the screaming black headlines returned.

The German onslaught had begun. One after the other, Holland, Denmark, and Belgium fell to the invaders.

Every day seemed to be a new drama unto itself, the morning headlines out of date by noon. No one around town could remember anything like it. The Wehrmacht was unstoppable, and a large mass of French and British soldiers was soon trapped, their backs to the English Channel.

On a Friday afternoon toward the end of May, as the school day was finishing up, the king of England himself came on the radio, his speech carried by several stations out of Milwaukee and Chicago. He spoke slowly, with long silent gaps between his words, as he described a "decisive struggle" where defeat would mean the "destruction of our world as we have known it and the descent of darkness upon its ruins."

Two days later, well after supper on a cool and drippy Sunday night, the radio was turned up for the nasal tones of the president. He was not popular in Marie's house, and her mother could do a wicked imitation. But not that evening.

He began with grave words about "this moment of sadness throughout most of the world."

> Tonight over the once peaceful roads of Belgium and France millions are now moving, running from their homes to escape bombs and shells and fire and machine gunning.

After a lengthy explanation of American military preparations, he finished by describing the prayers needed for "the restoration of peace in this mad world of ours." He made no request of God to bless America.

* * *

It was during the dizzying crescendo given off by an unraveling world that the air lost its chill and everyone's lilacs came into bloom. So many were planted around town, almost at every house. The soaring fragrance was inescapable.

By the end of May only the most dilatory in their weekend chores had not yet removed their clunky storm windows and put up screens. An almost wayward pleasure of freshness and renewal drifted through the newly opened windows.

In any normal year the sensory overload made it difficult to avoid feeling unhinged. For those who lived through the string of days from the middle of May of 1940 into the middle of June, there would never be anything like it again. Boyd, Don, and Marie would each carry forever within themselves a defining mark left by those weeks when their childhood formally ended, a moment of heady intensity and a never-again matched sense that the world they were about to enter was coming apart.

* * *

Memorial Day came on a Thursday, a bright and mild morning for Boyd and Marie to march with the band a final time, which they both loved to do. In those days, Memorial Day parades were not for spectators, but were an event for participants, who after a brief program at the school would join the procession.

The warming sun was behind the marchers once they all had made the left turn and headed down Main Street. Their destination was one of the cemeteries, where there would be a ceremony for those honored dead from the Civil War and the Great War.

Up front, ahead of the school band, was the legionnaire honor guard dressed in their smart dark blue uniforms, Ernst a flag-bearer. Behind the band were all the school children and other groups of townspeople.

Old Mr. Silverness was the only spectator on his side of Main Street. He stood alone in front of his drugstore wearing his pharmacy smock as the parade passed by, a little after ten o'clock.

June arrived, a switch flipped, and it was summer. Temperatures soared into the nineties for the week of graduation. The heat only added to the disorientation of lightheaded high school seniors trying to keep a balance between the pensive and the manic. Each day, the shimmering air was thick with the majestic disaster unfolding across the Atlantic. So far away but with an unshakable looming quality, it made for a slight pungency that drifted into the rest of the sensations and emotions that were overpowering each boy and girl being told that life was about to begin.

* * *

The evening newspaper arrived a little after the end of the school day.

Monday:

Tuesday:

Wednesday:

On Wednesday afternoon the boys took the playing field together for the last time, wearing the heavy flannel uniforms shared between the school and the summertime American Legion baseball team. With Boyd on the mound and Brownie at shortstop, they defeated Berlin in a play-off game on neutral grounds, in Beaver Dam, and won the Wisconsin Little Ten Conference Championship.

The next day was graduation. By early afternoon the temperature was again above ninety degrees, a haze settling over the town. Anyone taking a stroll up and down the sidewalks would have heard the steady stream of radio bulletins coming through open windows. The Germans were pushing hard toward Paris.

* * *

That evening, hundreds gathered in the auditorium of the Van Brunt Memorial School, where the seating was in rows of wooden desks, two adults squeezed into each one. The great room was airless, despite the long row of six-foot-high screenless windows on the north and south sides left wide open. The only relief came from fluttering programs clutched by parents and relatives.

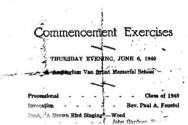

The class of 1940 was forty-six members strong, the largest in town history and a noted source of pride that year after the shrinking classes of the previous decade. The scholastic honor roll consisted of two boys and six girls, neither Boyd nor Don among them. Marie was the class valedictorian, an honor that did not include giving a speech. She did, however, sing alto in a small ensemble of seven senior girls and four senior boys, including Boyd. After they performed Stephen Foster's "Come Where My Love Lies Dreaming," Boyd carried his tuba onto the stage and played a solo.

When the applause for Boyd ended, Mr. Edgar G. Doudna, Secretary of the Board of Regents of the Wisconsin State Teachers Colleges, stood and walked over to the podium.

He looked down at the boys and girls in the class of 1940, and began:

Here we are in a critical time.

A bloody war being waged, and hatred undermining love.

It is no time to give advice on success in life.

* * *

Eight days later, German troops entered Paris.

CHAPTER FIVE

Media Vita in Morte Sumus

Wednesday, July 8, 1942

FATHER ANDRIY PICKED up the certificate and held it. At the top there were two lines in large printed font, one in Roman script and the other in Cyrillic: Testimonium ortus et baptismi, Свідоцтво уродин і хрещення.

He dipped his pen. Above the two large printed lines he wrote, in an oversized German cursive, "Birth and Baptism." At the very top of the paper he recorded that Myroslaw's document was the ninety-seventh of its kind that he had completed in the first half of 1942.

A little farther down, in the vertical columns, he scratched in Myroslaw's day of birth, the name of his father, Mykhailo, the name of his mother, Yevdokia, and the names of Myroslaw's grandparents and godparents. Underneath those entries, Father Andriy added in large German words: "Baptized and Confirmed."

Toward the bottom of the paper he put his signature and added an official stamp in blue ink.

Myroslaw took the document. He would keep it on his person for the rest of the war, along with an identity card received from the Germans a few weeks before, tagging him as Ukrainian and designating him as a laborer.

* * *

Whatever heavenly realms Myroslaw perceived at the age of twenty-two may have seemed unchanged during that summer. But the earthly world around him had, for the third time in his short life, heaved up another form of grim existence. A new misery had descended, altogether different from the twenty-two months of cold terror under the Soviet regime and light years from the more familiar wretchedness of his first nineteen years on earth.

A little more than a year before, in the predawn hours of a Sunday morning in June, three million soldiers had made a surprise attack against one million soldiers along a front extending a thousand miles. Within weeks, the Russian empire's reach into Galicia had melted back to the east. In a willful statement of departure, the Soviets had removed themselves from the area only after an outburst of widespread murder, the prisons near Myroslaw's village left filled with the tortured bodies of those who had more recently disappeared from their homes.

The invading Nazi troops that overran the area were welcomed and even cheered. Such emotions would give way once intentions became known, which did not take long.

* * *

For centuries, conquering armies from outside empires had passed back and forth through Galicia. Myroslaw had heard the tales.

This time, his Halychyna would be invaded three times in five years, twice from the east and once from the west. Through it all, there would be a continuing rupture of unrelenting wickedness.

Layer upon layer would be spewed out from Central Europe to the east, a broad area that was the unmatched centrality of the Second World War, both as a conflict and as an epoch.

* * *

The supreme leaders of the two forces that invaded Myroslaw's Halychyna were both, by everyday sensibilities, unquestionably deranged. The madness of each was distinct, but they shared a clear-eyed understanding of the effectiveness of sowing fear within a compliant citizenry through pronouncements of threats presented by others, along with the importance of displaying a strutting belligerence. Each had overseen the development of their own individual rationale, however queer if not pathological, for the state's use of assassination and the murder of civilians both as a geopolitical tool and as part of modern warfare. The alliance of the two as the opening gambit of the Second World War remains a stone in the shoe for those who prefer the lofty arc of wartime narrative familiar to English-speaking peoples fond of special relationships.

The armies of the two invading forces would finally clash, starting three months before Myroslaw's twenty-first birthday. The combat was feral. Not since the Thirty Years' War, three centuries before, had there been so few boundaries between violence among soldiers in combat and violence aimed at those not in arms. The practice would eventually spread like a contagion to all sides participating in the Second World War, wherever and by whomever it was fought.

Wherever the *Ostfront* passed, the war was intensely local, extra fuel provided not by alignments of shared cause but by a kaleidoscope of repulsions that changed its dark forms depending on context and whim.

* * *

For the new conquerors from the west, Galicia was a land of *Untermensch-en*, inferior and meaningless lives to be placed on the other side of a divide, fit only for removal. One group was to be exterminated. As for the other groups, mainly the equally subhuman Poles and Ukrainians, there was the potential, at least for the time being and depending on need, for their use as forced labor.

The foulness that descended on the area brought no unity among those so savagely oppressed. For many Ukrainians and Poles, the arrival of the Germans allowed for a full blossoming of their inexhaustible strife over homeland primacy. The subplot was very useful to the newest conquerors, who were able to hold to their own elevated standards of depravity, aimed everywhere but with a special target of the most reviled "others." No pause was taken by those Ukrainian and Polish visionaries of ethnic national identity. They kept themselves in self-sorted groups and excreted their own localized ethnic cleansing, one against the other. The Poles and Ukrainians of Galicia would continue killing each other throughout the war, and even for a period beyond.

* * *

The new terms of life for Myroslaw began with being cataloged. Everyone knew the raw hierarchy, set within bright lines and with no accounting for ambiguity. By the time they got around to him, the stakes were understood to be a matter not of comfort level but of survival. There was no one in Galicia who was not in need of protection.

For Ukrainians, what had started as a recruitment to come and serve in the homeland of the newest conquerors had, within months, become a manhunt for men and women to be deported into Germany as laborers. The most marginal, like Myroslaw, were the most ill-served by the ones who not only embraced the primacy of group ethnic identification but asserted themselves as leaders of such a thing. The stain of that particular failure of leadership toward those in the most need was common across each of the groups deemed subhuman by the Germans.

* * *

By the summer of 1942, Myroslaw was living in a place where light and shadow had reversed roles. Lumination came only from vague slivers no more than an obscurity, fleeting representations of humanity. For a very few, occasional shards of brightness brought some concealment from the black umbra that had enveloped the land. But such refuge was impermanent, as a shaded place is against the midday sun. The darkness was almost complete, days filled with fear and death. There was no symmetry, and no equivalence, and no mercy. Things just were as they were. And they were horrifying.

There can be no doubt that Myroslaw and everyone around him knew of the rounding up of men, women, and children for their immediate murder, families who had shared the very same homeland across a long history extending back generations and hundreds of years. The extermination of Jews in Galicia would be virtually complete by the end of the following year. It was a massive operation, accomplished with bullets and open pits dug in the earth. It could not have been done without assistance. The Germans would see to it.

Some Ukrainians participated willingly, others perhaps even eagerly. There were those who were indifferent. Some were nudged, some were ordered, some were forced. The Soviets had undoubtedly helped the Nazis by inculcating into the local society the "see something, say something" hoodlum culture of denunciation. Some would readily identify Jews. Others would do so reluctantly, under threat. Some would give a warning to Jews. A few would help Jews leave the area. Likely there were Ukrainians who at one point or another had responded in every one of those ways, depending on the situation presented by a particular moment.

A broad spectrum of participation ran from eager and willing to reluctant and forced, and an equally wide range of active and passive activities contributed to the heinous German undertaking. Peasant men, women, and children were requisitioned for certain activities. The Germans had a need to feed those who were shooting all the Jews, so cooks were required. Pits had to be dug. The elderly had to be carried to the place of their murder. Young peasant girls were useful for the assignment of walking across bodies to pack them down and make more room.

Whatever Myroslaw saw during those days, or heard, or knew, or did or did not do, he took to his grave.

* * *

A pause.

In recent years, often at this point in such a chronicle, it has become a practice to include one or more detailed and gut-wrenching accounts of some of the murderous cruelty that took place involving the innocent, often children. There is no shortage to draw from.

Such presentations are aimed to startle and shock, to grab a lapel. Each is horrific, each stands alone as an unfathomable obscenity. All are human stories that deserve to be read, even as language fails and the words of slaughter and savagery all fall short in expressing what went on every day of the war in so many places on the European continent.

But gruesomeness does not explain.

In the time of Homer, evil could be addressed and accounted for through the gods. Today, the word only ends a conversation. Sometimes that is the intention.

The sediment from those years continues to be painstakingly dug, although in reality the process has only barely started. The embedded fragments allow an intimacy with something that cannot be quantified. Shovels are not always welcomed by those currently on the land. And those who wield the shovels have sometimes sought things other than understanding. The digging often does not go down deep enough, into the older soil and broader bedrock so poisoned with the toxicity of contrived and false separateness.

Few places on earth have a historiography so marred, riven by apparent ground rules requiring one to choose or otherwise be assigned to a particular side. Much of the discourse is aimed at driving out ambiguities, complexities, and, most of all, human sameness, as though to do otherwise would run the risk of either diminishing the immensity of what happened or discoloring a particular national or ethnic mythology. It is not unusual to come across fearless attempts at navigating the territory on the head of a pin in order to set the record straight regarding either the uniqueness or the equivalency of atrocities, as though acts of cruelty and barbarism, including those within a war, can be ranked for superiority or a particular status. The shrillness of competing victimhood and the sweeping pronouncements of villainy suggest a curious deafness to the echoes from the past, the frightful sounds about otherness in designated groups along with the dehumanizing tones of righteous absolutism aimed at an exclusionary historical record to be owned and used.

It is the vocabulary of a small animal mind.

Tribalism is a pestilence of human thought, a primitive being's inability to stop itself from making the blind reach into a dark hollow. The continued spread of its infection across every continent is perhaps the greatest surprise delivered by a twenty-first century so sure of its global aspirations.

From without or from within, all group identities are forgeries.

We still pretend not to know that.

Respice humilitatem nostram.

* * *

Halychyna was no longer a place for the living. At some point that summer, Myroslaw packed a few belongings into a cloth sack and, in the middle of the night, slipped out of his family's house and left the area. He would never return.

How far he was able to go before capture is not known. But he was found and deported to Germany, as *Ostarbeiter*. By November he was eight hundred miles west of Galicia, in an area known as Moselle. Since 1940 it was considered to be a part of Germany, as it had been before the end of the Great War. Its French-speaking young boys were being drafted into the Wehrmacht to fight as Germans.

Such a matter of national ethnic identity was of no concern to Myroslaw. Now a rail-yard laborer for the Germans in a place called Basse-Yutz, he only hoped to survive.

CHAPTER SIX

Don't Say Anything

Friday, November 27, 1942

SNOW HAD ARRIVED the day before, making for a white Thanksgiving. The temperature then plummeted overnight. It was in the midteens on Friday morning when Herb took Boyd to the county courthouse in Juneau, just before the 5:30 a.m. reporting time. Wisecracking boys were stomping around and snorting out steam in the predawn darkness. But nothing could ever overcome the loneliness and vulnerability that comes with standing in the iron cold of the first blast of winter, never mind the reason for being there.

His draft notice had arrived two weeks before. He had known it was just a matter of time. Earlier in the year the minimum age had been lowered to twenty, and large groups seemed to be heading out every month. Boyd was one of nine from town who had arrived that morning, part of the latest batch of 109 boys from eastern Dodge County.

* * *

It had been the strangest year he had ever known, and he would always remember it that way. The life into which Boyd had been carefully raised was one that was promised to be a progression from, through, and into the familiar. The message from school, his church, and his parents was one of reassurance, that he would always be tethered by a thick and sturdy guy wire that ran both behind and ahead of wherever he was.

Even a full year before Pearl Harbor, when he was just out of high school, something had changed. There was a growing sense of being moored somewhere as the certainties of the past loosened and drifted off into the distance. Boyd would never forget the constant sensation during those months of just biding time, a day-to-day existence that did not seem quite real. By the middle of 1942 there was no longer any unity between the present and what had come before. The future was a blank. The only certainty was that Friday's early-morning trip to the courthouse in Juneau would inevitably come.

* * *

The summer after his graduation from high school, he had worked for a few weeks at the canning factory, during the pea pack. Then he had joined Brownie, helping Julius get the old stone building ready for the butcher shop. The two of them had worked side by side, digging and doing other demolition needed to convert the building, which had last been a local brewery. It was sweaty and dirty work. The two boys had gone at it hard and had fun doing it. Don would be well set for the future.

A few months later, Boyd had started a job at the factory where his dad worked, and where he would greet Marie every morning. She had started working there as a secretary after homesickness had gotten the better of her during the fall of 1940, her parents letting her quit the secretarial school in Milwaukee and come home. She had been there long enough to learn shorthand, which she was able to put to good use.

It was shortly after that when she and Brownie had become an official couple. He had signaled his seriousness, in the fashion of the day, by giving her a watch. Boyd was dating a girl from his church, but it was not very serious.

* * *

By 1942 the world Brownie and Boyd believed they were entering right out of high school no longer existed. Their lives had never gotten started.

Rationing had begun. It was difficult to accept having to face shortages, this time contrived, only a few years after life had started to pull away from the barrenness of the Depression.

The very first item to be rationed, just weeks after Pearl Harbor, was rubber. The trove Ernst had been collecting in the basement of his store was now worth a fortune. Indeed, on the Sunday afternoon of the Pearl Harbor attack someone had knocked on the front door of his home, wanting to speak with him. They wanted to know if he would sell them an extra pair or two of galoshes right then and there. He told them to try again at the store on Monday.

Food products were next, a slow item-by-item introduction, with sugar first on the list. Coffee rationing was scheduled to begin within the next two days, in time for Christmas. Given the all-day intake of Herb and Lylle, some changes would be brought. Nationwide gasoline rationing was going to arrive a few days after that, a limit of four gallons a week.

Closer to home, on the previous Friday, the War Production Board had taken 40 percent of stored butter stocks out of the marketplace. There had been an eruption from local farmers and grocers alike. Two days before Thanksgiving, the butter situation was still on the front page of the afternoon's edition of the *Beaver Dam Daily Citizen*.

Boyd's parents read the Beaver Dam newspaper every evening, as they would for all of their lives. A few columns over from the page-one story on butter was an item about a local Christmas party being planned for children of needy families in the area.

Just above that was some news about how Peoria was conserving rubber. Alongside the front-page stories on butter, rubber, and local needy children, was the following:

Thousands Of Jews To Be Killed

Nazi Gestapo Chief Orders Half of Jews in Poland be Exterminated

By Sidney J. Williams

United Press Staff Correspondent

LONDON — Heinrich Himmler, head of the Nazi Gestapo, has ordered that one-half of the large Jewish population in Poland be exterminated by the end of the year, reports from the Polish underground movement to the Polish government-in-exile here said today.

Bloody Program

The first step in the bloody program, it was said, would be to kill 50 per cent of the thousands of Jews living in ghettos established by the Nazis. The remainder would be "liquidated" later.

There were 3,113,900 Jews, or 9.8 per cent of the total population according to the 1931 census, but the Germans during more than three years of occupation have reduced this number by killing thousands outright or permitting them to die of starvation and disease.

Special Nazi "liquidation" battalions, commanded by the notorious Elite Guard, were said to be carrying out Himmler's program. These squads were dragging Jewish victims from their homes or seizing them in the streets and driving them to village and town squares in mass roundups for execution, the reports said.

Old men and women and cripples were singled out to be herded to cemeteries where they were mowed down by firing squads, Polish sources said. The Nazis made no attempt to prove that the Jews had committed any crimes or violated German regulations.

Jews who were not executed immediately, it was reported, were packed into freight cars— 150 packed to a car that normally was large enough for 40— to be shipped to undisclosed points for liquidation.

Brutal Torture

The floors of the cars were covered with a thick layer of lime or chlorine sprinkled with water and the doors were tightly sealed. In some cases the trains reportedly remained on a siding for more than two days before departing, and many Jews died of suffocation. The dead were left in the cars with the living.

Polish government quarters said the Nazis were temporarily sparing young and relatively healthy Jews to be used as slave labor. As confirmation of the reports they cited German figures reportedly announcing that only 40,000 food ration cards were printed for Jews in Poland for October, compared to 130,000 in September.

Polish Jews will not be the only ones to suffer from this latest Nazi pogrom, since thousands of Jews from Germany, Austria, and former Czechoslovakia and some occupied territories have been transported to Polish ghettoes after having been deprived of virtually all their wealth and personal possessions.

* * *

After his induction into the Army on that cold Friday morning, Boyd had one more week at home. He left town in early December on a special train that would deliver him and hundreds of other boys to Fort Sheridan, north of Chicago. A few days after that, he shipped out to Camp Chaffee, Arkansas, and began basic training. He spent Christmas Day on KP.

Three days into 1943 and with almost an entire month's experience in the Army, Boyd sat down with paper and pencil and wrote to Marie, passing on some specific advice for Brownie.

Sun Jan. 3, 11:30 P.M.

Hi Marie,

Writing this in day room. There's a radio in here, ping pong table, tables for writing & playing cards. Wrote to Brownie quite awhile ago. Received a carton of cigs from him a couple of days ago. In there he told me to write so evidently he hadn't received my letters when he sent them but I know he got it by now cause my mother said he called & said he got a letter from me.

Mail service here has been terrible. This is a brand new camp & we were the first big bunch to come in here so everythings kind of mixed up yet. This armored div. is highly specialized & motorized; it's rated next to the Air Corp so It's a darn nice outfit to be in. It's of the commando type in fact we've fellows here teaching who were in that commando raid on France. Everything here is new & modern — one of the best camps in the country. It's located 10 miles north of Ft. Smith, Ark. & about 12 miles from Tulsa, Olk. Along the Ark. River. That's the bad part. Cant have much fun cause the towns are so far away altho they've a 24 hur. Bus service running into Ft. Smith & back. But we as yet haven't been allowed to go into town, then it's so far you just get in & you've got to come back.

They've got 7 chapels, 7 theaters, a $150,000 field house & a service club where dances are held about twice a wk. Beens so busy haven't a chance to get around much. Been to only one movie. They also got post exchanges all over where we mail letters, buy just about everything you need including beer. This field house is the best I've ever seen. I'll be playing basketball in it next wk. Playing on our company basketball team. This outfit is plenty tough. Keep you busy all the time. In just as good physical condition now as I was when I played football.

I really miss Brownie — this is the first time we've been separated— guess I always expected him to be around.

Weather's about like late spring is in Wis. Rains alot & usually gets cool then. Last couple of days temps been about 75. New yrs day we got up at 5:30 and went on a 15 mile hike with full field packs strapped on our back which weigh 50 lbs. Got out in the hills, had a religious service, pitched tents, dug foxholes, & everything & then marched back at nite. Nice way to break in the new yr. What did you do New Yrs. Eve? I was in bed at 10:00. Couldn't sleep tho. It kind of bothered me that I wasn't celebrating. This is our day off & I really appreciate it. Oh! Oh! Chow time — finish this later.

It's 2:15 now. Have good food here. Shortage of milk & butter tho. Both are shipped in.

Don't say anything to my parents about this. If I stay in this outfit expect to go into combat in six months or less. Before we go will be on manuevers in the Calf. Deserts. Doubtless I won't be able to get home until after the war the way it looks now. Have a chance for Officers training after basic tra. & also a chance to transfer to the Air Corp. If I don't like it too well here probably do one of those things if possible.

So far I've given you a nice account of this place but Marie it's still the army & I don't like it. Get along O.K. but I'll never be in love with it. I'm talking from experience now. Tell Brownie to stay out as long as he possibly can. Pull strings, pay off, anything. Take all the deferments he can get. That is if he can't enlist in the Air Corp. Tell him to forget about what people say if he gets a deferment. They won't praise him either when he does get in the service. If they get too smart—lay one on them. Tell him to think only of himself cause that's what everybody else is doing. There's graft even in the army & plenty of it. I know it's hard to make him think that way. In this world now everybody's working for themselves & looking out for themselves. You've got to take care of yourself—nobody else will.

When your in the service there's only one attitude to take & that's this — "we've a job to do & the quicker we get in the spirit of the thing & work together, the sooner we'll all be able to go home." It's tough to keep that in mind all the time — disappointment is frequent, but that's it. If your still in civilian life like Brownie is, stay there as long as possible. Don't let anybody ever kid you this war isn't being fought for our freedom, to save democracy or anything like it. If it was people would be a lot more aroused then they are & I'm not just saying that.

That's why I wanted to write to you especially. Try to convince him about all this. I thought different before too but now I know. I'm not writing this way because I'm homesick, disappointed, or in a mood; it's the truth. Use me when you talk to him. It would be a good idea not to show or talk to just everybody about this or this letter. He'll have to go sometime & you'll have to make the best of it. It's just that I want you two to be together & happy as long as possible & not separated by the evils of the world. Sometimes I could write a book.

By the way, you remember my cousin Geo. Lindemer who took us to Madison when we were freshmen — well Mom writes that he's engaged to Betty Beottcher, the ministers daughter. How about that? Say "hello" to everybody at the office for me. What's going on in town? Hows Kate? Miss those trips west we used to take. Got a Xmas card from Anne Janz.

Have an awful lot of return mail to write. Spend most of my spare time writing & that isn't much. Most of the fellows here are alot older than me & married. Marvin Nitschke, Jerry Baerwald, Gishgowski, & Ray Gadow are all here. See only Jerry tho & him only about once a wk. How's "Butch's" hand? Until next time.

Love to all, Herb

CHAPTER SEVEN

Well, Right About Now

Sunday, August 8, 1943

2:00 P.M.

Hi family,

I'm in at Howes — have been since last nite. Dollye & Bill are playing cards while I'm writing. We went to the First Baptist church this morning. Went to 11:00 services. Boy! Do they have some loud ministers down here. They practically blow you out of the church — Sing good songs tho, you know all those old kind that got that negro rhythm in them. Such as "Give me that old time Religion" — I get the biggest bang out of that cause there's good harmony in them.

HAVING LET HIS mother know that he had been to church that morning and then making the obligatory mention of the hot weather, Boyd went on to describe how much baseball he was playing. He also apologized for forgetting his parents' twenty-fourth wedding anniversary. Everybody in camp was saying that the war was won, and that everyone was "just waiting for the big shots to call it off." He added "I'll be glad when the day comes. I am 21 now & it's time to get situated." Boyd continued:

Well, right about now Donald & Marie are being married. He sent a letter to me and asked me to be his best man tho Marie had asked me when I was home. He offered to pay my ticket home & everything. I planned on

doing it but then suddenly we were put on the "alert" &
that means that no one can travel more than 15 miles
away from the post on a 3 day pass, which I would of used
to come home on. It threw a monkey wrench in the works
& I felt very bad about it cause Don & I had always
planned it that way. I'm going to send them a telegram
tonight. I gave them two sets of glassware before I left,
anticipating this would happen. Glad I did now. Don't
exactly like the idea of getting married now but that's
they're business. I'm very happy for them.

* * *

Brownie had been inducted into the Army in March, one of eleven boys from town and part of that month's county quota of 139. In April he was shipped out to Camp Butner, near Durham, North Carolina, and was now home on a week's furlough, having just completed basic training. He was due back in camp at the end of the week. Everything had been hastily set, the four o'clock Sunday ceremony to be officiated by Reverend Schwertfeger.

It was an afternoon of unabashed perspiration. The church was always an oven on hot days. After the ceremony, Marie's parents had a brief reception back at their house while a few photographs were taken outside on the front lawn.

Then it was off to the Community House and a dinner at half past five, with places set for thirty-five. When the meal was completed and the invited guests had departed, there was still some daylight left. Before they headed to the hotel in Beaver Dam, Don drove around town. By instinct he headed down to the city park, its perimeter road once an oval track for horse racing.

A large picnic of some sort was taking place, and Brownie pulled over and parked. The two newlyweds got out of the car and strolled across the grass toward the area where everyone was milling about.

Decades later those who watched Don and Marie approach from their car would recall how the sun was low and the light had a curious quality, coming through the tall elm trees and splashing a soft gold tint onto everything, even the air. There were smiles everywhere as people began drifting over to greet the young couple, saying hello and offering congratulations.

It was so good to see Don in town again. Don looked so good in that uniform. Marie looked so nice. It was so good of Marie and Don to stop by.

Brownie was taking an obvious pleasure in every moment as he and Marie slowly walked around hand in hand, drenched in the radiance of the peaceable late-summertime dusk. He took time to have a conversation with every person who approached, to the point where Marie's impatience was starting to show. It was obvious to those who were watching that she just wanted to take him away, for herself.

* * *

Time had an oversized presence in those days, never gracious or compassionate.

Marie had turned twenty-one in April. Don was still a month shy.

Never should those so young be forced to hold each hour of every day as though another one will never come again.

Part Two

RISING

August 1944

CHAPTER EIGHT

The Dark Waltz

Monday, August 14, 1944

SITTING IN THE brush on the side of the road, Gilbert Decaudin was reminded of his days in scouting. Except, of course, for the old Hotchkiss machine gun from the Great War on the tripod in front of him.

The warm midmorning sun was behind him, and he had just noticed a pleasant mix of aromas starting to drift over. Lunch was being prepared by his father, Robert Decaudin, a former railway worker recently appointed cook for the resistance unit living in the nearby woods.

Gilbert had turned twenty the previous December. He had been studying to be a teacher until a month before, when he received orders to go to Germany and work under the forced labor regime known as the STO (Service du Travail Obligatoire). After managing to escape a July 17 roundup of *refractaires*, those who refused to go to Germany, he and his father had fled into a life among the maquis. They joined the FFI resistance group known as Groupe C134, led by the sturdy Claude Vougnon.

Next to Gilbert, also on watch duty, was a twenty-five-year-old English pilot who had escaped from the Germans and was being hidden by the maquisards. They both knew a few rudiments of each other's language and were able to communicate, although not without difficulty.

* * *

Their job was to be on the lookout for Robert Schreck, alias Mirabeau. The twenty-two-year-old Schreck was a friend of Gilbert's. Earlier that morning

Mirabeau and four others from Groupe C134 had gone out on a mission to a nearby village, Noidans-le-Ferroux, to stop a local French official from handing over a requisition of cattle to the Germans. If any Germans were trailing Mirabeau and his small force when they returned, Gilbert was to use the machine gun to sweep the road. If the old Hotchkiss worked.

In the late summer of 1944 the upper eastern corner of France remained the backwater of the war it had been since the days of surrender in June of 1940. Far from British airfields and close to Germany, rural life during the occupation was as poisonous as the conditions in urban areas of the country. But unlike the cities, it was possible to eat, even for the maquis living in the forest. The peasants in the area continued to cultivate the land, and despite the constant rapacious designs of the Germans, food was obtainable.

Shoes were another matter.

The weaponry of the resistance groups was scant and ancient, apart from what could be taken from the Germans. On the morning of the Allied invasion in June, there had been a single parachute drop, and twenty guns had been distributed. Throughout the summer, expectations of additional arms drops would be raised and then dashed.

* * *

Gilbert's thoughts of lunch were interrupted. Someone hidden across the road was whistling a tune. He recognized it.

C'est la valse brune (This is the dark waltz)

It was the signal for recognition used by the maquis in the area. Gilbert responded by whistling the next part of the refrain:

Des chevaliers de la lune (The knights of the moon)

Out stepped Simon Doillon, striding across the road in his usual shorts and open shirt, a dozen boys behind him.

During the summer of 1944 it was rare, at least in that area of rural eastern France, to see teenage boys out in the open. Like Gilbert, they were refractaires. The minimum age for STO participation had been lowered in February from twenty-one to sixteen, and many boys had left their homes and gone into hiding with the maquisards. Some in the area still took their chances during the daytime to work in the fields with their families, but would then spend their nights in the woods.

* * *

Gilbert had met Simon Doillon once before, and knew him to be a close friend of Claude Vougnon. He led Simon and his young crew back to the maquis camp in the woods, where he listened while Doillon proudly explained to Claude how he and his band of boys had just completed rounding up all the Citroen automobiles in the area, hiding them in various patches of thicket and woods. The few local Citroens still in running order were being commandeered by Germans. Not anymore.

Claude Vougnon was twenty-eight years old, two years younger than Simon Doillon. The two could not have been more different in appearance and background. The dark and curly-haired Doillon moved in the manner of a relaxed athlete, and he spoke in a low, soft tone. Vougnon's blond hair was thin and straight. He moved his bulk with intensity, and his voice was high pitched.

They were, however, a tandem, and very much alike in their style. Both had a reputation for discretion and not being given to outward displays of emotion, other than their furious contempt for les Boches.

Claude was also a refractaire. He came from a family that grew fruit trees. He was solidly built, with a Henry VIII–style beard that went from ear to ear, framing his blue eyes and a ruddy peasant face. He wore jackboots, taken from a German soldier who no doubt had no further need for them, along with riding breeches and an old-style dark blue tunic of the Foreign Legion. The Germans had put a price on his head of a million francs.

Simon had a lithe build, with a reputation as a natural leader who carried himself with the grace and manners of an aristocrat, which, in fact, he was. His mother, Simone de Vaulchier, was from one of the more illustrious families in France, and a descendant of King James I. The family heritage and Simon's "patriotic heredity" were well known, as were his reserved and sometimes aloof ways. The natural distance he maintained from others, even those nearby, also kept him apart from the uncompromising French politics that even in such an isolated area often crippled attempts at cohesion against the occupying enemy.

* * *

After lunch, Gilbert was just settling back into a turn of guard duty at the edge of the forest when he heard the sounds of a machine gun coming from the railway five hundred yards away. Thinking of Mirabeau, still unreturned, he went back to the forest camp and proposed that a group go and check things out. His father volunteered, grabbing a German Mauser and a khaki jacket weighted with cartridges and grenades. Three others joined, and Gilbert led the group toward the railroad.

Arriving at the track, they found nothing unusual, only the cars Simon's group of boys had hidden. Gilbert and the others continued on, under an overpass, then uphill along a forest of locust trees. After crossing some farmland, they spotted Mirabeau, downhill from them, approximately fifty yards away. He was sitting on a road, shirtless, next to three armed Germans. They could see that he was bleeding from his back, from what appeared to be several gunshot wounds.

Gilbert's father started to charge. "Let's go!"

The others objected. "No. No further. We'll be exposed against this slope."

Ignoring them, Robert Decaudin rushed ahead, yelling, in an apparent attempt to startle and distract the Germans holding Mirabeau, who jumped up and tried to run away from his captors.

Unseen were twenty Germans hidden in some nearby bushes. They opened fire. Gilbert heard his father scream as he was hit, and saw him go down. He rushed over to find him writhing in agony, severely wounded at the base of his neck. Gilbert lifted him upright by his shoulders and held him, trying to slow the bleeding.

"I'm done. Leave me alone. Go away, go away."

His head sank down.

Gilbert shouted back up the hill. "My father is dead! What should we do?"

Meanwhile, one of the trailing maquisards had noticed that his own gun, another German Mauser, had jammed. They yelled to Gilbert to turn back, and he rejoined the others and headed back to the woods.

Halfway to the encampment they were met by Claude and Simon.

Gilbert demanded they all return to fight the Germans; there must be revenge for the killing of his father. The remaining three who had set out with him vowed their readiness to join. Gilbert began suggesting ideas for an attack.

During Gilbert's outburst, Simon stood silently at a distance from the others. With his right arm straight down, pistol in his hand, he kept himself apart and only watched the agitation of Gilbert and his small group play out. Perhaps for that reason, no one took any steps toward the Germans.

As the minutes passed, Gilbert grew angry and soon began venting at Simon's passiveness. Saying nothing, Simon stepped away and began walking with Claude. After they talked between themselves Claude returned a few minutes later to say it was time to go back to their base in the woods.

By now in a tearful rage, Gilbert accused everyone around him of cowardice. Claude grabbed him by the shoulders.

"Simon believes the Boches are too strong against an attack. You and the others would only be killed."

* * *

In the days to come, Gilbert found himself unable to forgive Simon Doillon for putting an end to the chance to avenge his father's death. His bitterness increased when he learned about a young red-haired sergeant belonging to a Wehrmacht company stationed in Noidans-le-Ferroux. Gilbert was told by some of the villagers in Noidans-le-Ferroux that the German boy was boasting about having killed his father.

Gilbert made sure he knew the red-haired Wehrmacht soldier by sight.

CHAPTER NINE

Consequent to a Time of War

Sunday, August 20, 1944

O N A LATE Sunday afternoon in eastern France, a train lumbers directly toward the lowering sun, straining as purposefully and stupidly as the heavy-footed mastodons that once roamed the same land. Across the Continent the dark armored beasts are in motion every hour of the day, unaware of their impending mass extinction from the terrible landscape of modern war.

Metallic grunts and groans come from up and down its great reptilian length, burdened that afternoon by a cargo of weaponry and hundreds of young male human beings who wear the green-gray woolen German uniforms of war.

Myroslaw is among them.

Except for the rhythmic clatter of the wheels, it is a silent journey. Most of the soldiers tightly packed together are lost in their own thoughts. Some are able to look out at the countryside as the lengthening shadows spread outward across the rolling meadows between ridges of thick forest. In the distance the occasional tiny cluster of simple houses surrounds a lone steeple. They are passing through a frontierland. For some the sight triggers a pleasant twinge of false familiarity.

The terrain has been gradually smoothing since the crossing into France from Germany two days before, after going through a fifteen-mile passageway between the Vosges Mountains off to the right and the Jura

Mountains to the left. Known as the Belfort Gap, it is part of the natural east–west connection from the plains of Paris to the Rhine Valley, a strategic corridor for conducting war on the Continent since the days of Julius Caesar and his conquest of Gaul.

Whether Myroslaw or anyone else on board cares about such history is doubtful. But likely at that very moment on Sunday afternoon, men all over Europe and in a few places in America are studying maps of the Belfort Gap, along with other potential routes of escape for the German forces fleeing eastward.

Myroslaw's troop train is, of course, heading in the opposite direction.

* * *

Years later, Myroslaw never made clear whether what happened many months before that train ride had been an all-out Allied bombing mission or some sort of strafing raid. Perhaps he did not know himself. But what had mattered were the explosions, the destruction, and the chaos all around, providing an opening for him to make a break for it.

His escape was short-lived. He was captured again, and ultimately ended up in a camp in East Prussia, where since the early part of the year he had undergone military training along with other Ukrainians, Poles, Russians, Tatars, and Belarusians.

And now Myroslaw is on a troop train heading into France.

* * *

The final leg of the long journey, a two-day trip from Strasbourg, finishes early Sunday evening. A final sweeping ninety-degree turn to the right, toward the west, and the train comes to a halt a few blocks south of the center of Vesoul, France.

With its ten thousand residents, Vesoul is far and away the biggest city in the entire *département* of Haute-Saône. A few centuries before, the area was one of the earliest French industrial centers, but the forges, clockworks, and mills are long gone. By the mid-1930s, Haute-Saône's population of just over two hundred thousand was but two-thirds what it was in the early 1800s. With almost half of the land forested and rivers fingering out in all directions, 70 percent of the people lived in rural areas, dispersed throughout 583 small villages.

Haute-Saône is one of the most remote regions in all of France. It is a land of passage.

* * *

Myroslaw is among more than seven hundred Ukrainian soldiers to jump off the train, all dressed in the German *Feldgrau*. Also disembarking is the unit's German command force, which consists of several hundred officers, noncommissioned officers, and regular soldiers, many of the latter noticeably over the age of forty. Combined with the Ukrainians, openly treated as the Untermenschen they are considered to be by those same Germans, the collective bearing is not one of an elite Aryan force of warriors. The heavy weaponry being unloaded, though, presents its own dangerous demeanor.

Some of the local citizens furtively observe the offloading and overhear the arrivals speaking an odd-sounding language, definitely not German. Rumors are spread that a Hungarian Honvéd heavy artillery unit is being deployed in the area.

Within hours, the assessments are almost uniformly revised to say that the soldiers are Russian, a report that is also provided that night directly to Bermont, the leader of the FFI Groupe V (*V* for Vesoul). He sends an alert around to all of the resistance groups in his jurisdiction, advising them to be on their guard against an attack.

* * *

The unit arriving in Vesoul is a battalion from the 30th Waffen-Grenadier-Division der SS (russische Nr. 2). The entirety of the 30th Waffen-SS Division (Russia No. 2) consists of approximately nine thousand foreign soldiers, conscripted by the Germans despite their being of a lesser "race." Most had been collected into a camp in East Prussia, near Deutsch Eylau, where military training had begun in early February.

By July the Ukrainians had been gathered with other foreign conscripts, including Poles, Russians, Armenians, Belarusians, and Tatars, and organized into a single large brigade under one command.

The Germans also added the remnants of more than a dozen auxiliary police units, known as *Schutzmannschaft*, previously deployed near the Ostfront before being withdrawn as the Russians advanced westward. Overall, those from the Schutzmannschaft units made up about a third of the brigade. The regiment consisting of Myroslaw's Ukrainian battalion and two other battalions included what was left of three such Schutzmannschaft units, each approximately one hundred soldiers in size.

Three days before their arrival in Vesoul, while Myroslaw's battalion was still in Strasbourg, what had been a freestanding "brigade" was designated as a Waffen-SS unit. For reasons of apparent importance to German leadership, the designation of the new Waffen-SS division had been made officially retroactive to August 3.

* * *

Not all of the units within the division are as ethnically segregated as Myroslaw's battalion of Ukrainians. One detachment in the division's fourth regiment would be cataloged that month by the Germans as including "447 Ruthenians, 53 Russians, 15 Ukrainians, 65 Poles, and 3 Tartars." More than half the 30th Waffen-SS Division are Belarusian.

As for the arriving Ukrainians, the only item on their uniform indicating that they belong to the Waffen-SS is the black collar with a double cross on the right side.

Moving the entire 30th Waffen-SS Division requires thirty-one transport trains. As of Sunday, only a third of the division has entered France. On the day before, a different battalion of Ukrainians arrived in Besancon, a large city thirty miles to the south of Vesoul, in the bordering département of Doubs.

* * *

The arrival in France of a unit of foreigners under German command is not an unusual event. Russians, Poles, and other *Osttruppen* have been part of the Germans' defense force in France since 1943, and have faced the Allies all summer since the June invasion. Even in an outlying area like

Haute-Saône, the Germans had long before placed a Cossack unit with a particular reputation for crudity and ruthlessness. Across the Continent, there were "foreign" Waffen-SS formations drawn from almost every European nation and ethnic nationality.

Desertion is a constant problem. The performance of such soldiers in battle ranges from immediate surrender to a bitter willingness to fight to the death—the latter if the troops believe defeat will mean repatriation to Soviet authorities. Earlier in the year the Western Allies made a significant blunder when they dropped leaflets over France promising those from Soviet-controlled countries that if they surrendered they would be swiftly returned to the "Russian fatherland." One Polish general described the leaflet drop as ensuring that those soldiers in France would fight the Allies to the last man.

* * *

Like soldiers everywhere, the arriving Ukrainians are young and include teenagers. Most, if not all, have at one time or another been in some form of German prison camp or forced labor unit. All of them also lived through at least a period of Soviet rule. For those from the lands east of Galicia, a childhood under Moscow authority included witnessing and enduring a famine that had killed millions.

Where they came from, they did not have the luxury of facing but a singular evil. Each carries his own story of parents and relatives being taken away under one authority or another, and sometimes more than one. Most of them ended up in East Prussia earlier in the year because they had been rounded up, either forcibly extracted from their homes, ordered to report to local authorities, tracked down in hiding places, or removed from trains and other public spaces.

Some took up the fight to resist the Soviet occupation. No doubt many were among those who initially welcomed the Germans. Others wore the Soviet uniform and fought against the Germans, ending up in a prison camp. It would not be unusual if some had done both.

* * *

As the autumn of 1944 approaches, Myroslaw and the others in his unit have now spent fully a quarter of their lives on a blighted dark trail of terror, disappearances, violence, and early death. Things witnessed. Things done to each of them. Things they did to others.

Those arriving in Vesoul that evening are children of a European society that, fostered through its elites, bred self-definition based on the divide between one's own group identity and the otherness of similarly designated groups. For the Ukrainians, depending on the location, those others were the Poles, the Russians, the Jews, the Romanians, the Hungarians, the Lithuanians, and anyone else not the same. From their intellectual and spiritual betters, the boys learned the perverse discipline needed to look the other way when confronted with a more complicated reality, such as Ukrainians with different dialects, doctrines, and family relations, or even facial features discolored generations before by proximity to the alien.

Theirs is a world of hierarchies, the original sin of Western civilization, amplified as always when poverty and ignorance are societally accepted as both unavoidable and defining forces of nature.

* * *

So it is that the arriving Ukrainians hold a firmly ambiguous perspective as to which side of the Ostfront is the correct one to submit to. The only offerings for them are servitude and a short brutish existence with a likely violent death. Under what passes for guiding principles held on both imperial sides, the young Ukrainians have no individual worth. Their existence alone is enough to attract the aggressive malice that is the lifeblood of the two powerful forces locked in a mortal struggle off to the east. For them, there is no clarity as to which of the two regimes, both built on implacable hatred, presents the greatest terror and deprivation to humanity. Theirs is not a world that allows a free indulgence in pondering if there is a moral equivalence between the two regimes. There is no apparent side of rightness.

Such ambiguity will, several decades after the war, cause a bewildered disdain from those possessing the confidence required to make judgment on young lives in a human existence light-years away from the protective roof over the heads of those living in a peculiarly self-righteous later age.

* * *

The arriving boys have already been swallowed whole by the war's one ever-present constant, the ceaseless ironies that pelt down and drench like a cold November rain. As all those obscure always come to know as the timeless core of wartime experience, it is a continual near-drowning in the inexplicable, the trivial, and the profound, usually bitter and almost always foul. The black ironies infect the hours of every day. The topic will be avoided by the great ecclesiastical histories of the war, as though it does not signify or is otherwise unsightly.

Whatever comfort or bravado is provided to the arriving Ukrainians by their tribal myths, which are many, on this Sunday in eastern France they are the ones isolated by their own otherness. They are reviled by those who command them. The sight of the uniforms they wear stops people cold with fear and hatred. To the ears of the local citizens, the sounds they make are from another world, and their odd-looking appearance is presumed to be Russian, a most unwanted identity that will be assigned to them over and over throughout the next several weeks.

No Jews are to be seen in Haute-Saône, thanks to the efficiency of French authorities in achieving the removal and shipment to their death in a fashion that likely brought admiration in parts of Berlin. It is the arriving Ukrainian boys who are *chuzhi*.

They have no state, no nation. Some among them wish for one, for their kind and their kind alone, as a homeland is meant to be.

Most, however, just want to eat, and to live on.

They are not there with even a pretense of a cause, only their own base needs and their comradeship with each other. They have clothes and shoes, and they are fed. They are alive. And they will kill to keep it that way.

Theirs is a common soldier's reality of the Second World War, all across the Continent.

* * *

Each of the arriving Ukrainians had, at one moment during the past year or so, often in a hellish setting, been given a choice from the powerful. Serve or death.

That choice is their fortune, a gift of temporary value accorded to a designated slave "race," a grouping just above the most hated "others" in Europe.

That choice is also their sentence.

For the German commanders casting their eyes that Sunday night on the Ukrainian soldiers, there is increasing worry that such Untermenschen will betray.

For the Russians who will soon come looking for them, they are already traitors.

For those looking through the enhanced lens of comfortable distance and certainty of judgment, the uniform is seen. They are collaborators, all of them, and always will be.

* * *

Two and a half weeks before, Myroslaw and thousands of other Poles, Ukrainians, Russians, Cossacks, Tatars, and Belarusians in that division took the following oath:

> I swear to God this sacred oath, that in the struggle against the Bolshevist enemies of my homeland I will render unconditional obedience to the Supreme Commander of the German Armed Forces, Adolf Hitler, and as a brave soldier will be ready to lay down my life at any time for this oath.

And with that, Myroslaw's unit was ordered to proceed west, into France.

* * *

The Sunday night arrival of the Ukrainian battalion in Vesoul is later than had been planned. The delay is due to railway sabotage, Myroslaw's troop train the likely target. A bomb went off on the track as the train was approaching, a deafening explosion that startled everyone on board as the train came to a stop short of the damage. The Ukrainians had been brusquely ordered off by Sturmbannführer Hanenstein, the battalion's despised German commander, and were forced to do the grueling repair work to the track right then on the spot, *macht schnell,* under the day's hot sun.

They were also ordered to seize the first five French citizens they encountered and hang them. The Ukrainians had objected, and for reasons that remain a mystery, the German commanders withdrew the order, uncharacteristically losing their usual interest in savage retaliation.

* * *

Disembarking complete, the Ukrainian and German soldiers line up before marching through Vesoul in full parade to a narrow triangular meadow a little more than a mile to the southwest of the city, where they make camp. Tents are pitched, and the Ukrainians are informed that new orders will be given in the morning.

Very late in the evening, twenty-six-year-old Major Lev Hloba gathers in his tent with three others, Captain Polichtchuk, Captain Zintchouk, and Lieutenant Wozniak. They continue a conversation begun a few weeks before, while still in Germany, when they discussed the possibility of making their way to the Allied army coming from the west. It is time to revisit the idea and come up with a plan.

The four agree that any action they might take will require assistance from the local resistance. Despite the obvious dangers and difficulties, they have to make contact.

Not a single Ukrainian in the battalion speaks French. For most, including Hloba and the other three, even their German-language skills are only the most basic, acquired in prison camps, in labor units, and during the past few months of training.

Wozniak volunteers. He will attempt to make contact with the French partisans.

The four of them agree to keep their plans within a close circle. Hloba warns that each Ukrainian officer is being watched closely by the Germans; any carelessness about what they have just discussed will likely result in immediate death.

Finished with their meeting, they stand facing each other, and as though a formal occasion has just passed, they warmly shake hands.

* * *

At about the same hour as Hloba's meeting, across the Atlantic it is still Sunday afternoon in the flat emptiness somewhere between Albuquerque and Kansas City, where Boyd stares out the window as his train heads east.

Also at about that same hour, more than a thousand miles to the east of Boyd, Don is getting ready to board his own train, knowing that he will soon be facing the famous scrum at Washington's Union Station, where on some days two hundred thousand passengers pass through. Seven decades later, the busiest airport in all of the United States will have only a little more than half that number of daily passenger boardings.

When Boyd and Don make Chicago, which they will do at separate times, they will each get on the first available train to Milwaukee, where each will change to yet another train for a final rattling hour to complete their respective trips from west and east.

Neither is aware that the other is heading home, best friends who have not seen each other in almost two years.

Marie knows that the unplanned reunion of the boys is about to happen. Most of the town probably knows about it already, too.

* * *

The two boys traveling home to Wisconsin are crossing a country that is reaching an almost single-minded national madness of productivity. Even so, both of them will pass through areas that in 1944 are as distinct from one another as some of the countries in Europe, although not necessarily by virtue of ethnicity.

It is the final days in America for a lingering nineteenth-century coherence, of internal boundaries and deep-rooted local enterprise. A tectonic cultural shift across broader society has begun, a force unleashed that in later years will stampede far beyond the initial embrace of scale and standardization wrought by the war. The consequences for the boys' small hometown and thousands of others will not become apparent for another thirty to forty years, when efficiency, once considered merely a means to be utilized along with many others to reach societal goals, will gradually devolve into an objective in and of itself as the centerpiece of a puzzling monotheistic devotion.

* * *

During the agitated summer of 1944 the phrase "America at war" is not so much a martial injunction as an unaffected description of everyday citizen involvement, a stark contrast to twenty-first-century throat-clearing invocations of those same words as a vague pretext for otherwise unacceptable actions by government officials. The small factory where Herb works, normally a sleepy producer of equipment for cow stalls and a few models of "radiator furniture," is pushing out electrical switch boxes for navy landing craft. The other factory in town, famous among farmers for its grain drills, is now known for tank transmissions, pilot houses for submarines, and the utility trailers favored by military engineers.

The canning factory where Boyd's mother occasionally earns extra money recently had its government-set output target doubled from the year before. Starting in the spring, a barrage of appeals were issued throughout the county to "every man, every woman, every boy, every girl of workable age" to help in the fields and in the processing plant. The labor problems continued through midsummer, ultimately solved thanks to some German prisoners of war temporarily brought in and encamped at the county fairgrounds in Beaver Dam.

In the evenings around dusk, the German boys lined up in rows behind the four-foot-high wooden snow fence that walled them off from the local citizenry. Facing the road, they linked arms and sang as a choir. Word spread, and people came from miles around to listen to them each night. One evening in early August, just after dark, the prisoners were marched double-file to the train station, about a mile away. Much to the delight of the local teenagers tagging along, the prisoners kept their cadence by singing as a choir. According to news reports the Germans were shipped from Beaver Dam to an "unknown destination."

The summer has brought another surprising sight to the local fields of Wisconsin. The state government began bringing in foreign workers, mainly to help with the pea harvest and sugar beets: seventeen thousand from Jamaica, eight hundred from Barbados, and three hundred from Mexico. For many, their presence provides the sight of exotic hues in the skin of human beings never before seen.

Earlier in the summer the federal government commenced a new campaign by putting out an initial call for what were termed "outdoor people" to help officials locate milkweed beds throughout the state. Whatever its importance to the annual rituals of whimsy during a walk in the golden first days of autumn, milkweed floss is now urgently needed for use in life jackets and aviator flight suits. It grows in abundance in the marshy land surrounding Boyd and Don's hometown, and the county has been given ten thousand bags to be filled, the type normally used for holding onions. The bags can be picked up at most of the high schools in the area, where they are to be returned when full. The government will pay fifteen cents a bushel.

* * *

As both boys have heard about in letters from home, there are shortages of just about everything. The one local exception, for those in on the secret, is rubber footwear. There is plenty kept in the basement of Ernst's corner store, away from public view but available for sale to those in the know. People come from all over, even as far away as Milwaukee, and Ernst is profiting nicely off his prescience.

The state of tires on Herb's car is a constant worry, with prospects unlikely for replacements until after the war. He has taken to riding to the factory on Boyd's bicycle. Not that he has much choice, as gasoline rationing for most families was reduced earlier in the year to two gallons a week. The nationwide speed limit is thirty-five miles per hour.

In war as in peace, Julius extends no allegiance to speed limits.

* * *

Julius will soon become involved in his own top secret war project. With Don gone and no other help available, he has become desperate to find someone to help him in the butcher shop. In a few months he will obtain special permission and extra gas coupons to drive twenty miles each day to the Schwartz Ballroom in Hartford, the site only a few years before of performances by Tommy Dorsey and Benny Goodman, where several hundred German prisoners of war will soon be living. Starting in the fall and into the following year, every morning Julius will pick up two prisoners of war, both of them experienced butchers, and bring them back to town to work alongside him in his shop. And during the whole time Mother Brown will constantly worry about them trying to escape.

It is a time of small farms. Julius provides those farmers with custom butchering and meatpacking services, turning the slaughtered animals into various cuts and meat products, some of which he also sells in his retail store. Although five decades have passed since the tidal wave of German immigration into Wisconsin in the late 1800s, daily life in the area is still infused with the culinary habits of *das deutsche Volk*. Alongside the bland suppertime anchors of potatoes, bread, and coffee there is usually some sort of sausage.

Of the latter, nothing has taken root more broadly than the tangy yet mild *sommerwurst*, or, as known in the New World, summer sausage. Cured, it keeps well even during the warmest months, hence its name.

Julius will discover that his German helpmates can make a *sommerwurst* more delicious than most. Producing good summer sausage is an art, requiring a steady hand and just the right combination of a particular grind of meat joined with a variety of spices. Recipes are a valuable property, and closely guarded.

Early on, Julius observes an obvious surreptitiousness employed by the German prisoners while making summer sausage. Convinced that they will never share the recipe, Julius decides not to ask for it.

Instead, he spends the next several months in a drawn-out surveillance operation, a casual sideways glance here and a secret peek there, keeping careful notes of what he sees, batch to batch, and writing down what is being done with all the variables.

Like most men of action, Julius is sometimes prone to haste. But he is also nothing if not tenacious. Even, when necessary, with his own patience. Eventually he succeeds in piecing together the summer sausage recipe of the German prisoners of war.

Decades later, when it comes time to leave the business, Julius will sell the recipe to a young man in Dodge County starting his own meat locker business. That summer sausage will continue to be available for purchase into the twenty-first century.

* * *

Sunday is always a day of ritual, and the rites of the Sabbath extend well into the afternoon.

On recent Sunday mornings, Marie feels a pang of guilt for how thankful she is that, since her grandmother's death a few months before, the family now only attends the English service, at nine o'clock. No more occasional visits to the German service at ten thirty.

The worship service has its exalted place during the day, but there is no shortage of holiness assigned to the big noontime dinner that follows. More often than not, in Ernst's home fried chicken is on the menu, a meal of legendary status because of the way Marie's mother pours heavy cream over the chicken during its last moments in the black cast iron frying pan.

Sunday also means the afternoon radio news programs. Ernst has the habit of turning the radio up loud enough for everyone in the house to hear, even though he himself ends up napping through much of the broadcasts. After the midday dinner he inevitably drifts into a relaxed slumber, cigar smoldering on the table next to him and sections of several Sunday newspapers thrown down one by one around his favorite chair.

The sight is not one of an upright Main Street businessman, his white hair mussed in several directions, glasses down on the end of his nose, and his mouth open with the always troublesome dentures in plain sight. They never had fit well. A few years back, one Sunday in church he had sneezed, the dentures flying out and landing near his shoes. A proud man, Ernst refused to acknowledge what had happened and would not bend down to pick them up, leaving that for his son George to do.

* * *

No doubt as background to Sunday afternoon naps everywhere, Douglas Edwards begins the day's CBS broadcast of *World News Today* with the headlines, rattling them off one after the other:

> Allied headquarters announced today that elements of fourteen German divisions and parts of four others have been caught in the Normandy pockets and are being blasted to pieces by artillery fire.

> The Germans say American forces have crossed the Seine, northwest of Paris.

> In the south, the Seventh Army has sealed the doom of Toulon and Marseille by a twenty mile advance toward the Rhone Valley.

> On the eastern front the Red Army is hammering at four salients as the Germans report a new attack in the south.

> Here at home, Russian ambassador Gromyko has arrived in Washington for the world security talks.

> And the War Department announces another raid by the B-29 super-planes on industrial areas in the vicinity of Yawata on Kushu Island, on the Japanese homeland.

> And now for our first news direct from overseas, Admiral takes you to London . . .

* * *

Later that day Marie's parents will be leaving for Chicago on their annual fall merchandise-buying trip for the store. They are not due to return until

Wednesday, leaving Marie to take care of her ten-year-old sister, Ruth, and her younger brother, Billy, who is eleven.

Billy is a mongoloid. Or at least that is how everyone describes him. To Marie, he is just her baby brother, a sweet chubby boy who takes obvious pleasure in being playfully lazy as a way to show independence. Ernst sometimes slows his speech and increases the volume of his voice when talking to Billy, as though dealing with an imbecile. Billy's inevitable response to such displays is a heavy impatient sigh as he would say, "Ohhhh, Paaaa."

Saturday was the annual flower show put on by the American Legion Auxiliary, and it had been a big day for Billy. He had entered the miniature-flower category and won first prize, second prize going to the ten-year-old son of the owner of one of the hardware stores on Main Street. Oh, Pa.

Billy is excited about Don coming home on furlough. He loves Don, who has always been good to him. Since the wedding day a year before, Billy has taken to calling his sister Brownie, instead of Marie or, as it comes out, "Rie."

* * *

Don had been home on furlough in April. And while those around town who could handle the arithmetic were no doubt doing some private chortling, Marie is reaching the point of futility in her painstaking attempts, in accordance with good social taste of the times, to wear every type of clothing that disguises or at least downplays her condition.

In June, she was almost three months pregnant when she and Mother Brown traveled east to see Don. Marie had never been so hot in her life. The crowd at the train station in Washington was something that had to be seen to be believed. Don came to meet them from Camp Pickett, south of Richmond, and they all spent a few days in the same room at a seedy hotel. They went through the Smithsonian and walked around doing other sightseeing until Marie had to rebel. The three of them then traveled south for a few days at Don's base, where it was even hotter. She was miserable the entire time.

And then to top things off, in the following week's newspaper, which always listed who was visiting whom and who was traveling where, someone left out any mention of Marie going along with Mother Brown to visit Don. That had certainly gotten noticed around town.

Her pregnancy becoming visible was the signal for her to quit working, something she was not happy about. Marie loved her job as secretary for the sales manager at the smaller factory in town. It gave her pleasure to work with numbers, and she loved being around friends like Addie, the secretary for CJ himself, who ran the whole factory. He could be a stuffy sort. Not too long ago he had been so proud that he had gotten a sales order all by himself from a farmer who needed some cast iron bowls for use as drinking cups in his cow stalls. Addie had caused quite a stir, and a lot of red on CJ's face, by writing out the paperwork as an order of "20 Cow Bowels." The giggles always start at the first mention of that incident, and will do so even many years later when both girls are in their eighties.

* * *

It has been a hot and dry summer. Sunday is yet another warm day. Nothing can be done about it, except maybe go downtown to see a movie at the theater, the only air-conditioned building in town. The white clapboard house stays fairly comfortable in the heat, as it did even during the string of ninety degree days the week before. Six large elm trees stationed around the front and back help, as do the canvas awnings over the windows on the south side of the house.

In the evenings, there is nothing quite as pleasant as sitting on the screened front porch, the sun setting behind the house. On a good night people walk by with full purpose as they head down to some activity at the city park. A few hours later, many will make their return trip past the darkened porch in a full stagger, always great entertainment.

Since early August, the talk has been of drought. There are even warnings of an ice shortage and ice rationing.

Marie always marvels at the effect weather has on people, herself included. A few days of extreme heat, like the previous week, brings a daytime hush as things around town come to a sudden halt, almost like they do during a big snowstorm in the winter. On Friday, a front had passed through, taking the extreme heat with it. The change always reaches into her sense of well-being. Part of it is the air turning so fresh again. But mainly it is that things no longer feel off track. Nothing brings comfort more than a return to normal.

In the summer of 1944 few things are more welcome.

* * *

Even far from its physical realm, the Second World War brings a depleted form of existence, a life entirely within a ravenous present tense that brutally severs connections to that which is past. As with verbs in the English language, the war has no future tense.

CHAPTER TEN

Evening Arrivals

Monday, August 21, 1944

Tᴴᴇ sɪɢʜᴛ ᴏꜰ human beings wearing uniforms and standing in crisp formation has always brought a queer thrill to a certain element of mankind. Whether, on that Monday morning in eastern France, the exacting German standards for such displays were achieved by Myroslaw and the rest of the battalion as they stood, in an open field, will remain unknown. They were waiting for the appearance of Sturmbannführer Hanenstein.

The lean and hatchet-faced Hanenstein began his lecture with some reminders: All of the soldiers standing there are considered to be an integral part of the German Army. The battalion is in France to fight against terrorism. The terrorists are armed criminals. The terrorists aim to diminish the power of the German Army, which makes sacrifices in the struggle for the establishment of a new order in Europe. Because the French terrorists are serious criminals, they must be destroyed without pity.

Hanenstein added a warning about leaving the encampment: the terrorists will kill without mercy all who wear the German uniform.

Then came a few final words: The unit will be in the current position for an indeterminate period. Be ready to depart at any moment.

That would be all.

* * *

After Hanenstein's performance, Wozniak slipped away from the camp.

He was soon approached by, of all things, an old Ukrainian named Hroza. A political refugee who settled in France after the Bolshevik revolution, he kept an orchard in Echenoz-le-Meline, the village to the south of the encampment. Hroza had happened to overhear some of the newly arriving soldiers speaking Ukrainian but was reluctant to approach the camp.

Wozniak brought up his desire to speak to someone with the local resistance. Hroza avoided giving a direct answer. He also warned young Wozniak to use great caution when asking such questions.

Hroza then went on to suggest, though, that Wozniak might consider making a careful inquiry at the dairy operation located very near the encampment. Hroza also hinted that a preliminary contact might be made.

Later that day, Wozniak went to the dairy. He made his approach under the guise of asking permission to use a nearby field for the soldiers to play soccer. Greeting Wozniak was Simon Doillon, wearing his usual white shirt and green shorts, the enigmatic smile on his face an indicator that Hroza had made the alert to Doillon.

* * *

Simon Doillon was not attached to a particular FFI unit. He had worked with Claude Vougnon's Groupe C134, but operated at a distance while also helping to supply various resistance groups in the area. The Doillon dairy operations provided Simon with a freedom of movement that, along with his perfect German, allowed him to mingle easily among the occupiers. Bermont, leader of FFI Groupe V, thought of Simon as a natural-born charmer, skilled in achieving mutual understandings and sympathies from others.

It had been only a week since his friend Claude had broken up Groupe C134. He and Simon had become impatient with their current situations and had decided to make an attempt to join the Americans. Hearing of this, Bermont had offered both Simon and Claude positions as his lieutenants in Groupe V. Claude had accepted, but Simon had turned the offer down. Instead, he continued to operate the family dairy while still thinking about heading south to the approaching Allied forces.

Groupe C134 was turned into two smaller maquis groups, and Gilbert Decaudin, just days after losing his father, was put in charge of one. The new group took its name from Gilbert's alias, Cesar. Their home base was in some woods not far from the ruins of a twelfth-century abbey and its grand chateau, a few miles south and west of Vesoul.

* * *

Doillon broke the ice with Wozniak by asking, in slow and simple German, for a cigarette. He then invited Wozniak to the back room of the dairy to have a glass of wine. Simon hid his language skills, communicating with the same crude and elementary German used by Wozniak, which they both augmented with numerous hand gestures.

Their conversation began with banalities, Simon asking a few questions. But their talk soon shifted to the war, and then to the battalion's arrival.

Wozniak described his unit as being composed of Ukrainians who hated their German commanders, hated the German uniform, and hated the Germans overall for their barbarous behavior in the Ukrainian homeland. He said they were prisoners who had agreed to serve the Germans in order to keep from starving. He described how Ukrainians had nothing in common with either the Russians or the Poles. He accused both of wanting to Russify and Polonize the Ukrainians. Wozniak's passion was mainly reserved for the topic of escaping German and Russian oppression. He claimed that nowhere else in Europe were Germans as hated as in Ukraine, describing them as wanting to destroy the people of Ukraine at the root.

There is no firm account as to who broached the topic first. But at some point in the conversation, by one side or the other, the question arose whether the Ukrainians would ever take their arms and equipment into a fight against the Germans. Wozniak told Doillon that only his Ukrainian commander could make such a decision.

Doillon said little in response but agreed to another meeting at ten o'clock that same night.

* * *

Wozniak returned to the Doillon dairy in darkness. With him was Major Lev Hloba, the battalion's highest ranking Ukrainian officer.

Hloba was a lean five foot nine, with a thin mustache, dark eyes, and a full head of thick ebony hair. He presented a straight-backed military bearing, enhanced by the riding pants he wore as part of his uniform.

As the conversation began, Simon was very guarded. But as the back-and-forth continued he gradually showed his sympathies while deliberately stoking the fires about a rebellion against the Germans. Echoing Wozniak, Hloba described a Ukrainian perspective of oppression by Poles, Russians, and Germans, and, in particular, the brutal experiences under both the Germans and the Soviets. He recounted the experience of his men being prisoners of the Germans, the hardships, the threat of starvation, and the training in East Prussia that had begun in early February.

Hloba and Wozniak said they wished to see the last of France and "the terrorists and Communists who infested it." Simon took the opening and responded. "And if these terrorists, these Communists, just happened to be patriots, like yourselves, who wished, like you, to free their country from the yoke of foreigners . . . and if the Nazis had, in France—as in the Ukraine and in Poland—killed and massacred with savagery?"

It was not long before Hloba was open in describing a readiness to a mutiny by the battalion against its German commanders. The discussion entered the sphere of planning a revolt, and then became a negotiation.

Doillon insisted that the Ukrainians could not just switch sides and then join the partisan forces. If the FFI were to provide directions, shelter, and supplies, several specific conditions had to be met.

The first was the most contentious: The German command force had to be liquidated. There would be no prisoners taken. Second, the FFI would not participate in the mutiny, but the time and place had to be coordinated in order to move the unit into hiding. Third, after the mutiny the Ukrainian battalion would operate subordinate to the FFI command structure, possibly split into several companies.

The terms were agreed upon. The mutiny would take place on either Thursday or Friday.

Doillon then added a final point. He said that he did not have the authority to make the final decision to commit the FFI to such an undertaking. He needed to consult with his superiors for final approval.

Simon knew that Claude was meeting with Bermont the next morning. He would invite himself along.

* * *

During the same two hours that Hloba and Wozniak were with Simon at the Doillon dairy, Boyd was in Milwaukee, getting ready to board another train for the last leg of his three-day journey home. Upon his arrival at the Milwaukee Road Depot, one of Milwaukee's two grand train stations, he had been greeted by the newsstands spilling over with displays of various front pages that all cheered the war's progress. Most of them were trumpeting a proclamation by British general Montgomery that "the end of the war is in sight."

He had not been home since February, and there was plenty to catch up on. Madison and other cities in Wisconsin were making plans for "V-Day" celebrations. Boyd's beloved Brewers were in first place, two games ahead of Toledo. None of their games that summer were being broadcast on the radio, supposedly due to the war. He always enjoyed going with his pop to see them play at Borchert Field. Unfortunately, the team would be out of town for his entire furlough.

In between all the articles pointing to an approaching end of the war, there were shadows. There had been a sudden new outbreak of polio, twenty-four new cases in Milwaukee alone. The devastating disease that attacked children was so little understood that doctors were reduced to talking about treatment and prevention as though they practiced in an age of bringing the four humors into balance.

Things had turned dark again in London. German robot bombs were striking with impunity, and the Germans were boasting about a future "V-2" weapon soon to be unleashed.

* * *

The trip home had begun a few days before when he stepped onto an early-morning train in Kingman, Arizona, from beneath the curved roofline of a station that looked like the Alamo. In every direction was desert, and off in the distance a few craggy snowless mountains. He had gotten used to the sight, exotic but hostile to Midwestern sensory prejudices, skewed as they were toward a more well-rounded mix of modesty, approachability, and proportion, traits as satisfying in terrain as they were in human behavior.

Even as a boy he was moved by the presentation of land. Its form and arrangement would register within him in a way that was closer to scent than sight, a willed enlargement of human perception that was a once-common sensory reflex useful to understanding the world. In later decades it would lose its hold on most, as demands diminished for noticing anything other than the inescapably obvious.

As it was with all the railroads during the war, the timetable for the Atchison, Topeka and Santa Fe was an approximation. The equipment was laughably advertised as being "completely air-conditioned," and Boyd was consigned to long clattering hours in overheated stickiness. The assault of an ever-evolving mix of odors of a distinctly personal nature could be fended off only when he or someone else would light up a cigarette, a difficult task for those unfortunate ones who had to travel standing in the aisle as the packed train jerked from side to side.

Growing up, Boyd had been out of the state only a handful of times, mainly to Chicago and, many years back, a lone car trip with his parents to the Dakotas. In the past year he had seen more of the country than he could have ever dreamed. Wherever he went, he carried on his person a map of the United States, forty-one inches by twenty-seven and very handy, he thought, because it listed all towns with a population of over two thousand.

Recently Boyd had made an important personal decision. He liked traveling. He informed his parents that he intended to do a lot of it after the war.

* * *

Boyd had left Camp Chaffee the year before to go through basic training all over again, entering the army air force after surprising himself by passing some tests that qualified him to enter school to be a pilot. In January, around the time he had gotten a Dear John letter from his girlfriend, he was informed that the program was oversupplied with future pilots and that no more new entries would be accepted.

After a few months of waiting things out at Jefferson Barracks outside of Saint Louis, in April he was shipped to an army air force training base in Kearns, Utah. On the trip out west he saw his first mountains. He wrote his parents about it:

> . . . Went straight across Missouri into Kansas. Even Missouri was nice scenery because of the green fields with spring coming on, and then into the flat lands of Kansas. Acres and acres of fields just being worked for crop plantings. One field is so enormous it seems like it would take days to complete a full sowing operation.

*Then gradually as we went into Colo the Rocky
mountains came upon us. It was truly thrilling & I
think I'd get more of a bang out of it every time I went
thru them. We hardly ever hit large towns naturally
saving time that way.*

*The trip by train amounted to roughly 1800 miles &
as the crow flies the distance would be around 1400 miles.
Pueblo, Colo was one of the largest towns we went thru.
The scenery was terrifically beautiful as we circled around
in the Rockies. Its springs of rushing waters, rocks,
snowcapped mountains with clouds seemingly clinging to
them, and shrubbery all blending in made it all look even
more beautiful than the pictures we've seen.*

In June he traveled to Arizona, assigned to the gunnery school at
Kingman Army Air Force Base. He arrived on the day after the Allied
invasion at Normandy, and that same evening he wrote a letter home:

*. . . It's probably a good thing I left Kearns as that was
a overseas replacement depot and I couldn't have stayed
there much longer without getting on a shipment to a port
of embarkation. As to this gunnery school, at the present
Jim and I intend to flunk out intentionally. I have no
intention of being a gunner and in the first place I passed
the exams to become a pilot and I want that or nothing.
Of course if passing the school means staying in this
country longer than the other way, I'll do it that way. I'll
play it just as I see it as time goes along. By now you know
I've only one aim and that's to be a domestic soldier until
the fireworks are over or at least stay in the states as long
as possible. Five months ago I had no idea of being here
now, so now I'm congratulating myself that I missed that
big show that's going on over there right now. The Air
Corps been trying to railroad us men that transferred ever
since they found they had enough pilots.*

* * *

The following week Boyd took his first airplane ride.

It lasted two and a half hours, an orientation flight that circled several
times around Boulder Dam and then flew through the Grand Canyon at a
low altitude, just above the Colorado River.

That first flight would always stay with him. For the rest of his life he would be smitten with being up in a plane. His general opinion of pilots would be as close to worshipful as he would ever be about another human being.

* * *

Unlike anything he'd experienced before in the army, Boyd was now very busy. Up at four thirty every morning, he attended classes all day plus an hour of physical training, and then studied late at night as he had never done before. He puzzled his way through the mechanics of complicated gun turrets, learned the operation of a .50 caliber machine gun, and spent hours in practice shooting. There were repeated tests on aircraft sighting and recognition. The best part of each day was spending a couple of hours up in a B-17.

By the end of July, Boyd had completed the "Flexible Gunnery School" training course. While a small army air force band played, sharing the same stage that he and the other graduates were streaming across, Boyd was given a handshake, a diploma, and his gunnery wings, which he was proud to wear.

* * *

Then nothing.

Several times he warned his parents in letters that he would be home soon on furlough. But no new orders came, only rumors, the lifeblood of soldiers.

Twice a day he and the other boys all went out and stood at attention with the expectation of finding out where he was headed next. But it would be just another glorified roll call. Boyd came to believe the army air force brass cherished having the boys stand in formation even more than officers from the armored forces did back in Camp Chaffee.

In early August he learned that he was headed to Plant Park in Tampa, Florida, an army air force personnel replacement center, where he would probably be assigned to a B-17 crew. But still no orders came, only repeated processing and paperwork. And more standing in formation.

The delay caused him to miss the big celebration of his parents' twenty-fifth wedding anniversary. The gathering for Herb and Lylle was held at the church. It had gone on well past midnight, featuring what was described in the newspaper as an "impressive devotional service," and included a ladies quartet singing a favorite of many, "Love at Home."

Kindly heaven smiles above, When there's love at home;
All the world is filled with love, When there's love at home;
Sweeter sings the brooklet by, Brighter beams the azure sky;
Oh, there's One who smiles on high, When there's love at home.

His mother loved the old-style Evangelical hymns, an attachment Boyd shared. The sweet harmonies moved with an inner reasoning that said more than the words about inward strength. He took great pleasure in singing the assertive bass lines of those hymns, the confident upward and downward fourths and fifths anchoring the hearty refrains. Few things were more gratifying than singing the bottom pedal note during a drawn-out amen to finish.

No doubt his mother was pleased that four of his dad's six brothers had made it to the celebration. Two of Herb's brothers, Jesse and Albert, had married Lylle's two sisters, Gertie and Elvie. Another brother, Reuben, was married to Nona, a cousin of Lylle's who was as close to her as a sister. All the cross-marrying probably explained his mother's boundless enthusiasm for large family gatherings, something Boyd did not share.

While not regretful that he had missed his parents' anniversary celebration, he was, however, very disappointed that he would be arriving home too late for threshing time on his uncles' farms. Few things were more fun and satisfying than working outside in the dust and dirt, and nothing quite beat the good weather and festive all-hands production of threshing, with plenty to eat and drink all day. It was also one of the rare times his mother tolerated beer drinking within her viewing proximity.

* * *

The final mile of Boyd's trip home was signaled by a slow, shaky pull along the south edge of town, passing by the single-wire wooden poles leaning forlornly, left behind from the high age of the telegraph. The canning factory crept by on the left side, just before the train crossed over the old timber and concrete bridge perched high above the river. Soon, gliding past on the right-hand side, almost an arm's length away, was the loading dock where Boyd often watched the trains pass as he put the final nails and wire onto packing crates of barn equipment about to be shipped.

Only then was the small gray wooden depot in sight, just ahead.

His parents would be standing there, his dad towering over his mother, who always shrunk herself by hunching forward a little bit. Both wore glasses that were too big. Like most middle-aged men, Herb never went anywhere without wearing a broad-brimmed hat, which, combined with his slim stature, somehow gave a false impression of lankiness. Boyd's mother would no doubt be talking, and talking, while Herb would feign listening with the usual contented smile on his face. Restrained and polite, like most everything else Boyd's dad did.

The train came to a halt, and there was a half hour or so of daylight left. Boyd stepped off into evening air that still held a radiant warmth, which he always found so pleasing on summer nights.

Lost over the years is a description of how Boyd reacted when he was told that Brownie was on his way home. But the next day, when Don arrived on the same early-evening train from Milwaukee, Marie greeted him with the news. Brownie gave out a loud hoot.

* * *

Returning home from far away does something to the pitch of voices. The tones and rhythms penetrate more deeply, more soothing than any of the words. A familiar home-cooked meal calls for a stroll, stepping out into the sweet breath of early evening and the dreamy late-summer fade of light. For Boyd, the elusive moment between day and night in later years would be regularly grasped and reserved for solitude and the contemplation of matters held close.

In those years, the nighttime air of late August sometimes carried a faint, almost buttery scent, set adrift into town from the nearby fields being harvested during daylight hours. No further invitation was needed to start out under the cover of the elegant vase-shaped elms lining most of the streets.

The houses pass by, each one different from the next. A slow pace allows both feet to recall each imperfection and crack in the sidewalks, knowledge gained at a younger age when the tactile was much more important.

Down Vine Street, over to Hubbard, then up Maple. Perhaps a turn on Finch Street to walk past the darkened brick school building and, across the way off to the east, the football field. As twilight dissolves into darkness, distant laughter takes on a sharper edge. The calm is inevitably broken, a faceless hello shouted out from behind darkened porch screens, smiling overtones suggesting knowledge of some childhood antics better forgotten.

The stealth of a turning point adds to the disquiet, a nameless apprehension caused by a dizzying tug from a newly discovered larger world. It pulls hard even when surrounded by the older touchstones that gave shape and still bring comfort. The moment is both unsettling and agreeable, strictly reserved for those coming of age, a brief awareness that never comes again.

* * *

Early the next morning, in eastern France, Simon Doillon leaned on a large stack of firewood while making his case to Bermont with passion and thoroughness. Claude Vougnon was also there, and the three were standing together just inside a wooded area along the road to Chazelot, a village nestled into a valley eight miles south of Vesoul.

Simon pressed hard for Bermont to give his agreement to what he had proposed to the Ukrainians the night before. He wanted Bermont to take the Ukrainians under his command. The sudden infusion of an entire battalion of trained men and their weapons would be an opportunity like no other, a resistance group with the ability to militarily challenge the Boches.

Bermont was the *nom de guerre* of thirty-four-year-old Pierre Bertin, a professional military man since he was twenty-two. A graduate of Saint-Maixent military academy, he was a rarity, an active-duty officer who had taken up arms alongside partisans, always willing to adapt his military training to the impoverished and often imprecise world of fighting as an insurgent.

He had been stationed in Grenoble, part of the so-called French Army of the Armistice originally left in place in the unoccupied areas of France and in colonial areas. When his unit was dissolved by the Germans in 1942, Bermont had remained in Grenoble, keeping in contact with his dispersed company while organizing provisions of food, equipment, and ammunition for resistance efforts.

Then an old story. The timeless way of authoritarian control is to press a societal descent into a climate of fear. Something is seen. With the encouragement of those authorities, something is said. After Bermont was denounced, he barely escaped capture by the Gestapo. He made his way home to Haute-Saône in October 1943.

* * *

The reality of French resistance as a messy and ambiguous story never quite makes it into the impregnable romantic construct of the Second World War. Few words are so elastic in meaning as "collaboration" and yet so sharply pointed in utterance. Within Haute-Saône, as it was across France, what citizens thought and did was a complicated mix. The number of those involved in resistance was, at best, tiny. The partisan forces were never monolithic, nor were their operations structured as suggested by the various organizational diagrams and flowcharts that seemed to bloom after the war.

In Haute-Saône, the maquisards had a reputation for thuggery. Their indiscriminate theft and violence served to push the local peasants away from supporting the resistance effort, a gift to the occupiers. German reprisals were also effective, to the point that in early 1944 a prefect in Haute-Saône wrote "less and less do the terrorists enjoy the complicity of the rural population."

Bermont helped reverse this with the emergence of FFI Groupe V starting in mid-1944. In May he had been made responsible for the FFI not only in Vesoul, but also with regard to a number of smaller maquis subgroups in the area. On paper, his position was part of a tiered FFI command structure that extended from London into each département in France, while the reality was an alphabet soup of groups beyond the FFI. He worked mightily to bring some order and comity to the area's resistance.

His headquarters were on the banks of the Saône River, a forest hut built for him eight miles due west of Vesoul. Bermont became well known for his bicycle travels around the region, along with his ability to secure personal connections, including with the local version of the FTP (Francs-Tireurs et Partisans), the military branch of the French Communist Party. The latter was no small achievement, even in sparsely populated Haute-

Saône. He also developed contacts within the Vesoul police and with local farmers willing to supply food to maquisards.

* * *

As the dark-haired Bermont listened to Simon, his initial reaction was mixed.

He knew that the war's long quiet in Haute-Saône would soon be ending. Just within the past few days there had been a sudden increase in German troops moving through the area. Vesoul was a junction point for several major roads and railways running northeast from Dijon, as well as the route from Paris to Basel. If a full retreat was going to be on, as appeared to be the case, huge numbers of German troops would likely be coming from the west and south through the area, many headed toward the Belfort Gap. That would probably signal the end of the days of restricted sabotage, up to now, limited by orders from London to railways and telephone lines.

Bermont believed that a new phase of resistance would likely begin, one of combat. The idea of the FFI Groupe V having its own armed and trained battalion was attractive, if not audacious. On the other hand, it was also a question of whether the time was right.

In many parts of eastern France it was a morning ritual to listen to the news program broadcast out of Switzerland at a quarter past eight. The BBC was listened to as well, but the Swiss were considered more truthful. The BBC's reputation suffered from its attempts to preach spontaneous insurrection, viewed by some in France as a simplistic British recipe for anarchy. Bermont was confident from the news reports that, as of Tuesday morning, the Allies had not yet reached Paris, and that almost a week after the landing in the south there had not yet been a breakout from Marseille. The Allies could not be counted on to liberate Haute-Saône anytime soon.

A few weeks earlier it had become known among maquisards in that area of France that the Germans had received formal orders to burn down any village where they found signs of the resistance. There would be a high risk of severe reprisals directed at the local population while the Germans were hunting down a rebel battalion.

Bermont concluded that such a momentous decision would have to be made by someone in the FFI with authority at the national level. He already had an appointment to see Paul Guepratte, alias "Bouchery," a former reserve officer and railway inspector and FFI Commander for the

Haute-Saône département. Guepratte was considered a direct representative of the overall FFI command in London.

* * *

Each taking a separate route, Bermont, Simon, and Claude rode their bicycles to Quenoche, a few miles farther south and east. It was still midmorning when they regathered at the old mill that served as Guepratte's command post.

The presentation was made by Bermont, who while doing so observed Simon's discipline in keeping his own excitement in check, intervening only to answer questions. When the presentation was finished, Guepratte was hesitant to make a decision, for the same reasons as Bermont. He suggested a meeting with the Ukrainians that evening.

When Guepratte and Simon arrived at the battalion's campsite just outside of Vesoul, they found the meadow cleared.

The Ukrainians were gone.

* * *

Simon made inquiries in the immediate area. He soon learned that the unit had decamped and marched back into Vesoul, reportedly to board a train headed to Dijon, fifty miles to the west. He and Guepratte returned to the Doillon dairy, where a uniformed Ukrainian appeared.

Wozniak.

It took only a brief exchange to convince Guepratte. Simon was given the authority and a free hand in finalizing arrangements with the Ukrainians. Guepratte urged him to get to Dijon as soon as possible, giving him money and a formal accreditation to present to his FFI equivalent, who was responsible for the département of Côte d'Or.

Wozniak dashed off again and barely made the train departing Vesoul.

* * *

The next day, Simon and a local mechanic and friend of his named Bloch made the drive to Dijon in an old gasifier pickup truck. Doillon made contact with the local resistance, but even with the accreditation from Guepratte, he only met skepticism and was rebuffed in efforts to obtain any cooperation and assistance.

The snub turned out not to matter. The Ukrainians were nowhere to be found in Dijon.

Simon returned, discouraged, and appeared at Bermont's command post in the woods along the Saône River. He gave his report. And in a change of heart, he then accepted Bermont's previous offer of a deputy position in Groupe V.

The Ukrainians were not mentioned again, and the matter was considered closed. There were many other things to do.

* * *

Haute-Saône was no longer a placid backwater of the war. With each passing hour, more and more Germans were moving eastward through the area by every means possible.

All the energies of Groupe V were now occupied by planning and coordinating full-scale guerrilla activities.

On Wednesday, one of the maquis groups under Bermont, Groupe X113, carried out an operation of significant sabotage, using explosives to damage a major railway line about twenty miles west of Vesoul. The tracks were being used by numerous trains carrying German troops and heavy armor.

The next day a report reached Bermont from the mayor of Fresne Saint-Mamès, indicating that a "battalion of Cossacks" had arrived the previous evening. Their journey east toward Vesoul had been forced to a halt by the damage inflicted by Groupe X113. The unit had then marched a few miles to the east, arriving in Fresne Saint-Mamès at six in the evening. The mayor reported that he had been ordered by the Germans to set up the bivouac area for the unit. He estimated that there were 750 "Cossacks" in the German-commanded unit. Bermont passed the information on to Guepratte.

CHAPTER ELEVEN

Beatitude

Friday, August 25, 1944

FOR MYROSLAW'S BATTALION, the last week of August had been a mad series of movements back and forth. For Hloba and a few others, it had also been a week of a wild swing from hope to despair. Each day brought a new sense of impending doom into an already tense mix of confusion and suspicion.

* * *

The week had begun with the triumphal return to camp Monday evening by Hloba and Wozniak from their meeting with Simon Doillon. Pleased with themselves and impatient about moving ahead with the next steps, the two had given a report of the discussion to Polichtchuk and Zintchouk.

On Tuesday came Hanenstein's order to decamp and march back into Vesoul and the train station. Hloba had been thunderstruck, and tried to learn their destination. But the Germans were silent, making no secret of their distrust of him and the rest of the Ukrainians. Only at the train station in Vesoul did Hloba learn, from the stationmaster rather than the Germans, that they were headed to Dijon, more than fifty miles to the west. Wozniak had then gone off in search of Simon Doillon and had found him, along with his commander, Guepratte. Wozniak had just made it back before the train pulled away.

On Wednesday, with the same suddenness and lack of explanation, the trip west was abruptly cut short, in Gray, about half the distance to Dijon.

The battalion was soon on another train heading east, under new orders to return to Vesoul. Rumors had them going back to Germany, some saying that they would become part of the Siegfried Line defense. Hloba and the other three conspirators were not so sure about such rumors, fearful that the Germans had somehow gotten wind of their plan. To them, German concerns about a rebellion were becoming apparent, and any realistic possibility of a mutiny was probably lost forever.

* * *

As he stared out of the train as it headed east back toward Vesoul on late Wednesday afternoon, Hloba was furious, a deep anger against an entire world.

Looking out at the countryside, a stray thought intruded into his consciousness. What a beautiful world it was. He found himself taking in the blue and green tones spread under the tranquil late-summer sky, the verdant plains stretching away from the Saône River and fingering their way into the unbroken chain of rounded hills and dark green forests.

It was a strange moment, to be reflecting on such beauty while immersed in such a dark unknown and likely terrible fate that lay ahead. He surprised himself by somehow drawing an unfounded optimism.

* * *

The train carrying the battalion came to a stop twenty miles short of Vesoul, in Vellexon. Earlier in the day some French terrorists had done significant damage to the main rail line a few miles to the east. Myroslaw's battalion was ordered off, and after organizing themselves and their equipment, they marched four miles to the village of Fresne Saint-Mamès. It was six in the evening when they settled in and were informed by their German commanders that they would remain there for a week.

Thus the arrival of the battalion of "Cossacks" as reported to Bermont by Monsieur Rollin, mayor of Fresne Saint-Mamès.

* * *

At week's end the Ukrainian officers found themselves quartered in a building on the main road in the tiny village of Fresne Saint-Mamès, fifteen miles west of Vesoul. Nearby was the town's lone church and its squat twelfth-century steeple, a short walk from where Myroslaw and the rest of the battalion's soldiers were encamped.

Meanwhile, the tensions between the Germans and Ukrainians had become so thick they were even apparent to the ever-watchful locals, who observed a silent wariness between the two groups.

On that Friday evening of such an unquiet week, Hloba gathered his small band together, expanded to include a few more beyond the original group of four which had consisted of himself, Wozniak, Polichtchuk, and Zintchouk. Some trains were still running eastward. Hloba had begun to wonder if they were being held at Fresne Saint-Mamès until more German troops could be spared to guard the Ukrainians. He was now of a view that their very survival was at stake. Decisions needed to be made.

They discussed two options.

The first was to confront and eliminate the Germans and then set up a foothold in a nearby forest where they could try to hold out. The second was to attempt restoring contact with the French partisans before initiating any action.

The small group ended the evening with agreement that they would not be able to survive on their own. Wozniak was designated to venture out again to find Simon Doillon.

Hloba told him to do so at any cost.

* * *

In Wisconsin, the week had been like no other.

It was a perfection. Life does not often provide such felicity and plenitude of being all at once.

hree Classmates On Furloughs

A coincidence and unplanned reunion is in progress here this week when three servicemen, representing the Army, the Navy and the Air Force arrived home

Boyd and Don's reunion expanded with the unexpected arrival of yet another pal from the class of 1940, Johnny, who had come home on shore leave to visit his wife and baby.

The boys were front-page news. They were reported to be "making the most of it."

In that ungenerous climate, there are but a rare handful of days, and in some years none at all, when nature seems to take a short breather and delivers an almost perfect state of equilibrium between the intense grip of summer and the slide of autumn. Such unnamed exquisiteness was given to the arriving boys.

What a time they had.

The entire town seemed to be caught up in the marvelous happenstance, an unbridled joy that was spread everywhere. It was one back-slapping greeting after another. Cars would stop in the middle of the road while someone inside would holler out at them.

Boyd and Brownie were inseparable, making the rounds together as Marie tagged along and took photos while they posed at various houses.

Very few boys their age were in town anymore, a noticeable absence, unlike the cities so crowded with young men in uniform. Parents of other boys off in the service made a point to come up and greet them, as though a warm conversation and the inevitable brief tender touch on the lapel of the uniform would bring their own sons just a little closer. Boyd knew that his parents did the same when others visited home.

As of June, there were six million American boys overseas. Neither Don nor Boyd had such orders yet, but both expected them to come soon. Boyd knew that once he was in Florida he would be sent to some further training before going overseas for combat duty, either in Italy or England. As for Don, Camp Pickett had been full of rumors, and the scoop was that something must be up, that their time was coming.

During the week it went unsaid that it was the last visit by the boys before they headed off to the war. But the poignancy hovered, a visible luster that surrounded them all week, at least for those who looked hard enough.

* * *

The news reports each day injected a noisy and exhilarating backdrop to the week. Frenzied headlines shouted out how the Allies were racing across France from the west and the south. Only a month before, daily progress had been measured in a few hundred yards. Now it was jaunts of twenty to forty miles, the newspapers becoming hard-pressed to come up with stirring new verbs to describe a German Army in full retreat into eastern France.

On Friday came one word, not normally part of the town's lexicon.

Paris.

Americans were in Paris.

Paris was liberated.

It was not that anyone around town had any particular feelings toward the French, much less anyone even having traveled to Paris. But on that Friday, the word was said out loud over and over. The word brought another sublime overlay to the week. It was not a feeling of pride or even a turning of the tide, but something more important: a promise of return, the trajectory of life being set back toward normal.

For the boys and Marie, the news fit perfectly into the week. It returned them to what already in their young lives felt like another age, those breathless days surrounding their high school graduation when the Germans had been on the march.

They felt the electricity all over again. They talked about it. It was the same exotic location and the same war. It was so distant back then. And it had now taken over their lives. They were now so much older, they said.

There was much that each of them wanted back, strong feelings about things taken from them that needed to be returned. And maybe now that would happen with the war ending soon.

Perhaps the best news of the entire week, right on the front page of Friday afternoon's *Milwaukee Journal*, was a report that no less than the US Army saw the war with Germany coming to an end before October.

* * *

A mild Friday evening would always draw a steady stream of foot traffic, good for business, good for feeling connected. There is ritual in the sociable flow of people moving up and down the street on Friday nights. To hurry is to miss the point. And perhaps a few laughs.

Foot traffic comes out of the popular Armstrong & Paul ("Good Lunch and Tavern"), and the natural route crosses the street toward the river. And, Ernst hopes, into his corner store in the Oddfellows Building, constructed in 1878 and so proclaimed among the bricks near its roofline. Ernst shares the building and a common landing, three steps up from the sidewalk, with Frank Bossman and his drugstore. Two doors down is Adam Port's bakery, almost shy in appearance next to the magisterial floor-to-ceiling windows looking into Herman Wilke's hardware store, whose son had come in second place to Billy at the flower show. A few more paces to the east and a friendly wave is likely to come from one of the chairs in Fred Westfall's barber shop, in operation since 1892. Then another tavern, then the air-conditioned Pastime, where there is a single center aisle, five seats to the right and four to the left. Showing that Friday evening, at 7:00 and 8:50, is the 1936 movie *Comin' Round the Mountain*, with Gene Autry and Ann Rutherford.

The congenial air of late summertime dusk somehow subdues sharp edges and brash colors during the delicate fade into twilight. In the remaining glow of the day, the streetlights blink on but never quite overtake the much brighter inviting light coming from inside the stores. The warm night is gentle as it washes over the amiable end-of-week serenity on Main Street, a full display of the deliberate evenness that was once the American culture of the small town. It thrives that evening along tens of thousands of main streets, from the Midwest to both coasts.

It is as distant from the twenty-first century as the Great Flood.

* * *

At that very moment, all across the planet, an incalculable mass of supplications are being offered, each a prayer of despair for events to hasten forward, for the ongoing storm to reach its end. But closer to home, as the achingly sweet week of perfection draws to a close, there is an intense quiet wish for the hours to stop, the soulful yearning for things just to stay forever in that moment.

Since the ancients, man has been tantalized by the elusive nature of time and the mystery of eternity. It is easy to imagine the first such roiling thoughts by an early human, a tilt of the head at some ephemeral wonder of life witnessed in the unearthly sheen of the last warm rays of the day, or perhaps a lonely glance upward at the cold celestial infinity after life tore open a dreadful first vision of a savage domain.

Splendor and terror can both be too big, a wicked thing to bear for the fresher senses of the young that are their province alone, before the sounds slowly begin to fade and the colors gradually turn pale. Never again will being engulfed by deep friendship, love, and the comforting equanimity of an unsensational street scene feel so profound, nor, as so many will later discover, will the terrors of looming menace ever again be so tangible that each breath of air takes on a metallic taste.

When awash in a single moment so vivid, there are unaccountable twinges, something beyond ordinary perception. The past and future are both subsumed and even the presence of the now is lost, all of those eternities abruptly supplanted by a brief awareness that is greater than knowledge. An imprint is left, about one's self and about one's world. The mark can be hidden, but it can never be erased.

Clerics emerged after the war to define for us its crimes, and continue to do so, dispensing received wisdom from a learned distance. Always ignored, though, is the grossest offense.

Everywhere on earth, they are all too young.

The war is nothing but a thief of youth, taking payment for the hubris and failures of those who inevitably keep themselves, and their own, apart from the miseries they have brought to the multitudes.

CHAPTER TWELVE

Chance and Necessity

Saturday, August 26, 1944

O N SATURDAY MORNING, Wozniak boarded the earliest train heading east to Vesoul, making sure his departure went unnoticed. He made it all the way to the Vesoul station unchallenged, an achievement of note in an area not only infested by the Gestapo, the local fascist militia, and informants of all types, but also now swarming with German soldiers transiting the area. No doubt the uniform was helpful, but it was more likely plain luck.

He left the station in Vesoul and walked several miles without incident to the Doillon dairy. Simon himself was present, and they went upstairs to talk, over some coffee.

It was early afternoon when Jean Reuchet, head of the FTP for Haute-Saône, arrived at the Doillon dairy. However uncommon it was in France for Communists to join forces with the De Gaulle–led FFI, Reuchet had good working relationships with both Bermont and Doillon. Earlier that week, Simon had poured out the story of the Ukrainians to Reuchet, including his frustration with Guepratte's hesitation and the lost opportunity of the rebel battalion. As usual, they commiserated about the absence of assistance from the Allies.

Informed that Doillon was in the dairy's upper level, Reuchet climbed the steps and came upon the sight of Simon with an amiable look on his face while having coffee with an officer in a German uniform. He approached the two just as Wozniak was explaining the battalion's situation and his own orders to reestablish contact. The unit would soon be heading back east. He recounted Hloba's concern that the Germans had somehow learned of the planned mutiny, and the growing conviction that once in Vesoul, where there was a German garrison, the Ukrainians would be sent to Germany where they would all be executed.

Simon told Reuchet to grab a coffee. He said that they would soon be leaving, that he would be taking Wozniak back to his unit, and that Reuchet could come along. The three of them went outside and got into a dairy truck. Wozniak was hidden in the back alongside Reuchet and his bicycle, among empty milk cans. Simon fired up the coal-burning gasifier and they headed toward Fresne Saint-Mamès, fourteen miles to the west.

* * *

A few minutes into the journey they came upon a German roadblock. Simon showed his papers, and the truck was allowed to move on. A few miles later there was another stop, and once again they were allowed to proceed.

About halfway to Fresne Saint-Mamès they crossed a railroad bridge, about five hundred yards short of the entrance to the village of Raze, where they came upon a detachment of Cossacks. As they got closer they could see the unit was in chaos, the apparent aftermath of a skirmish with some maquisards.

Simon maneuvered past the Cossacks, who ignored the truck.

As they entered Raze, Wozniak's luck ran out. The dairy truck was stopped by Germans. Wozniak was found and recognized. He was unable to show any authorization for leaving his unit, and the Germans ordered him off the vehicle. Simon and Reuchet were astonished when the Germans sent them on their way without even checking their papers. Reuchet got out of the truck and onto his bike and headed back to Vesoul, while Simon continued on to Fresne Saint-Mamès.

* * *

Questioned by the Germans who had stopped him, Wozniak coolly insisted that he was out looking for wine. While his story was very believable given the Ukrainians' reputation for alcohol intake, the

Germans pushed back. Wozniak held to his story. Not hiding their frustration, the Germans sent him back to Fresne Saint-Mamès, to go before Sturmbannführer Hanenstein.

When asked by Hanenstein to justify having left the encampment, Wozniak repeated his story about buying wine. Shaking his head as he spoke, Hanenstein said that he knew exactly why Wozniak was with the French, why he was out in an area full of insurgents and terrorists.

But then Hanenstein stopped. There were no more questions. Wozniak was taken back to his quarters.

* * *

Hanenstein was in no position to go any further. He was a man in a standoff. As was Hloba.

Hanenstein knew the Germans were outnumbered. They would not be able to defend themselves against any sudden action against them by the Ukrainians.

But the Ukrainians, too, were at an impasse. There was no way for them to hold out very long by themselves, alone in a foreign land.

Hanenstein placed guards around the building that housed the Ukrainian officers. Their presence and their surveillance meant that it was not until Saturday evening that Wozniak was able to report to Hloba on his contact with Simon.

* * *

When Simon and his gasifier truck reached Fresne Saint-Mamès, he went to the mayor to alert him of the situation. He did the same with a few other trusted residents, making arrangements for providing the battalion with supplies and assistance in a safe hiding location, should that be needed.

Simon then attempted to reach Hloba. He approached the building where the Ukrainian officers were housed and saw the German soldiers all around. Keeping his distance, he slipped into a building directly across the road. Furtively waving from an open window on the first floor, he caught Hloba's eye, and soon they begin to communicate via hand signals. It took some time before Simon understood Hloba's message that they would probably have to wait until morning before they could meet. For the rest of the night, Doillon continued to stand near the open window, keeping watch.

At five in the morning Hloba noticed the German guards walking away. He called out to Simon, who ran across the street, into the building, and upstairs into Hloba's room, joined by Wozniak and the others. They locked the door.

Then commenced what Hloba would later call "the council of war."

Simon began, giving his agreement on behalf of the FFI to move forward with the terms negotiated earlier in the week. Hloba and Wozniak were both anxious, insisting that the Germans suspected something was afoot and that they needed to act.

The mutiny would take place that evening, the night of Sunday, August 27. The Germans would be eliminated, and Simon would then lead the Ukrainians to the place he had chosen for them to hide. He explained how he had made arrangements for the battalion to encamp in one of the nearby woods and had worked to ensure that they would have a food supply. His plan was to leave Fresne Saint-Mamès and return at five o'clock in the afternoon with a map and other information.

And so things were agreed. It was half past five on Sunday morning when Simon got up to leave the meeting.

* * *

Simon was back at Bermont's command post by nine o'clock, reporting that the mutiny was set to take place that evening at the encampment. He described the arrangements he had made for support of the battalion in the aftermath. Wasting no time, Doillon then started out, back to Fresne Saint-Mamès, grabbing a crust of bread to eat on the way.

He arrived to find that the Ukrainians had once again vanished.

CHAPTER THIRTEEN

Solemn Rituals

Sunday, August 27, 1944

O N SUNDAY MORNINGS there were no official rules as to seating during church services. But in practice most of the darkened oak pews may as well have been formally reserved, if not privately owned. A good thing, too, given the spiritual vertigo that would set in while sitting through a sermon in a spot different than one's usual location. Happily, the seating arrangements were so deeply ingrained among the congregation that such unfortunate mishaps would only happen to those regulars who, although they knew better, would arrive late to a crowded Christmas or Easter service.

For Marie, pregnant or not, the pews were never comfortable. A softer Lutheranism that included cushions would not arrive for another four decades.

When Don was home, Marie would sit with the Browns in their usual location, third pew from the front row, just to the left of the center aisle. Otherwise she stuck to her own family's spot, off to the right and under a balcony, where she had fidgeted as a child. Her father had long ago settled into the second pew, the site of the famous projectile sneeze.

In a small community the lines blur between ritual, habit, and requirement. The prearranged seating ensured a quick study for any notable absentees and provided for a critical contribution to the information network activated throughout town most Sunday afternoons.

Dial service would not come to the town for another five years. All calls were directed through the central telephone office on Main Street, above the furniture store. Lift the receiver, turn the crank, and offer a prayer the call would go through anyone other than the chief operator, who some said could scowl right through the phone line. Boyd was one of several in town who took delight in imitating Edna's well-known snarl as she directed a call. Whether she focused only on the connection and location information or extended her interest to the content of conversations was a matter of speculation.

Liturgically speaking, the epistle and gospel had their place, but central to all the worship services in town was the gaze of other congregants. It was on Sunday afternoons that the theological divides of the morning were smoothly crossed by telephone, including with Marie's mother. Reports were shared about no-shows at the morning services, new illnesses, unfortunate fashion ventures (often involving a new hat), and the occasional tsks and tuts about someone's peevish child. It made for a well-informed community and allowed the town to start its business each Monday with few surprises.

* * *

On that Sunday morning, Marie was still basking in the glow of the week. She was proud to be sitting next to Don, who was wearing his crisp khaki uniform with the sergeant stripes all but jumping right off his sleeve. He was still only a hair taller than Marie, but since going into the service eighteen months before he had undergone a transformation, filling out and hardening into a thicker version of himself. But he remained a full mix of his dad and his mother, who sat on the other side of Don, never far away.

Sunday was supposed to have been one of the biggest days of the summer, the annual railroad picnic down at the city park. The event, put on by the Old Line Service Club, the local employees of the Milwaukee Road railroad, was always an elaborate production and a full day of activities, including two ball games. In unusual deference that spoke to the importance of the picnic, there had not been either a Saturday night dance or the usual Friday night city band concert, both events held off until Sunday.

But an all-day rain, welcomed by many farmers, meant that the ball games were washed out, the band concert canceled, and the usual races called off. The afternoon's steady downpour also helped to increase the odds of Ernst fading into a nap during his favorite news programs.

* * *

Douglas Edwards began his afternoon broadcast of *The World Today* with the headlines, in the usual staccato format:

> The Allies are giving the Germans a steady drubbing as the enemy retreats toward the Reich.
>
> General Patton's armored columns have made new advances between the Marne and Seine Rivers.
>
> In Southern France, Toulon is now completely ours, and the Allied bag of German prisoners has passed the twenty-three thousand mark.
>
> Paris is swinging back to normalcy, despite some enemy sniping and a bombing attack by the Luftwaffe. General DeGaulle narrowly escaped death or injury yesterday when thousands of Parisians were thrown into panic by wild flurries of gunfire during a parade.
>
> On Europe's eastern front, Soviet troops are moving deeper into Rumania.
>
> The Hungarian underground radio has called for a vote in Hungary . . .

The first news report, direct from Paris about the day's events in France, included a specific mention of how beautiful the day had been.

CHAPTER FOURTEEN

We Drink, Drink, and Drink Again

Sunday, August 27, 1944

AFTER SIMON'S DEPARTURE at five thirty Sunday morning, Hloba had a few moments alone in his room to consider what had just been agreed.

His solitude was soon interrupted. He was informed that a German captain had arrived in the encampment area earlier that morning, likely coming from Vesoul. Whatever communication he brought must have been important, because all German officers in the battalion had been awakened and summoned to a meeting.

Hloba was also told that rumors were swirling around the soldiers that morning about the Ukrainians stationed to the south having had a bloody battle with the Germans before going over to the French partisans. Hloba dismissed it as "field fables," not realizing until later that day the rumor was true, and the subject of the early morning meeting of German officers.

* * *

New orders from Hanenstein arrived. The battalion was to prepare for a departure that morning at seven o'clock. They would be going to Vesoul, on foot.

First light was still half an hour away. Once more alone in his room, Hloba had a chance to reflect on things. As the bell in the nearby steeple began striking six o'clock, Hloba came to a realization.

The Germans knew.

He was now certain that the battalion was being returned to Vesoul, where they would be disarmed and then executed. There was one hour left to do something.

* * *

Hloba went to tell Polichtchuk, Zintchouk, and Wozniak to leave the building and go out to the local café, already opened to accommodate the Germans. He then slipped away separately and managed to find the home of the village mayor. He hoped to get a warning to Doillon.

Responding to Hloba's knocking on the front door, the mayor appeared, still half asleep but impeccably polite. Using a combination of bad German, worse French, and a generous amount of frantic gestures, Hloba insisted that the mayor had to get word to Simon Doillon about the sudden change in orders.

The mayor only shrugged his shoulders, smiling kindly. His repeated response to everything Hloba said was "I know nothing." The back-and-forth went on for a while, Hloba's agitated insistence facing off against the mayor's impervious friendliness. Hloba became convinced that the mayor, in fact, knew nothing. He angrily slammed the door closed and left.

Twenty minutes wasted.

He ran and caught up with the other three coconspirator officers having coffee, joining them at their table. At the other end of the café a few German officers were seated. The proximity presented a challenge to conducting a discussion, so the Ukrainians interspersed their quiet exchanges in between volleys of deliberately loud laughter and boisterous jokes.

Hloba explained his assessment that they must confront the Germans during the march. He was convinced that once they were in Vesoul they would all be facing a quick death. The others agreed. The decision was made.

He furtively pulled out a map of the area and pointed to the intersection of the road to Vesoul with a railway. He kept his instructions simple.

"When the end of our column goes beyond this point, I will launch a flare. At the green signal, you will order the soldiers to fire on the Germans. No prisoners!"

He said they would then head for the nearest suitable woods. And they would somehow reestablish contact with Simon Doillon.

The others nodded in silence.

* * *

A waitress brought over a few bottles of wine to start their day along with the coffee, a gesture not inconsistent with the reputation of the Ukrainians. Hloba and the others waved for her not to do so, indicating they did not have the money to pay. The waitress managed to communicate to them that she knew they were not German, and invited them as brave men to drink to their health.

For Hloba, it was a welcome sign of the handiwork of Simon Doillon.

* * *

A few minutes before the seven o'clock departure, the four Ukrainian officers stood up to leave. They had agreed to split up and make just a few others aware of the planned action.

Hloba was the last to leave. At the door of the café, he was approached by Hanenstein.

Facing Hloba with his memorably small eyes and slender Prussian countenance, he gave Hloba a leer and a wicked smile.

"So you drink?"

Hloba responded, "We drink, drink, and drink again!"

But he was no longer looking at Hanenstein as he spoke the words, walking past him and out through the doorway.

* * *

As Hloba headed toward the rest of the battalion, still organizing itself in preparation for the march to Vesoul, he met the battalion doctor, a sturdy little man with a short pointed beard. Kapandse was Georgian, and very sympathetic to the Ukrainians. He despised the Germans with all his soul, an enmity that had advanced into a vicious hatred after the Germans had discovered that his wife, Maria, whom he loved very dearly, had been smuggled on the journey from East Prussia. She had been forcibly removed somewhere in Germany. He did not know what became of her.

Kapandse spoke a mix of Russian and Ukrainian, and greeted Hloba with curses about the Boches.

Hloba responded agreeably. "It is time for the Boches to see."

"You speak well," said Kapandse. "I also think like that. I would also like to drink Boche blood once." He then burst into a cruel chuckle.

Hloba again replied. "Well, we will drink Boche blood."

"I'll be ready. I want from you the order."

"Today at ten o'clock. Near the village of Noidans-le-Ferroux. Be ready."

"I have five Boches in my medical group. I'll take care of them."

Hloba continued walking toward the battalion.

* * *

The sun was just above the horizon as the unit was ready to depart. The wary Germans had deliberately directed a wide spacing between the soldiers, groupings separated by a distance of more than a hundred yards. The entire column extended almost two miles.

Hloba, on horseback, was in the section at the front. Right behind was Captain Polichtchuk's company, followed by a section of German military staff, some of whom rode in the column's lone automobile, which had brought the German captain from Vesoul a few hours earlier along with the news of the rebellion of the Ukrainian battalion to the south.

In the middle of the long column was the battalion's store of arms and ammunition, this time under the watch of a small German force. Following behind was the headquarters company, then the wagons of heavy weapons, heavy machine guns. and trench mortars, followed by a third company, under the command of Captain Zintchouk. The last part of the column was the group responsible for feeding the battalion.

* * *

On full display that Sunday morning was the surprising horse-dependency of the great German war machine. It was a spectacle, a cavalcade of a thousand men and three hundred wagons and carts pulled by the sweating and blowing horses.

The pace along the asphalt road was slow, and it took more than an hour for the entire column to pass by, had there been any spectators out in the open. The sky overhead was a cloudless crystalline blue, the indifferent early-morning bliss of late summer bathing the rolling fields and patches of forest. Even with so many men and horses and so much equipment of war on the move, the march had a quiet tranquility, interrupted only by cries of birds and the occasional shout in German attempting to move things ahead at a faster pace.

The heat of the day was gradually making itself known. In their woolen uniforms, Myroslaw and the rest of the Ukrainian soldiers trudged on, quietly lost in their own thoughts. There was no reason to hurry, not with all those rumors. A few Ukrainian officers knew about the plans and the signal flare, while the ordinary soldiers like Myroslaw knew nothing.

* * *

Near the front of the convoy, Hloba was at one with the rhythm of the horse he was riding. Once more, he was deep in reflection.

He found himself struggling with the realization that the very existence of almost a thousand men trailing behind was in his hands, a fate unknown to most of them. It weighed heavily on him.

As he rode on, he considered that weakness was never in short supply, and he wondered what the attitude of the soldiers would be at the decisive moment. He himself had been resolute and without any hesitation in giving the orders to his coconspirators. Would the Ukrainians follow their Ukrainian officers? Would they lose their cool?

Their deep hatred of the Germans was not in question. But would they have the courage to raise their hand against them?

As for those few officers in the know, he sensed at that moment that they, too, were each considering what lay ahead, when they would throw themselves on the Germans and make them pay for all of the humiliations, all of the atrocities they had inflicted on fathers, mothers, brothers, and sisters, and on their homeland.

Looking around, Hloba mused about the Germans. He observed they had frowns on their faces, suggesting to him an uneasiness and apprehension. Perhaps, he thought, the poor devils were sensing somewhere deep in their soul the approaching end. Perhaps that was the reason for their wanting to hurry the march along, as if they could remove themselves from the arms of an unknown death.

* * *

Hloba had binoculars and was able to monitor the column's progress all the way back to the rear. It was midmorning when the leading section of the long parade began to approach the village of Noidans-le-Ferroux, just about the halfway point of their march to Vesoul. He made another check toward the rear.

At last. The final group at the end of the column was crossing the point where the asphalt road intersected with the railway.

It was time.

With a nod of the head to an assistant, Hloba gave his order.

The rocket was launched, the flare darting up with a whistle. High above the column, it etched an arc of green fire and smoke against the deep-blue background.

Nothing happened.

There were Ukrainians holding weapons who knew what the signal meant. But no one dared to shoot. Nobody wanted to be the first.

In the grouping behind Hloba someone barked out an order.

"V dya-haj-te sho-lo-my!" (Helmets in place!)

The Ukrainian soldiers in the section followed the command as a matter of rote. They put their helmets on.

On a horse next to Lieutenant Hryntchouk, who had given the order, was a German officer, Obersturmführer Bentz. He had not understood the words, but seeing the Ukrainian soldiers respond, he, too, started to put on his helmet.

Hryntchouk did not let that happen. He turned, raised his gun, and emptied the contents of its magazine into Bentz's head.

The German tumbled off his horse.

The Ukrainians in the section took his example. They began firing on the Germans next to them. They fell, one by one, onto the sunbaked asphalt road.

The mutiny was on.

* * *

Hloba steered his horse toward Hanenstein, who was unaware of what had just transpired. He approached the Sturmbannführer, pulled out his pistol, and shot him once in the head and again in the stomach.

The lone German automobile in the caravan, containing a group of German officers, started to pull out of the column. Wozniak, nearby, realized the imperative of stopping any Germans from escaping and he fired into the car, which came to a halt. Several German officers got out and attempted to flee on foot, but within steps they were lying dead on the ground, gunned down by other Ukrainians.

Gunfire crackled as the attacks spread toward the rear. Like a flame inching its way along a fuse, the hellish melee advanced down the length of the column.

In the center of the long parade line, the Germans realized what was happening and moved about to organize a defense. Polichtchuk, with a submachine gun slung across his shoulder while holding a Mauser in his right hand and a revolver in his left, prowled up and down the column, shouting for the Ukrainians to attack the Germans. One of the German officers, Hauptsturmführer Muller, took aim at him but instead hit a younger Ukrainian soldier named Petrovski. Polichtchuk turned and shot Muller and moved on to the next section, toward the rear.

The fighting in that area turned into a wild storm of hand-to-hand combat to the death, as shooting was impossible in such close quarters. The final killing blows were often delivered by the butt of a rifle to the head.

* * *

A Homeric telling of the scene would have had the gods overhead, spellbound as they looked down upon such vicious fury by mere mortals on a narrow battlefield little more than the width of a road, all the combatants wearing the same uniform. The battalion doctor, Kapandse, strode up and down the column with a revolver in his hand. Whenever he came upon a German lying on the ground, he would fire point-blank while screaming, "The time has come that I drink your blood."

The maelstrom made its way down to the heavy weapons company, which during the march toward Vesoul had been surrounded by German guards. Lieutenant Boiko, who was with the company, shouted out an order in Ukrainian to open fire on the forest away from the road. The Germans, not understanding what Boiko had said were willing believers of what they saw the Ukrainians in the company do and automatically jumped into the ditch alongside the road to face hidden attackers in the woods.

And that is where they lay as the Ukrainians turned and fired their weapons onto them.

* * *

The fighting was reaching its climax when in the distance there appeared a company of Wehrmacht soldiers. They had been stationed at Noidans-le-

Ferroux, assigned to guard the railroad track. Drawn by the sound of guns but uncertain what was happening, they were tentative and cautious in their approach. Hloba raced over in front of them on his horse, shouting, "Ja, Ja, terroristen, terroristen!" Spurred on, the Wehrmacht company charged ahead, running in the field toward the road.

Half were mowed down by gunfire and the rest, reaching the road, were taken in hand-to-hand combat to the death.

At the end of the column was the last section, five hundred yards apart from the rest. The signal flare had not been seen. The Germans in the rear grouping had been warned of the ongoing mutiny by a few who had managed to flee the onslaught up ahead in the long column. The Ukrainians in the section were disarmed, turned around to face the west, and started on a march back to Fresne Saint-Mamès.

When the group reached a turn in the road that abutted some woods, two armed Ukrainians emerged, one at the front of the group and one at the rear. They opened fire and began shouting at the others to kill the Boches. The weaponless Ukrainian prisoners rushed the Germans. Once again, death was delivered by brute strength of hands.

* * *

It was all over in less than an hour.

A two-mile stretch of road was left littered with German dead, including twenty-five SS officers, seventy noncommissioned officers, and more than two hundred German soldiers. The body count also included the Wehrmacht company of two officers and ninety-seven soldiers spurred on by Hloba to make the charge into their death.

One Ukrainian had been killed and six were wounded, of whom two would later die.

The Ukrainians failed on one part of their bargain with Simon Doillon. Three Germans managed to escape, including a captain.

* * *

The Ukrainians regrouped, picking up their dead and wounded, and went back on the march as soon as possible. They left the roadway to head north on a narrow path through a field. The sun was high overhead when they reached some thick woods a little more than a mile to the northeast. Hloba ordered the unit to stop. They needed to get some bearings as to what they had, where they were, and where they should go. Guards were posted on the perimeter.

Inventory was taken: 820 men, hundreds of horses, and several hundred transport wagons. Their arsenal included 4 antitank cannons, 41 mortars, 21 heavy machine guns, 120 light machine guns, 130 machine pistols, 700 rifles, 1,000 mortar rounds, and 6,000 grenades. There was three days' worth of food, and fodder for at least some of the horses.

The battalion was assembled, and Hloba spoke. He attempted to explain what had just taken place, describing how the Ukrainians would be joining with the French in the liberation of their homeland from the Germans. He stressed the need for strict discipline and its importance to the fate of the battalion. He advised them to be ready to go on the march again very soon, because the Germans would be looking for them.

With impeccable timing, the mayor of Fresne Saint-Mamès appeared.

He was no longer the man of affable ignorance awakened earlier that morning by Hloba. He offered to lead the battalion into a larger forest where there would be less danger. He also indicated he would restore contact with Simon Doillon.

CHAPTER FIFTEEN

Knights of the Moon

Sunday, August 27, 1944

IT WAS HALF past one on Sunday afternoon when Gilbert Decaudin came upon the scene.

He and four others from his small band of maquis had been in Neuvelle-lès-la-Charité, a village of two hundred people a few miles to the south, best known for the ruins of an abbey founded in the twelfth century. They were met there by the Maillo family, who told them that "the Russians just killed their SS officers at Noidans."

Gilbert and the others rode their bicycles to the spot between the railroad crossing and the entrance to Noidans-le-Ferroux.

The sight was one of horror and it filled him with joy, not yet two weeks since the death of his father. He had known something was in the air about a possible mutiny but was amazed at what he saw.

Every five yards or so, in the road and along both sides, lay the bodies of German soldiers and SS officers, most with their jaws and necks at unnatural angles. Some were already barefoot, a few even partially undressed.

He observed that the surprise must have been total. There was no sign the Germans ever had a chance to regroup. It appeared they had fallen wherever they had been stationed in the long column.

Under Gilbert's direction, the weapons and ammunition left behind were collected. He and his group were joined by some from Noidans-le-

Ferroux, and there was soon a happy commotion of horses and carts taking the German bodies away. The villagers agreed that their local cemetery was not to be desecrated with the Boches. A few days earlier, the Germans had forced them to dig trenches near the village as part of a defense preparation against the coming Allied armies. The German corpses were thrown into a few of the narrow ditches, which were then filled.

* * *

When the cleanup was completed, Gilbert entered Noidans-le-Ferroux and came upon a few villagers tending to a seriously wounded German captain. The medical care was being led by a nurse from Paris, a woman by the name of Charrière.

He gave serious consideration to killing the officer on the spot. Indeed, the longer Gilbert stood there and thought about it, the more he concluded it was what he should do.

But he could not bring himself to kill the German.

He left, faulting himself for not having the needed courage.

* * *

The search was on for the missing battalion.

At six in the evening, Noidans-le-Ferroux was surrounded by German armored cars. The commander of the detachment entered the village and came upon the wounded German captain, who explained that the French had not been involved in the incident.

The Ukrainians were the terrorists. It was the French who had treated his wounds.

* * *

In war chance and necessity always govern.

The failure that afternoon of the Ukrainians to liquidate each and every German, and, a few hours later, the human limitation within Gilbert Decaudin meant that the village of Noidans-le-Ferroux would not take its place alongside the atrocity of Oradour-sur-Glane.

As surely it would have, had death come earlier that day to a German captain.

* * *

For those who lived through the events of that Sunday in eastern France, the rich-blue sky and the scorching brilliance of the day would forever remain a vivid and lasting marker. The long day's sun was getting low when Gilbert and his fellow maquisards loaded their bicycles with part of the cache of arms they had collected. They started on the trip back to their encampment in the woods but soon came upon several German tanks, part of the forces dispatched from Vesoul out on the hunt for the missing battalion. Spotted carrying the weapons, Gilbert and the others were fired upon, forcing them to leave the road and crawl through the brambles in the fields between Noidans-le-Ferroux and their camp.

Gilbert would always remember the day's fading light as it made way for the first appearance of the stars he knew he would soon be sleeping under again, once he reached the woods. At that moment he came upon a body in the field.

A German corpse had been missed in the hurried cleanup after the massacre. He noticed the uniform was not SS but Wehrmacht, a sergeant.

In the dim light he looked more closely. And then he recognized the pale young face and the red hair.

It was his father's killer.

CHAPTER SIXTEEN

She's Mine

Sunday, August 27, 1944

THE PERFECT WEATHER of the day in eastern France was not matched in Wisconsin. Or perhaps it was, but in a different way, at least from the farming perspective of many in Dodge County. All Sunday, through the afternoon and into the evening, the rain fell.

Attendance at the park was sparse during the day, and activities confined to the bingo game under the shelter of one of the park buildings. The Old Line Service Club would have to return most of the hot dogs and refreshments they had procured for the day's picnic.

But all was not lost. The evening dance went ahead as scheduled, starting at eight o'clock. Unlike the afternoon, a large crowd turned out, staying dry inside the large white dance pavilion, built two years before the Depression had hit. The music was provided by Les Marose and His Seven-Piece Orchestra, a band from Mayville. They performed the day's favorite tunes from a stage at one end of the pavilion's main hall.

* * *

As they had all week, the boys stood out in their uniforms. Everyone seemed to be coming up to buy them a drink. Marie, Don, and Boyd sat for hours over beers, smoking cigarette after cigarette under the yellow lightbulbs strung along the wooden rafters overhead.

It was an evening of boisterous nonsense. Stories were traded back and forth about days gone by and about a larger world that not too long before may as well have been a discussion of the moons around Jupiter. There was no shortage of swagger and confidence in the boys, and a lot of talk about what the future would bring.

Boyd liked to talk about how exotic the land was out west, and he was always ready to describe his plans for traveling the country after the war. He said he was even thinking about going to college. His sister Blossom was about to start her final year at North Central College in Naperville, Illinois, and he was very proud of her. Maybe he could do the same after the war. After all, he had passed those tests to get into the pilot's program, which would have meant taking courses at a college.

To Don, nothing was as good as the old hometown. Waiting for him was his dad's business. He wanted so much for things to be back like they were, so that everyone could just get on with life again. No arguments there.

It never took much for talk to drift to how the war was taking so much of their best years away from them. But of course there was a job that had to be done, no doubt about that. And afterward, well, then life would get back to normal.

Boyd and Don had already begun a well-worn routine in their letters, a back-and-forth about who would be the first to get to Berlin. It continued that night, not something Marie liked to hear about, no matter how much the boys seemed to laugh and enjoy the give and take. On the other hand, it now seemed to be quite a stretch, with the war in Europe ending soon, certainly no later than Christmas. Don liked to say that the Russians were giving the Germans hell and good for them. Boyd personally agreed with that assessment and hinted a bit ostentatiously that he had heard things in his "official" briefings that he got when he was out west.

Never far from any conversation that week was Marie's baby, due in the first days of the new year. Don made no secret how much he was pulling for a boy. He said he would call the baby "Butch," since Julius was a butcher. Boyd liked to poke fun at Brownie about wanting a boy. He would argue with him, saying how sweet a daughter would be, something Don should be wishing for. Back and forth they went, until Boyd finished off the Sunday night debate, the words staying with Marie for the rest of her life.

"Brownie, I'll tell you what: if it's a boy you can keep it, but if it's a girl she's mine."

And they all threw their heads back and laughed.

CHAPTER SEVENTEEN

Knights of the Moon

Final Stanza

Sunday, August 27, 1944

ARLIER THAT SUNDAY afternoon, in one of the war's unceasing displays of the absurd, high-spirited French peasants could be seen striding alongside soldiers wearing German Waffen-SS uniforms. The mayor of Fresne Saint-Mamès was in front, leading the column north.

The Ukrainians were exhausted and hungry, and the scorching sun overhead was taking a toll. With more than three hundred horse-led carts packed with clothing and ammunition, it was slow going on narrow paths and unpaved roads. A brief but violent afternoon thunderstorm passed through, soaking everyone, but the long parade pressed on toward a well-hidden spot chosen by Simon Doillon, a large tract of thick woods just to the east of the village of Confracourt.

Simon had caught up with the battalion and joined the march. He remained insistent about avoiding any main roads because of his fears over the open target presented by the long column to both German and Allied aircraft. The battalion was now prey to everyone. Its only allies were a haphazard assortment of weaponless peasants and some maquis. Already on the hunt for them that afternoon were units dispatched by the Feldkommandant of Vesoul, including ten heavy Panzer tanks, seven light tanks, and four hundred French troops from the hated but well-dressed fascist militia known as the Milice.

* * *

The rainstorm meant that eight hundred soldiers with horses and wagons would leave tracks. The route of escape was soon discovered. Around six o'clock, some of the *miliciens* caught up with the trailing end of the battalion. There was a brief skirmish while the last of the Ukrainians scampered across a small bridge across the Saône River, in Cubry-les-Soing, a mere two hundred yards west from Bermont's hidden command post.

The German armored force in pursuit of the battalion soon arrived at the same bridge. It was too narrow to cross, a posted sign of a six-ton weight limit successfully facing off against the fifty tons of a heavy Panzer tank. The trailing end of the Ukrainians was still about half a mile away. But escape was assured, at least for that day.

* * *

Myroslaw's battalion reached the safety of the Confracourt woods at seven o'clock. Simon introduced the Ukrainians to Claude, the two of them serving as interpreters for Bermont, who did not speak German and had just entered the woods. Joining the group was Jean Reuchet from the Communist FTP, who had shared the brief ride in the back of the Doillon milk truck with Wozniak the day before. That afternoon, Reuchet had spotted tanks departing Vesoul and assumed it had something to do with the Ukrainians. He had rushed to Bermont's command post with the news.

Hloba noticed that Bermont had promoted Simon to captain, part of Bermont's efforts to ensure it was the French that would be giving orders to Hloba. Bermont wanted it made clear that the Ukrainians were now subject to the structure and hierarchy, such as it was, within the FFI.

After a lengthy attempt to communicate, with some initial misunderstandings, Bermont was able to direct the Ukrainians into establishing a line of guards around the woods and the entering paths. The battalion's horses, always remembered by the French as the short horses of the steppes, were set to graze in a separate clearing.

The area had already been prepared with some supplies. In response to Simon's pleas, a few of the local mayors had committed to furnish what was needed. Someone had brought in pigs, and there was plenty of cattle in the pastures nearby. An energetic former French Army noncommissioned officer named Girardier was designated as head of the unit's commissary.

The Ukrainians wounded in the fight that morning were transported to a hospital in nearby Rupt-sur-Saône. Those requiring surgery would be operated on, without anesthesia. Two would later die. The attending local physician concluded that every Ukrainian in the battalion he examined was recovering from typhus.

* * *

As Sunday's nightfall began to descend over the woods and the battalion, and their French counterparts were beginning to settle in, a small group of Ukrainians went off with the body of young Petrovski, killed during the mutiny. They walked a distance through the forest and came upon another clearing, surrounded by birches as well as some large oaks that looked to be a century old.

A grave was dug, a prayer recited. Together the handful of young men sang a mournful requiem, its words known well to them, a poem about death in a foreign land:

> Chu-yesh brat-te mie
> To-va-ry-shy mie
> Vid-li-ta-yout sie-rym shnu-rom
> Zhu-rav u vy-ri
> Kly-chute, croo, croo, croo
> V chu-zhy-ni oom-ry;
> Za-ky morr-re pe-re-le-chu,
> Kry-layn-ka zi-tru
> Kry-layn-ka zi-tru
>
> (Do you hear my brother
> My friend
> The cranes are flying off
> In a gray winding string
> They call, croo, croo, croo
> In a foreign land I will die;
> By the time I cross the sea,
> My wings will have shed
> My wings will have shed)

Me-rekh-tyt v o-chackh
Bez-ko-nech-nay shlackh
Hyn-ne, hyn-ne v sy-niykh khma-rakh
Sleed po zhu-rav-lyakh
Kly-chute, croo, croo, croo
V chu-zhy-ni oom-ry;
Za-ky morr-re pe-re-le-chu,
Kry-layn-ka zi-tru
Kry-layn-ka zi-tru

(The never-ending path of the cranes
Faintly glimmers in my eyes
Before disappearing
In the gray misty clouds
They call, croo, croo, croo
In a foreign land I will die;
By the time I cross the sea,
My wings will have shed
My wings will have shed)

The tomb was covered, an Orthodox cross planted. Someone said, "Sleep, my boy, sleep and dream of the freedom of Ukraine." They turned and walked back to the encampment.

* * *

On the last Sunday of the summer of 1944, the war was only entering its full bloom.

By the time the Allies invaded France, five million Jews had already been murdered by the Germans, accomplished with invaluable assistance from helping hands across the Continent. Another million Jews awaited being put to death.

Having already killed and enslaved millions and gained notoriety because of their use of torture techniques such as waterboarding, for which prosecutions would be brought after the war, the Japanese were continuing a biological warfare experimentation program on Chinese civilians.

In London, crackpot theories of "race" and empire, more worthy of a mad despot than a democratically elected prime minister, had fueled and then obfuscated a famine that during the previous eighteen months had killed millions in India, a bewildering incident of abysmal cruelty and scale that somehow still remains shunned from the received narrative of the Second World War.

Along the Ostfront, since the spring, two million German soldiers had been killed, wounded, or captured, or were otherwise missing. In the same short span of time, almost a quarter of a million soldiers of the Red Army had met their death, more than half the number of American soldiers that would be killed in action during the entire Second World War.

The outlook for the war was bright; its varied and rich swirling pools of death would continue seething until the very last day of the conflict. In Belarus, where almost a million Soviet prisoners would die, the war would kill almost a quarter of the country's civilian noncombatants. The war's death toll will include more than four million Ukrainian civilians, with another two million civilians having been sent to Germany as forced labor. In Russia, the number of deaths from the war was heading toward a final total of twenty million, most of them civilians. Most estimates suggest a similar number for the Chinese killed at the hands of the Japanese.

A million bombs were waiting to be dropped by the Allies onto Germany's cities. By spring the Americans would commence the process of indiscriminately burning alive anyone who had the misfortune of living in one of more than sixty Japanese cities.

Extremes had ascended to the throne, and the war's newfound reach was going well beyond what were thought to be boundaries of human behavior. The same was true for technology. Long-held fundamental human notions of time and distance were being encroached upon as never before. Supply lines of unprecedented scale, speed, and regularity connected places like Detroit and Vladivostok, San Francisco and Calcutta.

In England, the world's first programmable digital computer was in daily operation, used by code breakers. Only a few weeks before, the Germans had advanced the human race and its wars into the jet age. In ten days, the first ballistic missiles launched in anger would target Paris, then London.

Before the month of August was over, an American general named Groves would make his final decision on the site for the first nuclear explosion in human history. With a comedy-of-the-gods touch, he would choose an area in New Mexico, rather than a military training area in California, in part because the latter would have required discussion with another general named Patton, whom Groves considered the most disagreeable man he had ever met.

* * *

That evening, while the war was pushing computers and jets to begin their life-altering assault on time and distance as pillars of human experience, in a large clearing in the dense woods of eastern France there was a torch-lit scene indifferent to modernity, a moment that could have taken place when the weaponry of the day's battle was made of bronze.

Tents were going up, trenches being dug. The porcelain blue of that long day of war was all but gone, a half-moon directly overhead as the sun set. A bull had been slaughtered, and a field kitchen was putting out smoke. Vast amounts of wine were brought in.

The day would prove to be a marker. A victorious battle was celebrated as though it were a beginning. But for many, if not for most, it would denote the final destruction of the familiar and the ancient which until that moment had governed each of their short lives.

* * *

Beneath the stars, hundreds of young men mingled in the flickering shadows. Their unlikely connection was the result solely of chance and necessity. Two distinct groups, each steeped in their respective peasant cultures that were as alien to one another as they were distant from the present century.

Yet they were all the same. All of the boys, Ukrainian and French, carried the timeless gift that war presents to youth, the iniquity of an early familiarity with death and suffering, including bringing it upon others. On that Sunday night they also shared that which cannot be known except by experience: the wartime exhilaration of finding oneself still alive.

* * *

The two units were a contrast, one formation in uniformed Teutonic spit and polish, the other in desperate need of shoes.

There was one notable exception standing on the French side.

With a panache that had turned heads and added a unique pageantry to the evening, Bermont had arrived in the forest wearing his uniform from the 159th Regiment of the French Alpine Infantry. The dark-blue tunic was unlike anything worn by anyone else that night, from its colorful insignia of an edelweiss flower to the accompanying beret correctly worn at an angle straight down over the right ear, as only officers in the unit did. Bermont had last worn the uniform on November 27, 1942.

With improvised pomp and formality, the battalion of Ukrainians was designated as an "official" unit of the FFI. They had already christened themselves the Ivan Bohoun Battalion, after a seventeenth-century Cossack colonel who had fought in uprisings against Poles and Russians.

To their French counterparts, they would forever be known as "le BUK."

* * *

The wine flowed, and there was a mix of make-do language and friendly shouts not always understood. The night was its own brief and intense self-contained reality, such as the war delivered everywhere with regularity, with only the most tenuous connection to a past or future much beyond yesterday and tomorrow. The battle over, glasses were raised to proud French and Ukrainian nations emerging after the war.

For one group, liberation would soon arrive. It would come with a national diminishment to be borne with great difficulty by the country's elites. The crippling scar would continue to disfigure well into the next century.

Among the other group, few would ever again set foot onto the land of their fathers. They would be old men living in other countries when a muddled liberation would come, forty-seven years later, rapidly infected by competing versions of identity and history. From east and west, those playing the Great Game as unctuously as in the time of Kipling would foul things further with their own timeless pollution.

* * *

The day's events in Haute-Saône had no effect on the broader course of the war.

Except for those in the world fortunate to be surrounded by protective water, the Second World War was local. From that perspective there was great significance to what happened. Without firing a shot, the FFI's Groupe V had gained an entire battalion of armed soldiers that could be directed against the Germans. Hundreds of German soldiers would never take another breath, including an entire cadre of SS officers. Both of these things had been accomplished without a drop of French blood being shed.

Bermont would always believe that after the mutiny, the Germans in the area were burdened by having to reckon with a phantom battalion. The garrison in Vesoul had to fear an imminent attack on the town, even before the Allies were in reach. In his view, the mere presence of le BUK was a force of moderation against the potential in Haute-Saône for the brutal reprisals that the Germans were always at the ready to deliver with their characteristic knack. Only two days after the mutiny, to the south in Doubs, the Germans would burn three villages in response to partisan interference with their efforts to seize all available transport for the retreat.

* * *

As for Myroslaw, in a few days he would turn twenty-four years old and also begin his sixth year of being surrounded by the war's inferno. Whatever clamor was around him that evening was no doubt thick with the tribal mythos so intrinsic to his young sense of being, as much a part of him growing up as walking and breathing.

At the same time, the moment may have also brought a sense, perhaps more of a primal understanding, that all pathways back to the familiar noisome existence that was his world before the war arrived were now gone. For him, and most others in le BUK, the terrain of life had shifted mightily that day, not unlike the flow of a river yanked across a fault line by an earthquake.

* * *

There is an irresistible, almost narcotic pleasure drawn from assigning the ways of the heroic to deeds done during battle, if only to transmute some greater meaning and elevated moral lesson from so much killing and dying by the young and obscure. An enduring pretense conveys that individual soldiers are moved forward to take actions in battle because of a larger political rationale or even an ideology. It is a canard that has survived thousands of years because of its utility in constructing the necessary but equally false binary overlay for a war. It also allows a separate humanity to be designated for others, in particular by victors over the vanquished.

What transpired in Haute-Saône was not a reach for glory. Nor was it an undertaking for a larger cause.

What burst open that Sunday morning was a furious and reflexive act of survival, intertwined with a necessary measure of hatred, and buttressed by the nearby presence of comrades in arms and their needs of the moment.

It was not unlike most of the killing, so dense, during the Second World War.

But what made the mutiny and massacre remarkable, breathtakingly so, was how it encompassed an entire swath of the Second World War's basic table of elements—a single incident so extreme, so ironic, so fortuitous, so savage, and so life-altering.

And, ultimately, so deliberately unremembered.

* * *

Around midnight, as the moon was setting, Bermont stole away from the gathering, leaving the forest to head back to his hut near the Saône River. He carried with him a message from Hloba for delivery to the Ukrainian battalion forty miles to the south, which had mutinied the day before.

If he heard the growl of the lone B-24 flying low overhead, painted glossy black to make it difficult to see, he did not make a lasting note of it, despite the rarity of such an appearance in the region, at least up until that point in the war.

* * *

Nights of moonlight were preferred for parachute drops. But there was no such fortune for William Bales, the veteran twenty-three-year-old pilot from Lampasas, Texas. Heading south and east, he had just passed over the area of Dijon. Despite the darkness, Bales was able to observe a large number of convoys heading northeast. The German retreat was now a twenty-four-hour-a-day operation.

Bales steered his ship just beyond Paul Guepratte's command post, toward a valley alongside the Ognon River, which was Haute-Saône's southern border. He reached the drop zone, code-named Onion, a few minutes before one o'clock in the morning. Spotting a triangle of bonfires used to convey the signal letter *L*, he maneuvered the plane down to an altitude of 350 feet for the first run. After a bull's-eye drop of containers and packages, he returned three minutes later at seven hundred feet, dropping his three Joes.

In less than fifteen minutes over the dropping zone, he and his eight-man crew had completed Operation Messenger 35. They would be back on the ground in England before five o'clock in the morning.

The three parachutes during the second pass delivered two Americans with the Office of Strategic Services (OSS) and a Frenchman trained by the OSS. They were met on the ground by an operative with the British Special Operations Executive (SOE).

None of the four would ever cross paths with le BUK. But a single message they would send to London four days later would steer the fate of Myroslaw and the rest of the Ukrainians, as well as Simon Doillon.

Part Three

PASSAGE

September–October 1944

CHAPTER EIGHTEEN

Uniform Failure

Monday, August 28, 1944

B Y FOUR O'CLOCK the next morning the hunt for the battalion was back on. The area was overrun with the Milice, wearing their uniform of a blue coat, brown shirt, and blue beret. Hours before sunrise they had begun searching villages, entering homes, and questioning occupants.

The location of le BUK was soon discovered. Several hundred *miliciens,* feared and loathed by their fellow French citizens, started to gather and face the woods where the Ukrainians and the maquis were encamped, holding their machine guns as though planning an attack.

As the day went on, word spread about the formidable weaponry of the Ukrainian battalion. Enthusiasm for heading into the fray waned. By late Monday afternoon the Milice leaders decided they had no stomach for making an attack, concluding that the Ukrainian battalion was a matter of German dirty laundry. At six o'clock Monday evening, they formed a column in the road across from the woods and set off on the march back to Vesoul.

Upon arrival, the French commanders of the unit reported to their German overseers that "it had been impossible to precisely locate the place where the traitors were holed up."

Simon decided the battalion should be moved to a new encampment. That night he led the unit from the forest near Confracourt to another thickly wooded area known as Forêt de Cherlieu, seven miles to the north. Moving a three-mile-long column of men and supplies in darkness was arduous, complicated by the need to avoid major roads. The carts were noisy, and they did not stand up well traveling on narrow paths across stony fields. Stops were required for repairs, and there were times when the entire battalion had to take cover to avoid discovery. They did not arrive at their destination in the forest until five o'clock on Tuesday morning.

* * *

Tents were pitched, and the horses were put to pasture. The Ukrainians slept while some of the FFI stood guard. A steady rain was falling when they were awakened at noon. Lunch was prepared, with supplies brought in by the French. During the afternoon, weapons were cleaned, laundry was done, and the soldiers washed and shaved.

There was discussion that le BUK needed uniforms that looked different from what the Germans were wearing. Claude suggested that Simon's father ask his old friend Friquet, a cheesemaker who lived just to the east of the forest in the village of Bougey, to dye the uniforms blue.

Friquet agreed. Each soldier had an extra set of tunics and pants, which were collected. Friquet went into Vesoul to get some quiet advice on dyeing, and soon closed the doors of his cheese factory, putting his large vats and cheese-drying racks to a new use. On the door he left a note to those who delivered milk:

Do not be curious, my friends.
The less known, the better.
Come back tomorrow.

After two days and nights of effort, the uniforms remained unchanged from their original color—goose shit, as some of the locals referred to it. Inside the cheese factory, stubborn traces of blue dye were left behind and could not be removed.

The Germans had been questioning people in the area. Friquet did not reopen until after liberation.

The failure of the dyeing operation would save Ukrainian lives, several times over.

* * *

On Tuesday, le BUK went into its first action. At ten o'clock in the evening, a group of Ukrainians went out into the rain on an ambush planned and directed by the FFI. The objective was to destroy a German radar post.

The raid was unsuccessful. Two Ukrainians were killed and four injured. Eight Germans were also killed.

On Wednesday, another group was sent out into the night under the command of Captain Zintchouk, a detachment of two companies, one of which included Myroslaw. They were accompanied by Claude Vougnon. German units were reported to be passing eastward along the N70, the main route from Dijon and other points to the southwest. They took their positions and stayed all night, hidden in the brush just ten yards from the road, waiting for an opportunity to conduct an ambush.

But the evening was quiet, the highway only showing some life in the early hours of Thursday morning when a group from the Milice went by on motorcycles. The detachment let them pass. Better to wait for German targets.

Around nine o'clock a young French girl rode up on a bicycle and stopped in the road. She looked in the direction of the Ukrainians, a smile on her face. The boys in the unit were certain the girl knew of their presence. They remained hidden. She turned around and went back full-speed in the direction from which she came.

A few minutes later a German convoy appeared, four large trucks with trailers carrying antiaircraft guns, each vehicle holding approximately forty soldiers. Zintchouk sent up a red flare, the signal for the Ukrainians to begin firing machine guns and mortars at the trucks. The German trucks stopped, one catching on fire. The Ukrainians emerged from hiding and headed toward the trucks, throwing grenades as they approached.

An enormous explosion came from one of the vehicles, slaughtering dozens of Germans.

A German armored car pulled up to the trucks. As the occupants jumped out of the vehicle, they apparently saw no threat in the feldgrau-clad soldiers of le BUK, and instead began firing their weapons into some nearby woods. The Ukrainians opened up on the Germans, who then realized what was happening. A few survivors were able to flee. Left behind for capture were ten heavy machine guns, two hundred hand grenades, automatic rifles, ammunition, and three binoculars. A dozen Ukrainians were wounded.

The cost to the Germans was high. That evening they ordered, as the maquis would learn, forty-two coffins to be sent to the town hall of the nearby village of Combeaufontaine, presumably for those killed in the ambush.

* * *

The return to camp took several hours. The Ukrainians were slowed by having to deal with their wounded. Some were hidden with French peasants. As the day went on the Ukrainians had become dispersed and had to make their way over unfamiliar terrain. It was well after dark when they began straggling back into the Forêt de Cherlieu. Many were able to make their way back only because villagers had come out into the darkness and provided guidance, directing them toward routes that kept them close to stone garden walls.

One of the returning groups from le BUK was crossing the Paris-Vesoul-Belfort highway, Route N19, when they came upon another German-commanded foreign unit. The Ukrainians recognized the unit as comprising Don Cossacks, the largest of all Cossack groups and so-named for the major river that runs to the south of Moscow.

The Ukrainians passed by without challenge, safe in the uniform of *couleur caca d'oie*.

CHAPTER NINETEEN

Sick of These Traitors

Thursday, August 31, 1944

W HAT ARE THE Ukrainians like?"

"Splendid fellows, bursting to have a go at the Boches."

"Yes, and if the invasion had never come, or if the Boches were still winning the war, they would be bursting to have a go at us 'terrorists.' They are traitors, my friend. And their major, does he not mouth German propaganda?"

"He is anti-Communist. He wants to fight against the Boches, but he is not for the Russians. The men all say they were forced to fight for the Boches."

"They all say that. Every Pole, Cossack, Ukrainian, Austrian, and Pomeranian we have captured says he was forced to fight for the Boches. In my view, these men are all traitors. Another thing, I notice that ninety per cent of the Germans we capture say that they are Austrians, Poles, Czechs, or even Ukrainians or Cossacks forced into the Wehrmacht. The remaining ten per cent is German, but very anti-Hitler. I am sick of these traitors, but if they are fighting the Boches we must use them. The Russians will be capable of dealing with them after the war. After all, we are plus six hundred well-armed men, and the enemy is minus six hundred; therefore we are plus twelve hundred."

His benediction finished, George Millar, the SOE operative known as

Emile, turned and translated for the tall American next to him, an OSS agent named Douglas Bazata.

* * *

Millar's exchange in French had been with a robust balding stump of a man named Roger Menigoz, who had just burst in from the thunderous rainstorm outside. He was a maquisard who had come a long way in his search for Emile, whose testiness may have been related to Menigoz having interrupted a grand feast.

Millar had been in France since the beginning of June, a few days prior to the Normandy landings, arriving at night by parachute into a wheat field nine miles north of Dijon. In the early days of the war, Millar had been in a British rifle brigade before being captured in Libya by Rommel's forces. After escaping by jumping out of a train in Germany he spent much of 1943 making his way from Munich to Strasbourg, then through southern France and Spain, before the final leg back to England. In early 1944 he talked his way into the SOE and was now the well-known Emile.

Slender but sturdy of frame with, as is so common among younger English males, the facial features of a pretty girl, his physical appearance hid a determined ruthlessness. While not quite setting Europe ablaze, he had provided numerous partisans with training in the use of weapons and explosives. He arrived in France with two hundred thousand francs, paying forty francs a day to each of those in the maquis groups he helped organize. Through the summer, he directed more than seventy sabotage operations, mainly in Doubs, the département to the south of Haute-Saône. Consistent with the orders of French general Marie-Pierre Koenig, who had been since mid-June designated by the Allies as the commander of all FFI forces, the sabotage was limited to rail and communication structures.

Much of Emile's focus had been on practical improvements to the operation of resistance groups, along with providing important lessons (at least in the mind of Emile) on matters regarding the proper construction and use of latrines. Until August he had lived only in the woods, with the maquis, convinced that staying in the villages would present too much of a danger to himself and others. Emile's effectiveness was in large part related to his deftness in avoiding the French politics that so infected the resistance movement. Since early August the ranks of the maquis had been growing fast.

His successes had earned him a reputation, including among the Germans. Two weeks before, he had learned the Germans were actively hunting him down and had dyed his sun-bleached hair black with the hope of standing out less among the French.

Emile's contact with London through the summer had been sparse. Wireless communication was a difficult and dangerous undertaking given the legendary German skill at hunting down active transmitters. He had managed, though, to arrange for various grounds in the area to be designated for parachute drops, personally selecting the necessary French ground crews and organizing local stores and safe houses. He also appointed listeners for the BBC code messages, making sure someone in the local groups was monitoring broadcasts at least twice a day, every day.

* * *

Bazata first met Emile during that Sunday night parachute arrival into France, which took place at around the same time Bermont was leaving the woods where le BUK was spending their first night as newly installed members of the FFI. He was a part of a three-man Jedburgh team, one of eighty-two such groups dropped into France from June through August, most of them six months to a year too late to provide significant assistance. Jedburgh, which drew its name from a place in Scotland, was a joint OSS-SOE program that was ostensibly trilateral with the French. Following policy then in place as developed in London, the Jedburghs had been dropped in military uniform and were expected to keep wearing such, which horrified Emile.

The other two Jeds arriving with Bazata were an American radio operator, Richard Floyd, and an OSS-trained French captain, Francois Chapelle. Neither Bazata nor Floyd spoke much French, although Bazata claimed otherwise. Their mission, code-named Cedric, was to assist Emile in organizing and training the local resistance and to establish a link between London OSS headquarters and the maquis.

Douglas Bazata was a large man, his six-foot-plus presence enhanced by a glib forcefulness that at various moments annoyed, charmed, and frightened Emile, who had not been happy about the Jed team's arrival. Beyond Emile's natural dislike of large organizations, the arrival of the Jeds had created a suspicion, one shared for similar reasons by many

French, that the real purpose of the new team was to serve as a staffing extension and force of control reaching out from London. He was uncomfortable with having to change his operations from independent guerrilla activities to being a part of a larger enterprise.

But he also knew that with the Allied forces approaching, the war in that area was rapidly changing. The torrent of German soldiers in retreat had removed the life-and-death danger of attempting radio transmissions back to London. Bazata and his team were in wireless contact every day.

* * *

While the storm was raging outside, Emile and Bazata had just sat down to a relatively lavish meal that included roast duckling. They were the guests of two partisans who operated a mill near Rougemont, fourteen miles southeast of Vesoul. Like many other mills in France, it was a black-market hot spot. There was plenty of food, and Emile was enthusiastic about the mill's "beautiful bread."

The cars used for transporting Emile and the others had been hidden nearby. Guards were in place, and they had allowed the entrance of the thoroughly soaked Menigoz, known to be an energetic deputy of Simon Doillon while operating his own FFI Groupe 22 out of Forêt de Cherlieu.

Menigoz had spent hours trying to find Emile, who took him into a side room, along with Bazata, for their conversation. Starting with the tale of the Ukrainian mutiny, he made an urgent plea for Emile to convince London to make a drop of German ammunition for le BUK. Menigoz also requested a drop of antitank weapons, describing the Ukrainians to Emile as being afraid of tanks, as though such a thing was a particular peccadillo of theirs.

After Emile's ballad about traitors, Menigoz received the answer that he wanted to hear. This was followed by the usual European style of stiff-backed formal handshakes all around, a common practice that after only four days on the ground was already the source of much amusement for Bazata.

Satisfied, Menigoz went off into a night that was still gusty and rainy. Emile and Bazata returned to their meal, not happy about the duck having gone cold and the champagne having gone warm.

The next day, Bazata transmitted to Special Force Headquarters (SFHQ) in London:

```
1 September From Cedric C-3564/34
```

Have 500 Russians 20 miles northwest Luos. All their German officers killed 5 days ago. We can alter their Boche uniforms. Can you supply ammunition for Mausers light machine guns, Mayims 45 millimeter anti-tank guns. These Russians must be taken care of quickly if we hope to cause the thousands of surrounding Russians to revolt. No action here as yet. Rail traffic very heavy and damned well guarded. Munition train at clearing south Chevremont.

CHAPTER TWENTY

A State of Nature

Saturday, September 2, 1944

THE GERMAN RETREAT from the west had filled the main roads. The soldiers passed through on foot, on bicycles, and in any other type of transport they could find. The heavy traffic toward the east was also cutting through on secondary roads in the area.

Supplies to the forest where the maquis and le BUK were encamped had been cut. German forces occupied the access roads to the Forêt de Cherlieu and were congregating in nearby villages, directing trenches to be dug. Less than a mile away to the south was Melin, a village of fewer than a hundred people where three SS squadrons of Russian Cossacks had recently arrived. There were signs the Germans were planning to surround the woods and bring an all-out attack.

Early Saturday morning, le BUK began a bombardment of German trenches near the forest, allowing a detachment that included Myroslaw to head out toward Melin. The group was led by Captain Polichtchuk, along with Claude Vougnon. Polichtchuk was older than most, a military veteran who had served under the command of Austrians, Poles, Russians, Germans, and now the French. He had developed a reputation among the French as a colorful character, renowned for his breakfast of an onion and a cigar, chased by a gulp of vodka or reasonable substitute and followed by the utterance of a one-word command: "Forward." Polichtchuk was generous in sharing his day-breaking regime with

Claude, and the two of them had already completed the ritual by seven o'clock that morning.

At ten o'clock the Ukrainians attacked. The fighting did not last long. At both the center and the left flank of the assault toward Melin, the Cossacks gave way and fled into the countryside. The Ukrainians entered the village and came upon dozens of French hostages who had just been lined against a wall at gunpoint. What was about to happen was stopped. In the process, the soldiers of le BUK captured 37 Cossacks, along with 60 saddle horses, 2 carts of ammunition, 14 light mortars, and 150 rifles.

* * *

And so the summer of 1944 comes to an end in remote eastern France, where Myroslaw and other sons of Ruthenian parents engage in battle with Russian Cossacks while under the command of insurgents. Both combatant forces wear German military uniforms. None is able to speak the local language. Few are eloquent in the language of the uniform they are all wearing. Neither group in the battle identifies with a nation. Neither group fights for a cause. All of them are traitors in the eyes of someone, many twice over.

Analogs do not come easily. But they do exist, and contribute to a more complete, if unsettling comprehension of the Second World War as the calamitous upheaval it was, a conflict that became unbridled in its delivery of catastrophic suffering.

A once-proud republican form of government became a shambles, and with a practiced imperial reach brought perpetual, aimless war to the region around the Tigris and Euphrates rivers. Its military ventures, far from its capital, took place one after the other and soon extended into Syria and other areas. The repeated initiatives relied heavily on secrecy, mercenary soldiers, and a warrior class as detached from its general citizenry as the military undertakings themselves had become.

Notably, in the land then known as Mesopotamia, soldiers from places like Armenia served the empire well in a manner that in a later age would be called a "contractor." The mercenaries found themselves in chaotic clashes with nomadic tribes out of the east who fought with hatred and asymmetric methods.

Two thousand years later, in the same region there are mercenaries from lands that were once part of great Spanish and Portuguese empires across the Atlantic. They wear the military uniforms of one particular Middle East kingdom while serving under the military command of a different monarchy, in an armed conflict with a group rebelling against the government of yet another neighboring country. The mercenaries, or contractors as they are now called, do not speak the languages of the region and do not fight for a cause. The undertaking is made possible by the active support of the largest military power in the world.

For each and every one of the governments involved, from monarchies to the largest military power, the conflict is being carried out largely in secret, without public oversight. The military venture involves repeated incidents of slaughtering civilians and has led to the starvation of millions.

* * *

A forgetfulness comes with the ephemeral bursts of modernity, a distraction away from the larger truth that all societies make their own direction. No immunity is provided to any form of government. The nature of governance is but a small cog amid the much larger constant churn that sets the broad cultural frame of mind toward a particular path for advancement, for discourse, and for how people are to be treated.

A society can deliberately move itself toward higher knowledge. It may also fall prey to self-deception.

A once-strong ethos can disappear, lost with the natural passing of collective memory about an ungovernable war as it actually was, with its unyielding reach of darkness. The broader discernment of what war involves, and what it leaches into a society, can become warped, prodded by the hubris of high priests and oracles into a tilt toward a triumphant casualness when battle is taken up against vastly inferior technologies utilized by those perceived to be lesser beings.

It is a very old and unexceptional story. History leaves little doubt as to the fate of such conjured myths of supremacy. Demise comes, always sooner than expected by its practitioners, and never without a trail of savagery and tears.

It was less than a lifetime ago when young Ukrainians and Cossacks far away from their homes knew this to be a truth, wearing identical uniforms as they attempted to kill each other on a Saturday morning in eastern France.

Bellum omnium contra omnes.

CHAPTER TWENTY-ONE

Of What Is Yet To Be

Saturday, September 2, 1944

IN WISCONSIN, LABOR Day weekend provided a hazy finale to the summer. Saturday was Don's last full day at home. Boyd had left town earlier in the week, departing on Tuesday for Florida. The two boys had been herded outside for a couple of photos, just off the side porch at Herb and Lylle's.

Some final kidding, some small talk. See you in Berlin.

* * *

In those days when the weather was right a front stoop served as a social extension of the house. Marie and Don spent much of that afternoon on the wooden steps descending from the front porch. No need to go anywhere, no need to do anything. Far better to stretch the day, take all of it in, savoring every breath and every moment.

The afternoon mail came. Few things were more worthy of an idle thumb-through than the latest *Life* magazine. Stone-faced Cordell Hull was on the cover, and inside were tales of what television would be like after the war.

A little later, the paperboy came by with the afternoon *Milwaukee Journal*, with its front-page pronouncement that Americans were eleven miles from the Rhine, at least according to the Nazis.

There were some final pictures to take, over on the sunny west side of the house: Don with Marie. Don with his mother. Don with Julius. Don with his fourteen-year-old sister. Don with both his parents.

Ritual out of the way, it was back to the front stoop, now starting to lose out on the slant of the late-afternoon light. Marie and Don each took one last photo of the other, posed between the discarded newspaper and magazine.

* * *

The unassuming announcement of autumn never fails to startle, a few early crisping leaves scraping across the pavement. Always a shock to hear while in the stupor of late-season warmth that feels borrowed from somewhere. But then there is a realization of the sun's low angle. It was not like that just the other day.

The light itself seems different, as it was that Saturday afternoon, a tired and garish end-of-summer glare that marks the weariness of something about to leave the scene. Cleaner golden tones will emerge in the upcoming weeks, but not just yet.

Only one season always makes such a gentle entrance. The signals of its approach are almost tender, yet they bring the sharpest reminders of passage. From the start, nature fills the long turn known as autumn with a taunting beauty that adorns the bleak and unwanted lesson it presents, about the inevitability of departure, change, and loss. Only the most unfeeling are not made to ache with a rootless yearning and a nostalgic melancholy, as though the future is already the past.

As it will always be for Marie, every year for the rest of her life, when the first days of fall arrive once again.

On Sunday, she and Don said goodbye.

CHAPTER TWENTY-TWO

Do Not Drop Bodies Tonight

Saturday, September 9, 1944

3 September From Cedric C-3717/48

>   Our inspections show extreme lack of
> organization Haute Saone. Despite Boa says
> scattered chiefs have gathered all chiefs
> together harmoniously. Now have plans laid to
> correctly arm FFI and begin serious operations.
> However, all droppings in Haute Saone north
> Besancon-Belfort road must come through us. This
> is vital to retain achieved unity. Await arms
> anxiously as the Boche are very rife but nothing
> can be done with present arms nor can we defend
> ourselves or civilians after sabotage. Have
> coordinated with Boa on grounds. Do not use
> field again for men Saturday. Boche attacked
> Roderick container depot. Will verify losses
> later. They might have been averted. Roderick
> moves southeast Besancon Monday. Cut Besancon-
> Belfort Friday night. Troop train derailed. Many
> convoys north on Besancon-Belfort, Gray-Versoul
> roads. Sabotaged an artillery convoy tonight.
> Too busy to change from civies.

4 September From SFHQ to Cedric C-4915

>   Hoping to serve Onion tonight with arms and
> tomorrow night with arms and a special mission
> of 9 officers headed by American colonel. Object
> of mission collection of hot intelligence for

maquis and SHAEF. They have 8 W/T sets and full equipment. Very competent and cooperative. They will cover all your area and work to Emile and Boulayas instructions. Has Boulaya left you for another region. Hope you will all give them all possible help. We promise you do all possible to serve you but weather alone holds us up. For your information Germans have evacuated Plateau de Maiche and we are concentrating maquis and SAS and eventually American forces to the north of the Plateau. Elements of 7th Army are at Lons Le Saunier. Will warn you of arrival of bodies.

4 September From Cedric   C3827/11

Am missing broadcasts of 31 August and 2 September. Sorry ask for repeat but have moved good deal and reception sometimes bad. Regarding Uncle Sam - safehouse at Chateau at Libarre 9 kilos southwest Montbozin - BBC message Coupole always ready for you. Password 'Je cherche le plus beau counter cest un marchand gevin.' Verification of assault. All containers and other stores burned not taken by 100 uneasy Germans Loham maquis chief killed, 3 wounded. Further south 5 truck loads and armored Boche car attacked maquis. Only 5 latter present. Boche dispersed after 2 hours fighting.

5 September From Cedric C-3932/38

Have no uses for all 9 officers. Shall try to catch them personally. Shall give all aid possible knowing he will do likewise as we get on beautifully. Boulaya left yesterday. Weather wonderful.

6 September From SFHQ to Cedric C-182

Very disappointed you won't take intelligence mission but abide by your wishes about receiving unwanted men. However mission had strong approval of General Koenig and they are armed to the teeth and will bring arms for you. In addition they have with them Russian speaking parachutist who should be help to your revolting reds. FMFFI requires explanation from you unless you can immediately alter your decision and accept. Aprt from intelligence mission would you accept tomorrow 12 combatant Frenchmen with arms and rucksacks. Reply to this emergency channel tonight. Give also as soon as possible large grounds for dropping first, one to 5 hundred parachutists, second, large daylight operation. These are possibilities at any moment.

6 September From SFHQ to Cedric C-6480
Propose sending large night operation of 10 planes to you tomorrow. This operation takes priority over all other operations. Will be 150 containers.

7 September From Cedric C-4095/44
Thousand thanks for containers. Rolling now. Out all small roads area. Russian cavalry passed last night. Convoys not so heavy today. Will you send arms again soon possible. Can use all available. Shall have lights this time as we have cleared Boche from our field. Send Onion, Turnip. Lovely battle last night.

8 September From Cedric C-4188/17
Drop 12 Frenchmen, 12-man mission on Iris.

8 September From SFHQ to Cedric C-629
Must give coordinates ground Iris and reply tonight through emergency channel. We will drop an American OG party 201 men instead of 12 French men along with 9 fighting intelligence mission. Latter known as Marcel Mission.

9 September From Cedric C-4324/49
Important do not drop bodies tonight. Boche has flooded all of us for week.

CHAPTER TWENTY-THREE

Mission Marcel

Saturday, September 9, 1944

THE PHRASES CAME over the BBC at one thirty in the afternoon, a grand thing to hear. They were broadcast again at seven thirty and eleven thirty in the evening.

"Ne louvoyez pas sur rail." (Do not tack on the rail.)

"Quatre fois avec neuf amis." (Four times with nine friends.)

The coded signal was announcing a drop near Vesoul.

* * *

The "Russian speaking parachutist," touted by London three days before in the message to Emile and Bazata, was twenty-seven-year-old Lieutenant Walter Kuzmuk, who had grown up in Chicago. A week after his official start with the OSS, he found himself on a late-afternoon drive to Harrington airfield, seventy-five miles north of London, about to take a nighttime flight over France that would end with a parachute jump.

During the car trip he met the commander of his upcoming mission, Lieutenant Colonel Waller Booth.

After introductions, Kuzmuk took up setting the record straight.

He did not speak Russian. His parents were from Poland.

Booth was dismissive.

"It doesn't matter. You are a combat veteran. You seem to be angry. That's enough. Welcome aboard."

Booth had his own worries.

When he and Kuzmuk arrived at Harrington around six o'clock, Booth breathed a sigh of relief upon learning that there had been no phone calls for him. Until the doors were closed and the plane had taken off, he would remain fearful that the mission he had worked so hard to put together would be scrapped.

At forty-one, Waller B. Booth Jr. was an old man reaching to get himself into some war. He was also a Princeton man, 1926—president of his class, an athlete, and a noted stage performer. Before the war he had been a tour and cruise director until being personally recruited into the OSS by fellow Princetonian Allen Dulles.

In mid-1942, Booth was sent to Spain, but in early 1944 the OSS chief for Iberia had him removed from the region, his presence deemed prejudicial to relations with Spain and Portugal. Booth was welcomed by OSS operations in the United Kingdom and put in charge of the Proust Project, a combined OSS-SOE training program for French operatives to be parachuted behind German lines.

By mid-July, Proust was winding down, and Booth began a push to get himself into France. He wanted to prove a few theories he had about irregular warfare, pitching it as an "experimental mission." He was also itching to get into some action.

Booth ran into opposition from all corners, including his own commander's initial objection to an intelligence official of such a senior rank going into the field, along with concerns about the vagueness of his proposed mission. Once past that hurdle, his proposed mission was then personally rejected by French general Marie-Pierre Koenig, as leader of the FFI, because it involved placing intelligence agents to operate in a liberated zone.

Undeterred, Booth made numerous trips around London lobbying, calling in favors, and getting past each objection he ran into. By late August, though, his biggest problem was that German-occupied soil in France was rapidly disappearing. Marseille fell on August 28, twenty-six days earlier than projected under invasion plans, and Allied forces had reached Grenoble three months earlier than what had been planned.

* * *

Bazata's message about the "five hundred Russians" had been an unexpected gift, providing a new opportunity for Booth to push himself and his self-styled mission onto a drop and into the war.

And then along came Kuzmuk, who had been with the 82nd Airborne Division, stationed in Nottingham, until a few weeks earlier when he was recruited into the OSS while in London on leave. Just a few days into his new position, as he was preparing to leave his London station one evening, he overheard two officers complaining that their proposed mission was blocked because there were no agents who spoke a Slavic language.

Kuzmuk introduced himself, and he became a "Russian speaking parachutist."

* * *

Two planes were required to carry the nine-man Mission Marcel Proust, the B-24 carrying Booth and Kuzmuk taking off from Harrington at nine thirty. Also on board, along with twelve containers, were two Frenchmen and an American naval lieutenant, twenty-eight-year-old Mike Burke, who had worked with Booth on Project Proust and had also helped the lobbying effort to find a location for the mission.

As the plane reached its cruising altitude of eight thousand feet, the trip turned bitterly cold for the passengers. The engines were too loud to allow a conversation, so there was little to do except sit on the floor of the plane in the darkness and ponder one's fate.

Burke settled himself with his back against a side wall and his knees pulled up to his chest to keep warm, an effort aided by an occasional sip of cognac from the flask he had been given on the ground.

* * *

German soldiers were now pouring into Haute-Saône. All roads big and small heading toward Vesoul were thick with Boches. Many parts of the region had reached a "saturation point," as Emile put it.

Four days before, Bermont had met with the famous Emile and had learned the news about the imminent drop. Emile also informed him that the Allies were less than thirty miles south of Vesoul. For once, Bermont was looking forward to the sound of cannon fire.

After the meeting, he set out to make sure the maquisards in his area were fully prepared for the parachute drop, getting the logistics set and making sure someone was listening for the coded signal. Bermont decided that le BUK should move from Forêt de Cherlieu back to the woods next to Confracourt. He told Hloba of the decision, adding that the battalion would be needed for the upcoming drop.

After the first few days of participating in ambushes, Myroslaw's battalion became inactive and bogged down by a kind of lethargy. While Bermont saw the Ukrainians as disciplined and brave, he thought they had no sense of partisan warfare. Years later he would wonder whether it may have been better if the battalion had been dispersed among various maquis groups, as was the original idea of Simon and Reuchet.

On the other hand, while less than two weeks had passed since the mutiny the war had already entered an altogether different era. Whatever could be said about le BUK could also be said for insurgency operations overall, in particular OSS and SOE operations, as the original opportunities and their relevance were being swiftly overtaken by the eastward push of the Allies and the great retreat of the Germans out of France.

* * *

An overnight march toward the south by le BUK began, with Simon and Claude leading the way. The battalion first had to cross route N19, the Paris-Vesoul-Belfort highway, where there was heavy traffic from German units heading east. With no hope of fighting their way across, the Ukrainians waited through the night. It was six in the morning, after some armored German units had passed by, when there was finally an opening to begin crossing the highway.

A German guard detachment appeared. When the Ukrainians opened fire the Germans fled, and the battalion was again on its way south, the soldiers disappearing one by one into some woods on the other side of the road. As the last few were crossing the road, they encountered a car carrying a German general, who apparently only took note of their German uniforms.

At ten o'clock everyone was across, and they made camp for the day in some woods a mile beyond the village of La Neuvelle-lès-Scey.

* * *

The battalion now had three cars at its disposal. Simon and Hloba used one of the cars and a French driver to head east for a meeting with Bermont to learn more about the upcoming drop. Afterward, as they were returning to their camp, they came upon a number of retreating German units heading east. Hloba and Simon observed a certain astonishment on the faces of some of the Germans as they watched the unfamiliar officers in German uniforms heading west, toward the enemy. German soldiers saluted as the car went by.

Entering a stretch of road that was free of German traffic, they came upon two maquis scouts on bicycles. Told that German MPs were at a bridge just up ahead, controlling all traffic heading west, Simon stationed himself at the rear of the car with a machine gun, while Hloba sat up front near the driver. When they approached the bridge, the Germans waved them to stop. Instead, the driver floored it, and the MPs jumped aside to avoid being run over while shooting at the car as it sped by.

* * *

The seven-mile journey south to the Bois de Confracourt, a couple of miles east of the village of Confracourt, was completed in time for the Ukrainians to settle in the day before the drop. Trenches were again dug, and guard posts established.

In between the village and the large forested area was a meadow, designated for parachute drops of containers and given the code name Aquarelle. The drop area had no radio-transmitting station to assist a pilot in finding the small field. The area surrounding the drop field was crowded with Germans. Bermont arranged for a double ring of protection for the drop zone, the immediate area covered by a nearby maquis group known as D'arc and an outer perimeter of security against German intruders staked out by le BUK.

Everyone was in place just before one o'clock in the morning on September 10 when a low-flying plane could be heard approaching.

* * *

Hours before, the plane had entered French airspace in a thick cloud cover. But at the drop area the night was clear. At the helm was a veteran pilot, twenty-one-year-old Henry Gilpin from Cleveland, who had to visually locate the field by looking down on the moonlit pastoral landscape, using the features in the terrain around Confracourt. The most prominent was the Saône River, in the moonlight, a silver ribbon bending its way just off to the south and east.

Standing with those waiting for the arrival, Bermont was struck by the beauty of the evening, a perfect night. A half-moon had begun rising at midnight. The ground was dry.

The plane approached and made a turn over a nearby village to the west before heading toward the field just beyond Confracourt. To those on the ground it appeared Gilpin was using the church bell tower in the village for alignment.

The reception lights were turned on, three red, a hundred yards apart, which showed the direction of the wind. A fourth light, white, flashed in Morse code the letter *D* as the identification signal. From the air the signal lights were dim and difficult for Gilpin to see, but he managed to make the first drop in a pass at an altitude of 670 feet. The signal lights on the ground were turned off, only reappearing after he had brought the plane around for the next two drops, both done at just under four hundred feet.

A little after one o'clock, just six minutes after he had made the first drop, Gilpin gunned the ship's engines and started back to England. Bermont would always believe there had been three planes, rather than a single plane making three passes.

* * *

As the low groan from the departing B-24 tapered off in the distance, directly overhead there were repeated loud slams in the still night air as the chutes opened up. Bermont marveled at the sight of what appeared to be large flower petals descending. The designated collection teams sprang forward to recover the containers and parachutes so no clues would be left behind, and another team met the arriving operatives. Everything was loaded onto farmers' carts normally used to transport crops, driven by the owners themselves toward the prearranged caches hidden in the nearby forest.

The second plane never made it to the drop area. In addition to more containers and four additional officers, it had also been carrying the mission's wireless transmitters. The arrivals would be unable to communicate with London.

Another stroke of luck for Booth, and it would suit him just fine.

CHAPTER TWENTY-FOUR

The Day of Glory Has Arrived

Sunday, September 10, 1944

A S HE LOOKED at the deep shadows cast against the moonlit stone walls of Confracourt, Booth was reminded of a stage set from *Cyrano de Bergerac*. After a few hours' sleep, the light of day would reveal to him the abiding grace of the rolling wooded countryside that surrounded the village.

It was a little after noon when, having made sure the presence of the three Americans was witnessed by local citizens, a few of the maquis led Booth, Burke, and Kuzmuk out of the village on a one-lane dirt road. After a mile or so, their route tunneled into thick woods. They passed by a series of ill-dressed French guards and entered the world of the maquis.

Simon and Claude had joined them as the tour began, heading toward a series of clearings within the forest, where there were separate encampments for the maquis and the soldiers of le BUK. The first order of business was for Booth to conduct a ceremonial inspection, of sorts, maquisards standing for review in their version of a disciplined order while wearing ragged mismatched clothing of French, German, and a few other vague origins.

* * *

Simon Doillon brought over Hloba, who spoke English and was introduced to Booth. The Americans took note of Hloba's slight build and that he carried himself with a upright flair that played well against his discreet mustache and riding uniform with its wide belt, dark pants slipped into heavy boots.

The touring group continued walking.

As they neared a Ukrainian kitchen crew, Kuzmuk said to Booth, "They're speaking Polish! I can understand what they are saying!"

Booth turned to Hloba and explained that Kuzmuk was part of the group because of his knowledge of the Russian and Polish languages.

Hloba addressed Kuzmuk in Russian and saw only a lack of understanding.

He tried Polish and got the same result.

Kuzmuk then spoke up. In what he had once thought was the Polish language, he asked "in pure Ukrainian," as Hloba later remembered it, whether the battalion cook standing nearby was good at borscht.

* * *

At two o'clock, Booth conducted another makeshift ceremonial inspection, this time of the Ukrainian soldiers, giving a short speech about their service in the fight against the Germans. He said he hoped it would continue until the arrival of the American troops, and that the men of le BUK would then receive a long and well-deserved break. Booth also declared that Kuzmuk would be detached to serve as his liaison to le BUK.

News arrived in the forest by messenger.

German troops had entered and occupied Confracourt. Maquis scouts had been out and learned that a force of several thousand Germans, including tanks, was approaching all sides of the forest, reportedly under orders to wipe out the maquis and le BUK.

The Ukrainians dispersed to take up their designated positions of defense.

For the Americans, there was nowhere to go. They remained in the woods, Booth and Burke spending the night with the maquis, Kuzmuk in another clearing with le BUK.

* * *

A thunderstorm passed through that evening, bringing black sheets of rain. But the denizens of the forest, almost a thousand strong, awakened the next morning to rays of sunshine poking through the leafy canopy overhead.

The air had been cleansed and refreshed, the birds singing as though in a world of peace.

The Germans had other ideas.

They started the new day with a barrage of artillery and mortar fire at the front edge of the forest, an attempt to clear a way into the woods. With Simon and Claude in command, the Ukrainians went into action alongside the motley group of local partisans. Using the training provided to them by the Germans, they operated German weaponry that hurled ammunition at German soldiers, delivering a rejoinder with their own machine gun fire and several rounds of mortars.

An hour and a half after the initial exchange, a lone German armored car began advancing toward the forest. Fifty yards behind it were two companies of German soldiers. When the car got within 150 yards of the forest, the Ukrainians opened up on it with machine guns. The Germans inside jumped out and retreated, leaving the car behind while the two companies behind it unleashed a rain of intense machine gun fire into the woods. The Ukrainians responded at once with their own volley from machine guns and mortars, and then upped the ante by firing antitank guns.

As the battle raged, one of the Ukrainians made a dash to the abandoned armored car. He managed to start the engine and drove the car into the woods. Inside were fifty bars of chocolate and almost a hundred boxes of canned meat. Food supplies to le BUK had been cut off for two days, and the unexpected haul was welcomed right then and there, even while on the receiving end of an almost constant spray of machine gun fire.

* * *

Several times the German companies advanced in an attempt to enter the forest, once almost getting to the edge of the woods before being stopped. More than one area on the perimeter of the forest had come under attack. But at the end of the long day, the Germans had retreated back to Confracourt. One Ukrainian had been killed and two were seriously wounded. The Germans left behind sixty of their dead in the flat meadow outside the forest perimeter facing the village.

At dawn the following day the Germans again attacked, this time with heavier artillery, including 88s. The Ukrainians responded with volleys from their antitank guns and mortars. In the afternoon, on the side of the woods that skirted a small road heading south, the German troops began a new advance toward the forest. They got to within fifty yards when the Ukrainians surprised the Germans with heavy antitank fire, all but destroying the entire German company, more dead littering the flat meadow outside the forest perimeter facing the village.

There were no more attempts to reach the woods. For the rest of the day the Germans continued their artillery bombardment, and through the night they lobbed mortars that would burst in the trees above, showering those below with shrapnel and slivers of wood.

* * *

In the forest, things had turned bleak.

Everyone was exhausted. There was little food. Ammunition was running low, not enough to defend against another sustained German attack.

For hundreds of boys barely out of their teenage years, it was a night of unbounded weariness, with little rest. The air in the forest was thick with human thoughts about death at a young age.

Mike Burke bedded down underneath the trees and pondered his own mortality. Looking around, he observed how the maquisards and the Ukrainians all seemed resigned to the grim fate that likely awaited everyone at dawn.

* * *

The next morning the German guns were silent. At first light, it appeared that they had pulled their troops back to the edge of Confracourt.

A villager soon appeared in the distance, walking alone on the long dirt road from Confracourt into the forest. He carried a message from the Germans. All of the men and young boys of the village had been locked in the town hall. If one more shot came from the forest, they would all be executed.

There was much discussion in the woods as to what to do next, and it was decided to take a gamble.

The German fear of being captured alive by the French *terroristen* was well known and well grounded. Booth wrote a note, signing his name along with his rank, "Lieutenant Colonel, United States Army." It gave an ultimatum to the Germans: if they surrendered they would have the American guarantee of being accorded treatment as prisoners of war under the Geneva convention, something that the Germans knew would not be available upon capture by the French terrorists.

A white cloth was attached to a stick, and Burke and Kuzmuk stepped out of the forest.

They began a slow walk toward Confracourt, each making his way in a separate wheel track worn into the dirt road. The white flag was held up high as they approached the village to deliver the message.

As he walked, Burke found his mind wandering. One stream of thought tried to figure out what day of the week it was. He was looking at the wheat fields alongside the road when he realized that at some point during the night the Germans had removed their dead. He focused on the hope that death would be immediate if someone opened fire on him.

* * *

The final five hundred yards was a descent from a slight rise in the road, allowing Burke and Kuzmuk to look into the village. They could see no soldiers and no civilians.

Like every small town and village in France, as in America, a prominent place was given a stone monument listing the local dead from the Great War. Unlike in America, more than a million French boys had died in the conflict. Confracourt was a village of fewer than two hundred. There were sixteen names on the memorial.

One name would be added for the Second World War. During the previous night, thirty-year-old Andre Bazeau, a member of the local maquis who had been responsible for airdrops near Confracourt, was killed by the Germans after being captured and tortured. Among other things, the Germans had been interested in information about the local French terrorists and le BUK. Bazeau's beaten body would be found in a field the following day, his fingernails gone and both hands almost severed, presumably by wire twisted into his wrists, along with wounds in his back indicating he had been hung on meat hooks inserted into the muscles in his shoulder blades. He left behind a wife and young child.

* * *

Warily entering Confracourt, Burke and Kuzmuk saw no guns poking over walls or out of windows. Everything was quiet and motionless. Burke caught a glimpse of some movement off in the distance. A few German soldiers were climbing into vehicles as they began to drive away, toward the northeast.

The hot sun was beating down as Burke and Kuzmuk walked through the quiet empty square and over to the steps of a church, where they sat down. As they continued to look around and assess the situation, a few villagers appeared. Then a few more. And then some more.

Someone went to find the hostages, found them unguarded, and released them.

Soon it was an actual crowd that began to mill about in the open space in front of Burke and Kuzmuk. They sat and watched as a gradual realization began to set into the minds of the gathering villagers. More than four years of occupation were over. A young woman brought over a bottle of *pineau*, a local fortified wine, along with some glasses. She sat down with Burke and Kuzmuk, and the three drank to each other.

* * *

Burke sent someone from the village with a bicycle back to the forest to spread the word that the Germans were gone. Soon a stream of maquisards and soldiers of le BUK began to enter Confracourt. In the lead was Simon Doillon, sitting upright on a slow-moving horse. When he reached where most of the villagers were gathered, he stopped and solemnly made the announcement that Confracourt was liberated.

The joyous laughter, the weeping, and the hugging spread from one to another, and it was not long before "La Marseillaise" was sung. Burke spotted Bazeau's wife, standing off to the side, certain about the fate of her husband even though his death had not yet been confirmed. For the rest of his life, Burke would always remember Bazeau's hearty handshake and greeting of *bienvenu* after Burke's landing the night of his parachute drop into France.

Burke sat and took all of it in, witness to a pure splendor as the joy was spilling out everywhere in front of him. He spotted Simon off at the outer edge of the square.

Simon was still atop the black horse. Once again he was keeping himself apart from all the others in a self-effacing manner, fierce yet modest and courteous. As was Simon's way. His was a form of leadership forever too rare.

By the afternoon, flags were being unfurled, and flowers and other greenery had begun to bedeck the homes in Confracourt. Fruit was brought out, as was wine. In the open area near the church there was a brief ceremony, the entire village turning out. Along with leaders of the local FFI, Hloba was invited to stand up near the church as the mayor addressed the crowd. His speech included recognition of the soldiers of le BUK, noting that several had given their lives for the liberation of French soil. Some children came over and handed flowers to Hloba.

* * *

In the decades that followed the war, the understanding of the localness of the European conflict as essential to comprehending the Second World War was lost. Much of it was an erasure, mainly at the hands of those with a preference for history as a temple of worship and a grand forward arc. In France, there is no one story of the resistance. There is no one story of collaboration. And there is no single story of liberation.

Paris had nothing on the celebration in Confracourt, which lasted three days. Certainly, the great city did not include the participation of hundreds of young men dressed in German military uniforms. Floating through the air during those days were voices in song, the sweet lilt of old French folk tunes mingling with the beguiling modes and hypnotic melisma from a world more than a thousand miles to the east.

* * *

Missing from the celebration in Confracourt was a lone company from Myroslaw's battalion. They never made it to Vesoul, either a matter of chance or some German commander's necessity. Five Ukrainian officers and about a hundred Ukrainian soldiers had stayed behind.

A few days after the mutiny, all of them were gathered together, disarmed, and executed by the Germans.

CHAPTER TWENTY-FIVE

Silent, Brooding, Everlasting Fate

Saturday, September 17, 1944

IT HAD TAKEN less than a week for the entire western half of Haute-Saône to be liberated. During that time Booth and Burke tried various methods, including handwritten notes carried by maquis messenger, to get word out to Allied troops about the battalion of Ukrainians dressed in feldgrau.

Even so, as Allied soldiers entered the area there was a close call when a French army company spotted them and some shots were exchanged.

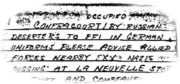

On a Saturday morning, five days after Confracourt was freed, the soldiers of le BUK were told by their French commanders that they were being given one month's rest. They were ordered to move out of the forest and make camp on the grounds of a large chateau and seven-hundred-year-old abbey in Neuvelle-lès-la-Charité, three miles south of where their mutiny had taken place. The Ukrainians took their wounded to Vesoul, where they would be given care at a US Army medical facility.

* * *

No one knew what to do with le BUK.

As an initial matter, they were not prisoners of war. That alone made them different from the thousands of other non-German soldiers surrendering throughout France.

And then there was the question of what they were.

To many, including most Americans, they were Russians.

To the Russians, they were Soviets.

To the British, they were not Ukrainians, the empire instructing its representatives well into the following year that "Ukrainians are not recognized as a nationality."

To others, at least some of the soldiers in le BUK were Poles. But that view depended on whether they had come from the correct side of a boundary line rejected twenty-five years before after being proposed by a British foreign secretary whose other claim to fame was being labeled a "gas bag" by the chief of His Majesty's imperial general staff.

Assigning group identity, so necessary for framing one's self while putting others in a designated place, is always a scurrilous undertaking.

* * *

Kuzmuk was ordered by Booth to remain with le BUK, in large part to keep them from getting crosswise with the American and French troops passing through the area. He would spend most of his days riding around in an almost continuous search for food to supply the Ukrainians.

For Hloba, and for most of the soldiers like Myroslaw, the time at the abbey was a welcome period of idleness. The surroundings were beautiful, even if the seasonal rains had begun a few days before. It was a comfortable life. The morbid darkness of the Ostfront was a constellation away.

But the days were also draped in a gray shroud of uncertainty. The farmers in the area saw this firsthand, and would long remember it. They knew about what the battalion had done and were friendly and open to the soldiers of le BUK, who began to offer whatever they could, including their horses, in exchange for a drowning or two in the local eau-de-vie.

Kuzmuk became very fond of the Ukrainians, and the feeling was mutual. His assessment, at least as related in later years, was that most of them were anti-Communist, a dogma he apparently spotted within those hundreds of boys, concluding that it was the reason for their willingness to fight under the Germans against the Soviet Army. Kuzmuk also had no doubt as to their hatred of the Germans. After the liberation of Confracourt, he witnessed some of the Ukrainians coming across a group of stragglers behind a retreating Wehrmacht unit. They promptly tore the Germans to shreds with an antitank gun. The action upset a nearby OSS operative who wanted the Germans alive for interrogation.

Like Emile, both Burke and Booth would repeatedly be taken aback by the enthusiasm within the resistance for killing German prisoners—no second thoughts, no questions asked. Various meanings can be drawn, both from what they saw and from their respective reactions. But what was going on in eastern France in the autumn of 1944, as it was elsewhere in Europe, was more than life having become very cheap and easy to extinguish. Recognized or not, the larger essence was that an entire civilization was entering into a state of full collapse, the war's dark turbidity only increasing its foul spread as the winter approached.

* * *

A few days into their encampment the Ukrainians were visited by a Soviet delegation. They represented themselves to Hloba as being from the Russian embassy in Paris and made inquiries to him about repatriation of the battalion. Hloba replied that the men of the battalion did not consider themselves to be Soviet citizens. He informed them that the battalion would remain in France to help achieve the total liberation of French territory.

The visitors left and did not return.

* * *

On September 19, Kuzmuk was visited by two American lieutenant colonels. Some Russians had approached the US Seventh Army Command Post, newly located in Vesoul, and demanded that the Ukrainians be returned to them. Kuzmuk was informed that the soldiers of le BUK were to be handed over under an agreement between the United States and the Soviet Union.

Kuzmuk responded with a strong plea on behalf of the Ukrainians, saying that turning them over to the Russians meant certain death. The two lieutenant colonels returned to Vesoul.

The next day, Colonel William Craig, head of G-1 (personnel) for the US Seventh Army, arrived at the abbey. The four companies that made up le BUK were brought out. They stood in formation in front of the ornate steps leading to the chateau entrance.

Craig turned to Kuzmuk and ordered him to get the Ukrainians to turn over their arms. He added that he had brought a truck and wanted to begin transporting them to the Russians.

"OK, but give me a few hours to get away."

Having gotten Craig's attention, Kuzmuk continued. "I will not disarm them. If you want them to go, you had better come with a battalion. You will have trouble."

"What do you mean? They won't accept an order from you?"

"No one. Come on, let's talk to them."

* * *

Kuzmuk addressed the Ukrainians. When he got to the part about what the US Army had decided would be their fate, there was a noticeable flutter in the ranks.

Craig appeared to take the point. He told Kuzmuk to tell the Ukrainians that he would take volunteers.

Kuzmuk stopped himself before saying anything further to the Ukrainians. He again turned to Craig and insisted that those who volunteered to be repatriated must be separated. If not, they would be killed by the others.

"It's as serious as that?"

"They do not want to return to Russia, and they will not. They prefer to be killed here."

Kuzmuk then conveyed Craig's call for volunteers. About twenty Ukrainians accepted the offer and stepped forward. They were removed from the abbey.

* * *

Bermont learned what was going on, presumably from Simon, who was still, along with Claude, considered a commander of le BUK. He took up negotiations with the Allied command post in Vesoul, making his own case against turning the Ukrainians over to the Russians. With Simon at his side, Bermont was vehement that the battalion was part of the FFI. It was therefore a French unit. He insisted that it was not up to the United States military to conclude otherwise and then turn such members of the FFI over to the Russians.

The argument took hold. And at the same time a solution emerged.

The Allied forces entering the area from the south included a group called French Army B. During those days the unit was renamed the French First Army, reorganized so it would ultimately be composed of several hundred thousand soldiers, including those from the FFI who were being brought into regular army service to continue the fight against the Germans.

It is unclear who thought of it first, although it was most likely the brainchild of Bermont, former (and future) career French military officer, given that it required the personal approval of the commander of the French First Army, General Jean de Lattre. The idea was put forward to offer the Ukrainians a chance to serve as part of the French Foreign Legion.

* * *

Booth was summoned to Vesoul for a meeting at Seventh Army headquarters. Told about the pressure from the Russians to turn over the Ukrainians, he argued strongly against such an action, saying that it was essentially a death sentence. He reminded everyone at the meeting that he had been a witness to le BUK fighting hard against the Germans.

During the discussion that followed it became clear to Booth that the Seventh Army staff was divided. He realized that some had sympathy and understanding toward the arguments against turning the Ukrainians over to the Russians, including from Colonel William Quinn, head of G-2 (intelligence), and Colonel Craig, head of G-1 (personnel), the latter having had his encounter with Kuzmuk in front of the Ukrainians.

After negotiations with Bermont, they agreed that le BUK would be turned over to the French. The Ukrainians would be offered a chance to serve in the French Foreign Legion and to participate in the drive into Germany. For the Seventh Army, the decision had the happy effect of putting the entire matter out of its hands, including having to deal with the Soviets about repatriation.

Within days, by at least September 22, British liaison officers in the area reported back to London that they had observed the Ukrainians being interviewed by French officers with a view to incorporating them into the French Foreign Legion. While it had not been General de Lattre's intention, all of the Ukrainians ended up exclusively in the French Foreign Legion's well-traveled 13th Demi-Brigade, which was in urgent need of an infusion of young men. The 13th DBLE (13e Demi-Brigade de Légion Étrangère) had fought in Norway in 1940 and had then taken part in battles in Africa and Syria, including facing Rommel. Its next combat was in Italy, before joining the August southern invasion of France.

Four days later the Ukrainians left the abbey, the promised period of rest turning out to be considerably less than a month.

* * *

In the first days after Confracourt's liberation, Booth had met with the commanding officer of the 117th Cavalry Reconnaissance Squadron, part of the US Seventh Army, explaining the situation about the Ukrainians. Booth also used the meeting to achieve informal agreement that a reinvented Mission Marcel Proust could be attached as an additional unit to the 117th Squadron. Once he was confident that the new undertaking was established, he and Burke made their first radio contact with OSS headquarters since the night of their parachute drop into Haute-Saône.

Hloba, along with a few of his officers and Kuzmuk, paid a farewell call on Booth and Burke. Simon and Claude were also present for the lunch gathering, as they would no longer be with le BUK because Booth had arranged for them to join his small team as part of the new version of Mission Marcel Proust.

* * *

In less than a month, Simon would be dead, killed by a German sniper while out on an advance reconnaissance mission. Claude Vougnon would weep for two days.

Simon's body would be left to rot on the ground for three weeks, unrecoverable, as the drenching autumn rains arrived and Allied progress suddenly came to a halt.

* * *

Of the twenty or so from le BUK who volunteered for repatriation, little is known as to their fate, although most likely they were either executed or sent off to spend decades in a gulag. In 1994 a letter was received in Haute-Saône from one of them, describing an imprisonment of twenty-five years.

As for the hundreds who joined the French Foreign Legion, they were initially kept together as a unit, the result of an intervention by Kuzmuk on their behalf. Still wearing German uniforms, along with black berets, their first action was an early October advance to take a particular hill from the Germans. It did not go well, and they suffered many casualties. The Ukrainians were then scattered throughout various units of the 13th DBLE, as had been originally intended.

Over the next several months the Russians would continue to press the French on repatriation of their "Soviet citizens" and, in particular, le BUK. On November 9, *Pravda* reported that "Soviet war prisoners, forcibly placed by Hitlerites in units of the rank, killed their German Commanding Officers and the guards, and then went over to the side of the approaching allied units, and heroically fought in their ranks against the Hitler troops." A problem existed, though, compelling Soviet representatives in France to take steps "to free the Soviet citizens from the French camps for her prisoners and to start sending them home," adding that "in the Marseilles region . . . there is permitted the infamous recruiting of Soviet citizens into the service of the Foreign Legion located in Africa." The next day, *The Times* of London repeated the *Pravda* report almost verbatim.

In December, the Russians would up the ante, making the French turning over the soldiers of le BUK an express condition for their own return of French citizens from Alsace-Lorraine who had been prisoners of the Germans. Initially, the French Army commanders refused to provide inspection opportunities, but the pressure continued. During the months leading up to V-E Day, most of the Ukrainians left their units, while the French helpfully cleansed their records at the same time so that they would be silent in the event of any Russian request to screen personnel documents as part of their search.

A few of the Ukrainians from le BUK finished the war with the French Foreign Legion, and even continued in the next decade to serve in postwar French Indochina, where CIA operative Walter Kuzmuk, stationed nearby, would unsuccessfully try to connect with them. And where Soviet operatives would continue to chase down those members of le BUK.

* * *

The faded and deliberately obscured record suggests that a very small number from the battalion were neither repatriated nor recruited into the French Foreign Legion. Only a fortunate few somehow managed to slip away and find refuge elsewhere in the fall of 1944.

One was Hloba, senior-most Ukrainian officer and leader of the mutiny against SS overseers.

Another was Myroslaw.

CHAPTER TWENTY-SIX

The World Left Behind

Friday, October 13, 1944

BOYD HAD NEVER known such October mornings. Not yet noon, the temperature was already above seventy. The air was deliriously perfumed. Combined with the colorful vegetation he found so intriguing and the sight of so many prosperous people, it all made him feel that Florida was nothing less than an amazing and glamorous playground.

He marveled at how it rained late each afternoon for about fifteen minutes, and then the sun would come back out. As a boy he had learned how to watch a sky. In Tampa, Boyd discovered the particular pleasure of observing the puffy tropical clouds that were always present, their squint-worthy brightness against the blue so much whiter than the clouds back home.

Two weeks before, he had finished up a letter to his parents:

... Got a letter from Brownie. He's still talking about that furlough. I can't get over it either—even now it doesn't seem possible. I guess no one in the service could have had a better furlough than we did. We sure ate like kings. You certainly have a lot of colds around. Guess we'll

*all have to go south every winter after the war's over. I'm
so sleepy I can't hold my head up and it's only nine
o'clock. Love, Boyd*

* * *

Boyd had already made the pronouncement to his parents that the time he
spent in Tampa was the best of his two years in the service. Stationed at
the Plant Park Replacement Depot, he spent his mornings raking and
fixing up the ball diamonds and his afternoons playing baseball, football,
and basketball. He felt like he was living the life of a small boy again.
Volleyball was a popular game with the officers at Plant Park, and it was a
point of pride with him that while playing he had been able to become
acquainted with quite a few majors, captains, and even some colonels.

Shipments for assignment to air combat crews went out twice a week,
and he had managed to avoid every one of them. He had heard that most
gunners did not last two weeks at Plant Park before being shipped out.
But each time his name came up, one of the officers he had made friends
with while playing sports had managed to fix things.

The morning of Friday the thirteenth brought the sad acceptance that
his name was not going to be scratched from the day's list. It was too late
for anything to be done about it. He knew that before the day was over he
would be part of a combat crew destined for shipment overseas.

The train for Gulfport Army Airfield in Mississippi would be leaving
in the early afternoon. He got himself packed up and ready for the eight-
block trip to the station, taking one last walk over the drawbridge that
woke him most evenings when it came clanking down after midnight.

* * *

A thousand miles to the north, the temperature that morning had started
to drop into the fifties. In the early afternoon it began to rain.

Don had finished packing everything into a single canvas bag. Carrying
a full field pack, he stepped outside the barracks at Camp Kilmer, New
Jersey, leaving behind walls marked up in pencil by those who had already
passed through.

Arrived May 6 — Left May 9

Arrived July 11 — Left July 16

When Brownie had returned to Camp Pickett from Wisconsin in
September, there was no longer any doubt that his unit was headed

somewhere. Preparations had started for a move, inventory being taken and equipment checked and packed. Weekend passes were stopped. And then one day they were told that all outgoing letters had to be left unsealed.

On the fifth of October, everyone in the outfit had boarded a train heading north. Since arriving at Camp Kilmer they had spent their days filling out multiple forms and drawing new equipment, including gas masks. They all underwent physical examinations and got a series of shots.

Now it was time to get in line to board a ferry, which would take them to another boat that would take them to the war. Brownie made a mental note that it was Friday the thirteenth.

* * *

In early September 1944, the Allies were less than an hour's peacetime drive from the Rhine River. They were facing enemy forces that were in almost complete disarray.

In mid-September, as abruptly as anything that happened in the war, the momentum of the Allies vanished. The Germans were given a chance to regroup. And they did.

As for the small area of Haute-Saône not yet freed of occupiers, an area just west of the Belfort Gap, liberation would not come for another two months.

By late October, the exhilaration of the late summer belonged to an ancient era. There was no more talk about the war ending before Christmas.

* * *

Many explanations have been offered for the almost trancelike state that seemed to seize Allied leadership as the season turned, with no effort made to take advantage of the historic rollback of a military force that was in very un-Germanic chaos. References are often made to logistical challenges, the distraction of an ugly mid-September failure at Arnhem, or the unusually heavy fall rains in eastern France. None rings particularly true, alone or in combination.

The Allies' inaction gave a breather to the Germans. It meant that every single mile of advancement to the Rhine would have to be fought over.

As it turned out, some of those miles to the Rhine would also have to be refought. Almost three-quarters of the bombs that would fall on German cities during the Second World War had yet to be dropped.

There would be plenty of war waiting for Boyd and Don.

* * *

The train was waiting alongside the brick Italian Renaissance–style rail station with its grandly arched windows. Boys in US Army Air Force uniforms were milling around outside. Names were called out and small groups gathered, one of which included Boyd. There were introductions and big open-spirited handshakes all around.

With that, a B-17 crew was formed.

Together they got on the train.

* * *

When he met the rest of the crew, Boyd took a deep pleasure, as he always did, in the variety of places from where the others came. They all seemed to be from someplace so exotic. He savored their unusual accents, enjoyed their mannerisms, and appreciated their experiences and perspectives that were so unusual and different from what he knew at home.

He always thought it was a funny thing, how hometown locations would stick with him before names did. The introduction of the crew was no different. As he would relate to his parents a few days later, the pilot was the youngest of the new crew at twenty-one years old, and he was from Georgia. The copilot was from South Bend, Indiana. The radio man was from Annapolis, Maryland. One boy was from Michigan, another from North Carolina. They still needed an engineer and a navigator, although at that point, Boyd still was not sure what everyone on a crew did.

He learned that day he was to be the tail gunner on their ship.

From the start, he thought they all were swell fellows. Before the train pulled out, they were told they would be together as a crew until the end of the war.

And they were.

* * *

Two days later, Boyd would make the first long-distance telephone call of his life, to his parents in Wisconsin. The operator had told him that it would take two to three hours for the call to go through Chicago, so while he waited, he picked up a pen and started a letter home anyway.

Nine pages of excitement spilled out, much of it about his being part of a crew and flying six hours each day, even if it meant that he would soon be heading off to England or Italy.

> *...I think I'm in better condition and healthier and happier than I've been since I've been in the Army. It just seems since I had that wonderful furlough it put a spark in me and everything's been going my way since.*

* * *

For Don, Friday had a late finish, starting with an evening ferry ride to the New York harbor. The boat was crowded and the trip was silent. As they approached the slip in darkness and a drippy autumn rain, the engine stopped and the boat glided in. Don and the rest filed off. Group after group was brought in.

The hour was late. Fog had started to close in all around, and not much could be seen beyond a few yards. The damp air was pea-soup thick as Brownie and thousands of others all stood in formation. Many wondered where the big ship was hidden. Red Cross volunteers went up and down the lines with doughnuts and coffee, wishing everyone good luck. Somewhere behind the surrounding murk an army band played, adding to the eeriness of the moment.

Last names were called. Soldiers responded with their first name and middle initial. There was one step forward, then a turn, and then the onward stride through the fog to a point where a gangplank extending upward could at last be seen.

One by one, each boy took his last step off of American soil and up the ramp. It was almost impossible to make the ascent without staggering under all the weight of the field pack.

At the top was the entrance to a ship the length of two football fields. Each soldier was directed to go below the deck.

And that is where Don and almost five thousand other boys spent their last evening in the land of their fathers, squeezed into their quarters and listening to the noises of the harbor, a wakeful night of fear and excitement.

* * *

On Saturday morning the sun briefly came out, then disappeared again. The boys could see other ships, still tied to the docks. Those that would be in their convoy were painted with a vague bluish-gray coloring, twenty-five ships in all, including six other troopships and ten escort vessels.

A voice ordered all the soldiers below deck, where the boys crowded around the portholes to look out as the ship swung out onto the Hudson River and passed the Statue of Liberty.

They had not yet been told their destination, although there was plenty of speculation.

The boys only knew they were heading to the war.

Part Four

OTHERWORLD

December 1944–April 1945

CHAPTER TWENTY-SEVEN

Closer and Closer

Thursday, December 7, 1944

THE INTRUSION OF the Second World War into the lives of Boyd and Don had been gradual and continuous. At some unidentifiable point, the war had become a large ungovernable presence throughout their society, altering how it functioned, how it looked at itself, and how it established worth.

When the boys left Wisconsin after their August furlough, shortages piled upon shortages. An absence of spare parts left many radios unrepairable, which meant fewer people were listening. The paper available for writing letters or used for publications had a cheap feel. Certain food products seemed to have taken on an odd and unfamiliar taste. A special fortitude was needed to face the niggling chaos awaiting anyone planning a trip or making a visit to a large public place.

By the autumn of 1944 a shabbiness had descended, along with a constant fatigue from it all. More than just the inability to buy a new refrigerator, or to see a new house going up, parts of life had gone missing.

But it was a comfortable and even prosperous deprivation. Whatever the strain and daily sacrifice, Herb, Julius, and Ernst were each doing far better financially than at any time since before the Depression. An exceptional geography had placed their nation between two oceans. For those fortunate citizens the physical realm of the conflict was elsewhere. The war remained an abstraction, a tiring disturbance of the senses like a skin rash or a lingering odor. Disagreeable and at times offensive, but on those shores it was hardly debilitating.

* * *

The remoteness of the slaughter and ruin had allowed for a romanticism about the war to take root on American soil, heavily fertilized by government and business enterprises. Upon Boyd's arrival overseas it soon began to rub him the wrong way, as it did many other boys. He would admonish his parents accordingly in his letters home from Europe.

Nurtured initially in the great remove from the physical actuality of the conflict, the notion of an American idealism as the omnipresent overlay during the Second World War would flourish in its aftermath. Passing decades brought more distance from the war, and by the turn of the new century the contrivance of a particular American élan at home and on the battlefield would become almost mandatory within the putatively established narrative of the Second World War. The more recent feel-good embrace of a noble simplicity that did not exist would, in the early twenty-first century, pair well with a worshipful detachment of society from its military.

The elevation of the American Second World War experience, toward a mythology of winsome days filled with sturdy leadership and a collective ardor devoted to a grand cause, would have seemed downright bizarre during those unruly years to a citizenry then more given to a flinty sincerity leavened by cynicism. Ignored in later years as ill-fitting within an uplifting narrative, the complicated American wartime temperament was a necessity if not a strength during those days. Those living through such a time perceived themselves in a world gone mad, having to endure one of the greatest and most dangerous failures of mankind. For them, it could not end a day too soon.

* * *

As each boy headed across the Atlantic or Pacific, the entrance into the *demesne* of the war was a staged passage, through progressively greater levels of ruin and wretched distortions of human existence. Every new step of exposure brought an initial disbelief, a slack-jawed gaze at the latest presentation of something they never thought they would see. All this well before any introduction to the terror of combat and those first moments when the war commenced its molten cold penetration into one's personal sense of being.

Don's Atlantic voyage would be memorable for how bad the ship reeked below deck. The air was almost unbearable as the digestive systems of thousands of boys unsuited to the pitch and roll were in constant and very productive rebellion.

On the twelfth morning after leaving the New York harbor, green shores could be seen emerging through the mists off in the distance to the east. Only the day before had they been told they were approaching England.

For most of Wednesday, October 25, Don's troopship poked its way along the southern English coast before entering the harbor of Southampton. Darkness was settling in as the last of his regiment disembarked. The boys were transported to the nearby resort area of Bournemouth, where they stayed, sometimes up to ten in a room, in what had once been hotels and private homes.

* * *

Except for the initial unsettling sight of barbed wire and pillboxes set out on the British beaches, where Don and the others would go each morning for training activities, the three weeks at Bournemouth were a gentle introduction to the war. The nights were spent at dance halls and Red Cross centers, and many of the boys experienced a new taste in a glass or two of bitters consumed at the local pub. Arf and arf, the boys joked.

New orders came. It was time to move out. Don's company of eight officers and 150 enlisted men took a train from Bournemouth to Southampton. At two o'clock in the morning on November 19 they boarded another and began their crossing of the English Channel. With gray clouds overhead and very choppy waters underneath, they transferred to a flat-bottomed landing craft and headed to the shores of France, where the ramp banged down with a deep thump onto a beach of pebbles. Don and the others were invited to step out.

The well-fed American boys wearing clean clothes took their first steps onto a continent at war. There had been no warning of what they would see.

They had also not been told how difficult it would be to cross the first hundred yards from the beach to the port roadway. Weighted down by a full field pack, each boy had to maneuver around bomb craters, large pieces of boats, ships on their side, stray shells and guns, crates, and burned-out tanks. Once beyond the beach area they started moving in a column on the road heading north, where they were met by the shocking sight of what the war had done to Le Havre. "Really beat up," Don would say later.

What he saw was an abandoned city. Home after home was destroyed, only fragments of streets and intersections remaining. As the boys walked as soldiers in their orderly column, they became part of a larger moving throng, having been joined by wandering sullen-faced refugees.

It was their first look at the war's crushing degradation of people. For some, the sight would be remembered as having provoked an unconscious apology. For others there was a realization that the newsreels and newspapers back home did not even begin to convey the atrocity that the war had brought upon humanity.

Up the road, a truck convoy was waiting to remove the boys from the shattered city. They were taken to an encampment in the Normandy countryside.

* * *

It rained the first seven days they were on the Continent. Where they stayed was soon christened Camp Mud. They stood in mud, trained in mud, and slept in mud, four to five inches deep.

The rain kept coming. It had been decades since France had seen such autumn rains. Thanksgiving dinner for Don required standing in a long line that snaked out of damp tents, where they were given turkey and all the fixings. He and the others in his outfit were then directed outside, where they stood in ankle-deep mud and ate, the cold downpour collecting in the compartments of the trays they held while eating. The mashed potatoes were made soggy by the rain, but the holiday meal was an important small comfort, remembered years later as having been eaten that day with enthusiasm and gratitude.

Two days later, Brownie and his mortar squad left camp and headed east by truck. Many of the others in his regiment climbed onto "forty-and-eights," the stubby French boxcars named for the forty men or eight horses they were designed to carry. Two hundred twenty miles later they were all in Belgium, just outside of the city of Tongeren, thirty-five miles from the front.

More greetings from the war: streaming overhead was an almost constant parade of German buzz bombs, a fantastic beast to behold, its long tail of sparks shooting out from behind as it gave off a low grinding whir.

In their new position the boys heard for the first time a distant whump-whump-whump, the muffled thunder of artillery that rolled across the countryside toward them at all hours. At night the flashes could be seen, like a storm off in the distance. The war was waiting for them.

Don had time to write some letters, including to his brother in law.

Somewhere in Belgium
Thurs. nite, Dec. 7, 1944

Dear George,

Well son, it's just about time I wrote to you. I imagine you wonder just what I'm doing over here, so do I sometimes, just as I'm wondering what your doing in Panama is that right? Boy kid for you to leave the states so soon surely surprised me. You'll have to let me know how your doing and can you get any liquer and drinks a sailor usually goes for down there. By your address I'll be damned if I can figure out what your in. As you probably know I hit England first and was there for some time and then to France and then now here. Lot of mud over here and in France, more than I've ever seen. You ought to try sleeping in it once. Had a good trip over, only bad part is we rode on a Limey Luxury Liner good boat but the sailors aren't like ours that were on the boat that took us across the channel. Gambled a few nites here in a tavern and made a little, anyway enough to send Marie $100 for a present for her and the baby. You know it won't be long and I'll be a papa and you an uncle. I guess you know I am sweating that out too. I can't get that cable from them too soon. Do you play any cards or shoot dice or haven't you learned that yet? Well George I have seen a little of the world and will probably see Germany too some day but buddy I'll take our home town to any part of the world. Well son this V-mail is too short so I better quit. Take care of yourself and write soon. Merry Christmas George. I'll try and write again before then. Cross your fingers its a boy George if we both pull it may be. Love, Don

CHAPTER TWENTY-EIGHT

Splendidly

Saturday, December 9, 1944

TWO DAYS AFTER writing to George, Don entered Germany. The convoy of trucks began moving at seven thirty in the morning. The drivers were "Negro soldiers," whereas Don and the others were "soldiers." Skin pigmentation rendered so much apparent otherness that it precluded them from going into battle alongside Don, to fight against those of whatever "race" the Germans considered themselves to be.

At least until the US First Army became even more desperate for replacement infantry riflemen than it already was.

The procession of vehicles snaking its way through falling snow entered what had once been a city, a place settled by Celts before the time of Jesus Christ and once the home of Charlemagne, eleven bloody centuries before Don's ride on that December day.

Aachen was the first German city captured by the Allies. Brownie was able to get a good look at what remained of Aachen after a merciless artillery bombardment, much of it at point-blank range, followed by vicious urban warfare that brought heavy losses to both sides.

The battle in Aachen had also pushed the war past another significant threshold. For the first time, German civilians were now joining the throngs of French, Belgian, Dutch, Polish, and other refugees wandering across Western Europe.

Never in his life, Don would later say, did he think he would ever see a city so large "just pounded to the ground." As he rode through Aachen he guessed it had once been the size of Green Bay or Wausau, and he tried to envision those two cities left without a single building standing.

From Aachen, the procession continued south. Moving at a deliberate, slow pace, each truck was kept sixty yards apart from the next. As the convoy entered the final stretch toward its destination, an angle in the road two miles north of the German village of Lammersdorf, the approach was lined with manned antiaircraft batteries, another first-time sight for the new arrivals.

The reason for the placement of the guns became clear at a little after two in the afternoon, when two German planes made a strafing run at the line of traffic. One of the planes was hit by antiaircraft fire and the German pilot bailed out. The arriving boys were well positioned to watch the gently descending pilot get shot up from a number of directions, his body riddled with bullets as it floated to the ground.

Another introductory greeting from the war.

* * *

At the detrucking point, Don jumped out and gathered with the rest of his company in a nearby assembly area covered with snow. What had been a light snowfall earlier in the day had turned into a driving snowstorm that was transforming the landscape into a serene Christmas-card scene of rolling fields with hedgerows, an occasional farmhouse, and clumps of fir trees being decorated in white. They began the single-file trek toward the east.

Approaching one of the entry points into a thick forest of interlocked pine trees standing upward of seventy-five to one hundred feet, they were told to stay on the right side of a string, the demarcation line for where mines had been cleared. Before they entered the woods, small white cloth strips were tied to the back of everyone's field pack to help guide the soldier following behind.

Once inside, the absence of daylight was almost complete. A thick mantle of snow clung to the tops of the trees and shut out whatever few rays might have normally found their way through. The boys were warned to be on the lookout for tripwires near wherever they stepped, and for booby traps the Germans had strung into the trees. They soon learned that the best technique for walking in the darkness was to hold on to the handle of the shovel poking out of the backpack worn by the soldier in front.

The arrival of new soldiers at the front was never a surprise to the unseen Germans. It would not be long before there was some sort of greeting.

* * *

Since crossing the channel, Don's introduction to the war's savage havoc had been mainly visual. But it was the noise that delivered the demonic reality of what he had just entered.

Nothing would ever compare to the first exposure. The wild mix of metallic shrieks and whiffles seemed to come from every direction. Artillery was no longer a distant thunder, but a deep godlike bellow, at times so loud it brought tears to the eyes, like a blow to the head. The deafening roar tore the air and made it move, followed by piercing screams that were not of the human world. In the background were bursts of small arms, and the occasional bowel-loosening rip of the German burp gun.

The throbbing noise of the war made muscles twitch, for some to the point of paralysis. It would stun and it would humble. And it brought terror to silence. Many of the boys discovered a newfound fear upon hearing the once harmless snap of a branch, a foot stomping in the snow, or the soft flutter and cry of a bird taking off close by.

The war's noise would always be beyond replication, never within reach of any radio or television portrayal or movie re-creation.

* * *

The boys had been ordered to dig in with as much separation as possible. That way, they were told, fewer of them would be killed from a single shell.

And so the first evening at the front, spent in a frozen hole.

German mortar shells fell throughout the night. The frosty air did nothing to stop cold sweat.

Fear is not a simple emotion. For each boy it was now an ever-present part of his life, something that had to be tended to regularly, like a matter of personal hygiene. There had been no training for the absolute aloneness, for terror so immense that it could be felt seeping into every mental and physical function.

The first night in Germany made some of the boys vomit. Others pissed their pants. Few slept.

* * *

As Don's regiment was moving into position across a several-thousand-yard area of front line, arriving boys occasionally came face-to-face with what was left of the units they were replacing, weary and bent men, hollow-eyed and unshaven. They came out of the snowy woods at an almost stationary pace of mortal exhaustion, some too weak to bear the weight of an overcoat. It was an encounter, a few of the arrivals thought, with real-life Willie and Joes trudging out of a Bill Mauldin drawing.

Another introduction to the war: the sight of other young Americans with a vacant stare, shuffling with an unyouthful countenance as though they consisted of pieces barely held together. As the new arrivals would soon learn, everyone who spent any time in the maw of the war, in Europe or the Pacific, would be broken in some fashion. Sometimes it stayed just below the surface, sometimes it went deep. Sometimes it blew apart where everyone could see.

But no one emerged unbroken.

* * *

Each of those badly aged souls leaving the forest had once been a fresh-faced arrival. Those who were departing that December afternoon had been similarly jarred on a cold and rainy October day by the sight of the soldiers they were replacing, nervous bearded men in torn, muddy uniforms walking beneath personal gear hanging from trees, where it would sometimes land after the wearer had stepped on a mine.

Don's outfit was relieving a division that had lost a third of its soldiers in a matter of weeks. They had been ground down in a merciless defeat, following similar failed attacks by other American divisions in the same place, all of it starting in September.

The stench inside the forest was almost unbearable. Left behind were bodies of those who had once been alongside. The corpses of American boys would stay there until months later, after the spring snowmelt. Some would be found on stretchers, mute testimony of awful calamity and agony. It was a particular skill of the Germans to booby-trap the American bodies left on the landscape, after stripping them of cigarettes and useful clothing, sometimes even before death had come.

The departing soldiers had been ordered to a new location, where they would take the place of another unit that had been resting. An always wishful high command had been assured by the best intelligence that in the upcoming mid-December days, that area would stay quiet.

The destination for those boys leaving the Hürtgen Forest was another heavily wooded area several miles to the south, a place known as the Ardennes.

* * *

Meanwhile, Don's company settled in. They were near the village of Germeter, close to the center point of the Hürtgen Forest, an extra emphasis always to be placed on the first syllable.

The Biennial Report of the Chief of Staff of the United States Army to the Secretary of War for the period of July 1, 1943 to June 30, 1945 includes the following sentence:

> East of Aachen troops of the First Army fought splendidly through the bloody Hürtgen Forest, taking heavy casualties and inflicting heavy losses on the stubborn enemy.

No doubt General George Catlett Marshall Jr. himself did not write those words. It is unlikely that the great man would have even had occasion to read that particular sentence. Rightly so, for it is impossible to imagine anyone with some knowledge and a modicum of honesty doing so without bile rising in their throat.

* * *

There has never existed on earth a large organization that has not undertaken, as essential to its mission, efforts to shape a pleasing but false narrative. This is always done through the use of words that connote something positive while expressing no actual meaning. The word "splendidly" is high-level command-post language, an effete and evasive term used as a result of calculation made from a protected distance.

The American troops in the Hürtgen Forest did not fight splendidly.
They fought needlessly.

It was the troops, not the forest, which were bloodied, casualty rates that approached slaughter by virtue of orders that could only yield defeat after defeat.

The enemy was not stubborn. The American high command was stubborn. And inept, incomprehensibly dulled after the late-summer triumphal burst across France.

The murderous disaster of the Hürtgen Forest does not fit well within the accepted canon of the Second World War, an obscurity that is unjustifiable given the magnitude of what transpired over several months. The forest remains inexplicable as a military objective. The conduct of American military leadership during the campaign was nothing less than ignoble.

During the fall of 1944, thousands of American boys were sent into a place and made to fight in vain. This was done by an all-too-familiar combination of high-level detachment, vanity, insecurity, and incompetence, at that juncture on the part of very human beings named Cota, Hodges, Bradley, and Eisenhower.

* * *

To those ordained to the call of the magisterial account, the high-level command during the Second World War is rich with Olympian thoughts, delightful repartee, and clever bickering among those who directed the "pincer movements" and "wheeling actions" sometimes carried out by the curiously named "fresh troops." As did the political leaders of the day, the military leaders left behind a durable trail, much of it purposefully placed and, later, willingly grasped as the basis for a sanctified master narrative of the war.

As in physics, where the world looks profoundly different at the quantum level, the familiar top-heavy, smoothed-out vision of the Second World War does not scale down very well to the war's actuality, a world dominated by the small. Each of the nameless millions was animated from one day of the war to the next not by grand cause but by a complicated snarl of disconnected threads from their culture and broader society, sometimes illogical and contradictory, and constantly agitated by the tyrannical immediacy that was so misshapen by extremes, randomness, and a lack of control.

A certain blind spot thrives among historians of the war. It is manifest in the patronizing styling given to the war's obscure while assigning their experience an essential irrelevance, other than as a sprinkling of flavor into unvarying displays of a bromidic "big picture." What remains underexamined and little understood after all these years is the basket of entanglements that steered every individual through the maelstrom, collectively commanding the war's actuality and giving both the war and the postwar era its fundamental shape. The capture and identification of those entangled threads present a challenge to more familiar and comfortable methods of research and canonical exposition of the conflict. They are the dark matter of a still-elusive comprehension of the Second World War, pointing to a far more ambiguous and complicated reality, particularly on the side of triumph, than the coherent unfolding set forth under a relativity-like perspective.

Thus the middle of December, 1944.

Only the very thinnest of strands connect the cloister of the high-level command post to the realm entered three days before by the affable twenty-two-year-old son of a small-town butcher, desperate to hear word that he had become a father for the first time.

* * *

When Don arrived at the front it snowed for three days, wet and heavy, finishing out with a deposit of a glaze of ice. It then turned bitterly cold. Crusted snow was a dangerous business. Stepping on it often caused a large piece to sink, increasing the risk of setting off a mine, a special problem for medical personnel when trying to reach and remove casualties.

As Don's regiment had taken its position, some of the placements for rifle squads were so exposed they could be reached only in darkness or with the assistance of mortar units like Don's providing cover of smoke. A jeep was not much use where they were positioned, and moving Don's squad on foot required several trips back and forth in order to gather all the equipment and ammunition, each short jaunt allowing exposure to snipers seemingly always at the ready. An early lesson was that when mortars were engaged, it was a good idea to move from the position. The Germans were skilled at rapidly sighting in and delivering a deadly response.

The Hürtgen Forest battle area covered approximately fifty square miles, thick with tall evergreens standing cathedral-like across deep wooded valleys and plunging gorges. The narrow roads inside the forest were slick and twisting, some with sheer drops of twenty or more feet alongside. It was no place for tanks. Across to the east, on the other side of the steepest slopes, the Germans were ensconced on high ground, heavily fortified with an array of concrete "dragon's teeth," assorted wire barriers, thick-walled pillboxes, and dugouts. The trails and the firebreaks ran laterally across the steep slopes and were heavily mined. Booby traps were everywhere.

* * *

Orders had gone out on December 11, divisional plans for an attack to take place two days later. Don's regiment was to be part of a diversionary action, initially to convince the Germans a large buildup was taking place, and then to make an attack for the purposes of further distraction while another regiment to the south attempted to take several high-ground villages held by the Germans. These aspects were not communicated to the soldiers involved.

The commanding general of Don's division, by virtually all accounts well liked and respected, had a message distributed to all fifteen thousand soldiers who served under his command:

> You are about to enter your first combat.
> You are well trained.
> You are well equipped. You are well led.
> You are ready.
> Have pride in yourself and your organization.
> Move forward. Gain your objective.
> God is with you. Your family is with you.
> You shall win.

* * *

Since before the time of the pharaohs and continuing to the present day, the orthodoxy of all large institutions, secular and nonsecular alike, has been to venerate a rite of unction. It is an opportunity for self-validation of the high station of command, usually done in the guise of leadership, through a benedictory conveyance of an apparent truth that is often anything but.

Whether Don saw the general's message, or what he thought about it is not known, although the latter can be guessed with great confidence.

What Don already knew, and which would continually be on display over the coming weeks and months, was that the soldiers in his division were neither well trained nor well equipped. Nor were they well led.

Twice in the previous twelve months, while still in the United States, all of the privates in his division had been taken in "levies," thousands sent elsewhere to replenish other infantry units already overseas. The second drawdown had taken place at the end of the summer, when Don was in Wisconsin. Their replacements were arriving at Camp Pickett around the same time the division was ordered to Europe, and there had been little time or opportunity for training. The officers did not know the soldiers under them, and often the men barely knew each other. Once in Europe, the training that was done, while generously recorded in divisional and regimental command-post reporting, was little more than a matter of keeping the boys occupied.

As a result of the two large drawdowns, it was only a much smaller group within the division, mainly sergeants and squad leaders like Don, who had actually been together through all the training, going back to the early days in 1943 at Camp Butner in North Carolina. This was a story common to the units already positioned in the immediate area when Don's arrived. Hardly an American infantry division in Europe was not perpetually short of riflemen. The Allied "broad-front strategy" more often than not teetered close to dangerous fantasy in its almost complete disconnect from the ongoing performance realities in the areas of logistics and personnel. Within a week a murderous demonstration of the strategy's folly would begin.

As for how the boys were equipped, Don and the others in the division were heading into battle without enough machine guns. Their mechanical equipment had not been winterized. Lubricants in the guns froze. The Browning automatic rifle, the so-called BAR, had a well-earned reputation for freezing up, ice forming in the chamber. Some discovered that pissing on them while in battle helped return them to function.

American tanks were no match for German tanks. There were insufficient medical supplies. Radios functioned poorly. Replacement batteries were all but unobtainable, and phone lines constantly broke. At the front there was a shocking reliance on runners for communication, the casualty rate so high they often worked with a partner, as going in twos ensured a better chance of the message getting through.

Coming from a nation with a 1944 economic output three times that of Germany, Don and the other boys were as ill dressed for the winter as the ragged frozen troops under General Washington during the winter of 1777. American soldiers in the middle of the twentieth century had to wrap their feet with whatever straw, newspapers, or rags they could find. When Don's division arrived at the front, all individual possessions and clothing other than that being worn had to be turned in, under orders by someone in a higher-level command. The only clothing Don had was the uniform he wore, having to scrounge, like most of the dogfaces had to do, for some more items to wear for warmth. The doggies found that a towel worked very well as a muffler. Some tore up the cheap sleeping bags they had been given and used the liner as an extra layer to wear.

Don was able to secure some extra pairs of socks. He rotated them as part of the constant vigilance needed to keep trench foot at bay, although that was only effective if he was able to avoid getting his shoes wet. The boots Don wore were notorious for how they soaked up water and mud to the point of becoming impediments to walking. His socks were too thin, not made to take into account a need for protection against cold.

The footwear situation was a reason that trench foot had delivered a casualty rate of more than 5 percent to unit after unit in the Hürtgen Forest, through the late fall and into winter. Large rubber overshoes for the snow were not available to many at the front. Those overshoes that did arrive were of such poor design and manufacture that many chose not to wear them if mobility was required. The bottoms were thin, they provided no support, and the canvas uppers leaked. The standard gloves issued to the soldiers froze solid when wet, and prevented movement of the fingers necessary for firing weapons. The gloves were flimsy, wearing out after just a few days of use in the forest.

There were no white camouflage suits yet available to Don's unit for combat in the snow. The Germans had reversible garments, white on one side. Some of the other US divisions along the front were issued white snow capes, but they were too loose for fighting. The thin fabric was cheap, and would catch on nearby branches and rip. The material soaked up moisture that then froze and "rattled like a bunch of tin cans," rendering them unsuitable for use where silence was necessary, such as during the nightly patrols.

The clothing situation was so severe that it was repeatedly brought to the attention of high-level command, even personally raised by the commanding general of Don's division to his superiors, including the commanding general of the US First Army. The problem would not be addressed for another two months, when the weather started turning toward spring.

It is difficult to overstate how bitter the boys at the front were about their equipment and clothing. For many after the war, that bitterness never went away. It was as though the season's turn to winter had been an event unexpected by Allied leadership. The winter proved to be severe, but cold and snow were not abnormal elements of the season.

* * *

For the upcoming attack, Don's regiment was temporarily attached to another division. Such short-term transfer of units from one command structure to another was a matter of inordinate significance to the rear-echelon denizens of high-level command posts, meticulously recorded by those in clean and warm uniforms.

To the extent such a temporary change in higher-level command was known to Don and the rest of his squad, a doubtful proposition, it ranked in importance well below the daily challenge of defecating without being shot or setting off a mine. A packet of toilet paper was included in each Crackerjack-sized K-ration box, along with a few cigarettes, both items generally more welcome than the edibles, and extras were often parked in the webbing of a helmet. The toilet paper was of high importance to achieve completion of what was sometimes less than a blessed event, varying in performance from one extreme to the other. Dysentery, a word scarcely used compared to the more favored "the GIs," was a widespread intruder into daily life. Fear of snipers and the body contortions needed for a proper and complete wiping in such a setting made for a sizable challenge, the task perhaps surprisingly critical to a soldier's individual maneuverability and overall well-being.

* * *

The morning of Don's fourth full day in Germany, December 13, broke cloudless and very cold. The temperature would not get above freezing. His unit had moved into position in the darkness of three in the morning. At six o'clock, artillery firing commenced from the entire area of the regiment and beyond, a thunderous barrage coming from eight different American division and corps-level battalions toward the Germans.

After half an hour and still in total darkness, Don's battalion went on the attack, through the dense woods toward a complex of bunkers in an area known as Ochsenkopf. In a typical advance, riflemen went first, mortar squads like Don's providing support from behind. Mortar squads also had to be ready on a moment's notice for orders to advance and operate as a rifle squad.

Little had been communicated beyond the command to attack. The boys were shown no maps that day, given no information about how far away their objective was. They were not told their attack was a diversion. Many did not know what to do, other than to follow the fellow in front of them.

Moving on feet already numbed with cold, the boys stepped out into knee-high crusted snow, moving down a slope of land into the face of German machine gun fire coming from unseen concrete entrenchments. Sudden blinding flashes lit up the darkness, the advancing soldiers setting off trip wires hung from the trees that triggered flares. There was a quick image of other boys nearby, appearing frozen like statues, drawing even more German machine gun fire.

Everywhere, there was confusion, an almost constant stumbling and tripping. The depth of snow was uneven and invisible. One stray step and snow would come up to the waist. Bursts of gunfire seemed to be coming from all angles, as though the Germans had infiltrated whatever battle line there had been. Entire groups went in the wrong direction, wandering into areas declared off-limits because of mines.

It only took the first few steps for the new arrivals to get an introduction as to how young people die in war. They could see that sometimes death was swift and sometimes it was a slow slide. The boys became acquainted with the lonely, unseen cry of "Medic... medic," and sometimes calls to one's mother. On that day they learned early that the enemy would shoot at medical aid personnel. Some of them saw an officer killed by a German hand grenade as a medic was leaning over him to treat a wound. Others were able to watch some of the fellows they had gotten to know during the months-long journey get shredded by machine gun fire. For the first time, but not the last, some experienced the fellow in front of them being turned into a spray of pieces by a land mine. The boys received their first lesson that, unlike battle wounds in the movies, dismemberment was so ghastly and commonplace that it sometimes approached the level of morbid comedy.

One company in Don's battalion had just reached its objective before being forced all the way back to their starting position by heavy German gunfire. Some of the boys in that company had gone too far and were lost, never to be heard from again. Two other companies never advanced much beyond the point from where they had started.

* * *

The battle was over by late morning. The Hürtgen Forest had stayed true to the name given to it earlier in the autumn by American boys: "the death factory."

In the early afternoon the command post of Don's regiment received a visit from the commanding general of the division to which the unit had been temporarily assigned. The general was briefed on the morning's outcome, such as it was. Someone in a clean uniform made sure there was a written record that the general was "well pleased with the results."

* * *

Brownie had survived his first day in battle. His company came out of it better than most. Only three among their wounded had to be evacuated.

Another nearby company in his battalion had lost a third of its soldiers that morning. Later that day the commander of the same company would respond to a German call over the loudspeaker asking him by name to come over and pick up some of his wounded soldiers. He would spend the rest of the war as a prisoner.

* * *

The next day brought the ghostly combination of fog over snow. Where Don came from, it was considered a weather event so out of the ordinary it was thought to carry its own sense of portent. It soon became evident that something was different. That evening, the Germans went silent, a puzzling if welcome end to the usual nightly harassment of occasional flares and random bursts of machine gun fire. Even the cavalcade of buzz bombs sputtering overhead had stopped.

The merciful quiet continued through the following day and night.

Two hours before daybreak on the morning of December 16, starting at five thirty, the German side erupted with artillery. The shelling in Don's area was deliberately aimed to rip into the tops of the trees overhead, each blast causing the dreaded "tree burst," the much-feared downward explosion of hot metal and wooden shards capable of delivering devastating injuries and death to a fifty-yard-wide area. It put the test to the branches the boys had been taught to lay over their holes as protection.

The bombardment came from thousands of German guns along an eighty-mile front, a volume and intensity beyond anything seen in a long time. In some areas it stopped after two hours, but for Don's outfit the incoming continued all morning and into the afternoon, when snow squalls began, an unworldly experience of unmatched visual tranquility, combined with deafening noise and earth-shaking tumult.

Don's company commander, Captain Lawrence MacDonald, was among those killed during the shelling. He had just turned twenty-seven.

Very late that night, around the same time that Generals Eisenhower and Bradley were cracking a bottle of champagne at a villa near Versailles to celebrate Ike getting his fifth star, before they would play a few rubbers of bridge, the sky above Don was filled with the sound of German planes flying very low. Sightings of Luftwaffe during the previous months had been rare. They were thought to have been chased out of existence on the western front. Only once during the autumn had there been a German airborne attack as part of the fighting in the Hürtgen Forest.

The noise of the planes was soon joined by unusual flashes of bright light that could be seen even through the thick forest canopy. They appeared in rapidly increasing numbers.

Flares.

After that, some odd popping noises could be heard.

Parachutes.

* * *

In most historical accounts it is called an "intelligence failure," repeated almost as a liturgical intonation.

But it was nothing of the sort. What took place in December 1944, when the Germans managed to stage a major counterattack that was a complete surprise to the Allies, was something more common—and more dangerous.

The information about the counterattack existed and had been gathered, and in significant volume. It was analyzed, and then it was shaped and tuned up—not to present a reality, but to match and support the ongoing perception and wishful aims of those at the highest levels of SHAEF (Supreme Headquarters Allied Expeditionary Force) as to how the war would continue to unfold.

It would not be the last time that such an equation would bring about an American military debacle.

Equally notable was the amount of time it took for the magnitude of the counterattack to set in at the highest levels of Allied command, including on the part of the commanding general of the US First Army. He was not alone in exhibiting a level of fretting and indecision that, if displayed by the boys at the front, would have been actionable on the spot if it had not already resulted in a quick and violent death.

On the other hand, the fearful German attack at Ardennes, taking place just off to the south of Don's outfit, was a gift. Perhaps it even saved his life, as it brought an end to what had started in mid-September, what the Germans had come to call *die Hölle im Hürtgenwald.*

The long and bloody American failure known as the Battle of Hürtgen Forest was over.

It was not a famous victory.

CHAPTER TWENTY-NINE

The Holes We Sleep in Aren't Bad

Tuesday, January 16, 1945

AFTER FIVE WEEKS at the front Don was given forty-eight hours at a rest center. He made the most of every minute, and was finally able to put together a decent letter. Like Boyd and so many of the boys, Don wrote home foremost for the eyes of his mother.

> *Somewhere in Holland*
> *January 16, 1945*
> *. . . Here I am on my 48 hour pass and it's almost over with, as we go back to the outfit tomorrow morning sometime. I can't begin to explain how wonderful and perfect it's been since we got here. It's been like a dream to get back here and have 48 hours of complete relaxation — you can forget the Jerry, the fox holes, well, the war almost altogether. Right now I'm sitting in a big easy chair writing and listening to the radio.*

* * *

December 18, 1944 had presented a hesitant dawn that gradually unveiled an icy gloom. Dull gray clouds hung low. The temperature during the day would not escape the teens.

Where Brownie had been raised, an awareness was instilled early in life as to the long and orderly cycle revealed in the ebb and flow of each day's light. Such knowledge meant that it was never too cold outside for an appreciative moment taking in the ethereal glow of pastels on an icy mid-

December morning. For some in that treacherous wooded landscape of war, the day's first light during those frightening weeks would be remembered for how it cast a serene pink onto the same blanket of snow that later on each day would turn an angry red beneath the burst of flame from guns.

Don and thousands of other American boys were positioned in a meteorological area that happened to be a choice location on the Continent for collisions between moist wintertime weather systems rolling in from the Atlantic and frigid masses of air knifing down from northern Russia and Scandinavia. The result was an almost constant roiling brew of freezing mists, fog, heavy snow squalls, and punishing cold.

A rough-edged stillness had settled in while the war's newest fury was churning away off just to the south, a most frightening, desperate lunge of machines and men.

* * *

Off to his left and off to his right were German forces. In front of him, not very far away, there were more Germans, entrenched along a jagged line that would sometimes fold over on itself, bringing about startling confrontations that rarely turned out well for anyone. Coming from all three directions were occasional mortar and artillery reminders of a German readiness to do anything to protect the lines still streaming by off to the south, just below where Don's outfit was positioned.

Fortune had placed Don on the northern shoulder of what would become known as the German Bulge, which would ultimately extend forty miles to the south of where he was positioned and sixty miles deep to the west, behind him. While that battle raged, Don's division and the Germans they were now facing shared essentially the same mission, to be on guard, to patrol and harass, and to keep the other side out of the larger fight going on elsewhere. All were deadly tasks.

* * *

During the next few days a forbidding arctic murk crept in and hung in the air throughout the trees, a dense icy fog suspended over snow that served as the backdrop as each unit in his regiment took their turn moving out of the godforsaken depths of the death factory. Don's division completed a gradual shift into a defensive position along a two-mile front closer to the northern edge of the bulge.

The terrain was a bit more open in places, but only marginally less difficult. Nearby were a few villages, most of the houses little more than remnants of walls and shattered basement foundations, most civilians long gone. Farther back, near the regimental command post, there were some first-time encounters with a few German civilians. Someone in the proper boots and warm outerwear that Don did not have made sure there was an official written report reflecting that "a strict non-fraternization policy was put into effect."

> *I'll try and tell you how it's gone since I left the outfit. The only bad part of coming was the ride up here as it was quite cold and my feet were almost frozen but it was well worth the ride. When we did get here we could hear in the distance a dance orchestra and, boy, it sounded good. As we walked into a building where they were to orient us on our stay here, sure enough upon the stage were these G.I.'s playing and they were good, too. So between hopping up and down and keeping time with the band we could warm our feet to music. There were a couple of Red Cross girls there and they served us coffee and do-nuts and did that hot coffee hit the spot. Even seeing an American girl seemed good.*

* * *

If he had held them out to be examined by those citizens of Europe who saw themselves at a certain station within their civilizational hierarchy, Don's hands would have been tagged as proof of peasantry. Where he came from, they were called "working hands." In the small civilization of his community it was a term used as a compliment and with pride, translating into a strong grip and an ability to make and fix things.

Those hands served him well. With the move out of the Hürtgen Forest, the boys had to dig new trenches. Where usable bomb craters could not be found, frozen dirt was scraped and chipped, the excavation process sometimes hurried along with a grenade.

"The holes we sleep in aren't bad," Don would say. "We put a lot of work in them."

The favored technique was to make sure it was deep enough for three or four fellows to sit up. Then they would finish it off with careful placement of logs, which were then covered with dirt. It was a good idea to fill the bottom of the hole with pine branches, not only for comfort but also to serve as a floor above melting ice and snow, if it ever got warm enough for that.

Don and one of his buddies in the outfit, Fred, who was from Michigan and was also waiting to hear about the birth of his first child, worked together to fashion a stove out of a five-gallon can. They put grates inside and then included a chimney for the top.

"You should see that baby heat."

Like a lot of the fellows, he also made himself some little torches, putting gasoline in a small bottle with a strand of rope, which he would light after the gas was soaked up. He liked how they gave off light when he was in the shelter of a hole, sometimes even enough to write a letter.

But the smoke was always a problem. What Don really wanted, like many in the infantry that winter, were some candles.

* * *

A bitterly cold Christmas came and went, a day of blue skies and storybook beauty. There was a crunchy snow on the ground, and fir trees all around. Icicles hung across the bumpers of jeeps as though strung for the season, sparkling in the day's short period of sunlight. When the light hit just right they threw off a festive rainbow of colors. A holiday dinner of turkey was distributed, and for some it even arrived warm. A few of the boys tried singing some carols.

Some no doubt privately searched for a familiar Christmas whisper from the divine. What came down from above during the entire day was the guttural rumble of large formations of American and German warplanes flying overhead.

When the light of Christmas Day 1944 was no more, reconnaissance patrols were sent out.

* * *

During those days Allied leadership effortlessly spread its own fears and nervousness about more surprises coming from the Germans, a pitiful but common human reflex toward flailing and distraction after one's own monstrous failure has unleashed calamity and an unbound chaos. On Christmas Day, gas masks were handed out at Don's regimental headquarters, with orders from above that they be carried by "men of the command henceforth." Don and his squad did not get them.

I meant to write you last night but after thinking of that nice feather bed upstairs, decided to write today instead. It seems so funny that little things like seeing a table cloth on a table or electric lights or hearing a radio or eating off plates and drinking out of a cup with a saucer, or a thousand and one things that happen here, just make a fellow feel good all over. Everyone treats you like a king — they can't seem to do enough for you they think. It's really a grand feeling to be waited on hand and foot for a change. The meals are perfect. They are the closest to your cooking that I've ever tasted while in the army, so you can see they are good.

* * *

For the next six weeks, as a terrible battle was grinding away to the south and west, Don and the others were plunged into one of the exclusive deviancies of the war, stretches of tense boredom interrupted by sudden lethal violence. It was a full immersion into an acute wartime state of being, an altered human existence impossible to comprehend without experiencing.

There was very little to life. The taut immediacy was all-consuming, untethered to anything in the past going back farther than their arrival two weeks before.

More terrifying was that void that replaced any sense of connection to a future beyond the next several hours. It was an inhumanly tiring existence.

Everyone did patrol and guard duty. Sleep was something that was caught now and then.

And always, it was so goddam cold.

* * *

The days soon lost their meaning as a measure of time. Even the supple nerves of youth are easily chewed away in a constant saturation of fear, loneliness, and hatred. The only things that mattered were keeping warm, keeping one's terror under control, and keeping tabs on the fellow nearby.

Conversations were brief, usually some healthy gripes and an exchange of a few unanchored thoughts about commonplace things that once made up daily existence. Both types of utterances were as important to survival as food and water.

There were always a few boys for whom the various methods of self-trickery were not enough to keep some footing out beyond the ravening present. Almost every platoon, squad, and aircrew during the war had an example or two of someone being pushed past an internal boundary. Tragedy often followed, an easy mark for the war's wickedness in dispensing almost comically revolting sudden death or the worst imaginable mangling of certain body parts, the latter constantly feared.

Most of the boys knew that it was never a matter of weakness or strength, courage or cowardice. Everyone had that boundary within, and somewhere inside them it stood, always waiting to be crossed.

The weather alone was a punishing enemy for the reprehensibly ill-clad boys. It was not an easy matter to sit in a frozen hole with socks and shoes removed, bare feet elevated so the other fellow could give the massage needed to keep skin healthy and pink to avoid debilitating trench foot. Frostbite was never far away. Its appearance often presented a choice to leave or stay with the others on the line. As with trench foot, it is likely that cases often went underreported. As December turned into January, Don's company, like others, actually showed a decrease in the number of noncombat casualties. This is explainable not because of improved care but only because there developed, as the days dragged on, a widespread reluctance to leave the other fellow alongside in a lurch.

* * *

Don stank. They all did.

Whatever they wore never came off, other than their socks. Cleanliness was rapidly becoming a division-wide problem of both health and morale.

Well, the fellow told us that the town was ours during our stay here. He said we would have arm-bands to wear to signify we were back from the front and no one would bother us. That means M.P.s — and even those guys went

*out of their way to do things for us. They told us we would
stay in hotels and sleep between sheets and where we could
take showers and different helpful hints about the place
here. Then they took us to our hotel and it's a very nice
place. We registered and went to our rooms, and did that
bed look good. I plunked right down on that feather
mattress and gee, it was nice and soft.*

*After we got situated we went downstairs, listened to the
radio, and sat in these big easy chairs until dinner time.
And what a meal we had — chicken, potatoes, vegetables,
pie, bread and butter, jam, etc. The reason the meals are
so good is that the Dutch women make them and waiters
serve you and push your chair up for you to sit down and,
oh, it's perfect.*

*After dinner we rushed madly to get our shower. It was a
regular laundry outfit, too, so we talked to the Sergeant in
charge and he agreed to do our laundry for us while we
were in the shower. So for 45 minutes I sat and soaked
under a shower, washed my hair three times and just had
the best shower ever. When our clothes were dry they
brought them to us and it sure was a good feeling to slip
into clean clothes after about a 40 day stretch without
changing, although I did change socks during that time.
We stopped and got haircuts in one of the hotels by a
civilian barber for five cigarettes. And now I look quite
human and am clean all over.*

* * *

The new year arrived. As did the due date for Don's first child.

An icy murk had once again seeped in, a godless curtain behind which
the invisible Germans pushed hundreds of rounds of mortar fire onto
Don's regiment for three straight days, along with more than the usual
occasional sprays of small arms and machine gun fire. On the fourth day
the fog was chased away by an all-day storm that delivered two feet of
snow while five hundred rounds of artillery and mortar were crashing
through the day's delicate snow-globe shimmer.

Then came more cold. Then more snow. And then more cold.

Everyone shared in nighttime guard duty, the longest hours of anyone's lifetime. Few things were more miserable, an emphatically empty yet terror-filled experience of vague silhouettes and faint inscrutable sounds. There were occasional frantic exchanges of passwords-of-the-day, often botched. All of this while standing and shifting weight from one foot to the other in an attempt, without success, to keep one's upper body and hands warm. The few overcoats available were ridiculously heavy when wet. After a few hours they would freeze solid, like a board. Those who chose to wear them were under orders to do so only with the bottoms of the coats rolled up to avoid being confused with a German soldier in his far superior overcoat.

All physical activity brought almost immediate exhaustion, each step seemingly either uphill or downhill. Tramping through the snow required skills unknown to any athlete, just to stay upright while keeping both hands on a weapon and trying not to be seen or heard.

There were mines to be laid and raids to conduct. Patrols went through wooded areas where darkness seemed total, a pitch-black world of trip wires and Germans in hiding places, of sudden blinding flashes, shouting, and the violent splatter from a machine gun. The nighttime blackness of warm blood spurting across the shadows onto the glazed snow was a sight never to be forgotten.

> For supper last night we had fish and a bunch of other stuff I can't remember, only I know it was good. The coffee is excellent at every meal. Last night I went to Kay Kyser's movie "Carolina Blues," which wasn't bad. After listening to the radio I went to bed and did I sleep. Boy, it felt so good to sleep in between sheets on such a soft mattress with a pillow and pillow case. In fact, I slept most of the morning — just hated to crawl out of the bed.

> This morning I just shaved, washed, brushed my teeth, combed my hair and spent the rest of the morning until noon reading a story or so in Colliers and a Saturday Evening Post. This afternoon there was another movie and tonight, also, so I saw my share of movies. Had a coke and some beer and it tasted good. This whole thing is just like a dream. I'll never forget my stay here for a long

time. Whenever anyone sees that patch they have for an arm-band they are so friendly and very nice to you. Wouldn't mind staying here for two weeks instead of two days. But then other fellows wouldn't get the chance so I guess it's all for the best. Their purpose is to give a fellow rest, relaxation, enjoyment, entertainment and everything they can do to satisfy him — and they really do.

* * *

For each of the first twenty days of January 1945, a morning report was signed by Don's company commander, below the same succinct description of the day's activities: "Usual Combat Duties."

There was no usual.

German artillery never went quiet for long. The horizontal 88, a weapon unlike anything the Americans had, was so intimidating that for some of the boys they became an obsession. The Germans were accomplished at targeting food-delivery routes. Don's company was lucky if they got one hot meal every few days. More often it was once a week. They lived mainly on K rations and, sometimes, the despised C rations.

German homes were always deemed available for scavenging. During this stretch "usual" combat duties included going on hunts for sewing machines and any type of white cloth. A few soldiers who were handy with cutting and stitching worked with the recovered white sheets, napkins, towels, nightgowns, and curtains, the boys making their own snow camouflage capes and suits. Excess white rags and tape were also found and passed around, to give at least some measure of camouflage to the weapons they had to carry.

The Germans had loudspeakers and would taunt by showing off their knowledge of the names of the outfits. Similar taunts flew back from American loudspeakers.

Patrols were often sent out with the specific mission of bringing back prisoners. Those German prisoners who were not immediately shot after being captured were, for the most part, pitiful.

But when they were not prisoners, the Germans killed well. They killed with a swagger. And what they did with booby traps and various types of mines was ruthless, and always on the mind for most boys. Many had their own grisly story of someone else's misfortunate of running into one.

Hatred toward the Jerry came easy. It was a hate that was not part of a passion toward a larger cause, but one of a beast-like enmity born of fear, deprivation, and a base survival instinct. And for some of the boys it was better not to give much thought to just how easy the killing came.

I guess I'll have to cut this short and get ready to leave. It has surely been a wonderful 48 hours. Had pancakes, cereal, bread, butter, grapefruit juice, and delicious coffee for breakfast so I'm all set. Had a good night's sleep last night too.

Well, be good and don't worry about me as I'm very well and safe. Don

* * *

On the day Brownie returned to his squad, more than five hundred rounds of artillery and mortar shells rained down over the area where his regiment was positioned. One of the nearby companies was attacked by a dozen or so Germans, two with machine guns and the others with automatic weapons, who managed to take and secure what had been an American regimental outpost.

The following day it snowed again, and more German artillery shells fell. And so it continued. One cold day after the next, the same routine of patrols, raids, and guard duty. Occasionally there was a move into a different position along the front.

* * *

Around the middle of every January there always comes a moment of the pleasant realization, even if just barely so, that the days are lengthening. It was at that same time when German artillery and mortar shelling became much lighter in the area of Don's unit. Even the random bursts of small arms and machine gun fire favored by the unseen enemy were becoming more sporadic.

The German Bulge was soon no more.

Victory had come in the form of a gradual flattening of the German line back to where things were in early December. It had been the largest land battle in American history.

The battle was a collection of one-man stands taken up by thousands upon thousands of American boys mired in ineffable misery. For the first days and weeks after the Germans attacked, when it mattered most to the outcome of the battle, they were on their own, individually and in small groups. Success was achieved because of the uncountable small individual episodes of endurance, initiative, and decision-making, squaring off against indescribable fear, a desperate enemy, and unforgiving weather.

The epic narratives contain but a mite's worth of what was experienced and accomplished by individual platoons, squads, and other small groups, and by privates, corporals, sergeants, and lieutenants acting alone. The known tales are a fragment of what made up a great totality that slowed and brought defeat to the German initiative. Most of those confrontations, filled with the rawest of terror and violence, are lost forever and will never be known.

* * *

An episode such as the Ardennes inspires incantations about young hearts touched with fire, an almost envious crooning from afar about each boy having gone through the Second World War as a great lyric passage during his time on earth.

The reality was otherwise.

They were there and faced what they did because of someone else's failure. And they knew it.

It would have been most difficult during those days to find a boy who would not have traded it all away for a dry pair of dirty socks. And they would have done it in the decades that followed the war, when such a bloody debacle was still fresh in minds and the path in front of each still went out farther than that which was behind.

We are left to consider each of those individual boys and what they did in the forests of the Ardennes, and how they carried such things home and held them inside, someplace unreachable.

* * *

Precious little of the Ardennes victory can be attributed to Allied leadership.

In the first days of the German offensive, there was much high-level bravado on display, from Eisenhower on down, about the German attack having left an obvious vulnerability to a devastating counter-maneuver that would envelop and entrap the Wehrmacht inside the bulge of its own making. Fine words. But it never happened. No encirclement was attempted.

The attacking Germans were allowed an unchallenged and measured retreat that merely flattened the "bulge"—the only aspect of the battle's outcome, other than the vulnerable American troop positioning at its beginning, which belongs solely to Allied generalship and their staffs. The performance was unworthy of the boys at the front, who would have to fight many of those same German soldiers again, mile by mile all the way to the Rhine.

No doubt theirs was a difficult and complicated job. They were under much pressure. Nonetheless, during the most critical days of the German counterattack, the still-celebrated personalities that made up Allied leadership engaged in brazenly small behavior. With their detachment before the attack and with their frenetic spinning and posturing once it began, they abandoned those they commanded. And the boys knew it.

It cannot be said that those generals waged war in the Ardennes.

* * *

As the end of the month approached, Don's regiment was reorganized and repositioned, in a fanlike shape, as preparations began for a major attack toward the Rhine. His outfit then moved into the ruins of a bombed-out building just outside the town of Simmerath. Nearby was an intersection that had drawn so much German artillery it was dubbed "88 corner," one of many such addresses around Western Europe.

In the grim indifference of a wintry three o'clock in the morning on January 30, Don and his squad gathered in a wrecked building with others in his company and began to get ready for battle. Outside it had started snowing. The wind was picking up.

With little talk, the boys put on their snow suits, made up from white sheets. Some of the camouflage effect was already countered by dark splotches appearing from the smoke being given off from the gasoline lanterns used for light.

A shipment of new oversized rubber boots had arrived. There were few takers. The boots were too heavy for what they were about to do.

They were told their objective was to clear the Germans out of Huppenbroich, a small village a few miles to the southeast. They would be facing German tanks. Hand grenades, belts of ammunition, and satchel explosions were passed around. Most of the latter would be tossed aside a few steps into the battle because they were too heavy to carry.

Don checked over his squad, as did all the sergeants and other group leaders. Everyone checked and rechecked their equipment. As the hour approached in that chilled smoky room, there was obvious praying going on among the boys, each keeping close with their weapons of gray iron and wooden stocks wrapped with strips of white tape.

As the final minutes drew down to departure, one boy after another would reach into a pocket, take out a photo of a loved one, and give it a kiss.

* * *

At five in the morning they stepped outside into the darkness. Greeted by a blast of driving snow, the silent shuffle began toward the designated positions along the line of departure.

Minutes later they all stopped moving. No motion was allowed during the always godforsaken stretch of time waiting for the signal.

It came at half past five.

* * *

First they had to cross an open field. Snow depths were anywhere from six inches to six feet. Waiting for them was a German pillbox with a line of entrenchments extending out each side that held machine gun units. Once past the entrenchments the boys would encounter a descent into a ravine, from where they would have to make their way up a steep hill. Huppenbroich was on the other side, beyond yet another downward slope toward the road into the village.

During the previous weeks bulldozers had been used to clear snow from some of the roads. In depths of snow greater than a foot, mine detectors did not work, and the day before, six of the dozers were lost to mines. The road into Huppenbroich remained unplowed, and would pile up that day with more snow.

* * *

A rifle company in Don's battalion stepped out and began crossing the open field. The winds, at twenty to twenty-five miles an hour, were whipping the snow into drifts and made it impossible to hear. The cold air chewed at ungloved hands, and some of the automatic weapons being carried were already freezing up into a most untimely uselessness.

The initial steps were met with silence from the Germans. When the boys had advanced fifty yards, heavy artillery and mortar fire began to rain down. It was as if demons had been unleashed.

Lightening-like flashes shattered the darkness. Flares and mines were being triggered as booby traps went off, the snow and wind muffling the explosions. A chaotic strobe-like illumination overtook the field and revealed that the boys were passing through a formal sculpture garden.

Or so it seemed, until the realization came that the three-dimensional figures scattered about were once upright young males just like themselves, now long dead and frozen in various grotesque positions.

Somehow legs had to keep moving, one after the other through the uneven snow. Many of the boys who went down with wounds that day disappeared into the growing drifts. Medics had difficulty locating them. Some would only be found days later, dead from exposure rather than their wounds.

Don's division had no winter equipment for removing the wounded. The full-track vehicle known as "the weasel" was often used for such evacuation but did not function well in snow. The first day of the battle brought some quick improvisation by medical crews and engineers who fashioned makeshift sleds out of doors, skis, and cots, with horses put into use for pulling to safety whatever wounded boys they could find.

During an interview a few weeks later, the commander of Don's battalion bitterly recalled how more boys could have been saved if there had been winter equipment for evacuating the wounded.

* * *

An initial group made it across the field and maneuvered around the first line of German machine guns. It was left to two more companies behind them to take up the attack against the entrenchment. Next came the steep slope down to a narrow creek, before the heavy-footed climb to the high ground and starting point of the final downward entrance into Huppenbroich. All this into the teeth of what had become a full-on blizzard.

First light showed itself one hour after stepping off. All across the division's attack front, visibility would never be much more than a hundred yards. Many of the landmarks the boys had been told to use could not be seen. Telephone lines were constantly breaking and radios did not work when needed. The wind was wicked, steady out of the east-northeast, driving snow particles that lashed at any open skin and into squinting eyes.

Past the ravine it was a tramp upward through drifts that reached the knees and higher. The boys slung themselves forward into the wind, almost completely deaf and blind from the storm. The Germans continued their heavy shelling. In some places there were deadly tree bursts showering down. Many of the boys were so numb and tired that they no longer fell to the ground or showed any reaction to the artillery and mortar fire landing all around them.

It took almost four hours for the first group of riflemen to reach the entrance into Huppenbroich. The final approach was done in single file, down the right side of the road. A point man would break trail through the snow, which was knee- to waist-deep, and the others would follow behind. The group would periodically stop and get down for safety against German snipers, while also trying to hold their weapons above the snow to keep them dry. The soldiers would change places, someone else going on point. The grueling push through the fresh snow, lifting one leg after the other, would then resume. Squads behind the initial group were staggered to keep out of the direct line of fire from each other.

Behind them, on top of the hill, the mortar squads in Don's battalion set up to provide the initial support for the assault on the village. A little farther back, another group, including some from Don's company, had gotten pinned down on the upslope by German artillery. Someone found an open mineshaft, and a lieutenant from another company ordered all of them to take cover inside until tanks could be found and directed to provide support so they could continue up the hill.

Around ten o'clock a scouting party was put together inside the shaft and sent out to try and determine the German positions. They were spotted. A barrage followed and the mineshaft took a direct hit.

Twenty-two of the twenty-seven boys inside were killed.

* * *

Inside Huppenbroich was an SS unit, defending every building until the last man. The town was secured as darkness was settling in, twelve hours after the first group of riflemen had jumped off that morning.

The following morning, Don's company would report twelve boys as missing. Whether they were dead or had been taken as prisoners would take days, even weeks, to determine.

The war did not stop for matters of accounting. The next day it was time for another attack, toward some high ground to the southeast.

CHAPTER THIRTY

O Day of Rest

Sunday, February 11, 1945

SUNDAY MORNINGS IN February always had an inescapable downcast quality. A discouraging lifelessness would take over the town, broken only by the ceremonies of the day. The dour feel to things was reinforced by all the stores in town being closed, as they always were on Sundays. Church traffic was polite, much of it on foot and most of it a little itchy around the edges.

It had been a rough winter, with no end in sight. Well over a foot of snow was still on the ground. Those walking to church that morning had to deal with a dirty crust of leftovers from another four inches that had fallen a few days before. A pristine white mantle was the stuff of Christmas cards, given the coal-fired furnaces in most of the homes and the blue smoke released from the foundry at the large plant down by the river.

The interminable dreariness of the month never seemed to be heading in any direction. The 1945 version would offer only four clear and sunny days. That morning was not one of them.

There was something more, though, to the dull melancholy draped over of the community.

The town had an emptiness. Absences had gradually accumulated, now onward of three years. Almost a fifth of the town's population was gone. The void was visible and constantly felt, so many boys and quite a few girls for whom leaving Dodge County for places like Milwaukee or Chicago had once been a major excursion. Now those children were scattered all over the world, in places no one had ever heard of before.

Hanging in the air was something new that had entered the scene in the autumn. Each week now seemed to bring news of someone who would not be coming back home. Two weeks before Christmas it was nineteen-year-old Jimmy Marschke, killed somewhere out in the Pacific. In January came word that Earl Steffen, also nineteen, was missing in France. There was news of twenty-year-old Elwood Kreger missing in Germany. Toward the end of January, Otto Zander and his wife had received a few postcards from their boy William, sent from a prison camp in Japan. And just a few days before, the town's newspaper reported that twenty-eight-year-old Earl Mitchell, a well-liked supervisor at the wildlife refuge north of town, had been killed in Belgium.

* * *

The dank and cheerless morning greeted Herb and Lylle as they stepped outside on their way to the 9:30 Evangelical service. Much to the annoyance of both their children, Lylle always insisted on being among the first arrivals at any public event. She was unembarrassed if chairs for the audience had not yet been set up yet, and Herb would often find himself pitching in to help. A special form of damnation and woe was reserved for anyone keeping her from being at least twenty-five minutes early for Sunday morning services, whether she was playing the organ or not.

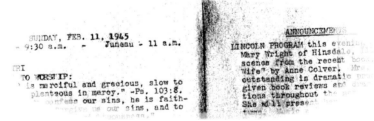

No gloom of any day, though, was ever a match for the vivacious presence of their ever-smiling daughter, Blossom. She was home that weekend from North Central College, now in the final year of her studies to be a music teacher. After supper that evening they would all be returning to church, where Blossom was to provide the musical accompaniment to a friend's dramatic reading, performed in costume, of scenes from the popular book *Mr. Lincoln's Wife*.

The program was part of a series of Sunday night entertainments arranged during the winter by the young people of the church. Already scheduled for next Sunday was a presentation by Mr. Bussewitz, the school superintendent, entitled "Famous Churches I Have Seen."

Church starting times around town were staggered. A block and a half away, down toward Main Street, Marie's church was already midway through its English service. The German-language worship would start at ten thirty.

Walking from one church to the other required passing by the home of the Presbyterians, with six tall white Doric columns standing guard in front of a red brick barn-like structure. Such a stroll at that hour would bring a good chance of catching bits of a muffled refrain, and the cold outside air always made the earnest quality of the sound inside more apparent. From each sanctuary the wavering voices seeping out were not always in tune and they carried no identifiable doctrine other than an eloquent admission of human frailness in the face of life's unknowables.

The gray morning would be the last chance until April to hear a stout hymn. Later in the week Lent would begin, the season of the penitent and the deliberately amplified diminishment of pleasure.

* * *

It had been ten days since Marie came home from the hospital. The christening was set for next Sunday, no doubt the reason that Ernst had bought himself a brand-new suit at Fred Ulrich's store the day before. Fred had left college in Madison the year before, taking over the clothing business on Main Street after his dad, who had been married to Ernst's sister Clara, unexpectedly passed away. Erwin had once been Ernst's business partner, from the early days of the century, until an amicable and well-advertised separation ("1932's Surprise Selling Sensation! Partner's Split-up! Ulrich gets the clothing! Schneider gets the shoes!"). Ernst had walked across the street from his own store and paid his nephew $31.50 for the new suit, about half of what he would spend that winter for coal to heat his home.

The baby had been three weeks late. The harsh winter and the practices of the day combined to keep Marie housebound since well before Christmas, something she had been most unhappy about. It was early on a Saturday morning in January when it became obvious that things long overdue were about to get under way. Ernst bowed out from the proceedings, saying he had to go downtown and open the store.

Transportation was left to Marie's mother, who did not drive very often. Mother Brown was called and joined the wide-eyed adventure of a twelve-mile drive to the hospital in Beaver Dam, not always within the thirty-five-mile-per-hour speed limit. The banks of snow alongside the highway on the west side of town were piled up so high that Marie felt at times as though they were whizzing through a tunnel.

The next morning both of the new grandmothers had gone from the hospital to church and jointly informed Reverend Schwertfeger about the birth, which he announced during the service. He drew an audible sigh from the congregation when he noted that the baby girl weighed eleven pounds, no doubt a fine lead item for the interdenominational debriefings conducted over the Sunday afternoon telephone network.

The morning service at Lylle and Herb's church began with a singing of number 56, "O Day of Rest and Gladness," also a favored opener at Marie's church, although the Lutheran version had many more verses, as was often their wont.

> Today on weary nations, The heav'nly manna falls;
> To holy convocations, The silver trumpet calls;
> Where gospel light is glowing,
> With pure and radiant beams
> And living water flowing,
> With soul-refreshing streams.

After another hymn there was the Organ Call to Prayer, a time for reflection just before the sermon. The congregation was directed to use the moment for silent prayer for those in service.

* * *

Thus a February Sunday, more dismal than most. Much of the morning's ritual, as always, was conducted under the solemn watchfulness of those not fully taken up with prayerful reflection. No doubt segments of thought were properly allotted to Sunday's noon dinner, with wayward musings about an afternoon nap.

It is the rhythm of the mundane that consoles and keeps one whole and sound. As must be done in February of 1945.

* * *

As a child, Don had been well instructed to remember the day and to keep it holy.

He awoke that Sunday morning to a nasty mix of rain, snow, sleet, and ice. Weather from hell, according to another soldier not too far from him who was writing in a journal.

Nightfall on Saturday had closed out twelve soul-destroying days of almost round-the-clock combat. The new day brought Don some rest, the intermission of labor as was told in the scriptures.

Redemption was another matter.

* * *

They had gone on the attack in a blizzard, and the combat carried on during the following days into periods of fog, mist, and a penetrating cold rain. Toward the end, the snow was gone, except for patches of what had been larger drifts. The rest was mud. To step anywhere was to slop through dirty slush and a deep goo.

* * *

When the offensive began, on January 30, Don's regiment had 149 officers and 2,966 enlisted men. Three days later the regiment consisted of 61 officers and 1,645 enlisted men.

The boys kept moving. There had been little time for rest, much less for sleep.

On the previous Sunday, his outfit had gone on the attack at four o'clock in the morning.

On Monday, they were on the move again before daylight. Things began with a walk through pitch-black driving rain, a blanket of thick wet darkness memorable for the way it surrounded and isolated each individual soldier during the final minutes before the attack, at the exact point in time when the usual sick, hollow feeling was retching its way up the throat.

On Tuesday, at a half hour before midnight, Don and his squad assembled with the rest of the regiment in a forest. They began to prepare for a middle-of-the-night attack. The town they were to take was spread along the eastern slope of a large hill, the scene where a few months before, another American division had been mauled in an ill-fated attack. His unit was to approach almost straight on from the west, first through dense forest, then over a hill, and then onward to an open and exposed descent toward the town's entrance.

A platoon of tanks had been assigned to the first group. When they started their engines, the loud rumbling noise drew an immediate response from German artillery. While still in the assembly area, normally a safe place, the boys were showered with tree bursts, shrapnel, and even entire tree trunks. They took many casualties while not yet even in position to start their attack.

The shelling continued through the night. Small groups in Don's battalion escaped the assembly area by sprinting in a zig-zag manner for a few yards before dropping. They would fling themselves down into any indentation in the ground that could be found, even something as slight as a depression left in the mud by tank tracks. Then they would get up and do it again. And again. And again.

The German barrage was so loud that shouts of command and cries for help could not be heard. At regular intervals the wounded had to be sought out by medics and removed. Boys carried stretchers and stumbled through the darkness over stumps and bushes, ignoring the bullets flying and trying not to think about mines underfoot.

It took until Wednesday morning for Don's unit to make it to what was supposed to have been the original line of departure. When the gray daybreak brought an increase in the intensity of the shelling, the advance was halted. Exhausted boys dropped into the nearest muddy hole or crater, many of them sleeping right through as the Germans continued to take aim.

* * *

At two in the afternoon they were awakened, with new orders to start another advance. It took time to find and gather the tanks. Hopping up onto them during a shelling was a challenge.

The procession got under way, the tanks out in front loaded down with boys holding their weapons. The rest of Don's battalion walked behind.

They were on an open stretch of road, the Germans having gone quiet. They reached the top of the hill that was about a thousand yards west of the town. All that remained was to make the final descent and push forward into the entrance.

When the tanks got beyond the crest of the hill, the Germans began shelling again. The lead tank was two hundred yards from the town's entrance when it was hit by three separate armor-piercing shells, and burst into flames. The other tanks behind the burning chassis turned around and headed back to the original line of departure, the infantry troops still on top. In the chaos, a few officers rushed over and began ordering everyone off, while at the same time the tank company commander refused all pleas for his unit to return to leading the attack.

Don's battalion regathered at the top of the hill. The platoons and squads were reassembled and dispersed away from the road. The attack would continue on foot, through the nearby open fields. Tired boys, by now aged far beyond years any of them would ever reach, started out toward the westernmost houses of the town. They gripped their rifles and moved forward in the face of German machine gun and other automatic weapons fire. The murderous noise was almost constant.

Somehow, through the fatigue, the damp chill, and the mud, legs had to keep going. A brief sprint, a jump here, a crawl there, or a roll, always done with one eye looking out for the slightest bit of cover from the unseen hot metal flying everywhere. Even while moving, the boys found no escape from sudden images popping up, sometimes directly in front, more often half-seen in the corner of an eye. A boy who just recently arrived, hardly known and in his first time in combat, flopping over after being cut down by a bullet. Someone else who only an hour ago talked about things back home, instantly blown into meat-like chunks after taking a direct hit from mortar fire. It all had to be ignored. There was no stopping.

On the immediate outskirts of the town, they came upon blackened tanks, twisted bodies half out of the turret with their arms splayed at strange angles, dead boys killed months before while trying to get away from their vehicles. The sight was but a hint of what was to come.

* * *

Those who made it into the town of Schmidt entered a netherworld. The boys had to maneuver around the litter of freshly killed Germans, some already missing their ring fingers. Everywhere there was foul wet slime and an overwhelming stench. Few buildings had roofs. Entire sides of homes had been ripped away, spilling out beds, dressers, dolls, toys, and other ballast of civilized human life.

Many houses were little more than piles of rubble, mixed well with rotting dogs, chickens, and other once-living things pinned alive during one or another period of destruction during the past months. There were heaps of broken lumber that had once been barns, the debris recognizable only because it was mingled with bloated horses, their heads crushed.

What had once been streets were a vague pattern of muck-filled craters and overturned jeeps and trucks. In between, there was the occasional flattened human corpse that had been repeatedly run over by vehicles.

In some of the open areas there were carcasses of dead cows along with scattered, once-frozen bodies of young Americans killed in November and left behind. They were now beginning to thaw.

The combat in Schmidt was savage, from one pile of rubble to the next. Gradually, the Germans gave way, but sporadic fighting continued through the night, and many Germans had to be cleared out in battle the next day. At noon on Thursday, Don's battalion was still fighting its way through the last houses in the town, joined by another regiment from his division.

At around the same time, the leadership of Don's division was getting reports of widespread grogginess, fatigue, and exposure across its thousands of soldiers.

* * *

As if facing a desperate enemy in unspeakable conditions was not enough, throughout the week the boys had to grapple with a demoralizing confusion put upon them by the antics of American generalship.

On Monday, one general had overruled another and brought to a halt an ongoing maneuver involving thousands of soldiers, one unit passing through another. As a result, one regiment spent almost an entire day standing in a cold drizzle, loaded down with their packs and weapons, under specific orders not to take shelter because they might have to move out again on short notice. New orders came that night, undoing the reversal. The maneuver originally ordered was to continue the next morning.

The reversal, overturning an order issued by the commanding general of Don's division, had been the accomplishment of a corps-level general who had been inserted into the situation by the commander of the US First Army. The latter was impatient over the slow progress toward securing the dams beyond Schmidt, the same dams that throughout the autumn he himself had failed to comprehend as an important objective during his obsession with the Hürtgen Forest.

Several times during the week he threatened the commanding general of Don's division with dismissal if a faster pace of advancement was not achieved. Later in the week he appointed yet another general, the commander of a different infantry division who just happened to walk into headquarters on a routine visit, to be in charge of the attack on Schmidt and onward to take the dams.

Sometime after nightfall on Saturday, the Germans abandoned the area, retreating to the east. Before leaving, they released twenty-two billion gallons of water held back by several dams, not as a sudden short-term catastrophic wave of destruction as predicted by US intelligence (and sought by Germany's chancellor), but far more cleverly, by damaging certain machinery and discharge valves to ensure a constant flow that would flood for almost two weeks. The front line on Sunday would remain where it was until close to the end of the month.

* * *

As Sunday morning's snow and frozen rain took turns pelting down around Don, he would more likely have felt rather than known, as the outcome of calculation, that about a third of the enlisted men in his company who had arrived at the front with him two months before were no longer around. He would not have needed an official accounting to know that five fellow sergeants in his company had been killed during the previous twelve days.

* * *

Hilmer Hobbs was from Saint Ansgar, Iowa, his hometown smaller than Don's. He and Brownie had arrived at Camp Butner in North

Carolina around the same time, in early 1943. Known to folks back home as Shorty, Hobbs had played basketball and football in high school, and he had worked on a neighboring farm until entering the service. Dead at the age of twenty, Sergeant Hobbs left behind a widow, Marilyn, whom he had married while home on furlough four months after Don married Marie. He was also survived by his parents, Lee and Agnes, who were already dealing with the loss of Hilmer's older brother, Merle, declared missing three years ago after his ship, the USS *Houston*, was sunk in the Java Sea by the Japanese in early 1942.

Erv Dykstra, from Michigan, the son of Fred and Pauline, had also been with the outfit since 1943. He had just been promoted during the first week of January. Death came to Sergeant Dykstra at the age of twenty.

Gerald Buckley was the son of Mary and William from Scranton, Pennsylvania. Sergeant Buckley was twenty-three years old when he was killed.

Milton O'Boyle, the son of Michael and Maude, had grown up in Crookston, Minnesota, not far from the North Dakota line. Sergeant O'Boyle was dead at the age of twenty-one.

Fred Bocanelli, son of Dominic and Adele from Winnebago, Illinois, was the old man of the bunch, killed at the age of twenty-seven. Sergeant Bocanelli had never finished high school, never married, and had been a roofer and slater before enlisting in 1942.

Others in Don's company killed during the previous twelve days included Ray Clark, known back home in Myrtle, Missouri, by his middle name, Sherman. He had volunteered during the blizzard on the first day to be a runner, and was killed by a sniper shortly after delivering a message to a machine gun section that had become separated from the rest of the company. He was twenty-one years old when he died.

Ernie Little was from Rising Sun, Maryland, and was one of those in the mineshaft on the first morning. He had been in the army six months, joining Don's company in early January as a replacement. He loved baseball and had played for the local team known as the Rising Sun Midgets. Dead at twenty-six years old, he left behind a wife, Annie, and two children.

Two of the boys from Don's company killed during the previous twelve days were still teenagers.

Joe Stone, dead at eighteen years old, was the son of George and Josephine, who lived in Cleveland.

Tilford Johnson was nineteen years old, killed on the fourth day of battle. Twelve months before he was still cooking and waiting on tables at Blackard's Sandwich Shop in Madison, Indiana.

* * *

On that ashen Sunday, a weary Don wrote to George about the things that mattered.

Germany Feb 11, 1945

Dear George,

Well, brother-in-law what do you think of your little niece. Or should I say big niece. Boy it sure did surprise me to hear she weighed 11 lbs. That's a really big girl. Sure does make me feel good to know they are back from the hospital now and are both doing fine. Wish this dam war would end so we could all get home and get back to normal. Well Marie writes they have finally heard from you and that they think your sailing from Panama to the S.W. Pacific & back. Sure hope you aren't running into too much trouble out there. I haven't heard from John W. in a long time but I think he's out that way too now. We're pretty darn busy over here & there is not much chance for writing. This infantry is a pretty darn rough & rugged life and you can thank your lucky stars your where you are. Hope the Russians keep on going & then maybe these dam Krauts will give up. I guess Herb is over here in the Air Corps someplace but don't know just where. See by the papers that we beat Beaver Dam, they must have a pretty darn good basketball team. Well be good George & write once. Love, Don

* * *

Brownie was right with his guess about Herb. On that Sunday, Boyd was in England. He had arrived the previous week, traveling by air.

The crew had not been told of their destination until the day before they started out. Boyd spent the night before the departure writing a few letters by flashlight while inside the brand-new plane, taking his turn to guard the crew's personal valuables already aboard. "Really a honey with all the latest accessories," he wrote his parents.

Their journey took them along the North Atlantic Route, one of four designated flight paths used to ferry planes and crews to England. It was the most difficult route in severe winter weather. They first flew in short hops up the East Coast, then on to Goose Bay, Labrador.

* * *

As much as would be permitted by the knucklehead tendencies of males that age, there was an inescapable mix of sentiments attached to the moment of leaving behind American soil and heading off toward the war. Each boy departed with his own full spectrum of thoughts, regardless of whatever the youthful drivel was coming out of his mouth. Unbeknownst to them, that moment of departure was also the final and permanent unfastening from the world that each boy, including Boyd and Don, thought he had been born into. Comprehension would only come later, often through an unexpected gut-wrenching realization of some sort that was most unpleasant. Boyd's experience was no different.

It was 969 miles from Goose Bay to Meeks Field in Iceland, on the other side of Greenland, which in the perspective of Boyd and the rest of the crew was akin to the other side of the moon. They were warned about how bad the storms were over the Atlantic that winter, but they were assured they would not be attacked by German guns. Since the ferrying operations had begun in 1942, not a single plane out of more than thirteen thousand flights across the Atlantic had been shot down.

Take-off was in darkness. They began their flight in a loose line formation with other planes, but it did not hold as the day went on. The pilot, Pinchback, kept their ship below ten thousand feet, which meant the oxygen masks were not needed in their unpressurized cabin. And thankfully, it also meant they could smoke. Like the others, Boyd was wearing an electrically heated flight suit, but he was still cold, as he always would be in the air.

From the very start, the plane was buffeted by winds, tossed about by an animal-like force of a completely different magnitude than anything they had experienced during their hours of flight training over Mississippi or Texas. The darkness gradually gave way, and the plane entered an indeterminate twilight, a wondrous indigo glow that was as much the last light of eventide as the first few strains of dawn. They were flying in something that was neither night nor day.

Boyd found himself staring in an almost hypnotic awe at the aurora borealis sweeping its patterns across the rich thick purples. The airborne sight of the northern lights was unlike anything he had ever seen from the ground. With the plane heaving around in the wild turbulence, he gripped tight to watch the great arcs of light, edged with all colors of the rainbow as they flickered and shifted in colossal rolling waves. The plane rattled and shook, but he fought to keep his gaze on what seemed so massive that it was almost too much to take in. The chop was as severe as he had ever felt, as though all control of the plane was about to be lost, and his head was sometimes thrown downward, an unwanted forced glance at the forbidding ocean just a few thousand feet below.

Just like that, it ended. The day got a little brighter, and the weather outside the plane turned dirty and gray. The air smoothed out a bit, and there was nothing more to see. He would never forget that stretch of time, how small he felt as they pressed on toward the war.

They made their pass around Greenland and latched on to a strong signal toward the airfield in Iceland. They had been told that flight times had a wide variance. Their journey dragged on. A sense began to develop that something was not right. They were only certain that they were somewhere beyond Greenland. Pinchback began watching the fuel situation.

Worries turned to a level of alarm that began to creep through fear and beyond, even into the beginnings of a wrestling match with an acceptance that they were going to run out of fuel while over water. It was a sudden and new perspective on the notion of an entire lifetime, and they had time to think about it.

Later on, nothing specific could be identified as the reason for changing their course, away from the direction in which the signal had led them. Other than that they were unable to find Iceland.

The tense final minutes of the flight were beyond anything Boyd had ever known in the first twenty-two years of life, and perhaps the next fifty as well. Not until they touched down were they certain there was enough fuel in the tank. Only afterward came the understanding that they had been following a ghost signal, the handiwork of some German U-boats and an ongoing source of B-17s disappearing as they headed toward the war.

It was a close call. But what left a mark on Boyd was something else. It was the first time he had to face the realization, a blow delivered somewhere inside of him, that someone was purposefully attempting to end his life.

A year later, Marie jokingly told Boyd that giving birth to an eleven-pound baby was a near-death experience. Boyd was quick to respond, not altogether as a matter of humor, that on about the same day he had his own first near-death experience and it was very real.

* * *

After a final flight across the Irish Sea to Wales, Boyd and the rest of the crew had to reluctantly part ways with their brand-new plane. They continued on by train into central England, to a combat crew replacement center in Staffordshire, where Boyd spent the second Sunday in February. On Tuesday, the boys would head to their assigned air base in the English midlands, about an hour north of London by train. Four days later, on Saturday, his mail caught up with him.

After reading some of it, Boyd wrote a letter.

Sat. Feb. 17 - 45

Hi Marie,

Just a note to let you know I heard via my mother &
am sending my best congratulations to you & Don. Sure is
wonderful & you can imagine how I've been wondering.
You see I got the first mail today & I knew the baby must
have come by this time. Had a swell interesting flight over.
Have a good field and very good chow. Will write all soon.
Don & I are very, very, close at times now - hope to hear
soon. By the way, I'm in England.

Love, Herb

CHAPTER THIRTY-ONE

Very Close Together

Tuesday, February 27, 1945

DURING THE WAR Boyd would write more than three hundred and
fifty letters to his parents. His letters early in the war were scratched
out in a pinched and uncertain scrawl, more often than not in pencil. By
the time he headed overseas his hand was confident and delivered an
evenly spaced flourish, usually in ink.

He had noticed much during his first weeks in England.

Hi Mom & Dad,

*We saw the sun today for most of the day which is a treat.
Got my things all fairly straightened out now, tho we have been
very busy. Sure is good to be settled again. Still can't tell you
much about England as I haven't gone to town or anyplace out
of camp yet. Have a 48 hr pass coming up near the end of Mar.
& then I expect to go to London, so after that I should be able to
tell you some good stuff. From what I've seen of Britain it looks
like the people have really suffered from the war. The war is
much more a part of the civilians here than in the U.S. Their
fuel for warmth is very limited as is their food. The clothes they
wear are the same ones that they were wearing five years ago,
probably made over several times. Everybody works at some
kind of work beneficial to the war effort including all the
women. The implements and conveniences of the people seem a
trifle backward, but then one forgets they've been at war five yrs.*

The people go about there work soberly & talk very little. They're very reserved & polite, don't have the looselessness, relaxed way we do. It's true they've lost a good percentage of the "cream of the crop" of the present young generation. From what I've seen of them I get an over-whelming impression that on victory day they'll, unlike the hilarious celebrating in the U.S., solemnly go to church & give thanks in all sincerity, for they have lost much.

* * *

Many months had gone by since Boyd last offered to his parents any reference to "we" when describing his interest in future travels or any other plans he was making for after the war. He now smoked, drank, and swore with the best of them, all of which would have horrified his mother. It was a commonplace, even timeless evolution for boys like him.

However, the hand holding the pen on that Tuesday belonged to a fundamentally different human being than the one who had awakened at the start of the previous day.

An altering had taken place. As it had for Myroslaw. And as it had for Don, and for all those who entered the physical realm of the war.

The imprint was deep. As with others, and as it has always been, an accumulation had begun, a collection that would be carried about for the rest of his life. Some of these things could only be shared with those who had been there. Only they could ever understand.

* * *

The briefing was at four forty-five on Monday morning. Boyd had already eaten breakfast, and he and the rest of the crew all sat together in a row on a hard wooden bench, ready to hear about their first combat mission. They were rookies and they felt like it, wide-eyed while looking around a crowded, smelly room full of rowdy noise and cigarette smoke.

There was a sudden silence, an unseen signal from somewhere. An officer strode out, more flamboyant than purposeful. A curtain was pulled back, revealing a large map of Europe and some colored lines extending from England to the Continent. Nothing was said, but a buzz started up, with a rapid buildup to a low roar. Quiet was ordered.

They would be heading to Big B: Berlin.

It might have been only the usual grease-laden charm of breakfast. But it did not sit well, and moments after the briefing, Boyd needed to make the first of several trips to the latrine, where he met a few of the others from the crew who had the same urgency. It made for some laughs, not unwelcome.

* * *

The airbase had been hurriedly constructed four years before, one of many that dotted the flat green countryside of the area known as East Anglia. Its crisscross of runway was a short mile to the northwest of Thurleigh, a small village not much more than a bend in the road, along which there was a pub, school, post office, and a church that had seen two major renovations, one in the thirteenth century and the more recent having taken place two centuries later.

The base at Thurleigh was home to what was officially called a "bombardment group," made up of four squadrons, each with twelve planes. Boyd and the crew were now part of a squadron that was called the Clay Pigeon Air Force, complete with its own logo and a reputation as a hard-luck outfit.

On the previous mission to Berlin, at the beginning of the month, the Clay Pigeon Air Force had lost three planes. One diverted to Sweden and the other two were brought down with flak, with at least fifteen boys killed.

The Berlin mission in early February had involved more than a thousand planes, a titanic daylight American raid following on the heels of a large nighttime bombardment by the British. The planes had been aimed at the civilian center of the city, with not even a pretense of a military target. The mission was still the subject of a lot of talk on the base when Boyd arrived, as was a bombing raid almost two weeks later to Dresden.

* * *

For their initial mission the crew was dispersed among several planes. Pinchback was to fly as a copilot on one ship, Boyd the tail gunner on another.

With a drumming precision that was hair-raising, the mass engine-start commenced at 7:35 a.m. Boyd was seated with the other gunners next to the wood-lined space they called the radio room. One by one, each of the plane's four engines came alive in an exhilarating ritual of vibration and noise that spread from one plane to the other, a great crescendo to a deafening chorus from more than 150 engines. He would never tire of it.

Fifteen minutes later, thirty-nine planes began maneuvering politely in a slow-motion square dance, positioning themselves for take-off. At eight o'clock they began thundering down the runway, each taking its turn with only a minute or two in between.

Few things were more exciting than the acceleration down the runway to more than one hundred miles per hour. First came feel the feel of tail lifting up, the plane vibrating more and more with each passing second. Then came the release, upward into the smoothness of the air. That split-second moment would never fail to stir Boyd. He was a Depression-era farm boy who would always consider flight nothing short of miraculous.

* * *

Next was the often harrowing process of getting into formation. The maneuvers needed were magnificent and scary at the same time, great beasts clumsily gathering themselves like buffalo lumbering into a well-ordered herd. Collisions were not uncommon as each plane made a blind climb through clouds. Boyd marveled at the intense concentration needed by Pinchback and the other pilots as they nudged their ships as close together as possible while trying to keep at least a fifty-foot clearance from the tail of the plane in front and between wingtips of planes alongside. Fifty feet, less than the familiar distance between home plate and the pitcher's mound.

Boyd's ship broke through the overcast that morning at fourteen thousand feet and then made its move to join the others heading to Berlin. Getting into formation took time, and it was almost ten o'clock when his plane left the airspace over England almost seventy miles due east of the Thurleigh airfield.

Half an hour later, they crossed the Dutch coastline. By then, Boyd had already taken his parachute and moved to the back of the ship, inserting himself into the tight quarters of the tail-gunner compartment. He settled into the kneeling bicycle position, his legs doubled back (good for praying, he must have heard a hundred times already). His heated suit was plugged in, as was his oxygen.

The compartment was not even close to being airtight, and he would always be cold on missions. Frostbite was a constant worry, creeping up unnoticed during a flight. Years later, in only a halfhearted jest, he would sometimes blame his grouchy intolerance of winter in the Midwest on those frigid hours he spent in the breezy tail-gunner compartment.

* * *

Of all the positions on the seventy-four-foot-long ship, the tail gunner was the most lonesome place to be. It suited Boyd just fine, as being alone always did. The extra strength bouncing around that came by virtue of being at the very back end of the plane never bothered him.

Boyd was one of many B-17 gunners who had once been set on becoming a pilot. Part of his affection for Pinchback dated to the days of training flights during the previous autumn, when in the skies over Texas and Arkansas he would let Boyd fly the plane for an hour or so at a time. Boyd liked to think of himself as more than just a gunner, taking seriously his observation responsibilities, the only one aboard with the visual perspective looking out behind. He relished the moments when, over the intercom, he would begin a quick report with "Tail to pilot . . ."

* * *

Air warfare was something truly new, only thirty years in existence. And yet, the formations streaming eastward over the Continent would have been understood by anyone looking up during the days of Wellington, or even three thousand years before, in the age of the Greek phalanx.

The boys called them ships, not planes. It was the war's most modern technology, but it operated as a vestige of the ancient past. On that Monday morning Boyd was one of more than twelve thousand young men of high spirit who had joined up in close ranks before moving toward the enemy in tight formation at a deliberate pace. As in earlier times, they were swarms of soldiers locked together in the airborne equivalent of arm's length. Almost two thousand separate pieces of silver armor gave off a glint in the morning sun as they advanced, an overlap of modern-day spears pointing outward for protection.

The war machines on the ground were intentionally grim and humanless in appearance. In the air that day was the only weaponry of the Second World War expected to wear a flourish of artwork, some of it as elaborate and personalized as the intricate decorative elements of wooden warships under sail or the colorful trim on shields carried centuries before. Under almost every window, where soldiers were stationed, some artist had taken time and pride to add a drawing and some words that connected to the young man inside being sent that morning to besiege the enemy's capital. As with the great infantry charge, the greatest fear was in a breakdown of cohesion, which could bring almost immediate mortal danger. Maintaining their alignment was a far greater priority than speed, and they approached Berlin that day at a controlled pace that could not be called a sprint.

From where he was on the plane, Boyd could see it all, a magnificent sight of grandeur and dread, while bracing for whatever enemy weaponry in those late days of the war could still be hurtled against the oncoming assault.

Boyd was one of the last on earth to experience the awful delight of the great formation charge into engagement with the enemy. There was nothing else like it in the war, and there has been nothing like it since. And there likely never will be again.

He would later try to explain to his parents the massiveness of what he witnessed for the first time that day, writing that the bomber stream "was 300 miles long, about the distance from Chicago to Minneapolis."

* * *

It was the sense of utter helplessness that was so terrifying about flak. There was not a damn thing they could do against it. Boyd knew how easy it was to pierce the shell of the plane. There were so many things that could go wrong from just a single small piece of hot shrapnel in the wrong place, from cables breaking to oxygen failure and fires. It did not take much of a hit to drain a fuel tank, kill a pilot or a gunner, or take off a wing. It was not worth thinking about the exposed belly carrying the bombs, or that the pilot gave up control of the ship to the bombardier in the final moments before their payload was dropped.

Boyd heard from some of the old-timers just how brutal and merciless the air battles with the Luftwaffe had been during missions a year or two before. Those days were over. But the old-timers also said that there seemed to be more flak now, probably because the retreat from France and in the east left the Germans with more 88s available to point upward and shoot.

From his compartment, Boyd was always the last to see the flak. He discovered on that first mission that what most everybody had said was true—when it hit the plane it sounded like hail on a tin roof. The noise was familiar to him in a ridiculous way, as a comfort-giving sound from his childhood. The plane would shake from explosions nearby, most muffled and some not heard, but almost all were felt in some fashion. Sometimes the flak would come up from the ground and then seem to boil for a few moments right alongside the plane, a phenomenon Boyd never fully understood.

And no matter how much he told himself it was coming, Boyd was never able to prepare for the dark sensation that was altogether different from the terror already in full agitation. Each mission he had to get through an initial moment—the same involuntary shudder he first experienced in the episode of the ghost signal on the flight to Iceland—as some internal part of him came to grips with the actuality of someone trying to kill him.

* * *

In the air, as on the ground, the war twisted and bent all sense of time. The immediate overwhelmed everything, obliterating any internal sense of duration. To pass through thick flak for only a minute, even thirty seconds, was to endure the span of a lifetime. Which is what they did that day over Berlin. Boyd had picked up the elaborate jargon used to describe the various degrees of flak. He recorded in his own personal notebook that it was "intense," and would later describe it as "so thick you could walk on it."

At five minutes to noon, Boyd felt the sudden upward jump of the B-17 as a result of its bombs being released. There were few sensations more welcome, followed as it was by the immediate sharp turn away and the start toward home.

For the trip home they were routed once again over Holland. Oxygen checks were done every five to ten minutes over the intercom, all the crew members taking their turn to acknowledge that they were still among the conscious. As the ship headed back to the base the oxygen checks that day were businesslike but laced with smart-ass remarks. With Berlin behind them, there was an unmistakable elation inside the plane, the primal exhilaration at still being alive. But there was also an element of cockiness, cruising through the air at more than 250 miles per hour, mission accomplished in a rugged and sleek airplane that was the very embodiment of American know-how and firepower.

Such were the thoughts of Boyd at the very moment when, in the haze off the starboard side of the ship, something shot up from the ground pushed by a fireball, arced high above them, and headed toward where they were going. A few blinks of the eye and the thing was already over England, which they would not reach for another hour or so.

They knew what they had seen, and the mood on the ship seemed to change sharply. At least Boyd's did.

At the sight of the V-2 leaping upward, Boyd felt like he was flying in a biplane. In the coming weeks there would be more sightings and several encounters with jets, which Boyd could only describe as unforgettable. They moved so fast, terrifying and magnificent at the same time. During those days, Boyd was not alone in his conviction, one that became lifelong, that if the Germans weren't knocked out of the war by summer, there might not be much left of the gallant masters of the air and their propellers.

Ten hours after the morning take-off Boyd was back at Thurleigh.

> . . . Seems funny to go out on a raid & come back & hear all about it on a news broadcast. By the way, if you want to know where I was yesterday just look at the headlines in today's paper. It was a place I always wanted to go to, to pay my personal respects to Hitler for causing me all this trouble of fighting a war. Paid my respects alright & in a mammoth way. Sometimes Brownie & I are very close together, only a few miles apart, upward, of course. 'Bout all I know for now. Will write again soon. Am well & very satisfied with everything. Love, Boyd

* * *

He had been to Berlin. He would have to tell Brownie.

CHAPTER THIRTY-TWO

The Awful Realm

Thursday, March 8, 1945

Their ship was named "Weber's Wagon." The moniker was a tribute to thirty-year-old Elmer Weber, an Illinois farmer. As the ground crew chief, Weber gave their B-17 nothing but his complete devotion. He and his mechanics often worked through the night before an early-morning take-off, checking and double-checking every inch of the plane.

During the nervous hour before engine time, Weber would stay with the crew as they cracked lame jokes and drank too much coffee out at the paved area where the plane was parked, known as the hardstand. He would stand there as they taxied away and watch them take off. As they approached on their return from a mission he would be at the same place, pacing as he waited for them. Like a mother hen, after a mission, Weber would have something to say to each one of them, always wanting to know afterward how things went and how everything worked.

* * *

Thursday's ritual of the engine-start had begun at a quarter past ten.

After carefully nudging their way through the clouds, Weber's Wagon and thirty-eight other ships from Thurleigh joined another seventy B-17s and formed up to make their charge over the Continent. Their target was the railroad yards in one of Germany's major cities, Essen, which had been home of Krupp manufacturing works and a frequent target. Only Berlin, Cologne, and Hamburg were on the receiving end of more total bomb tonnage than Essen. Bombing accuracy being what it was, there was very little left of the city. Three days after Boyd's mission, the city would undergo one last thorough sweep by a thousand bombers dropping four and a half kilotons of explosives on what was already a landscape of ruin, doing so just hours before it was taken by Allied soldiers.

By the time Boyd arrived in England the air war had become a siege of German cities, a ruthless gothic destruction that had little effect on advancing the war to a surrender. Consistent with the British experience on the receiving end during the Blitz, but contrary to war-planning expectations, the bombing did not cause a change of heart among the populace toward surrender or revolt against their Nazi masters. If anything, it pushed toward greater alignment of citizens with the German state, whether by physical need or by anger. And for that achievement, the cost in economic terms and in the lives of young American and British boys remained high.

March would be a busy month for all air crews, the war hitting its all-time peak for bombing, more than a hundred thousand tons of bombs dropped by American crews. Boyd and Weber's Wagon were out on combat missions almost every other day, and one day late in the month they went out twice.

* * *

The crew had been together since meeting on that Friday the thirteenth in Tampa. From the start, they had always gotten along well. They knew how to make one another laugh and had also learned where they had to be careful with each other. But as friendly as they were, things were different once the combat missions started, an intensity of connection that was now more instinctive, even sensory. They were attuned to one other in a connection that was something quite apart from friendship, an experience for Boyd unlike anything before the war or after.

Like Don's squad, what bound them together has sometimes drearily been called a brotherhood, a grossly inadequate word. They were joined in a tightly wound coexistence, a combined brute animal force and primal tenderness imposed by the moment of battle. And like those boys on the ground, they were held together by a shared secret knowledge that only comes from facing the inexpressible and terrifying aloneness of combat. The awful realm could be understood only by those who had been there.

* * *

Everyone had a different war.

Boyd's war was not Don's war, and neither of those two boys had Myroslaw's war. Boyd knew his fortune in being able to leave battle and return to his own space with a few personal items and a bed. But he too had hours that were filled with the same debilitating mix of tedium and fear while awaiting the approach of violence. In the air there was no hole in the ground to jump into for cover. Like Brownie, he was with others who counted on him to endure and deliver.

Boyd learned early on how difficult it was to keep functioning when a cold liquid fear entered the bloodstream. There were plenty of stories about those who froze up. It was understood that such things just happened, a line somewhere deep inside having been crossed. But no one wanted to fly with them.

Staying busy taking care of his guns and doing routine tasks made things a little easier, using one instinct to help overcome another. Laughter also helped—a lot. And when other things failed, Boyd learned that sometimes anger was useful to push the body and mind to overcome the terror of the moment. He was cautious about going to anger, worried it could cause him to make a mistake. But he saw it a lot in others, and understood it was about fear, something everyone had to deal with.

* * *

The skies on Thursday were overcast all the way to Essen, and he was not able to watch for various landmarks below to orient himself, which he sometimes did using binoculars.

Boyd knew from the briefing that they had been routed right over the US First Army. He spared a thought for Brownie that morning, knowing he was somewhere below, near the Rhine, as Weber's Wagon passed overhead.

So far from home, and so far away from everything they had known. What a world they now lived in.

There were mornings for Don when such a thought might have been mutual. During those weeks the boys in his outfit could sometimes hear the low growl of B-17s streaming overhead to the east toward their target. There would be the occasional upward glance.

Thursday, March 8, 1945, was not one of those days.

* * *

It had been a month since Don's division had broken through the fortifications known to the Germans as the West Wall, christened by the British as the Siegfried Line, where, so they sang in 1939, they were going to hang out their washing. The high ground beyond the West Wall and Schwammenauel Dam had provided a most welcome vista, a wide and level expanse that offered the first prospects in months of walking more than a few steps without going either uphill or downhill.

The same overlook also allowed the first glimpse of the other side of the Rhine River. Far beyond the wide plain was a small cluster of dark bumps marring the distant eastern horizon. The tiny black silhouette was a narrow range of steep hills known as the Siebengebirge. According to inimitably German myth, it was where Siegfried had slain a dragon and bathed in its blood to gain invulnerability.

The dragon's cave would be waiting for the boys.

* * *

For the past week they had been on the move. The snow was gone, replaced by a well-trodden slop. After Don's battalion jumped off in late February it rained every day, ensuring uniforms were constantly soaked, a good match for their heavy damp boots caked with dun-colored mud.

Each day, Don's unit was able to advance several miles. They took one town after another, places like Obergartzem, Firmenich, and

Kreuzweingarten. The names were such a challenge to the awkward American tongue that substitutes were used, and Don's regiment secured towns they would know instead as Bridgeport, Farmville, and Atlanta.

Hundreds of prisoners were being sent back westward for confinement. Many German soldiers were captured while hiding from the SS in barns and woods, trying to get away from those who usually led the more fanatical resistance sometimes encountered by Don's outfit. Unlike the days in the forest, there were plenty of German civilians to see, along with their sweaters, long johns, sheets, and any other available white cloth that hung outside houses in an attempt to declare that no Nazi soldiers were around, that there were no Nazis in the village, and that the villagers did not know of any Nazis. Some of the male civilians waving to the column of dogfaces passing through were observed to be red-faced, presumed by the doggies to be the result of exertion during the quick change out of their Wehrmacht uniforms.

Mobile warfare was a new experience for Don's unit. What was not new was the sameness of each day, the noise, and the crazy savageness of the violence. They were told little. They were given a direction to go, and they either went into battle or took up a temporary reserve position. When that was done, they would do it again.

It had been a very long time since days of the week mattered, or even existed, stripped away like so many other anchors of human existence. Only the smallest particles of a past identity and former serenities could still be found or conjured.

The pace was exhausting, physically and in other ways not easy to think about. They were in combat during the day. At night everyone had a stint on watch. Hot meals and sleep were both in short supply, unlike all the death and wreckage of every sort that was always around. They kept moving.

About the only good thing during that first week of March was the happy rumor that once the boys reached the west bank of the Rhine River there would be a break, some time to rest. To the north, naval craft, bridging equipment, and other stores were being assembled for a large coordinated initial crossing of the Rhine, but it would not involve Don's division.

* * *

During the very first hours of Thursday, shortly after midnight, the yelling had started.

Politely translated, the boys were requested to get up and be ready to move out as soon as possible.

Rain was falling when some trucks pulled up. Don jumped into the back of one after he and his squad had carefully loaded it up with their mortar equipment. Each piece was the responsibility of a designated squad member, the sight and aiming post usually carried by squad leaders like Don, while the bipod, baseplate, firing tube, and other parts were carried by the rest of the squad.

No one in the back of their truck had any idea where they were going. But wherever it was, someone was in a hurry, jerking their way forward in anxious fits and starts. They stopped in absolute darkness, except for other truck headlights flashing here and there.

The yelling started again, mainly for them to get their fucking asses off the truck *right now.*

A few from the greeting party jumped onto the back of the truck and started throwing every piece of their equipment onto the ground. That was something that was just never, ever done.

Someone in Don's outfit shouted at the truck driver, asking where they were. As he hurriedly turned his truck around to go and get another load of boys, the driver's deep and knowing voice cut through the damp air and the darkness.

"Youse at the Rhine."

* * *

More precisely, they were still a few miles west of the river, near a place called Queckenberg, where Don's battalion was gathering.

Rumors were flying. The Germans had left behind a bridge that was still standing, and the regiment was being sent across. The front was now on the other side of the Rhine River, just a few yards in.

The hurried waiting continued. Thursday's first light arrived, yet another filthy day of low overcast. A chilly light drizzle and some fog had replaced the steady rain of overnight.

Orders came around ten o'clock. Don and his squad jumped back onto trucks, this time headed to where all three battalions of the regiment were converging. They soon entered a traffic jam extending as far as the eye could see, all the muddy roads of the area choked with tanks, jeeps, soldiers on foot, artillery pieces, and ambulances. Everyone was heading to the bridge.

The sign next to the road said the name of the town was Remagen. A little more than twice the size of Don's hometown, nineteen hundred and forty-five years before, it had been a fortification along the Roman frontier line, aimed against barbarian Germanic tribes.

Their truck slowly maneuvered over the familiar German village gauntlet of loose cobblestones, abandoned equipment, and the occasional mangled body.

During the night they had seen the flashes in the east. By the time the boys arrived in Remagen that morning, the intensity of the artillery barrage gave the correct impression that every single German cannon, howitzer, and mortar in the area was targeting the river's west bank and the bridge.

The screams and whistles of shells were almost constant, the Germans letting loose with almost six hundred rounds that day. The level of noise was astounding even by the standards of their wintertime experience in the dark German forest, and it would leave a mark on many.

* * *

Adding to the din was the arrival of German planes. They were greeted by eager American antiaircraft units being set up near the bridge.

Four Stukas were the first to arrive, flaunting their gull-like wings and fixed landing gear. They ostentatiously soared upward through the low overcast before entering dramatic steep dives almost straight down toward the bridge, their trademark siren-like scream piercing through the thunder of the guns. Both sight and sound were well known, made famous in never-to-be-forgotten newsreels about the Spanish Civil War during Don's high school days.

But that morning the Stukas may as well have been from the kaiser's air force. Their days of delivering shock and awe were long past. The deafening wail of their "Jericho Trumpet," clever German engineering aimed at inducing additional terror, was just another bit of noise during a very loud day.

The first three Stukas were shot down.

The Germans would send ten planes against the bridge that morning, most of them Stukas, and the American antiaircraft units would destroy eight of them. The same fate would come to the German bombers that arrived with payloads they tried to aim at the bridge.

One pilot in the initial group of Stukas managed to bail out. As he floated down over the river all manner of .50 caliber antiaircraft machine guns and handheld rifles began firing in his direction. The spray of hot metal over the river was so thick and wild that it briefly posed a danger to the boys who had already crossed the bridge and were on the east side.

Whatever remained of the German air warrior attached to the parachute splashed gently into the venerated river.

* * *

Don's entire regiment was supposed to have been across the bridge before noon. Instead, after inching down the narrow streets sloped toward the river, they were sitting in a line of trucks, waiting. The delay was due to not only the traffic but also the need to sort out conflicting orders from a commanding general in one location and from his staff in another location, each contradicting the other as to whether the unit should motor over the bridge.

A little after high noon some trucks in front of Don's group that had made it to the west bank of the river took matters into their own hands. After maneuvering around the thirty-foot-wide crater just before the west entrance to the bridge, they motored across.

One battalion across. Don's was next.

His squad was ordered off the trucks. Their crossing would be on foot.

They were told to leave their mortar gear. It would be brought across later. If the bridgehead held. For now, Don and his squad were riflemen.

At both the east and west entrances to the bridge stood twin turrets three stories tall, castle-like in shape and the stone blackened by years of soot. Two sets of railroad tracks went across the bridge. In between was loose wooden planking that had been put down by the retreating Germans for their vehicles. The bridge emptied out onto the riverbank on the east side and then into a dark tunnel that went into the base of a wooded bluff jutting upward six hundred feet.

As Don and the others approached the crossing, the ground was shaking from the constant bombardment. Machine guns and other small arms were rattling away from across the river, tracer bullets visibly ripping through the air toward them. Geysers were shooting up alongside the bridge as bombs went off in the river.

The racket was ear-splitting, although somebody from Don's regiment was heard to say, just as he was about to take his turn to make the dash across the bridge, "Sure takes your mind off the war!"

Their orders were to run like hell, turn left, and be ready to start fighting. As Don and others got close to the bridge they were met by MPs, never the subject of sympathy, or any utterance other than scorn. But few boys crossing that day did not consider those MPs to be some of the unluckiest bastards on the planet. They took heavy casualties while sorting out the various lanes of traffic feeding into the bridge and then hurrying each group onto the bridge and across. The sight of them standing upright out in the open, arms waving and pointing while the shrapnel and bullets flew, was as incongruous as when the cop back home in Don's town, after church let out, would step out into middle of Main Street and direct traffic while wearing his Sunday-best suit.

* * *

The shells flew nonstop. There was one last dive into a gutter on the west side. Then they ran, into the cold drizzle.

It was almost four hundred yards of a full sprint, in zigs and zags.

The bridge swayed. Each time a shell ricocheted off its sides, the bridge gave off a shiver.

It was not easy to keep from tripping over the shrapnel scattered about on the planking, or the fallen American and German bodies in noticeably awkward positions, although they did occasionally provide cover for the living. The guardrails were broken, and there were holes and gaps in the planking, openings that went straight down fifty feet to the brown water rushing by. The chatter of gunfire coming from the east side was constant.

* * *

Don made it across. Once off the bridge he turned left and headed north.

The area abutting the river was a series of elegant mansions and chateaus, some with walled gardens. There were no white sheets hanging out, and sniper activity was considerable. Every house had to be secured.

One of the boys from a rifle platoon in Don's company made his gallop across the bridge and then, along with a few others, "busted in" one of the nicer homes along the river to check for Germans. A family was just sitting down to a midday dinner, the food still steaming. With the appearance of American soldiers, without a word they rushed down to the basement. The boys let them be, and they all sat down at the table and ate a hot meal before rejoining their outfit.

* * *

It was around three thirty in the afternoon when Don's battalion assembled in Erpel, a village a few hundred yards from the bridge. There were new orders. They were to secure the town of Honnef, four miles up the river to the north. The orders were given directly to their regimental commander, along with repeated personal assurances from high-level command that there would be no German resistance between Erpel and Honnef, that the advance would be nothing more than a road march in columns.

The three battalions assembled and started out one after the other, in the order they had crossed the bridge. Don's battalion was the second one to step off. German forces responded, providing all the boys a quick and sickening realization that hundreds of 20 mm and 40 mm antiaircraft guns had been repositioned downward toward them. Some of the German nests were in commanding positions, elevated and surrounded by sandbags.

Don's unit came under attack by ten 20 mm antiaircraft guns, all of them blasting away at once. Each battery had to be eliminated.

* * *

At nightfall, rather than settling down for a rest at Honnef after the predicted four-mile road march, Don's battalion was still on the outskirts of the first village to the north, Unkel, less than a mile away from where they had started.

In the fading light of a very long day of war, one of the last sights presented to those exhausted American boys was of Germans intentionally firing on their own soldiers as they fled. It was punishment from their commanders for not following orders to stay at their guns in the face of the machine gun fire pouring out from the approaching tank destroyers in front of Don's battalion.

* * *

The fight to secure Unkel continued into darkness. Phosphorous grenades had to be used to provide a few seconds of illumination to guide the boys through the streets.

The village was taken. But there was to be no rest.

The same general who had provided assurances of an unmolested march to Honnef was now complaining to the commanders of Don's regiment about the slow pace of progress heading north. At ten o'clock that evening, when told that the boys would be back on the attack two hours after midnight, the general ordered that the jumping off time be moved up, suggesting that German resistance be bypassed.

At midnight, Don's battalion was again on the move. As would be discovered throughout the bridgehead area, the overcast night and the sharp rise of the Siebengebirge to the north and east rendered a darkness so complete it was almost impossible to see one's hand extended out at arm's length.

A platoon from each company was sent out into the blindness to precede the advance. The rest of the battalion would wait for word from those initial groups before going on the attack. Some of the advance groups found it so difficult to see that they had to hold on to each other while moving.

It was almost dawn and the advance platoons were still missing when Don's battalion set out toward the north and east, single file, each company seventy-five yards apart. As another gray and cloudy day was emerging they met up with the advance platoons, who said they had stopped when they realized the enemy was all around.

As daylight increased, Don's battalion was spotted and pinned down as 20 mm antiaircraft guns once more opened up on them. Another day began with the familiar dive into trenches alongside a road.

From there, it was a matter of using grenades, mortars, and rifles to take out each one of the gun nests. Some of the Germans manning the guns were killed several times over. As each squad passed by, unsure if they were about to be ambushed, they would fire into the unmoving uniformed figures at their stations.

It was nine o'clock in the morning when they entered the next village to the north, Rheinbreitbach, on the southern edge of the Siebengebirge. The German resistance was intense, fighting over every room in every house. Not until just before darkness was Rheinbreitbach secured, more than twenty-four hours after Don had crossed the bridge. Only then could the boys get some rest.

* * *

The first nights on the east side of the Rhine were fitful. The German artillery and mortar continued through the darkness. When there was a pause, the distant sounds of approaching German tanks could be heard. Stray beams of lights could be seen ricocheting within the bleak natural confines of the Siebengebirge, truck convoys on their way from the east. They were bringing twenty thousand German soldiers.

* * *

News of what happened at Remagen burst across the United States. The unexpected crossing of the Rhine was given the rare three-tiered *New York Times* front-page headline reserved for only the most imposing events of the day. Eisenhower was unabashed in his rejoicing when he heard the news, offering not only encouragement but more divisions to get across at Remagen.

Within twenty-four hours he was overridden by SHAEF staff. Like most who are ensconced in close proximity to the apex of inordinately swollen organizations, the energies of SHAEF staff were always aimed toward a caution that was something close to self-parody, renowned for an aggressive intolerance of originality and anything requiring a new decision. A larger crossing of the Rhine was already being planned for the north. The events at Remagen interfered with decisions already made and threatened to require creativity and adjustment. As such, the Remagen crossing was cause for open dismay among SHAEF staff.

The next day an order from Ike was delivered by General Bradley to the commanding general of the US First Army. The advance from the bridge was to be limited to a thousand yards a day. Once the superhighway running north and south a few miles east of the river was reached, the troops were to hold in place until further orders.

* * *

Regardless of any orders, expanding the bridgehead was not a simple matter. Standing in the way was the immovable Siebengebirge, ever the rampart of barbarian tribes and a natural amphitheater for the drama of mythic doom so cherished by those who had assigned sacral powers to the dirty brown waterway now breached.

CHAPTER THIRTY-THREE

Not Anywhere a Thing More Dismal

Tuesday, March 13, 1945

TUESDAY BEGAN IN the Pacific. Before the day was over on the island of Luzon, twenty-four-year-old Lester Baerwald would be killed, eight thousand miles away from his hometown in Wisconsin. Les had been a year ahead of Boyd in school, a fine athlete and an all-around good guy. During his senior year he was the starting fullback on the football team, ahead of an impatient Boyd.

* * *

On the east side of the Rhine, at seven thirty on Tuesday morning Don's outfit launched an attack on some high ground to the northeast. The previous two days had been the first time since late February that they had remained in the same location, where they were able to watch the Germans methodically shell a nearby village that contained only German civilians.

The day would be a bloody one for Don's regiment. Thirty-one boys were about to die.

* * *

At an airbase north of London, Boyd clipped out the front-page story in Tuesday's *Stars and Stripes* about the mission he had been on the day before, on the Baltic coast. He would send the article home for his mother to save, as he did for most of his missions.

At the Tuesday morning briefing on some air bases in England, a teletype written by divisional commander General William Kepner was read aloud to crews who had been on the same mission:

> Evaluation of yesterday's bombing results on important communications and a/c centers shows that each of 2nd Division's targets was superlatively hit.
>
> I consider this to be not only the best day's work this Division has ever done while under my command but also one of the outstanding performances in the history of precision bombing.

* * *

In Panama, Marie's eighteen-year-old brother George spent Tuesday playing catch, shooting baskets, and, after the recent long stretch of shipboard dining, enthusiastically eating vegetables for the first time in his life.

In port for a little over a week, he had caught up with all of his mail from the previous three months, careful to read each piece in the sequence in which they were sent. Only the previous day he finished getting through it all and had mailed off a response to the V-mail Don had written to him a month before, on the second Sunday in February.

It would be fifty-eight years before George's letter to Don would be opened.

* * *

In Wisconsin, Tuesday dawned bright and unusually warm. Marie's mother thought the sunshine streaming into the house might provide enough light to allow for the rare successful indoor photograph.

She took the chance, snapping a picture of Marie holding her baby daughter, now six weeks old.

* * *

It had been quite some time since the outcome of the war seemed to be in doubt. And yet as the spring of 1945 came on, the conflict remained at full pitch, taking on the form of a complete global surrender to human regress.

Beyond count as well as comprehension was the number of ubiquitous encirclements of barbed wire from one end of Europe to the other, an astonishing amount of humanity spending every hour of every day, some for years, within such confines. They do not appear on most battlefront maps.

New grotesque methods and efficiencies for killing and wrecking were coming to the fore every week, some rushed into use for the sole purpose of being put into use. Mass incineration was now a calibrated tool of war. Across the Continent, rape and starvation had become a force of subjugation, east and west.

These activities were undertaken by all belligerents, with varying levels of magnitude and adroitness. After the war, some would defend against a critical examination of such acts when perpetrated by the victorious side, citing a good intent of heart. For those on the receiving end, there was no difference.

On the Ostfront, the raw bestial impulsions belonging to the eighth century were mauling the forces of malevolent fantasies of extinction suited to the fourteenth century. Both armies operated with an animalistic aggression. Both armies represented grand historic failures of humanity retched up by their respective societies for reasons inadequately examined and still not understood. Working together, they had commenced the great conflagration as they extinguished other nations. Turned one against the other, their savage furies delivered a fashion of war every bit a plague as anything that had ever before swept across the Continent, yielding destruction and slaughter on a biblical scale.

Only pretense from the commanding heights of distance would suggest that it matters whether there was, or whether there was not, some sort of equivalency represented by the two dreadful forces. The unanswerable and ultimately pointless question would be feverishly debated in the safety of later decades as an odd intellectual substitute for the more difficult and uncomfortably granular challenge of exploring how a society can take itself into such a dark abyss.

* * *

It would soon be the turn of a new season in Europe, a springtime of shattered trees and barren, pockmarked fields littered with rotting flesh and blackened metal. Each village seemed to have a steeple in ruins, destroyed because, while nearer to God, it also made for the best local overlook. To those in planes passing overhead at a low altitude, it was a bleak landscape of narrow twisting plumes of smoke. They were everywhere, thin wisps curling upward while torrents of human misery passed in between. The great civilian armies that were not to be found on battlefront maps would trudge over the broken land in a pitiable delirium, never toward a destination but only away from something.

In the western part of the Continent there were also other wanderers who came and went, mainly keeping to urban areas. Tens of thousands of American soldiers were adrift, having quit the war. They remained in uniform, moving about and sometimes carrying weapons. A staggering volume of desertions plagued the US infantry, enough to fill several divisions. Their existence has long since been wiped clean from the cultural memory of exceptional triumph.

* * *

With his usual sparse notation, etched onto the writing tablet liberated from the Red Cross at Dow Field in Maine, Boyd recorded that the previous day's mission had been to Swinemünde. He parenthetically added that it was a naval and military installation.

His ship had been one of thirty-seven planes from Thurleigh that joined more than four hundred other B-17s and two hundred B-24s, the long stream of bombers escorted by four hundred fifty-two P-51 fighter planes.

During the entire flight, Boyd did not see a single enemy aircraft. Approaching the target, they encountered what he later assessed as "spotty" flak. At one in the afternoon, Weber's Wagon dropped five one-thousand-pound bombs through a thick cloud cover. They were back at Thurleigh by five o'clock.

During the post-mission interview with the ground-pounders, done as always with the offer of a shot of something strong, Boyd reported that from his tail-gunner position he had observed an unusual amount of black smoke boiling up from Swinemünde through the overcast. So did several other crews, the smoke described as coming up to the level of the planes, which were at twenty-two thousand feet when bombs were dropped. Probably some burning oil, they were told.

* * *

On the ground, it had been a massacre.

Swinemünde was not a large city. Before the war it was known mainly as a resort town with a fine sandy beach. Its prewar population of little more than twenty thousand had swelled to at least several times that number with refugees arriving every day by land and by sea. The mouth of the river Swina was the entrance to the harbor, and on both banks of the river tens of thousands of refugees camped, and thousands more were crowded in the city center and wherever a train could be boarded. With the Russians less than twenty miles away, the port was in its final days of being a destination for those in the east for whom the only escape from the Red Army was a voyage on the Baltic.

The streets were filled, as one witness later recalled, with exhausted women wearing big boots and scarves, children, and old people who were sitting around everywhere. Many had been part of the trek from the east on foot, an endless wandering column of human suffering out of the Middle Ages. Some of the arriving women showed no response to anything, and would occasionally ask for someone to shoot them, having been raped several times by Russian soldiers and having lost their children. .Carts and carriages, once pulled by an animal or two, now seemed to take up every available space in the streets and courtyards of the city center. Hundreds more horse carts with crowds of refugees were outside the city center, waiting on the other side of the river.

Swinemünde's public facilities were stretched to the limit and beyond. Shelter was being provided in hospital corridors, school rooms and auditoriums, movie theaters, churches, and other buildings where space was available. Behind the beach areas there were public gardens, where many refugees camped out. There were throngs at various points along railroad tracks, those hopeful of getting on board one of the waiting long trains that would take them any direction but east.

* * *

The harbor was crowded that morning with ships of all sizes. People were jammed onto small vessels, into the cargo holds of freighters, and on a few larger ships that held thousands. Many had been out on the water for days, waiting in stuffy quarters for their ship's turn to disembark.

The refugees who had arrived by sea were there as a result of Operation Hannibal, the largest maritime evacuation in recorded history. It was begun by the Germans in late January, in response to the new Soviet Army offensive that had gotten under way once the German counterattack at Ardennes had fully run its course. The Kriegsmarine deployed everything from fishing crafts and merchant freighters to large passenger ships to evacuate a million civilians and half again as many soldiers. Each overladen boat had to run a gauntlet of air attacks, British-laid mines, and Russian submarines, while battling harsh Baltic wintertime conditions that would keep the deck and anyone on it coated with ice.

One of those evacuated by Operation Hannibal was Myroslaw's future wife. Three years before, in Galicia, Maria had been conscripted at the age of seventeen to be a servant for a German military family stationed in Kolberg, another Baltic port seventy miles to the east. Since November, Kolberg had been a Hitler-designated *Festung* to be defended at all costs against the besiegers.

Untermensch to the Germans, a traitor to the Soviets, and, like all women in Kolberg over the age of ten, trapped in a pandemic of rape, Maria somehow obtained passage on an escaping vessel and made the perilous voyage west, ultimately reaching Bremen. Years later, only the occasional burst of emotion, but never many words, would reveal glimpses of what she had seen and experienced during those days.

The refugees in Swinemünde included survivors of the worst sea disaster in history. Six weeks before, a Russian submarine torpedoed the MV *Wilhelm Gustloff*, killing more than nine thousand passengers, most of them women and children. Eight days later, the same submarine sunk the *Steuben*, another liner full of civilians and wounded soldiers, a loss of life of between three and four thousand.

Bodies were washing up every day along the Baltic coast, including those of small children in life jackets that were too big, their heads under the icy water like forlorn ducklings as their tiny lifeless legs bobbed up and down.

Decades after the war ended, the Baltic would continue to spit up pieces of human beings onto the shore.

* * *

In some areas around Swinemünde the sirens sounded a warning, approximately an hour before the bombers arrived. There was no panic, as such warnings were not infrequent. They had always been false alarms, triggered by bombers passing overhead on their way to much larger cities, including Berlin. In any case, there were no underground shelters to go to, as few structures in Swinemünde had basements.

At the outer reaches of the harbor, where a few obsolete naval antiaircraft guns stood watch, the sirens were silent until after the bombs had already begun falling through the clouds. The antiaircraft stations had no working radar, and the planes were not only invisible above the clouds but were likely out of the range of the guns. They were fired anyway, by boys in their early teenage years.

* * *

For an hour the bombs fell.

They came down at a rate of almost fifty per minute, one thousand six hundred tons of explosives raining onto the small crowded area that was Swinemünde.

One of the first bombs landed near the railroad station. It struck a train crowded with refugees, where an eight-year-old girl named Isa was sitting in a compartment along with her mother and brothers. The force of the explosion, which bent railroad tracks and tore the roof of the car away, made Isa's mother disappear, never to be seen again.

Ten-year-old Martin Kruger and his mother had spent the night on a road to the east, arriving on foot that morning in Swinemünde. They had decided to stay another day after being given a hot meal of sauerkraut. During the bombing raid, Martin was hit in the neck by shrapnel. He said, "Mama, what's happening?" Those were his last words before bleeding to death.

The refugee encampments in the park near the beach were on the receiving end of a thorough carpet bombing. The bombs detonated upon contact with the trees, showering the area with hot metal and bursts of deadly splinters.

In the harbor, the steamer *Andros* was filled with two thousand passengers. The boat had moored that morning after sitting for several days on the water, and refugees had just begun to disembark when the ship was hit by three bombs. The second bomb set fire to the vessel, its iron frame turning red from the heat of the flames. The third bomb split the bow. Five hundred seventy aboard the *Andros* were killed, many of them women and children who burned to death.

When the bombs stopped falling, according to several eyewitnesses, fighter planes appeared and did some low-level strafing.

* * *

Dazed survivors began to walk about. The early afternoon had turned dark, as though night had descended. Swinemünde was in flames, black smoke everywhere. The streets were gone, replaced by ruins and stone rubble. Strewn about were heads, limbs, torsos, and other pieces of human anatomy, some hanging from broken trees and stuck to fences.

Women were running around and screaming, searching for their children. The injured were calling out for help.

Many refugees had stayed with their carts and wagons holding their few possessions. They had been replaced by a large and gruesome garbage dump, piles of broken carriages and personal effects mixed with the remnants of human beings who had been ripped apart.

In the harbor area there were noticeably fewer ships. Thirteen had been sunk, including six of twelve transport vessels loaded with refugees.

The inferno burned uncontrolled. The city's electricity, gas, and water services had been destroyed.

* * *

Eight-year-old Isa was found alive in the train car by rescuers. When she was pulled upright, she saw her brothers, sitting nearby. The tops of their heads were blown off.

Legs, arms, severed heads, and other remains of humans and animals were in bomb craters that now covered the park and garden areas where refugees had been camping. The concussive force of the explosions had reduced the trees to broken stumps, from which pieces of human beings dangled.

After the raid the cleanup began. It had to be done in a hurry because of the threat of disease from such a volume of dead flesh spread over the area. Much of the work was done by the "cadets," boys in their early teenage years.

Dead babies and the bodies of children were sorted by size and stacked. One of the cadets found the body of a woman who had apparently been killed while giving birth. Her abdomen had been ripped open by flying debris. A dead baby girl was beside her with no apparent wounds, still attached to the mother by an umbilical cord.

The human and other animal remains found in the park and on the beach were buried on the spot, taking advantage of the craters and then filling them in. Hundreds of people had been trapped in the houses now destroyed. There was no recovery process, and many were left in the buried ruins, as were those in the sunken and burned vessels. For decades after the war, human body parts would emerge from the soil in the city's parks and gardens.

* * *

The bodies of sixteen hundred townspeople were identified and buried. As for the rest of the human remains, the city's cemeteries were too small, so they were taken to the side of a great hill known as the Golm and put into two mass graves.

Rounding out the day's tableau of collective human achievement was the sight of slave laborers and prisoners of war being directed by their German overlords to undertake the monstrous task of giving a burial to so many pieces of the nameless. They were ordered to do so by people in a land where there was a shared cultural fondness for giving a prominent place on living room walls to an image of their very own loving Jesus Christ, as so many American infantry soldiers would discover in home after home as they crossed Germany.

The exact toll of Monday's raid by Weber's Wagon and six hundred other American bombers would never be known. Estimates vary wildly, from a general consensus that at least four to five thousand civilians were killed, to some suggesting upward to five figures, and others insisting that there were more than twenty thousand deaths.

* * *

As for the military value of the raid, the port of Swinemünde suffered little damage. Its handling capacity was not disrupted, not even for a single day. No combat ship was destroyed in the raid. There was no damage to Kriegsmarine stocks of ammunition and fuel.

Soviet reconnaissance photographs showed the existence of hundreds of bomb craters in the area around the beach and harbor, and confirmed the sinking of three transport ships.

One month after the bombing of Swinemünde, General Kepner sent another teletype to air crews in England under his command, this time forwarding a special message from General Carl Spaatz, commander of Strategic Air Forces in Europe:

> Your well planned and magnificently executed operation of 12 March against Swinemunde is deserving of the highest praise. The town of Swinemunde was heavily damaged by concentrations of high explosive bursts which also destroyed a factory, several warehouses and installations near a seaplane base.... This devastating instrument bombing attack, made with great accuracy only a short distance from the Russian front lines, truly demonstrates the skill and determination with which your crews fulfill their duties. I wish to commend you upon this outstanding job by your command, and particularly wish to commend and congratulate the lead crews and air commanders who so carefully and efficiently conducted the attack.

* * *

Boyd would go to his grave without knowing what took place on the ground at Swinemünde. But there were other days, other missions, when he saw or he just knew from the circumstances what it was they were leaving behind.

There was always talk about such things among the boys. In April, they would go to the Atlantic coast of France, more than eight hundred miles *west* of the battlefront, joining a thousand other planes on back-to-back days to drop six kilotons of bombs on a target in liberated France where supposedly there were large German gun emplacements. The first day was a highlight for Boyd, with its thrill of being part of so many planes maneuvering into formation at eight thousand feet directly over Paris.

But the missions to France left questions, as he and many of the boys knew that any Germans would likely be in the shelter of concrete bunkers, while any French civilians in the area would not. The second day of those missions delivering destruction to French soil would include the first use by Eighth Air Force heavy bombers of a new weapon of war, called napalm.

After the war, Boyd would have little use for talk about war crimes. He would respond with an out-of-character surly dismissiveness, muttering as though talking to a fool.

"It was war."

If that did not stop the conversation he would sometimes add that he himself was a war criminal because of some of the things they did. He would sometimes finish by saying that it was the "big wheels who start these things and keep them going" who deserved punishment.

But it was also never that simple. During the war and afterward, it bothered him, and it was more than just a slight uneasiness.

He knew, and they all knew, that they not only were killing civilians but were doing so with deliberate intent by those giving the orders, no matter how the target was described.

Years later he would say that he considered it a good lesson in life that at such a young age he was able to observe the shameless use by the top brass of the phrase "precision bombing," while he knew firsthand that the reality was otherwise.

It was war. He was doing a job. It was terrible, all of it. Far more so, he thought, than anyone back home knew—or would ever know.

* * *

During one mission Boyd had a split-second encounter with a German fighter pilot whizzing by, what seemed like eye-to-eye contact. The brief moment hit him like a board to the forehead, leaving him with a crazy mix of feelings: respect and hatred, kinship and revulsion, and just overall disbelief at life—all in that brief split-second. It would always be difficult for him to describe.

* * *

The whole time Boyd was there he wished it was over. His life during those days brought him more laughter deep from the belly than he would ever experience again. While he was on his missions it thrilled Boyd to look out and see that he was part of a massive armada. He grew desperately tired, not only of the dangers, but of the fear that was a heavy weight that always had to be worn. Boyd carried no personal quarrel with the Germans. He believed with all his heart that the Germans were a menace to humanity that had to be stopped as soon as possible. If there had been any choice, at any time, he would not have been there. The death and destruction they left behind would be a lifelong disturbance. He was proud of what he was doing.

So many dualities. So much that was, and would always be, irreconcilable. It all ran deep.

Boyd would carry it home, like so many others. To be kept tightly clenched inside for the rest of his days. Theirs was a complexity of existence that Boyd had already known before the war and innately understood. As did Don. As did Myroslaw.

Their reality of the human condition would be pushed away by a later modernity, to a place outside the comprehension of a twenty-first-century society with its own paralytic obsession with immediate binary verdicts, even where none can ever exist.

* * *

Only the shallowest of truths about the Second World War are revealed in the lines and arrows superimposed on battlefront maps. Always absent are the columns of human displacement, as though irrelevant to the war's reality or the world the war was leaving behind. As for accuracy of military portrayal, the smooth broad sweep of the front is a fable, about both a connectedness and a cohesion that did not exist.

Like Boyd, and Myroslaw, Don had been raised to take in the set of the land wherever he stood.

A skill learned early in life, it was second nature to locate north and west, sniff the air and take note of any wind, give measure to the sky and the light cast while drawing in a feel of the ground underfoot. Done in an unthinking moment, the offhand proficiency was once pervasive across a society that could not easily avert itself from natural surroundings. Its practice would fade away within a generation, well before the later decay of map-reading and the not-unrelated demise of broader inclinations toward introspection.

Surrounding Don on that Tuesday was a terrain without subtlety. Its unfriendly tangle of vertical contours, storm-worn ridges, and brooding hills cut through by steep canyons gave the Siebengebirge its severe and sinister beauty. The compact range of uplands extended north and south for not much more than four miles. Its breadth was two and a half miles. Just beyond, on the east side, running north and south, was one of Hitler's superhighways.

Among the thirty or so hills of the Siebengebirge, a few perpendicular shapes of menace dominated, rising to a thousand feet above the Rhine in less than a few hundred yards. The most imposing of these was the Drachenfels, almost perpendicular on three of its sides, complete with a cave where Siegfried's legendary dragon had dwelled. The towering crags loomed with a dark Wagnerian presence, blocking light from the dismal and tilted world down below that was covered by thick woods interspersed with stark bare-faced knolls.

The cheerless setting had long nurtured Teutonic myths that attached romantic notions to vengeance and annihilation.

Atop the tallest summits were stone ruins, each with a clear sight of the bridge. In early March of 1945 the remains of medieval castles sheltered descendants of the ancient barbarians, zealous and desperate in their defense against those who had dared cross the river that they, like their ancestors, still revered as heroic.

In more immediate terms, Don had entered an infantryman's nightmare.

* * *

The topography was one of compartments. Five days after the crossing it was still impossible for Don's battalion to stay together, much less the entire regiment. In such tight quarters, the numerical superiority now pouring across the Rhine meant little. Armor was no match for the winding roads. German antitank weapons easily blocked progress, as did log barriers and other roadblocks, many booby-trapped. Where the woods thinned out and the slopes became more gentle, the Germans took advantage and hid themselves.

Everywhere were sharp angles, left and right, down to ravines and up from ravines. The terrain was as much an obstacle to progress as German snipers and mortar fire. Reaching any objective required a struggle through narrow and circuitous routes, as Rome's soldiers had learned almost two thousand years before. The only way to advance toward the holdouts on the highest ground was on narrow footpaths that ascended almost straight up, greasy steps once cut for hikers, less than a foot wide. Vehicles for crew-based weaponry could not be used, so mortar equipment and ammunition for squads like Don's had to be passed up steep slopes by hand, one soldier to the next, like a bucket brigade. At the higher elevations the ground was so steep that ten-minute rest periods were needed for the advancing boys to catch their breath.

It was combat in an otherworld. Never more so than in the dim first moments of the day when attacks were launched, making use of the shadowy half-light while generated smoke was threading its way through the unwelcoming passages. The only thing missing in the damp morning gloom was a few Valkyries flying overhead, choosing who would die and who would live for another day. They would have been preferable to the occasional low-flying German plane attempting to strafe the boys.

* * *

The entire battle of the Remagen bridgehead was strange. At times, for those on the ground within that confined area, it was an entrance into the surreal, many things never seen or heard before in a mishmash of sight and sound that was an almost supernatural display of human inventiveness and desperation.

Hitler's rage in reaction to the Rhine crossing was a rather standard affair. Some German officers were taken out and shot. There were orders for annihilation of the bridgehead area.

The chancellor liked Himmler's idea to use the V-2 weapon, apparently setting aside any sense of irony in directing the launch of the *Wunderwaffe* from Holland onto the *Vaterland*. Göring offered up pilots flying suicide missions against the bridge, an idea later cast aside after underlings informed him, no doubt carefully, that the arming system on the planes would preclude detonation in such a scenario.

Thus vengeance unleashed.

* * *

It was a spectacular array of war-making violence. For days thunder and smoke rolled through the river basin near Remagen, a gaudy bedlam of noise rattling up and down the Rhine-cut valley and into the sidelong ravines. Explosions of every sort made for a ragged drumroll that was almost constant. The earth near the river trembled. A soldier's distance from the front line now on the east side of the river meant little in terms of safety, with more danger from the artillery hitting the west side of the river. Engineers working on the bridges and those who crossed the river to make deliveries or evacuate the wounded bore much of the brunt, sitting ducks for the shelling being guided by German observers on the steep bluffs on the east side.

More than a hundred heavy German guns and howitzers, all of them larger than the dreaded 88s, had been firing away each day, trying to knock down the railroad bridge and to confound the American attempts to construct two additional bridges. Joining the barrage from miles away were huge German railroad guns, throwing shells that weighed as much as a 1940 Ford pickup truck. They were notable for sounding like a freight train as they passed overhead. On the east side of the river the dreaded Nebelwerfer had entered the scene. Its terrifying multiple-barreled gun launchers were known to the boys as the Screaming Mimi, giving off the harmonic moans of a wailing banshee while accurately saturating areas with rocket mortars.

The days after the crossing were filled with sounds never before heard, sights never before seen. Barrage balloons had sprouted after the crossing and lazed overhead. Long snakelike barriers were floated out onto the water in order to stop German attempts to send mines down to the bridge. Landing craft cruised constantly around the area, grenades dropped into the water like depth charges in order to discourage any German frogmen.

Sometimes the entire bridge would disappear, smoke generators at work to hide it during repairs. At night, boys on the heights of the east side could see an eerie glow rising above the river, the light reflecting back down off the usual low ceiling of clouds. The bridge was kept brightly lit against approaching German swimmers or small boats carrying explosives. It was the first use of what had once been intended to be an American secret weapon of night-fighting tanks, developed under a failed theory that a blinding light of thirteen million candlepower would cripple oncoming forces.

* * *

On the third day after the crossing, a few engineers on the west shore were tending to the construction of a new bridge. They stopped what they were doing and looked up at each other while they all had the same frightening sensation of the air being sucked away from around where they stood. They heard nothing approaching.

Not far away there was a great thunderous explosion. Like most of the boys, the engineers were familiar with the signature sounds of various types of armaments going off, but they had no idea what they had just heard or experienced.

Those engineers survived the first of eleven V-2 missiles that would be launched at the bridgehead area over seven days. Each one would hit the surface of the earth at more than three thousand miles per hour, the thunderclap from the fracture of the sound barrier arriving after the explosion. One rocket demolished a house three hundred yards east of the bridge, killing three Americans inside. Three of the missiles landed in the river near the bridge. Five others struck the countryside to the west.

* * *

Each day the narrow patch of sky over the river was alive with planes, a bizarre circus of technology, demolition, bravery, and suicide.

On the first day after the crossing some American P-38s had appeared overhead, their signature twin tail against the gray overcast easily recognizable to soldiers on the ground. Perhaps for some it was even a reassuring sight, given the fearsome reputation of the plane, known as "The Lightning," for speed and intimidation. When introduced five years before, it was the fastest fighting airplane in the world, once described by some Germans as *der gaelschwanz teufel* (the fork-tailed devil).

The P-38 could be seen chasing something smaller and twice as fast, like an old lumbering dog after a fly. For many boys on the ground, including those in Don's outfit, it was the first jaw-dropping sight of a jet airplane.

The fork-tailed devil had already been tossed aside by the war, like the Stuka. It was now only a showpiece of power from days gone by, like cavalry horses in the previous war, the battleship during the Second World War, and what would become of the aircraft carrier in the next century.

* * *

Almost 150 German airplanes of various types, including jets, were shot down in the air space over the Remagen bridge. The Germans tried dive-bombing. They tried low-altitude bombing and they tried high-altitude bombing. They came in singly, and they came in pairs.

A few days before, at around five o'clock in the afternoon, there was the remarkable sight of eight Stukas cruising in formation down the Rhine valley, making a steady and unhurried approach to the bridge at three thousand feet. They took no evasive action, even as they came under fire. Each one was destroyed.

On Monday, at around the same time that Boyd's crew was approaching Swinemünde, there were ninety separate German sorties over the Rhine, each plane diving at the bridge from either the north or the east, through the low gray clouds. The overcast and cold drizzle did little to muffle the loud carnage of twenty-six planes being shot down and another nine damaged.

There were now almost seven hundred antiaircraft weapons placed around the bridgehead area, and the number was still rising. Nowhere on earth was the air ever so thick with the thunder of metal being thrown at passing aircraft, the bridgehead area becoming home to the heaviest concentration of antiaircraft weapons at any time during the entire war. Some of the planes were not just shot down, but when caught in the spray of the withering antiaircraft fire, they appeared to disintegrate in the air while making a single pass.

* * *

Like Ardennes, Remagen was anything but a set-piece battle. The unexpected crossing did not fit with command-post plans or previous experiences. Securing the bridgehead in such an improvised, off-the-cuff manner was a remarkable achievement. The conditions faced by the boys were a constant challenge, including another miserable performance by a disconnected high-level leadership entangled in individual theatrics.

The record about what happened at Remagen, especially during the week after the first crossing, has already faded. And, as with Ardennes, no one will ever know the countless unaccounted for and unhonored moments of creativity, pluck, and iron resolve on the part of such unwarrior-like boys, those privates, sergeants, and others all below the rank of colonel who kept moving ahead in the face of deadening fatigue, fear, and confusion that was not their own doing.

The boys around Don knew no exultation after crossing the Rhine. In his outfit there were no thoughts that the war had somehow changed. Because for them it had not.

Their existence was uncluttered by strategic meaning. Their only motivating convictions were staying alive and having a thought for the fellow nearby. The war's immediacy remained predatory, annihilating anything having to do with an individual's past or future, a mercy as much as it was a torture.

For Don and those with him, the days approaching the ides of March

1945 were a numbing blur of digging in, moving out, patrolling, and doing it all again and again, always vaguely north and east, under the same dull gray skies and spitting rain.

The slanted ground beneath their feet seemed hateful. Nerves were ragged. A killing of some sort always lurked.

* * *

Tuesday closed itself out on the other side of the Atlantic.

For the sixth straight day the afternoon paper delivered to the front porch at Ernst's house had a bold page-one headline about the Rhine crossing:

Capture of Honnef Gives American Firm Anchor
for Rhine Bridgehead

Both Marie's dad and Julius followed the daily maps of the war. They knew the generals' names and they knew where Don was. She had been told, excitedly, that he was a part of the great crossing of the Rhine, which many said had changed the war.

Marie paid little attention to such things and was not moved by them. She only wanted it all to be over. And for everything to get back to as it was.

In the meantime, she wrote letters. Marie was always a dutiful letter-writer, even in her final years after her penmanship of elegance and grace, always a source of pride, fell victim to failing vision and shaky hands. In her stream of letters to Don, Marie regularly included snapshots of the baby. Always subject, of course, to the whims of getting the developed photographs back in time from the Silverness drugstore.

She had recently written a letter to Boyd and included a photo of Ann, now almost two months old. He put the picture up in his tail-gunner compartment, drawing predictable razzing from the others in the crew.

* * *

Just a few days before, it had snowed in Wisconsin, nothing unusual about that year's relentless winter continuing its drive into March.

But Tuesday had brought a sudden change, not only bright sunshine but an incredible sixty degrees, a leap of twenty degrees above what it should have been. And for the rest of the month it would continue, a freakish stretch of weather that belonged to late May, even early June. It was like nothing Marie or anyone else around town could remember.

Things began to bloom at the wrong time, and were finished before they were supposed to start. Her equilibrium was upended by the sight of trees budding out while the afternoon sun still hung so low in the southern sky. During such warm days the house would become unbearably stuffy because nobody in their right mind would put on screens in March. The only thing to do was to get scraped knuckles while fiddling with the stupid contraption on the storm windows that was supposed to allow a little bit of fresh air inside.

The right clothes for such weather were still all put away. It was far too early to take them out, even if it was unsettling to be perspiring so much.

Some people became lighthearted with the arrival of Florida-like temperatures when it was normal to have snowstorms. Marie was not one of them. She took no pleasure from being so disoriented by something that felt like it was stolen from another season. She never liked extremes, which only put her all out of sorts, and that alone would make her fearful. It was always hard for her in such moments to shake a feeling that something was dreadfully off.

She so wished the war would end.

CHAPTER THIRTY-FOUR

Quietus

Friday, March 16, 1945

FEW THINGS IN life have more healing properties than a good dose of March sunshine on the face.

Spring had emerged the day before, and Friday broke sunny with the promise of blue sky and golden warmth. The monochrome of the past few weeks was gone. The morning air was glorious.

Don had spent the night in the basement of an abandoned house. Getting a few hours of sleep on a dry floor under a roof was nothing less than luxurious.

Friday morning brought some quiet. For the first time since the boys crossed the Rhine eight days before, the background thunder of German artillery had gone still. The gaps of silence that morning sometimes lasted an hour or more. Even the airshow had slackened off, something already noticeable the day before.

Less than a mile away and now within reach of one day's efforts was the famous German superhighway. Don's unit was still in the snare of blind chambers, imposing slopes, and open ridges all used so diabolically by the Germans. Up ahead were SS troops who that day would be maniacal in their desperation to keep the autobahn from being taken. Heavy casualties and bitter hand-to-hand combat would be required to displace them.

Back behind Don, toward the Rhine, the streets of the tiny villages close to the riverbank were jammed with American armored vehicles. If he knew about them, and it's doubtful that he did, they might have offered something pleasant to think about, but not much more.

American tanks could not deliver what was needed most by Don and all those other weary boys, which was rest.

* * *

The standard practice was to keep a pencil and some paper in the webbing of the helmet, in a slot next to where many kept some spare toilet paper.

It had been a good long time since there had been a chance for Don to write home.

On that morning he wrote two short letters, first to Marie and then to his parents.

* * *

A little after midday, around one o'clock, Don was standing with another fellow just outside the entrance to a walk-in basement of a house situated on the side of a hill. The two were chatting with a medic, who was standing in the doorway. Brownie and the twenty-year-old medic had become friendly since their arrival at the front in December.

The three of them were talking about nothing in particular, just some of the usual small back-and-forth about something ordinary back home. Sustenance came from such conversations.

A sudden noise made all three of the boys turn at once.

An antitank gun appeared, more than a hundred yards behind them and down the slope. It was exchanging fire with a German tank that had made a surprise appearance up toward the crest of the hill, well beyond where they were standing.

Don abruptly broke things off.

"I better get back to my guys."

He turned and began walking away. He was no more than five or six steps from the basement entryway when the shell hit. There had been no sound of incoming.

It did not take long to find Don. A few of the boys from inside the house, which was now in shambles, carried him into what was left of the basement and laid him down. The medic who had been standing in the entryway talking to Don, and had just watched him walk away, came right over.

He sat down on the ground and took Brownie gently by the shoulders, pulling Don's upper body onto his lap.

Don was still conscious, but dazed. Occasionally he would say a word or two.

He had a gaping chest wound, and the medic knew from the sight of it that nothing could be done. He continued to hold Don and tried to make sure he was as comfortable as possible.

Don spoke again.

"Tell my wife I'm fine."

And then he died.

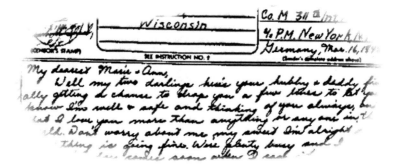

Germany, Mar. 16, 1945

My dearest Marie & Ann,
Well my two darlings here's your hubby and daddy finally getting a chance to drop you a few lines to let you know I'm well & safe and thinking of you always, and that I love you more than anything or anyone in this world. Don't worry about me my sweet I'm alright and everything is going fine. We're plenty busy and I sure hope the day comes soon when I can sit down & write you a nice long letter. I write every chance I get darling which isn't very often. Just keep your faith in our Lord sweetheart. He will see us through all of this & it won't be long and He will end the war. Been getting all your swell letters and Moms and also ones from Boyd, Gladys U. and John Manfreddi. Don't know when I'll get to answer them though. Received three more pictures of Ann the other day & they are really swell. Oh honey I love you two so much your my whole life. Fred received word the other day he is a Daddy too and is plenty happy. Your letters do so much for me my sweet, I can't begin to explain how good they make me feel. Everything you write darling really hits the spot with me. Everything about Ann is so good. Oh darling your perfect. Well my sweet must write the folks a quick V-mail and hope I can write again to you soon. Be good darling and take good care of our honey. May God bless you both and keep you always happy healthy and well. I love you so much my own little family of two. Always your very own Don

CHAPTER THIRTY-FIVE

A Numberless Sorrow

Friday, March 30, 1945

MARIE GOT THE telegram in the morning. It came on Good Friday, another weirdly warm day in the ongoing stretch of altered weather. Word about Don spread around town like fire.

Ed Frei, who owned the oil company on the southwest edge of town, had made a stop that morning at the meat locker shop a block off Main Street beside the river. After hearing the news directly from Julius himself, Ed just had to come home for a bit and collect himself.

His daughter, Rachel, was a friend of Marie's, both of them part of a loosely organized group of self-described gals who gathered together every month mainly to get away from their mothers. They would play bridge or sometimes poker, smoke cigarettes, and have a couple of drinks while sharing stories. They all had husbands away in the service, and most had new babies, Rachel included. Hearing the news that morning from her father, she wept.

* * *

At least one person from town took up the responsibility of calling the daily newspaper in Beaver Dam.

The afternoon's edition carried a brief item set out in an appropriately passive voice.

S/Sgt Donald Brown Killed in Germany on March 16th.

Word Received Today.

Life went on.

As Julius did at the end of every workday, on Friday he drove his helpmates, the two German prisoners of war, back to the camp at Hartford, a twenty-mile trip.

Whatever conversation took place in the car, either in German or English, will remain forever unknown.

By local custom, on Good Friday the stores in town were closed for a few hours during the early afternoon, even though none of the churches held services during that time. The tradition served to increase the Friday night shopping traffic, an eagerly anticipated pre-Easter rush. Ernst's corner store would be open until at least nine o'clock. In anticipation of a steady stream of customers, both he and Marie's mother went downtown to work in the store.

After putting her twelve-year-old brother, Billy, and ten-year-old sister, Ruth, to bed, Marie spent the rest of the evening alone, her baby not far away.

* * *

Boyd learned about Don in a letter from his mother. That same night he went out and got very drunk, a few crewmates all but carrying him back to his enlisted man's hut.

On the next combat mission, something unusual took place. The specifics of how it was accomplished were never made clear. Boyd never spoke about it, except to Marie shortly after the war.

The abridged version, and as it turned out the only version, was that the pilot, Pinchback, along with the others on the crew, came up with the idea for some switching of positions, so that at the right moment, Boyd was up in the front end of the plane and operating the controls for releasing the bombs onto German soil.

The story became a family fable, held with a ration of skepticism.

In a conversation six decades later, after Boyd and Marie had both passed on, the crew's radio operator brought up the incident unsolicited. He was in his mid-eighties when he told the same abridged version, plainly reluctant to provide any further details, as though mindful of some continuing risk of official consequences for such a stunt.

* * *

The war went on.

Boyd did not know it at the time, but his final combat mission was in mid-April. Weber's Wagon joined a force of more than four hundred B-17s to drop bombs on whatever rubble remained of Dresden. Just a few days after the great firebombing that took place on February 13, the trains had begun running again. A follow-up bombing of Dresden had taken place on March 2. The stated target for the April 17 mission was two railroad centers.

Heavy contrails from all the planes made for bad air-to-air visibility around the target area. Just two minutes after Weber's Wagon dropped its bombs, one formation of ships entered into a collision course with the formation in front of Boyd's group. Three B-17s collided with each other. One blew up, and another was seen going down in a dive. The third went down missing a wing. Only four parachutes were observed. Boyd had witnessed a similar collision between two B-17s on a mission nine days before.

On the way to Dresden, Boyd saw four German jets. They kept their distance from the stream of bombers, which was fine by him. The flak, he reported later, was "light, but very accurate."

What was left of Dresden's city center was well hit. Five hundred civilians were killed.

* * *

Perhaps as a reflection of his Depression upbringing, or his time in the war, or both, in later years Boyd reserved the word "waste" for strictly limited occasions. When he used the word, it was said with a notable sharp pronunciation that included a hiss. The context always involved a misuse of talent, resources, or people in a way he considered to have reached the level of unqualified human transgression.

It is doubtful Boyd was ever informed that hundreds of civilians were killed on the ground in Dresden during his last combat mission. On the other hand, unlike the air-to-air visibility the air-to-ground visibility was good that day. He could often get a look at the results of their work. He also knew that crews had gone down that day with their planes, and that it was the third bombing of Dresden since the February firestorm that was a frequent topic of conversation on the base.

After the war, Boyd deftly avoided speaking at length or in great detail about any particular one of the missions, other than perhaps the first to Berlin. He was skilled in deflecting conversations, and it took years for others to understand that it was his way of maintaining control of what might emerge from deep within. But from the moment of his return that day to the base at Thurleigh and forever after that, Boyd would always say that he never understood that last mission to Dresden. And then he would give the pronouncement, in a most unpleasant tone, that it was a "waste."

* * *

Ten days after his final combat mission he would put down the only words he would ever write to his parents about Don's death:

> . . .*You can tell Browns, & I will too in a letter, that I've already thought about doing what they asked. I've been trying ever since you sent the letter about Don, to find out from Intelligence and G-2 all I can about what happened. A Captain from Intelligence, whom I know quite well, has gone by plane on a tour around Frankfurt, Cologne, the Rhine, & those places to inspect things & see just what kind of damage our bombing has done. If he has time he'll see if he can locate Don's grave for me. Then another officer is going for a day or two soon—he will do the same if he has time. I may get a chance at any time to go along with them, alone, or on a pass, just depending upon plane loads and things. It's a pretty large order to fill but I may get a chance and fulfill it. At least I've been working on it and will continue so.*

Part Five

AFTERLIFE

1945–1997

CHAPTER THIRTY-SIX

Days of Victory

May 8, 1945

THERE WERE SOME false starts. But the official end came at last. It was a day of soft air and gentle warmth, memorable to Boyd if only because he already had his fill of how most days the blue sky over England would never hold, inevitably pushed aside by a mood-deadening sprinkle.

Boyd spent some of V-E Day in the air, along with the rest of the crew of Weber's Wagon, giving an air tour of the Continent. It was a task they would be doing a lot in the upcoming weeks, taking up ground personnel, WACs, and reporters on what were called observation missions, in between going on leaflet missions and transporting GIs who had been prisoners of war.

For the tours over the Continent, Pinchback would take the ship down as low as possible. The boys thought it great fun and encouraged it, demanding to go "hedge-hopping." As part of the tours during those first days of peace, it was almost mandatory that whenever they were over Paris they would buzz the Eiffel Tower. The ruins of Cologne were a popular spot for seeing total destruction. They often had to pull up to avoid hitting one of the twin spires of the famous cathedral, which was about the only building that was still standing.

* * *

Something happened during one of those flights around the time of V-E Day. It was never made clear whether it was a leaflet mission or an observation tour. A sight opened up on a low and slow pass to reveal a world that

Boyd did not know could ever exist. From a much higher altitude, while on combat missions, he had already seen what he had thought to be prisoner-of-war camps, surprised at the large and elaborate layout of fences, block houses, and watchtowers. He was not prepared for the sight of stacks of bodies. There were hundreds, if not thousands. Another slow pass, and a bulldozer could be seen working a trench for the bodies. On the ground there were walking dead people, living skeletons. The worst, and for some the most unforgettable part of the experience, was the ungodly smell that seeped up into the plane.

He later once said he thought it had been Buchenwald. The few times it came up, usually triggered by something on television, Boyd would never say much more than "I was there," followed by the silence of a closing gate. In the manner of his lexicon about the war, the use of the word "there" was not so much a reference to a specific place name but his confirmation of the undeniable existence of an unholiness that he had visited. After a few such exchanges over the years, it became clear that he had no other words to use, beyond that he had been "there."

What he had experienced in that brief low-flying pass over the camp did not deliver a sense of justification. Like most of the boys, Boyd was neither an intellectual nor emotional simpleton, and for him there was no made-for-television moment of receiving a new answer to the question of why we fight. Instead, what the war had delivered to him during that moment in the plane was another unwanted fragment of understanding about mankind. It joined other sharp-edged pieces he had collected, buried deep as something not to go very near.

* * *

Boyd was apparently not alone in his earlier prediction of a potential conflict, in responding to the end of the war, between the weary and phlegmatic British and the American appetite for celebration and hilarity. On V-E Day everyone was restricted to the base, except for assigned air missions.

The makings of a bonfire had been put together during the day on the ball diamond near the quadrant considered the home of Boyd's squadron. As dusk was settling in over the deep-green English countryside, kegs of beer were rolled out. The fire was lit and a brownish haze ascended over the field, mixing into the otherwise clean colors of spring twilight. In the background the airbase band played some tunes.

A separate celebration for officers had begun in a nearby mess hall, where unlimited Scotch was available. But it was not long before most of the officers drifted outside and strolled over to join the enlisted men gathered around the bonfire as the last wisps of light were fading on the first day of a Europe gone quiet.

Boyd stood with the others, drinking his beer and gazing at the great bonfire. No longer present in his life was the war's bullying world of the present tense, a destitute existence of living only in the immediate, unconnected to anything forward or back.

It was five years almost to the very day when the whirlwind had begun, those stirring weeks that had left on him and everyone else an indelible mark. He and Don had been seventeen years old. And now there was already a full generational gap between that boy and the self he carried that evening. Those days had been full of arrival and triumph, a sweet joy shared alongside Brownie, Marie, and the rest of the class of 1940, made electric by the end-of-the-world drama then unfolding in such a faraway place. He had thought he was about to start life. So did Don. So did Marie. It did not happen.

Never would he have expected that five years later he would be standing on a makeshift baseball field, four thousand miles from home and an unmeasurable distance from the world he had known.

On that evening, for Boyd, and for so many boys in England and on the Continent, triumph was left to others.

* * *

V-E plus one was designated as another holiday. The order restricting everyone to the base was lifted, and on a perfect summer night, Boyd was among the many who left the base and went first into Thurleigh, and then on to Bedford, a much larger city about seven miles to the south.

The boys could not have expected what they came upon. Someone appeared to have made it their business to find and string up over the streets every available light bulb, a dazzling assertion being made about a return of certain things. The war had made everyone exiles from light.

Under the incandescence there were crowds of formerly proper English people roaming about, raucous if not ready to hold their own against any conduct offered up by the notorious Yanks. Flags were hanging everywhere, and drinks were passed around. In the park a band was playing and there was dancing on the grass, along with other hearty activities consistent with an epic emotional release from years of darkness. Boyd wandered around, watching snake dances going up and down the streets. He had never seen such a thing.

The entire evening was most remembered, by him and by others, for a particular song. Its refrain was shouted throughout the night after each ribald verse by impromptu choirs of staid British subjects:

Roll me o-o-o-ver in the clo-o-o-ver;
Roll me over, lay me down, and do it again.

CHAPTER THIRTY-SEVEN

From the New World

Summer and Autumn 1945

ALWAYS A MONTH of unrest, April brought a cruel, punishing wind as the follow-on to everything that March had delivered to Wisconsin. When agitated by the breeze, the peonies so highly favored around town would lose their elegance and look blowzy. The lilacs came and went, the curtain call of a spring season even meaner and more fraudulent than most.

Summer was a slow starter. A cold June put the corn crop behind, always the source of complaint by farmers. Their state of mind was a frequent suppertime report delivered by Ernst, tales of whatever he heard when they came into town to do some shopping. He would sometimes add his own stock editorial, never to be even whispered inside the store, that those farmers seemed to be happier when they were unhappy about something.

* * *

Marie dutifully took her baby daughter in for a weekly checkup with the local family physician known to all by his first name, Doctor John, a toothy, larger-than-life man who wore gold wire-rimmed glasses and was given to mouth-breathing whenever he would lean forward and turn quiet to listen. His father, Doctor Adrian, had also served the community for decades, and had delivered Marie.

Without fail, each visit the baby would be pronounced healthy, and sometimes Marie and Doctor John would share a cigarette and talk a bit.

The frequency of the appointments made no impression on Marie, although she did notice that they spent more time chatting about goings-on around town than on the examination of Ann. Only many years later did Marie realize that the weekly checkups were actually for her, not for her baby, a small deception that allowed Doctor John to make sure she was holding up after the loss of Don. He quietly did the same with some other young war widows left alone with small children.

In July, Julius announced that due to the continuing labor shortage he would no longer make deliveries from his store, except on Saturday afternoons for larger orders. Before the year was out, he would put the business up for sale.

That summer was the first time since Herb and Lylle moved to town, almost fifteen years before, that neither one worked at the canning factory. Herb was still struggling to keep four tires in working order, but he was earning good money for the first time in almost twenty years. In June, they had traveled down to Naperville for Blossom's college graduation, a first on both Herb's and Lylle's sides of the family and the source of shoulders-back, chest-out pride. Blossom moved back home for a few months before starting a position in the fall as a music teacher in a school just outside of Chicago.

* * *

Since around V-E Day, Lylle's letters to Boyd did not hold back on her worries that he would soon be transferred to the war in the Pacific, converted to the infantry for the invasion of Japan then being planned for the autumn, which would involve more than a million American combat soldiers. While Boyd did not admit it to her, he shared his mother's concerns, and then some. Every day in April and May seemed to bring new rumors to the base about their fate.

A war-weary instinct combined with the rapid spread of accounts in letters from pals already in the Pacific made for widespread belief among the boys on the base that the invasion of the Japanese mainland would be a nightmare of blood and death, far beyond what had gone on in Europe. Everyone Boyd knew wanted no part of it and would have done just about anything to get out of going.

His unease was not helped when, in mid-May, the crew learned that Weber's Wagon was one of many ships being transferred off the base for ferrying back to the States. The boys took some last pictures with their ship, including with Elmer Weber himself.

A few weeks later came the godsent orders ensuring Boyd would be in Europe through the summer, no matter what went on in the Pacific. His bomb group was one of two assigned to the Casey Jones Project, taking high-altitude photographs for aerial mapping of the entire continent of Europe, to be conducted jointly with the British.

In June, new B-17s were brought in and stripped of gun turrets and other combat gear. Special cameras were installed for the photography, which was to be done at a constant altitude set at twenty thousand feet, covering a preset grid pattern. Like other gunners, Boyd was retrained and assigned to operating a camera.

Some of the countries they were going to be flying over were expected to view the photographic undertaking as the conduct of an unwanted occupying power and an impingement of their sovereignty. When the project began it was classified "top secret."

'Top Secret' Job?

To the B-Bag:
We of the 306th Bomb Group have been receiving clippings from home which have been cut out of some of America's most widely-circulated newspapers. The publicity contained in these clippings is roughly this: "The USAAF will occupy Europe an indefinite period, photographing and valley, to provide

As such things tend to be, the mandated secrecy foisted upon the boys was overdone and overwrought.

On Tuesday, July 3, 1945, a letter appeared in the *Stars and Stripes*:

We of the 306th Bomb Group have been receiving clippings from home which have been cut out of some of America's most widely-circulated newspapers. The publicity contained in these clippings is roughly this: "The USAAF will occupy Europe for an indefinite period, photographing every hill and valley, to provide a strategical map for invasion in the event of another war. This project is to be carried out by volunteer crews—former combat bomber crews."

Now, in the first place, we who are doing this work were given to understand that anything pertaining to the job was strictly top secret, and were given orders not to talk about it, not even among ourselves when not on duty.

In the second place, it is absolutely false in this respect: We as individuals, or as crews, definitely did not volunteer for the job. We are doing our job and acting under orders strictly.

In the last few weeks we have been doing our level best to console our families at home, our wives and sweethearts, by telling them that we have a job to do over here, which we cannot describe to them because it is top secret. We tell them we have no idea how long it will take, but, as we love them, they can rest assured we will return home just as soon as it is humanly possible to get the job done and do so.

Some of the folks at home have gotten the idea from these clippings that we are staying over here as long as possible merely to play around in London and Paris and have a gay old time. Many of the men have received rather cold letters from their wives which include these clippings, in which the words "volunteer crews" are underlined.

Signed by 84 Air corps officers and EMs.

* * *

Later in the summer the Casey Jones Project sent Boyd and some others to the Azores for several weeks. More orders came down from a distant command post that they were to behave on the ground as though they were in transit. No one in the Azores was fooled about what was going on, and the boys thought the orders were typically pinhead stupid. On the other hand, it was great fun to both ignore the order and to occasionally follow it in exaggerated ways. They had a lot of laughs as a result.

* * *

Short of going home, there was probably not a better way for Boyd to spend the summer of 1945. The weather had to be absolutely perfect for conducting a Casey Jones mission, something that was not a common occurrence. It made for a light work schedule. While the army was putting great energies toward the centralization of command and operations in Germany, being on the base at Thurleigh provided the pleasant sensation of being detached from much of the military regulation and discipline that so grated on Boyd and the others. It all seemed so very silly now that the war was over. They had a surprising freedom in what they did day to day, and they took every advantage of it.

Their photographic coverage responsibilities took them over western and southern Europe, all the way to Italy. Apart from the Casey Jones missions, they were able to get a lot of other flying time in, ferrying soldiers around the British Isles and to various locations on the Continent. Boyd became involved in an informal transit service, perhaps more accurately described as a black-market delivery operation. It turned out to be a lucrative venture, and he would carry home hidden on his person several thousand dollars in cash, more than his dad made in a year.

* * *

In hut number 19 on the Thurleigh air base, where Boyd and the other enlisted soldiers on the crew lived, that summer there developed a late-night tradition of each of the boys taking a turn at making a midnight snack for the others. It evolved into high ritual, the radio always set to the soft sounds of a particular music program coming out of Paris each night at eleven thirty.

Prepared with a flourish on the iron stove in the middle of the room, the fare served by each host would be on the order of buttered toast, a fried egg sandwich, or some items sent from home such as cheese, canned soup, popcorn, or sausage. The central culinary tenet was the use of as much butter as could be scoured up from the nearby countryside.

For young men in their early twenties, with a war behind them combined with a constant need to avoid seriousness, and an equal need to chow down whenever possible, the late-night sessions were close to ecstasy. Inevitably, one of the boys would lean back, hold up high whatever item was being eaten that night, and with a mouth full of food and a glop of melted something running down the chin make the official pronouncement:

"This . . . is better than sex." And they would all laugh.

* * *

Boyd was always captivated by every moment he ever spent up in an airplane. That summer he sent home a stream of enthusiastic descriptions:

> On those long trips we really live in the sky . . . we take along insulated containers & eat right up there when meal time comes.

On a Saturday afternoon in mid-July they had flown around the Swiss Alps:

> What beautiful country down there! . . . we had potatoes, peas, spinach, hamburger, bread, coffee, and pie way up at 20,000 ft. We ate our dinner while flying over Geneva Switzerland making it a full occasion.

Best of all, as he put it to Blossom:

> I flew the plane all the way back today. Pinchback usually always lets me fly back whenever I want.

* * *

The Casey Jones missions wound down as fall approached, and more boys were being sent home. By October, the weather had turned cold. A chill would arrive most late afternoons when the light was low in the sky, and the lengthening shadows gave the base a lonesome quality as it gradually emptied out for good.

After weeks of a frustrating wait, Boyd was tagged to get into the queue for heading back to the States, still hopeful of making his first Christmas at home since 1941. He went by train to Southampton and then crossed the channel by boat to Le Havre, exactly a week shy of one year after Brownie's arrival in France—unknowingly retracing the same steps

Brownie had taken. After spending the night just outside the port city, where Boyd was horrified by the destruction and human mess that was Le Havre, he moved on to a camp at an airfield near Perrone, north of Paris.

And there he waited. Encamped in the mud of France with no sign of when he would be departing, he turned bitter about not yet heading home. The moody November skies matched his frame of mind as he and a few others would take jaunts around France and into Belgium. Every place Boyd came upon presented only an ugly devastation along with a general ill-being that he just wanted to leave behind.

* * *

Eighty miles southeast of Boyd's late autumn encampment, near Reims, was an American quartermaster base where thousands of German prisoners of war had been organized into various companies responsible for salvage collection, construction, forestry, sanitation, maintenance, laundry, shoe and clothing repair, and railroad work. After the invasion of France, the constant need for American infantry troops was matched by a shortage of service troops to support the combat units. An emphasis had been placed on achieving 100 percent substitution of prisoner labor for that of American soldiers.

A major problem was furnishing guards. American soldiers were needed elsewhere. In France, small companies of "Polish Guards" were recruited from among displaced persons. They were given some training and deployed under the supervision of a handful of American servicemen. They were all issued a standard US Army uniform without designation of rank.

The American military jacket was not a crisp fit on Myroslaw.

He was one of the few from le BUK who somehow found a way to remain in France. He provided no explanation in later years. Hloba was another who stayed, and both ended up in Paris for a time.

* * *

Like millions on the Continent, it had been a long time since Myroslaw had any possessions. Of the greatest value were papers, always kept on one's person and carried everywhere. That fall he collected a few more documents, including a certificate of demobilization from the FFI dated October 2, 1945, signed by Guepratte as battalion commander. It was added to another certificate he received, signed by Bermont attesting that during Myroslaw's time with the FFI Haute-Saône, he was "particularly active in opposing the Germans" during attacks on a number of named villages, and that Myroslaw had "demonstrated great courage and a good example to his comrades."

The papers from the FFI were folded to fit into Myroslaw's pocket. When he was an ocean away from the war, the papers went into a drawer. They would not see the light of day again until after his death.

The sundry wartime papers of Boyd included lists of addresses, official documents, and keepsake slips of paper significant for reasons known only to him. Throughout his time in the service he sent home many photos. Some he had described in letters as deserving enlargement after the war, with a special few designated as worthy of being colorized. The entire collection of documents and photographs went into some shoe boxes and were put in the attic, next to Lylle's unfinished scrapbook of wartime clippings and his medals. All of it would await sorting after his death.

CHAPTER THIRTY-EIGHT

Immigration

Friday, January 4, 1946

P ASSING IN AND out of view behind huge dueling swirls of fog, the
famous skyline was bathed in the morning sun. It was a vision right
out of Boyd's schoolbooks, as was the scene of tugboats approaching their
ship through the mist hanging just above the water.

At ten thirty in the morning on January 4, 1946, Boyd was among
hundreds of boys standing shoulder to shoulder on the deck of a Liberty
ship, the SS *William Cushing*, as it sidled up to Pier 84. Boyd had made the
voyage with some fellows he knew from the Clay Pigeon squadron. One of
them had enough wits about him to take a picture just before the final
moment of arrival.

Boyd's turn to head home had come in mid-December. Departing
through what was left of the harbor at Le Havre, his voyage was slowed by
a stormy Atlantic, with great towering waves more than fifty feet high and
winds approaching hurricane force. He appreciated having familiar

company with him, although it was certainly a different Christmas, spent on the water for his fourth in a row away from home.

Boyd and the 583 other boys stepping onto American shores that Friday were among eight thousand GIs arriving in New York. Later that same day, ten thousand soldiers would enter San Francisco on nine ships, twelve thousand more in Los Angeles, and thousands of others in Portland, Tacoma, and San Diego. On the day before, thirty thousand boys had disembarked in New York, the crowd of vessels causing Boyd's troop ship to be held out at sea an extra day while eleven other transports docked after voyages from England, France, India, and Japan.

* * *

After almost two weeks at sea, there was the welcome sight of fresh newspapers. Each one confirmed that Boyd was entering a noisy land, a country of unrest and people simmering with a widespread willingness to disrupt against anything perceived as being foisted in their direction. From the front-page headlines alone, it seemed like everyone who had a job was in an uproar, with strikes imminent or already happening among meatpackers, Western Union employees, autoworkers, park department employees, and those in manufacturing plants making telephones and other electrical equipment.

Overseas the attitude had been no different, a palpable anger developing that fall among the several million boys not yet shipped home. As Boyd knew firsthand, the troop drawdown after the war had been a mess, operating on a point system that pleased few. Through the fall and into the new year there were demonstrations as well as riots involving tens of thousands of soldiers in Guam, Hawaii, Japan, France, Germany, Austria, India, and Korea. In England the week after his arrival home, five hundred American boys would confront Eleanor Roosevelt while she was in London for the first meeting of the United Nations General Assembly.

Whatever the desires of military leadership and the organizational problems that had combined to deliver the drawdown such as it was, they were met by a force carrying a broader theme, a loud and, at least in those days, very American reminder for all who cared to listen that those who served and fought were not warriors. The boys were hardly even soldiers. They were citizens who had finished their job. They wanted to get on with life, and to hell with someone's "occupation policy."

Some voices in Washington suggested that Communism was behind such unruliness among the boys.

* * *

After a few days at Camp Shanks in New Jersey, Boyd boarded an Erie Railroad train to Chicago. Before he did so, he grabbed several handfuls of travel brochures for places up and down the East Coast, from Maine all the way to Florida.

A week later, at Fort Sheridan in Illinois, Boyd was discharged from the Army. His separation papers, typed by a clerk, included a detailed description of his prewar civilian occupation as a "packer," where he "stenciled crates and helped shipping clerk prepare orders for shipment."

As he went through the discharge process, Boyd was recruited into signing up for a three-year commitment with the Army's enlisted reserve corps. He was given an official identification card, yet another clerk at a typewriter inserting Boyd's responses to questions, which included a description of his current occupation.

"Student."

* * *

On the Sunday after his first full week at home, Boyd was a featured speaker at his church, advertised as giving a brief talk during the Evangelical service about "some of his experiences as a bomber in the European theatre of war." That same afternoon, four blocks away, Ernst's Sunday rituals were set aside for a small celebration of Ann's first birthday.

Boyd was invited. And he went. It was his first encounter with Marie since the surprise reunion with Brownie. She would always remember how thoughtful Boyd was that day and that he brought a red-and-white-striped outfit as a gift for Ann.

* * *

At one time or another during the war, more than forty million people had been forcibly displaced. In 1945 there were seventeen million displaced persons in Germany alone, eight million of them forced laborers. Such figures do not include refugees and those otherwise displaced throughout the Continent by the war.

Out of such Old Testament squalor emerged a loosely organized system for sharing and processing information about those who were displaced. It was likely the very first time the world would see a working version of what decades later would be termed a "global distributed network." Makeshift and short-lived, getting every ounce out of what today would seem the crudest technologies, the enterprise was nothing less than a marvel of human effort by thousands who neither knew one another nor knew the particulars of what the others were doing.

During those days millions were searching for spouses, parents, children, and other relatives. Locator messages were everywhere across Europe, scratched with chalk or pencil onto any centrally located large wall, others more formally displayed on bulletin boards. Many were read out loud over the air on special radio broadcasts and were also printed in circulars published in the camps holding the displaced. From such messages, lists were developed that were then further circulated, not only on bulletin boards and broadcasts in Europe but in various media all over the world. There was no end to the ingenuous methods by which connections were achieved, and some of the accomplishments, in particular those involving children left behind by the war as refuse, were miraculous.

At a Toronto church in late 1945, someone at a wedding carried a folded-up newspaper over to a squat man with strikingly thick dark hair who had come from Ottawa to attend the ceremony. An immigrant to Canada two decades before, he was shown a list in the back pages of a newspaper, name after name of displaced persons. And he was asked about one of the names that appeared to be similar to his.

A few months later, on the other side of the Atlantic, a man with a physique much like the immigrant at the Toronto wedding noticed something on a bulletin board in France.

On the back side of a US military–issued card that identified him as a Polish Guard, a hand more inclined toward Cyrillic characters held a colored pencil with a dull point. Myroslaw made two attempts to scratch out the words "Duke Hotel."

In mid-March of 1946, Myroslaw's service with the US Army as a guard of German prisoners ended when, as officially recorded, he was discharged "on his own request." He remained in the area, having found work as a logger. Within a year he had obtained a French passport designating him as a stateless person and in the summer of 1947 was issued an immigrant visa for Canada before taking a series of flights through London, Ireland, Newfoundland, and Montreal.

* * *

Myroslaw made his way to Ottawa. On a September day he arrived at the intersection of Queen Street West and Duke Street, a bustling jumble of a neighborhood consisting of residences tossed together with shops, factories, rail-yards, and slums, all of it known as LeBreton Flats.

The sign on the window on the front of a tavern and boarding establishment said Duke House. Myroslaw walked in and for the first time in more than twenty years saw his brother Dmytro, known in that neighborhood as Dan.

* * *

Boyd's first weeks back home were off-putting. Both to him and to those around him. Things were fresh and stale at the same time, just like the town seemed too quiet and the people too noisy, both at the same time. Everything was unchanged, yet it all seemed so different.

He was in no hurry to start working, not with all that cash on hand. In late February he wrote to one of his crewmates about the dull life he was living, saying that he had not gotten drunk a single time since arriving back home. Others often described Boyd upon his return from the war as "distant" and "sour." As the weather got warmer, he would occasionally show up unannounced to help out at the farms of his uncles Reuben and Albert. He would work hard and not say much to anyone. And then after a few days he would be gone.

* * *

But it was altogether different being with Marie.

They already knew each other so well. She had her own stories to tell, her own feelings of being stifled. She had her own loss, one they shared. For his part, Boyd was always a good listener and good company.

By the summer they were seeing each other regularly. They avoided the ears and eyes around town by spending most of their first dates at the bowling alley in Juneau, a five-mile drive away. The place had four lanes, but they never once bowled a game. A short glass of beer was a dime, and forty cents would get them through an evening. They would sit in a booth, and they would talk.

When Marie got home at night her mother would always ask what they did on their date. The answer was always the same. "We talked. That's what we do."

They talked of what was. They talked of what had happened to them. They talked of life. And they began to talk of what might be.

"Which name should I use? Should I call you Herb? or Boyd?"

"I'd like you to call me Boyd."

The budding romance initially did not go over well with Boyd's mother. Lylle was not shy about expressing to others her discomfort over Boyd's involvement with a woman who, however nice and upstanding, not only had been married but also had a small child. Eye-rolling soon evolved into a loss of patience. It was up to Lylle's otherwise unfailingly gentle and sweet cousin, Nona, married to Herb's brother Reuben, to take her aside and set her into a different direction on the matter. And that was that.

* * *

Just before Labor Day of 1946, after spending another summer at home, Boyd's sister Blossom moved out again to start a new music teaching position, this time in Wisconsin, at a school in a small town south of Madison. During the first weekend of November, she went to visit the family in Illinois with whom she had lived during college. Initially feeling some discomfort in her chest, within twenty-four hours she was fighting for her life as the polio virus began to run its vicious course.

In the coming months, Lylle would take a room near the hospital, where she volunteered so she could spend more time with Blossom.

All of the cash Boyd had brought home went toward Blossom's care. It was gone within a matter of weeks.

Against very long odds, Blossom would fight death and survive, spending almost a full year in an iron lung. She would be left a quadriplegic, except for some slight movement of her left arm.

On a warm October Saturday in 1947, eleven months after she had been stricken, Blossom was placed into an ambulance for the drive from Illinois back to Wisconsin on winding roads cut from old Indian trails, Boyd and Marie following close behind in a separate car. They were met at the county line by an assortment of police vehicles from various localities. A convoy of flashing lights and blaring sirens escorted them the rest of the way to the hospital in Beaver Dam.

Six months later, an attending nurse in a hospital anteroom placed a phonograph needle onto a scratchy 78 rpm recording of Debussy's "Clair de Lune," the wedding music for Boyd and Marie. Blossom was maid of honor, positioned for the ceremony in a special wheelchair with the back down, her spine still a year of therapy away from being ready to bend into an upright position. Marie's brother George, who had begun working with Ernst at the corner dry goods store, stood alongside as best man.

The only other person present was the officiating minister.

* * *

Six weeks later, a twenty-four-year-old woman stepped off a ship that had just arrived at the Port of Halifax from Bremerhaven. Her long path to June 6, 1948, and that moment on a North American pier had been a nine-year odyssey, begun in Galicia when she was fifteen years old. The first six years were in close witness of three invasions, including a proximity to the horrific during the last year of the war, which she could never bring herself to speak rationally about. After a year living in the bombed-out wreckage that was postwar Bremen, she spent the next two years at a displaced persons camp in Aschaffenburg, Germany, just south of Frankfurt. Shortly after her arrival in Halifax, she was connected, through the Red Cross, to a posting for a housekeeping position in Ottawa. She boarded a train, landed the job, and began working for a doctor and his wife.

Maria's new course in life soon crossed that of Myroslaw. The following February they were married.

They both took classes in English, and within a few years they were citizens of Canada. Myroslaw worked for his brother at the Duke Hotel, sometimes tending bar but more often counted upon to keep order in the place, which in that roughneck neighborhood was a full-time position involving work with his hands. It took almost a decade, but Myroslaw and Maria managed to scrape together enough money to buy a house outside the flats, where they would raise their two sons and two daughters.

* * *

For Boyd, not much after the war turned out as he had expected.

He would never go to college. It would be several decades before he would travel outside of Wisconsin beyond either Iowa or Indiana. He would not have occasion to get up in an airplane for almost thirty years. He would never return to England.

Boyd and Marie had originally planned to move away so that he could use the GI Bill to get a degree and become a baseball or football coach. But they decided they should remain in town, mainly because of the obligation they felt not to move Ann away from Don's parents. It was a decision they would later regret, and they would infuse into their children the notion that their own futures were elsewhere.

After their second son was born, they moved in with Ernst, Marie following through on a promise she had made to her dying mother. The year before, Herb and Lylle had accepted an offer to move in with Buzzy, now a sixty-five-year-old retired school superintendent. They would pay a very modest rent in exchange for keeping the house clean and making the meals. The house had enough space for Blossom to have her own room on the first floor, and it was one block away from Marie and Boyd. Two blocks away lived Julius and Mother Brown.

And so things settled for several decades, Boyd and Marie's children growing up with three sets of grandparents as though it was a natural thing.

* * *

In the midst of a July hot spell in 1964, Boyd and Marie along with their three children and Ernst had just sat down to dinner in a sweltering kitchen, everyone on their respective mismatched chairs around the blue Formica tabletop. The telephone on the wall in the next room began to ring, and Boyd got up to answer it. The conversation was brief, and he was soon back in the kitchen.

"It looks like this is it. He wants me to come over and be with him."

Boyd went out the back door just off the kitchen. He got into the green station wagon parked on the gravel driveway and drove off to the hospital in Beaver Dam.

He sat with Julius through the night.

Together they watched Don's mother, and they waited. It was all over by morning.

* * *

Julius Brown had a matchless brand of hard-charging gusto and an uncanny ingenuity that was always in motion, building this, fixing that, and tinkering with the other thing. He thrived in the intricate gear-works of the self-contained small-town culture, which remained robust in the first decades after the war but was about to begin a long fatal slide, as it would without exception everywhere in the country.

A couple of years after the war's end, Julius knocked down the old two-story barn that stood behind his house, saving the lumber and using it to build, with his own hands, a cottage on the lake in Beaver Dam. He kept himself busy operating a farm outside of town, and eventually he would open up another meat locker and grocery store in a small crossroads village a few miles west of town, not yet having sold his summer sausage recipe. He fished and he hunted. In springtime he tapped trees for maple syrup.

Once a year he would come over to Marie and Boyd's and make his famous potato pancakes.

Julius let Boyd take over a good portion of the expansive garden acreage behind his house, and many tables in town enjoyed the output of beans, peas, cucumbers, squash, lettuce, onions, corn, potatoes, and various types of berries. Those who tagged along and attempted to help under the keen outdoor eyes of Julius or Boyd were given an initiation into the solace and salutary perspective on life provided through proper weeding technique and putting one's hands and knees into full contact with dirt.

Julius was in his sixties when he began working as an assistant to the local undertaker, retiring when he turned eighty. In his seventies, Julius again served as alderman of the third ward, this time avoiding physical scuffles with political rivals. In his later years he would finally give up deer hunting but still went along up north with the fellows to help out as cook. His hair never turned gray, although any mention of that would draw an immediate guffaw from Boyd about "shoe polish." Into his midnineties, Julius continued to make his own gadgets for rainwater irrigation of his tomato plants.

Few are able to live such a full and sturdy life. But one thing was always said about Julius, in the years right after the war, through the decades that followed, and even sixty-five years later by his daughter. He was never the same. The loss of Don was always just under the surface, a part of Julius no longer there.

CHAPTER THIRTY-NINE

Julius

Monday, February 24, 1997

A s BOYD KNEW so well, to a practiced eye the ever-changing light of each day transfigures and brings orientation, important to a firm grounding and a sense of place. Even the somber offerings of late winter's leaden skies can add a purplish depth and a clarity of line not otherwise perceived when gazing across flat farmland spreading out into the distance.

It was that type of February day. The overripe winter clouds hung low as Ann drove the familiar and numbingly straight road due west, to Beaver Dam and the hospital. She had visited Julius a few days before, but a call had come that afternoon.

Within hours of his appearance at the funeral home visitation for Boyd, Julius had come down with a full-blown cold. His condition deteriorated and two days later he was hospitalized. Now he had pneumonia, and he was slipping.

Marie's youngest son and Myroslaw's youngest daughter had already left the area, returning home out east. Ann, who lived in California, had stayed on to keep an eye on things for a few weeks.

Arriving at the hospital, she was told that Julius was no longer conscious. As she entered his room a minister finished up with whatever he had been doing and left.

Ann went over to Julius, spoke, and held his hand.

She felt a slight grip in return.

Over the next half hour, she sat, alone with him. His breathing gradually slowed down, and then it stopped.

Don's daughter, raised by Boyd, leaned over and gave her grandpa a kiss on the forehead.

Insignificant Mortals

It was a long, long war.

As with all the other nameless millions, it endured for the rest of Boyd's life. The Second World War was not just a divide in time, but an ongoing presence that framed the existence of each who lived through it, connecting itself to everything that followed.

Life in the aftermath was deliberately and even forcefully lived forward. But getting beyond the war's grasp would be impossible.

* * *

They are almost all now gone, those who came of age during those days of war.

Vanished, too, is the collective ethos that gave a distinct and purposeful shape to the course of postwar life in America and Europe. It was no accident that, for all its own very real struggles, fears, and violence, the second half of the twentieth century brought surcease from the ferocious traumas that during the first half of the century had ripped across entire Western societies: two global conflicts, epidemics worthy of medieval legend, a devastating economic depression, and state-directed mass killing of a magnitude that continues to elude understanding.

The decades-long intermission from such leviathan catastrophes, however wanting in perfection, was a historical oddity. It was not the result of grand geo-political strategies but a manifestation of the war's deep collective imprint on millions. On both sides of the Atlantic, the great ebb tide of the war's aftermath had a constant undertow toward stability as both a means and an end, even in the midst of an existential worldwide duel between the empires left standing and their spheres of influence. The terms of that contest required vast amounts of energy to be aimed toward an expansive notion of knowledge and well-being, at home and abroad, as the most integral elements of global security, a word not yet captured and narrowed for use in the locution of a cowardly belligerence.

* * *

More commonly than not, what each boy and girl had gone through in the war years remained hidden behind intensely private barriers, a posture difficult to comprehend in a later age given to self-branding as a virtue. As they have passed from the scene, there is now a void where there was once a broad understanding that what mattered coming out of the Second World War was what each had individually lost, not what all had won.

Those who held this basic truth collectively made up a great social force—understated and often unconsciously manifest, which made it no less powerful—and in Europe and North America it generated and sustained the character of the postwar era. Privation, not triumph, was the base ingredient in the robust primordial mix of expectations and especially the tensions of those first decades that yielded new institutions and understandings of governance, still with us today, however enfeebled.

* * *

Back home and out of uniform, Boyd was fortunate that he had served in a military willfully kept within the confines of the surrounding society, no matter how far removed from civilian life combat experiences turned out to be. He was a citizen who had served, never a soldier who was a citizen. His country would later soil itself by allowing and even encouraging a warrior culture to arise within a military that would become detached from the citizenry providing its remit. Such idolatry and tribal separation from broader society always helps to ease the way for smoother outlays of blood and treasure by those who would govern. Forgotten, though, is that the adoring construct of a warrior hero, as it has been since before the Bronze Age, is always a harsh and merciless sentence of isolation. For some who return from battle, it makes for an ornate entryway to a very private death row. The coming national torment about all of this has not yet arrived.

When asked in later years why he did not talk much about his own combat experiences in the war, Boyd's response always began "because everyone had it different, and there is always someone else who had it worse." The few times he briefly parted the curtain to reveal some of what had been seen and what had been done in those days, he did not use the word "combat." He had been in "battle," a place name and a much larger word about the human experience. Don had been in "battle." So had the next-door neighbor, seeing the worst of it at Ardennes but never talking about it.

Boyd would sometimes say, always in polite if vague terms, that it was not humanly possible for him to explain those moments of war. Left unsaid was the discomfort brought by speaking about such things, an almost visible flinch away from any question from someone who had not been "there" and would not be able to understand.

The very same was true of Myroslaw. As he framed out a life in happy Canada with Maria and the family they raised, his war was not reachable. Nor were the days of his youth, mired in a squalid bog of tribes given to the most base human behaviors from a prior millennium. His strict reticence was also demanded by the need to keep distant family members safe, out of the hands of eager Soviet authorities in the wretched land of his fathers. Myroslaw's health gave way at an early age.

In the eyes of a child, there was something frightening about the casual and outright cold reaction to death by Boyd and Marie and by Myroslaw and Maria. It did not matter whether a sudden passing came to a close friend or a relative succumbed to a long illness. Death brought little emotion. It was a part of life, just as the sun came up every morning.

Almost as chilling to those nearby was how neither Boyd nor Myroslaw ever evinced being afraid of anything. To observe such a phenomenon was to witness not an admirable display of bravado but a visible absence of something, as jarring as the sight of a missing limb. Both men confronted the sudden onset of their own end-of-life events with the same unbridgeable solitariness, a silent and bull-headed adjustment as though it did not matter if darkness was closing in or not. The war had allowed them, at an early age, the unwanted privilege of coming into contact with parts of themselves and elements of life that were far less pleasant to face than whatever would later come stalking.

There can be no doubt of the relationship between the final passing of so many who were so marked by what they saw and did, and the more recent outbreak of so many tinny voices peddling fear throughout

Western societies, often doing so, without shame, as a method for political advancement and pecuniary gain.

* * *

As Boyd's sons came of age there was still a military draft, along with ongoing American operations to degrade and ultimately destroy a vaguely defined threat across the Pacific. Boyd was no pacifist and, uncharacteristically, would show a blunt intolerance for such talk. He was also anti-communist, and had no quarrel with the domino theory. But as someone who had been "there," he was moved into certain actions by what he saw as a dishonorable casualness about waging war without an identifiable endpoint. What riled him most was observing that it was being undertaken only with the children of the unprivileged. He did his level best to make sure that his own were not among the chosen, even making attempts to call in personal chits with some on the local draft board.

* * *

Just as the end of the postwar era cannot be determined to be an exact moment, the death of a once-sovereign small town cannot be traced to a particular day, such as when the local weekly newspaper stopped publishing, when a new pair of shoes or an automobile could no longer be purchased within city limits, or when the top executive of the bank or factory no longer resided a few doors down from a mechanic, around the corner from a plumber, or across the street from a maintenance worker. Many nice people continue to live a good life in Horicon, Wisconsin, even if they have to drive elsewhere to buy groceries or come under pressure to merge their school system with that of another town. But the broad and dynamic peer-to-peer economic and cultural arrangements that were the pillars of a robust and self-contained Main Street life are now gone. As has happened across the country.

Explanations for the disappearance of such a thick strand of culture that was once a major portion of broader American society usually invoke efficiency and scale as inevitable forces of nature. They are too facile by half.

* * *

During the decades straddling the recent turn of the century, an unexpected government career in the field of international trade and economic diplomacy would provide endless hours in various Western capitals of governance: Washington, London, Paris, Brussels, and Geneva. Uncountable flights to the Continent would always include a final descent through the day's first upward rays of light and, without fail, bring to the son of a B-17 tail gunner a brief evocation of all that had led to that very point in time.

On the ground, the early years brought palpable encounters with ghosts from the Second World War. They appeared from time to time even after the Wall came down. Hallway conversations, sometimes in hesitant tones not always in full harmony with the orchestrated declarations of the negotiating table, offered personal understandings, narratives, and prejudices that more fully explained how and why things were. Each moment was a reminder that a vast and very human project of all nature of construction was still taking place. Something was being built. The work had begun decades before amid unimaginable devastation and ruin that was no longer visible but continued to have a lingering presence.

In later years, the once-discernible sense of purpose would fade in parallel with the emergence of a political gentry often inclined to confuse themselves with their appointed position. In each of the major capitals a certain scruffiness that once signaled an urban area teeming with ideas and discourse was replaced by the clean lines and banal architecture of new affluence. An acrid smog of monetization gone rampant seeped in, explained away or justified by most, at least by those apparently unaware or uncaring that positioning one's self within the comforts of its clammy overspread meant that stated beliefs and doctrines, whatever the subject and whatever the correctness, would no longer be taken seriously. The connection of the latter to the former, still not understood inside any of the capitals, would bring about one political disaster after another on both sides of the Atlantic, while also unwinding much of the fabric sewn in the war's aftermath.

The final years brought seniority, and with it, confirmation that there may not be a surer path to agnosticism than the unsought frequent exposure to the highest levels of governments and large businesses. A front-row seat was provided to displays of a well-ordered shrinkage in awareness of surroundings beyond the immediate, a preference to project rather than to see beyond one's self, part of an odd inability to cope with paradox.

In government, as in business, introspection is never a match for a smug oblivion to the long lines of context and the perception of others, both elements eagerly pushed aside by courtiers chanting their spells in the form of infantile calculations of value inevitably geared to optimization of the present.

* * *

The strong postwar current is no more.

The period that was a brief historical departure is now most certainly behind us. In the disjointed era that has followed we have been left with two Second World Wars.

One has become the object of veneration, reshaped and well-manicured over the years into a binary framework of correct and pleasing apportionments, devoid of nuance and capped by triumph. Great histories of that war abound, many stocked with an overabundance of research results, like the predictable interior of a big-box store arranged with a careful sterility into a savvy presentation that contrives the necessary grandeur and sweep. There are also specialty histories of that war, many tailored for a later narcissistic age and its desperate needs for starkly drawn heroes, villains, and myths. It is a war used by those devoted to establishing equivalencies, and by others equally devoted to scripting the exceptional, each in accordance with their own immediate aims and all of it quite beside the point.

There is another, strangely unfamiliar and distant Second World War, a complicated apocalyptic eruption and a most ungeometric conflict. Its numbers not only stupefy, they remain outside the range of meaning, like some ancient volcanic cataclysm so large it defies a mental image of its whole. For those who lived through it, life was an immersion in a staggering disaster, every day filled with ambiguities and absurd ironies in a complicated reality that was the antithesis of wishful latter-day projections of duty and leadership, and tidy notions of collaboration and resistance. The years have airbrushed away the preening mediocrity, and often much worse, of a detached Anglo-American generalship that like all human beings got most things wrong and a few things right. Also wiped clean was the bitter ambivalence of all those soldiers called to enter the physical inferno of that war, where there was little sweetness in battle to go along with the punishing aloneness of facing its deadly caprice.

Forgotten is the war's decades-long genesis within the blindness of privilege that does not recognize context beyond one's own, rendering the conflict inevitable by the early 1930s and widely acknowledged as such by the middle of the decade. Unadmitted is how much of that war's zeal was parochial, local squalls of hate acted out in countless areas across the Continent, each beset with their own depraved strife over the foreignness of others living alongside. What became the uncontrollable global reach of the war's obliterating darkness sprang from a prodigious human failure to resist primitive impulses toward group identities: "They" are this and "they" do that. "They" are not like us and "they" are a threat. Instead of enriching human life as adjectives and adverbs, the designations were allowed to metastasize into nouns and verbs in order to remove qualities of humanness and to provide self-validation through the threat of otherness. We now live in an age where polio and smallpox have been all but eliminated, while this far more deadly scourge has begun to flourish anew.

The Second World War is a disremembered war. It remains uncomprehended. And therefore it is still dangerous.

* * *

When Boyd set foot again on the land he had left only twelve months before, he was older at the age of twenty-three than most walking upright in the twenty-first century will ever be. Life's normal exposures and sequences had been hurled wildly askew. Like all the arriving boys, and like all those across the oceans who were displaced, stateless, or returning to a home, on that January day in 1946 he was as much an immigrant in a new and unknown world as his grandfather had been at the same age, landing in New York harbor on a similarly frosty morning in November of 1873. Little did Boyd know that the new world he and millions of others were entering, and together would deliberately construct, would not last much longer than his own lifetime.

His wartime story—like that of Myroslaw, Don, Marie, and Maria, or Lev Hloba, Simon Doillon, and Gilbert Decaudin—is remarkable only because of its ordinariness. There was nothing exceptional in the insidious theft of young life, and no uniqueness within the war's delivery of terror, drama, savagery, and death. They were not warriors. They were not heroes. They were not victims. They were not survivors. They just were.

The war of Boyd, and of the others, was not a good war.

The war just was.

AUTHOR'S NOTE

It had not even been twenty years since the war had ended. Memories were fresh, but held close by those whose gaze was still only forward. The three-letter word was never far from any overheard conversation, usually attached to "before," "during," or "since." For a boy of seven or eight, a day never went by without the war's presence being felt.

The questions always came easily, even when facing strangers. The answers did not. But the conversations never stopped and the habit of asking was never given up.

Three decades later a new spark was provided, quiet sideline chats about life and the war with negotiating partners from Asia to Europe, colleagues who had also become respected friends, particularly one in Moscow, whose father's wartime story deserves a wider audience.

A personal disdain for watching movies during long flights allowed for excessive periods of reading and thinking. But not until the last funeral was there the realization of a need to put it all down, for those who would follow.

* * *

Developing a book brings new and unexpected awakenings. For example, the past few years allowed witness to a startling deterioration in the function of a leading internet search engine, smarter and smarter algorithms yielding dumber and dumber answers, with a growing clutter of commercial surveillance detritus. Another unforeseen discovery, made while immersed in wartime newspapers, was how much understanding of culture and temperament was gained from the delivery of news accounts and how little could be gleaned from the commentary of wartime analysts, the hot takes and talking heads of those same days.

Conducting research in small towns from Wisconsin to Maryland yielded the conviction that every evening a toast should be raised all across the land to local librarians. As one long November day drew to a close at the public library in Beaver Dam, Wisconsin, the same person who had just given some steering toward Dodge County war-era materials stepped away to show someone in paint-streaked clothes how to use a computer to access an online job application. She then walked over to the front desk while providing commentary on certain English literature to an inquiring patron before she invited a developmentally challenged teenage boy to stand with her between two shelves, where for twenty minutes she gently steered him to certain books she thought he might enjoy exploring.

Much has quietly fallen into the lap of community libraries during the past two decades, unnoticed by those who have managed to separate themselves from public institutions. Particularly in small towns and rural areas, the libraries not only provide the increasingly rare dual sense of locality within a larger world, they are now almost alone in unashamedly infusing the notion—to anyone and everyone who comes through their doors—that a lifespan of formidable strength is achievable only through the continual development of an individual intellectual identity.

* * *

This book's tale of a disremembered war owes much to archival research provided by Frank Grelka in Germany, Veronica Langberg in France, and Rosalie Spire in London. Jean-Claude Grandhay, local historian of Haute-Saône, was also the source of useful information, including through his labor-of-love writings about the Vesoul region during the war. Ron Rose took some moments away from his longtime stewardship of the unique and marvelous LeRoy Meats of Horicon to share some of his expertise on meat processing and summer sausage. Tim Hoff of Hoff's Quality Meats in Brownsville, Wisconsin, did the same.

In Washington, DC, the research staff of the United States Holocaust Memorial Museum could not have been more helpful. The Ukrainian Canadian Research and Documentation Centre in Toronto provided access to the personal wartime papers of Lev Hloba found after his death. The staff of the *Beaver Dam Daily Citizen* newspaper was most kind in allowing a stranger off the street to search through their morgue for issues not available on microfilm.

A great deal of material was gathered during numerous visits to the National Archives and Records Administration outside of Washington, DC, in College Park, Maryland, years of immersion into the well-thumbed files contained in the facility's military record groups. Conducting research at NARA was anything but uplifting. Each and every visit provided a painful if familiar exposure to yet another emblem of the decades-long functional consensus in Washington regarding public works. Visibly underfunded and served by a harried staff, the national institution dedicated to the documentation of America's very being presented an operational ambiance stuck somewhere in the late 1970s—except for the coarse theatrics now commonplace in public facilities under the name of "security." Perhaps things have improved since 2013.

Any mistakes in the accounts set out in this book are attributable only to the author.

* * *

Finally, after all the conversations, with all the research and writing, and no matter all the hours of contemplation, this chronicle would never have come into existence without a loving sister, child of Don and raised by Boyd.

As for Boyd's youngest son, life could never have offered any greater fortune than to be married to Myroslaw's youngest daughter, to whom this book is dedicated.

Matthew Brown Rohde

January 5, 2017
Uniontown, Maryland
USA

NOTES

Page

xi   **Death and the Strong Force of Fate Are Waiting:** "And look, you see how handsome and powerful I am? The son of a great man, the mother who gave me life a deathless goddess. But even for me, I tell you, death and the strong force of fate are waiting. There will come a dawn or sunset or high noon when a man will take my life in battle too." Robert Fagles, trans., *The Iliad* (New York: Penguin, 1998), 523–524.

7   **A few of their high school classmates suspected:** Letter to author and siblings, November 2004. The reference to Boyd was unsolicited, the letter being written after Don, Boyd, and Marie had passed away.

8   **Twelve miles to the west was Beaver Dam:** *The Federal Writers' Project Guide to 1930s Wisconsin* (Saint Paul: Minnesota Historical Society Press, 2006; originally published by Duell, Sloan, and Pearce, 1941), 372.

8   **That week's edition included items:** *Horicon Reporter*, August 31, 1939.

10   **In 1939 he would earn eight hundred dollars:** 1940 US census records include information on wages paid. US Department of Commerce, Bureau of the Census, *Sixteenth Census of the United States, 1940, State of Wisconsin, Dodge County* (Washington, DC, made publicly available April 2012); Faith Meyer, *The History of the John Deere Horicon Works, 1861–1986* (Fond du Lac, WI: Action Printing, 1986), 25–26.

10   **At the larger factory the men earned:** Grain drills were made at the larger factory, which the townspeople referred to only as "Van Brunt" but was owned by John Deere. In 1911 the Deere company had bought the operations from the Van Brunt family that had started the business in the late nineteenth century. Nothing significant changed in operation after the purchase, the local company continuing its corporate existence. The plant would not get its first nonlocal manager until 1940, and would only change its name to "John Deere Van Brunt" in 1947. Walter Bussewitz and Allie Freeman, *History of Horicon* (Horicon, WI: Horicon Wisconsin Rotary Club and Chamber of Commerce, 1948), 79. In 1958 the name of the factory would change to "John Deere Horicon Works" when Deere & Company altered its corporate structure by merging with three of its wholly owned subsidiaries, including John Deere Van Brunt. Meyer, *History of John Deere Horicon Works*, 39. Not until the mid-1960s would the moniker "Deere" take hold over the use of "Van Brunt" as the preferred name when referring to the place where many people in town worked. In the twenty-first century, more than a thousand people are employed at a newer plant known for its production of lawn and garden tractors, located just outside the town's western city limits.

10   **As foreman, Julius made twice what Herb earned:** US Department of

Commerce, Bureau of the Census, *Sixteenth Census of the United States, 1940, State of Wisconsin, Dodge County* (Washington, DC.).

10   **Buzzy's salary that year was thirty-one hundred dollars:** Ibid.

11   **During the two years it took to construct the new building:** In 1948 the school superintendent from 1917 to 1947 wrote, "Of late years some church organizations have expressed surprise at the quick willingness of the school authorities to lend them dishes and equipment at any time the request is made. They might have forgotten, but the school had not, the kindness shown in the school's emergency." Bussewitz and Freeman, *History of Horicon*, 46.

11   **The town went ahead and set up its own telephone company:** Ibid., 88. The local phone company was sold to the Wisconsin Telephone Company fifteen years later.

11   **It had been only six years:** "Hope to Ease Bank Holiday Soon; 14-Day Suspension Ordered by State," *Milwaukee Journal*, March 3, 1933, 1. On the following day, a Saturday, Franklin Roosevelt was inaugurated to his first term, and on Monday all banks in the country were ordered closed.

11   **A plan emerged to circulate scrip:** Bussewitz and Freeman, *History of Horicon*, 88; *Horicon Reporter*, March 9, 1933. The Wilcox brothers were the sons of the founding family of the large factory in town.

12   **The plan would allow for food and other necessities:** Thirty thousand dollars of scrip was issued, in denominations of twenty, ten, and five dollars, one dollar, and twenty-five cents. All but $18.50 was ultimately redeemed. Collection of papers, Horicon Historical Society, 1979 (author likely to be local historian Wilton Erdman).

12   **For farmers, including Boyd's dad:** In 1920 alone, crop prices fell 40 percent between spring planting and fall harvest, and the agricultural trade balance turned negative in 1923. The postwar collapse in prices and income meant that farm debts became unserviceable, even while the rest of the US economy during the decade remained prosperous. David Orden, Robert Paarlberg, and Terry Roe, *Policy Reform in American Agriculture: Analysis and Prognosis* (Chicago: University of Chicago Press, 1999), 13–16.

12   **Employment at the larger factory:** Meyer, *History of John Deere Horicon Works*, 26.

12   **Throughout the 1930s, the size of the high school graduating classes kept shrinking:** The invitation mailed out for the thirtieth reunion of the class of 1938 was produced on heavy bond paper with formal embossed printing and conveyed its message in polite, if unusual, terms: "You are cordially invited to attend a reunion of all persons who were members of the Horicon High School Freshman Class of 1935, Sophomores of 1936, Juniors of 1937, and the Seniors of 1938." Author's personal collection.

12   **starting in 1936 and for each year that followed:** From 1936 to 1940, the value of the WPA sewer construction projects exceeded $100,000. The 1936 sewer project employed twenty-six; the 1938 project employed ninety-four. There were

also projects directed toward sidewalk construction and building tennis courts. Overall in Wisconsin, between 1935 and 1943, the WPA employed 43,000 people per year, creating 22,889 miles of roads, erecting 1,456 new buildings, and laying 1,588 miles of water pipes and sewers. Seventeen airports were built, 504 dams were constructed, and 63 million trees were planted. "Works Projects Administration, WPA Project Cards, Dodge County Wisconsin," Wisconsin Historical Society, http://content.wisconsinhistory.org/cdm/ref/collection/tp/id/78004. The Historical Society online citation assigns an incorrect name to what should be the "Works Progress Administration."

16 **Unrefined, as it surely was:** Greater eloquence about the now-lost American small-town culture of those days can be found in the 1946 wartime memoir of CBS news broadcaster Eric Sevareid, one of "Murrow's Boys." Describing his own hometown of Velva, North Dakota, he wrote: "Later, I read all the exalting literature of the great struggle for a classless society; later, I watched at first hand its manifestations in several countries. It occurred to me then that what men wanted was Velva, on a national, on a world, scale. For the thing was already achieved, in miniature, out there, in a thousand miniatures scattered along the rivers and highways of all the West and Middle West. I was to hear the intelligentsia of eastern America, of England and France, speak often of our Middle West with a certain contempt, with a joke in their minds. They condemned its tightness, its dullness, its bedrock of intolerance. They have much to learn, these gentlemen." Eric Sevareid, *Not So Wild a Dream* (Columbia, MO: University of Missouri Press, 1995; first published 1946 by Knopf), 7–8.

22 **The epic storms of violence:** Orest Subtelny, *Ukraine: A History*, 3rd ed. (Toronto: University of Toronto Press, 2005), 56–65, 176.

23 **Like his forebears, a national identity was not a part of Myroslaw's life:** However strange and even impossible it may seem to a twenty-first-century mindset, Myroslaw's lack of national consciousness was not uncommon in Galicia. Paul Robert Magocsi, "Galicia: A European Land," in *Galicia: A Multicultured Land*, ed. Christopher Hann and Paul Robert Magocsi (Toronto: University of Toronto Press, 2005), 13–15; Timothy Snyder, *The Reconstruction of Nations* (New Haven: Yale University Press, 2003), 152–153.

23 **a lingering remnant of a feudal past:** Galician peasants had been granted personal freedom by an imperial decree issued in 1848, which allowed ownership of land. It did not bring improvement in their lives. For most, it meant new tax burdens and also opened up avenues for exploitation, financial and otherwise, of the uneducated and already impoverished peasants. By the turn of the century, 80 percent of the peasant farms were less than five acres in size. Keely Stauter-Halsted, *The Nation in the Village: The Genesis of Peasant National Identity in Austrian Poland, 1848–1914* (Ithaca, NY: Cornell University Press, 2004), 21–22.

23 **Emigrants had to pass through Oświęcim:** Norman Davies, *Vanished Kingdoms* (New York: Viking, 2011), 458; Timothy Snyder, "A Core of European Tragedy, Diversity, Fantasy," *New York Review of Books*, November 10, 2011.

24   The arrival of the Depression during the same year put an end to immigration opportunities: Samuel L. Sharp, *Poland: White Eagle on a Red Field* (Cambridge, MA: Harvard University Press, 1953), 98.

24   The bishops of the Metropolia of Kievan Rus' had come forward: Subtelny, *Ukraine*, 99–101.

25   The countryside had few industrial sights or sounds: In the years after the Great War, the percentage of people in all of Poland who were dependent on agriculture was the same as in late-seventeenth-century England, about seventy percent. The percentage within Galicia would have been much higher. The peasants were without any significant political strength, even before taking into account additional constraints on behavior presented by the government's view of their ethnic or "racial" status. Sharp, *Poland*, 83.

25   The censuses of the day were tainted by agendas: Joseph Rothschild, *East Central Europe Between the Two World Wars* (Seattle: University of Washington Press, 1974), 35–37. Polish authorities aimed to minimize the numbers of those who did not consider themselves "Poles," and the potential variances were not insignificant. In 1931, Polish scholars estimated that 4.8 million Ukrainians were living in Poland while some Ukrainians suggested a number closer to 6 or 7 million. Sharp, *Poland*, 86.

25   The landholdings of peasants in Eastern Galicia were small: Almost 20 percent of the eastern Galicia's peasants held no land, and more than three-quarters of those who did farmed plots of fewer than two hectares. David R. Marples, "The Ukrainians in Eastern Poland under Soviet Occupation, 1939–41: A Study in Soviet Rural Policy," in *The Soviet Takeover of the Polish Eastern Provinces, 1939–1941*, ed. Keith Sword (London: Macmillan, 1991), 240–241; Sharp, *Poland*, 102.

25   The Great Depression had dealt the area a heavy blow: Subtelny, *Ukraine*, 429–430.

26   The region had a significant population of Jews: Rothschild, *East Central Europe*, 38–41; Rachel Manekin, "Galicia," *YIVO Encyclopedia of Jews in Eastern Europe*, 2010, http://www.yivoencyclopedia.org/article.aspx/Galicia; Samuel Kassow, "Shtetl," *YIVO Encyclopedia of Jews in Eastern Europe*, 2010, http://www.yivoencyclopedia.org/article.aspx/Shtetl; Volodymyr Kubijovyc, *Memoranda of the Sevcenko Scientific Society; Ethnic Groups of the South-Western Ukraine: Halycyna–Galicia Vol 1 1939, Ethnographic Map of South-Western Ukraine* (London: Association of Ukrainian Former Combatants in Great Britain, 1953), 1–6; Snyder, *The Reconstruction of Nations*, 133–137.

26   They wore black: A young American woman who in those prewar days lived among a similarly intractable unconnected mix of Jews, Hungarians, Poles, Czechs, and Ruthenians in a region not far from Myroslaw, off to the south at the edge of the Carpathians, observed in her 1946 memoir, "They did not look at all like the Jews of Western Europe or America, who often cannot be distinguished from the rest of the population. These were so different as to be almost alarming. . . . But the really noticeable thing about them was that they looked so urban." Eleanor Perényi, *More Was Lost* (New York: New York Review Books, 2016; originally published by Little, Brown and Company, 1946), 87.

26 **To the Ukrainians, *chuzhi*:** Andrew Wilson, *The Ukrainians: Unexpected Nation*, 3rd ed. (New Haven: Yale University Press, 2009), 125.

26 **To the north of Myroslaw's village:** During the postwar Soviet era the city was known as Lwów. Today it is known as Lviv.

26 **Around the time Myroslaw's parents were coming of age:** The 1911 Baedeker portrayal of Galicia, which it described as "the N.E. province of Austria," does not use the word Ukrainian: "[Galicia's] total population is about 8,022,000, including over 4,000,000 Poles (in the W. Part of the province), 3,000,000 Ruthenians (Little Russians; to the E.), 800,000 Jews, and 200,000 Germans. The Poles are Roman Catholics, the Ruthenians belong to the United Greek Church. Polish is the official and the school language." Karl Baedeker, *Austria-Hungary: Handbook for Travellers* (Leipzig: Karl Baedeker, 1911), 370.

27 **The old term *Rusyn* (Ruthenian):** Subtelny, *Ukraine*, 307. Wilson, *The Ukrainians*, 110.

27 **but the Ukrainian culture of Galicia:** Yaroslav Hyrtsak, "Historical Memory and Regional Identity," in *Galicia: A Multicultured Land*, ed. Christopher Hann and Paul Robert Magocsi (Toronto: University of Toronto Press, 2005), 96–198. Wilson, *The Ukrainians*, 109. Subtelny, *Ukraine*, 219–220, 307.

27 **one in five marriages during that time:** Bohdan Budurowycz, "The Greek Catholic Church in Galicia, 1914–1944," *Harvard Ukrainian Studies* 26 (2002–2003): 332–334.

27 **The earthly authorities offered by the Habsburgs:** Ibid, 332–333.

28 **A further complication:** Magocsi, "Galicia: A European Land," 19n16.

28 **A few years after Myroslaw was born:** The requirement entered into effect in August of 1925, pursuant to *Inter Sanctam Sedem et Poloniae Rempublicam Sollemnia Conventio, Acta Apostolicae Sedis*, vol. XVII, no. 8 (June 2, 1925), article VIII. Andrew Dennis Sorokowski, "The Greek Catholic Parish Clergy in Galicia, 1900–1939" (PhD diss., University of London, School of Slavonic and East European Studies, 1991), 200n664.

28 **As the Great War was ending:** The four empires that expired were the Habsburg, Ottoman, and, for a few years until they both soon returned in different forms, those of the Germans and the Russians.

28 **No decision came from Paris:** Margaret MacMillan, *Paris 1919: Six Months That Changed the World* (New York: Random House, 2002), 225–228.

28 **But throughout Galicia, its actions operated:** Snyder, *The Reconstruction of Nations*, 150–153.

29 **a violent and bizarrely spiritual intolerance:** Perhaps understandably, if also with an unappreciated irony, those extremists pressing for a Ukrainian national identity used language that managed to join Wagnerian phrasing with the lyricism of a Soviet tract. One ideologue of the time even asserted a "national Eros." Wilson, *The Ukrainians*, 129–131.

29   **organized ten years before:** The OUN was founded in 1929 in Vienna mainly by veterans of the brief 1919 clash with Polish forces. Snyder, *The Reconstruction of Nations*, 143.

30   **Its founding manifesto stated that the OUN:** "Resolutions of the First Congress of the Organization of Ukrainian Nationalists, 29 January–2 February 1929," in *Ukraine during World War II: History and Its Aftermath*, ed. Yury Boshyk (Edmonton: Canadian Institute of Ukrainian Studies, University of Alberta, 1986), 170–172.

30   **that was an occupying force:** During the 1930s, up to 80 percent of those considered to be the Ukrainian intelligentsia were killed or disappeared or were sent to the camps. Wilson, *The Ukrainians*, 146. Snyder, *The Reconstruction of Nations*, 142.

30   **Little of the fervor of extremist Ukrainian nationalism:** "There was no natural fit between the ideology of expatriate war veterans and frustrated intellectuals and the concerns of the 95 percent of Ukrainian-speakers in Poland who worked the land." Snyder, *The Reconstruction of Nations*, 152.

32   **within only twenty-five miles:** Frank Golczewski, "Shades of Grey," in *The Shoah in Ukraine*, ed. Ray Brandon and Wendy Lower (Bloomington, IN: Indiana University Press, 2008), 137.

35   **A "waiting war" it was called by some:** "Is It a War? Berlin Yawns; Even Hitler Is Bored Over 'No Shooting' Conflict, Leading Nazi Declares," *Milwaukee Journal*, November 5, 1939, 1.

35   **King Leopold of Belgium and Queen Wilhelmina of the Netherlands offered:** "Move For Peace Praised By Pope," *Milwaukee Journal*, November 11, 1939, 1.

36   **Twenty-four high schools from two counties:** Nine of the twenty-four high school bands at the festival were from towns with a population of fewer than a thousand people.

37   **He began with grave words:** Franklin D. Roosevelt, "On National Defense," May 26, 1940, radio broadcast, transcript, Franklin D. Roosevelt Presidential Library and Museum, http://docs.fdrlibrary.marist.edu/052640.html.

41   **Media Vita in Morte Sumus:** "In the midst of life we are in death." The phrase is the title and first line of a Latin antiphon that likely predated the tenth century. One famed translation and adaptation into a hymn was done by Martin Luther ("Though in the midst of life we be, snares of death surround us"), and another translation was done for inclusion in the Book of Common Prayer, by Thomas Cranmer, the Archbishop of Canterbury, who was later burned at the stake for heresy in 1556 on the order of Queen Mary.

42   **the unmatched centrality of the Second World War:** An almost delusional orientation of the Second World War has been fostered by fashionable histories portraying the conflict primarily in terms of what took place in the western half of the Continent, which, for all its own destruction, blood, and valor, was never anything more than an appendix to the Ostfront. Seven decades have passed and little remains known about the latter, while even less is understood—in part for want of trying and in part because of deliberate secrecy in the east about the conduct of war, something that in more recent years has come to be fully embraced by governments in the west, including the promulgation of "secret law" despite the resulting fundamental alteration in the nature of the government's relationship with the governed.

44 **For Ukrainians, what had started as a recruitment:** After the Germans entered Galicia, Myroslaw's future wife, sixteen-year-old Maria, moved to Lwów to live with her sister, hoping to learn the German language and find an opportunity that would allow her to permanently leave behind the impoverished countryside. Early in 1942 she would answer Hitler's call for a half million Ukrainian women to come and serve the women of the German "race" as household laborers. By midsummer she was on her way north to Kolberg, on the Baltic coast (today Kołobrzeg, Poland), assigned to care for the family of a German military physician.

44 **The Germans would see to it:** The ironies continually spat out by the war included death sentences from the SS and police authorities in Galicia for being a member of the OUN and for sheltering Jews. Pronouncements of carrying executions for both deeds would appear on the same posted public proclamation. Image of poster from January 21, 1944, in Boshyk, *Ukraine during World War II*, 79.

45 **A broad spectrum:** Wendy Lower, "Täterforschung im globalen Kontext," (paper presented at Local Participation in the Crimes of the Holocaust in Ukraine: Forms and Consequences, Bundeszentrale für politsiche Bildung, Berlin, January 27–29, 2009), 9–10, http://www.bpb.de/veranstaltungen/dokumentation /127465/perpetrator-research-in-a-global-context-taeterforschung-im-globalen-kontext.

46 ***Respice humilitatem nostrum:*** "Be mindful of our lowliness." The words are from perhaps the most well-known work of composer Thomas Tallis. *Spem in alium* is a sixteenth-century motet and a sonic wonder delivered by forty voices, each with its own separate part. The text was taken and adapted from the ancient Book of Judith, which has varying degrees of biblical acceptance among faiths.

Spem in alium numquam habui praeter in te,
Deus Israel
qui irasceris
et propitius eris,
et omnia peccata hominum in tribulatione dimittis.
Domine Deus
Creator coeli et terrae,
respice humilitatem nostram.

(I have never put my hope in any other but in you,
O God of Israel
who can show both anger
and graciousness,
and who absolves all the sins of suffering man.
Lord God,
Creator of Heaven and Earth,
be mindful of our lowliness.)

50   **Closer to home, on the previous Friday:** John MacCormac, "Butter Is 'Frozen'; President Plans a Food Chief Step; 40% of All Butter in Storage Is Set Aside for Forces and Lend-Lease Compacts," *New York Times*, November 21, 1942, 1.

50   **Two days before Thanksgiving:** By then, the butter situation barely warranted an inch of space in the *New York Times*, deep within the paper. "Butter Rationing Begins Unofficially in Stores," *New York Times*, November 24, 1942, 21.

56   **obligatory mention of the hot weather:** While going through basic training at Camp Chaffee, Boyd was in the 14th Armored Division and active in all the sports programs that were offered. As spring was turning to summer he wrote home: "The fellows in the Co. always call me 'that rugged man from Green Bay.' They connect Wis. and me with Green Bay because they've all heard about the Packers and because I happen to play football well they connect me with Green Bay." Boyd, letter to parents, May 23, 1943. During that summer, Boyd played the outfield and third base for the 62nd Armored Infantry Battalion baseball team, thrilled to be on a roster that also included several minor leaguers. It was always a special moment for Boyd when a jeep would be sent out to retrieve him from field maneuvers when a big game was to be played, including against various all-star teams that sometimes featured major leaguers like Warren Spahn. During this time he played his first baseball game at night, under lights.

61   **Introduction to the notes for chapters 8 through 25:** These chapters include the tale of a little-known wartime event that took place in remote eastern France and is drawn from a scant overall record that has faded. The main sources exist within broader personal accounts about the war left behind by some of the participants who were French (Jean Reuchet, Pierre Bertin, and Gilbert Decaudin), Ukrainian (Lev Hloba), British (George Millar), and American (Waller Booth, Michael Burke, and Walter Kuzmuk). There is a broad commonality across the French sources and the narrative recorded for the French by Hloba in early 1945, although each perspective differed, as did memories.

Care was taken to combine and bring the accounts into alignment, with a bias toward the most contemporary and firsthand sources as much as possible. Judgments on the reliability of descriptions were sometimes required. The time frames suggested by some accounts would not have allowed events to take place as they did, in accordance with what is otherwise broadly established. The same is true with regard to the varied accounts about the formation of the Ukrainian battalion. The endnotes that follow occasionally point out some of the differences between sources. No fictional characters, thoughts, or actions have been added. Nonetheless, all tales of war are imperfect, and the resulting chronicle of le BUK is no different.

SOE and OSS records contemporary to the period were also used. The colorful memoirs of two former OSS operatives, Waller Booth and Mike Burke, contain numerous verifiable errors concerning the mutiny of the Ukrainians, very much out of synch with the French accounts that largely comport with each other. Such a conclusion is not intended to demean either Booth or Burke. The mutiny had taken place before they arrived in France. The descriptions in their respective memoirs are based on a thirty-year-old memory of secondhand accounts given to them after their parachute drop into France. In the preface to his book, which preceded Burke's, Booth acknowledges that he had no notes to work from, and "as a consequence, it is very possible that a reader who was involved in, or associated with, some of the occurrences related may find inaccuracies." He also writes, "Further, there are deliberate discrepancies. I have substituted fictitious names when memory failed, occasionally attributed to one person acts of several and described scenes I did not witness, incorporating imaginary dialogue where I thought it was required." *Mission Marcel Proust* (Philadelphia: Dorrance, 1972).

In August and September of 1944 events were moving very fast in eastern France. There is reason to believe, from the broader record concerning those weeks, that Booth and Burke were likely told a version of the mutiny by members of the local maquis who did not actually participate in it, and who were not averse to embellishing things about themselves to suggest their connection to the resistance deeds of others. This was not an uncommon occurrence anywhere in France during the late summer and early fall of 1944.

61   **Sitting in the brush on the side of the road:** Jean Vartier, *Histoires Secrètes de l'occupation en zone interdite (1940–1944)* (Paris: Hachette, 1972), 223–224; Jean-Claude Grandhay, *Vesoul: 12 Septembre 1944,* (Vesoul, France: Imprimerie Marcel Bon, 1994), 16–17.

61   **Gilbert had turned twenty:** "Adieux a angirey pour le resistant Gilbert Decaudin" (obituary), *L'Est Républicain*, August 21, 2011, www.estrepublicain.fr /haute-saone/2011/08/22/adieux-a-angirey-pour-le-resistant-gilbert-decaudin.

61   **labor regime known as the STO:** Julian Jackson, *The Dark Years* (New York: Oxford University Press, 2001), 228, 529.

61   **After managing to escape:** In mid-July a London radio broadcast had incited a large Bastille Day display of French flags, and a few days later the Germans had responded with a roundup. Jean Reuchet, *Le Desarroi, le souffrance, l'espoir "vecu" par les combattants de la resistance de Haute-Saône* (France: Edition Crimee, 1996), 161.

61   **They both knew a few rudiments:** Vartier, *Histoires Secrètes*, 223–224.

61   **Their job was to be on the lookout:** Ibid.

62   **The peasants in the area continued to cultivate:** George Millar, *Maquis: The French Resistance at War* (London: Cassell, 2003, originally published in 1945 by William Heinemann, with an American edition published under the title *Waiting in the Night*), 144.

62   **On the morning of the Allied invasion in June:** Jean Vartier, "Des Russes Dans Le Maquis Francais," *Les Ecrivains Contemporains*, Octobre–Novembre 1973, 5.

62   **It was the signal for recognition:** Vartier, *Histoires Secrètes*, 219.

62   **Out stepped Simon Doillon:** Ibid., 224.

62   **The minimum age for STO participation had been lowered in February:** Jackson, *The Dark Years*, 530.

62   **Some in the area still took their chances:** Millar, *Maquis*, 307–308.

63   **The two could not have been more different in appearance and background:** Booth, *Mission Marcel*, 34.

63   **He was solidly built:** Michael Burke, *Outrageous Good Fortune* (New York: Little, Brown and Company, 1984), 42.

63   **Simon had a lithe build:** Ibid., 27.

63   **The family heritage and Simon's "patriotic heredity":** Pierre Bertin, *Resistance en Haute-Saône* (France: D. Gueniot, 1990), 217; Vartier, *Histoire Secrètes*, 231.

63   **After lunch, Gilbert was just settling back:** Vartier, *Histoire Secrètes*, 224–225.

64   **Ignoring them, Robert Decaudin rushed ahead, yelling:** Mirabeau was recaptured and treated by the Germans for three gunshot wounds. He survived the war and became an engineer. Ibid.

65   **As the minutes passed:** Ibid., 225–227.

65   **Gilbert was told:** Ibid., 223.

66   **Consequent to a Time of War:** "Whatsoever therefore is consequent to a time of war, where every man is enemy to every man, the same is consequent to the time wherein men live without other security than what their own strength and their own invention shall furnish them withal." Thomas Hobbes, *Leviathan* (Project Gutenberg, 2009; originally published 1651), chap. 23, "Of the Natural Condition of Mankind, as Concerning Their Felicity, and Misery," https://www.gutenberg.org/files/3207/3207-h/3207-h.htm.

66   **Most of the soldiers tightly packed:** Lev Hloba narrative, April–May 1945, pp. 2–4, Archives, Département Haute-Saône, Vesoul, France. In a 1984 magazine article written six years before the publication of his own memoir, Pierre Bertin, aka "Bermont," described the Hloba account as sincere but as having a tendency to magnify the role of the unit and the losses inflicted on the enemy. Pierre Bertin, "Les Comtois de 1944 vus par les Ukraniens," *Le Jura Francais*, Juillet–Septembre 1984, 12.

67   **By the mid-1930s, Haute-Saône's population:** Pierre Bertin, *Resistance en Haute-Saône* (France: D. Gueniot, 1990), 13.

68   **With almost half of the land forested:** Jean-Claude Grandhay, "Les Maquis Haut-Saônois dans leur Environnement Social," in *Lutte Armee et Maquis: La Resistance et les Francais*, ed. Francois Marcot (Besançon et Paris: Annales littéraires de l'Université de Franche-Comté, 1996; published collection pertaining to a symposium in Besancon, June 15–17, 1995), 279.

68   **Also disembarking is the unit's German command:** Rolf Michaelis, *Russians in the Waffen-SS* (Atglen, PA: Schiffer, 2009), 67.

68   **He sends an alert around:** Bertin, *Resistance en Haute-Saône*, 217. Vartier, "Des Russes," 5.

68   **The unit arriving in Vesoul:** Michaelis, *Russians*, 60–65.

68   **collected into a camp in East Prussia:** What was once known as Deutsche Eylau in East Prussia is, in the twenty-first century, a part of Poland known as Iława.

68   **military training had begun in early February:** Hloba narrative, 2–3.

68   **By July the Ukrainians had been gathered:** Antonio J. Munoz, *Forgotten Legions: Obscure Combat Formations of the Waffen-SS* (New York: Axis Europa, 1991), 259–261. Michaelis, *Russians*, 60. Hans-Joachim Neufeldt, Jurgen Huck, and Georg Tessin, *Zur Geschichte der Ornungspolizei, 1936–1945* (Koblenz, Germany: 1957), 63.

69   **made up about a third:** John Pecaroni, Captain, US Infantry, *PW Report # 3, September 11, 1944*. The report concerns interviews of captured prisoners that included 1 "Russian officer," 28 "Germans," and 158 "Russians" from a later-arriving regiment of the 30th Waffen-SS Division: "PW's state that 30 Div was formed in W PRUSSIA (POLAND) on approx. 26 July from a cadre of policemen (approx. 20 for each Co.) and the rest conscripted Poles and Russians." Ibid. Pecaroni noted that each company was said to be 150 strong.

69   **The regiment consisting of Myroslaw's Ukrainian battalion and two other battalions:** Claude Paillat, *Le Monde Sans la France, 1944–1945: Le Prix de la Liberté* (Paris: Robert Laffont, 1991), 719.

69   **what was left of three such Schutzmannschaft units:** Munoz, *Forgotten Legions*, 260. Michaelis, *Russians*, 60. O. Romanko, "Belarusian Collaborationist Formations in Exile (1944–1945): The Organization and Combat use," October 10, 2009, http://www.jivebelarus.net/history/new-history/belarusian-military-formations-in-emigration-1944-1945.html#lnko. Some writers have mistakenly portrayed Myroslaw's Ukrainian battalion interchangeably with a particular Schutzmannschaft battalion organized from conscripts in an area of Volhynia, eighty miles northeast of Myroslaw's village, the "102nd" Schutzmannschaft Battalion that had been created by the Germans in October 1942. As is the case for so many such units, records are scarce. Interviews two decades after the war by KGB officials of two individuals who were members of the 102nd Schutzmannschaft include descriptions of the unit's contribution to an autumn 1942 German massacre of Jewish men, women, and children in Kremenets. Their assigned duties included widening and deepening a preexisting moat for use as death

pits, and guarding the Jewish ghetto so none of those living inside, intended for murder, could escape. United States Holocaust Memorial Museum, "Central Office for the Investigation of National Socialist Crimes," files 7493–7497, reel 2682, RG 14.101 (Interviews of MDK and JKK; Ludwigsburg, Germany, February 1969).

In 1943 the 102nd Schutzmannschaft was sent to Vilnius and then Belarus, and was renamed the 61st Schutzmannschaft Battalion. Neufeldt, Huck, and Tessin, *Ornungspolizei 1936–1945*, 104. When the unit left Belarus, to be combined with thousands of other Ukrainians, Poles, and Belarusians into what would become the 30th Waffen-SS Division, the erstwhile 102nd—now the 61st—Schutzmannschaft had fewer than one hundred soldiers. Munoz, *Forgotten Legions*, 260. Romanko, "Belarusian Collaborationist Formations in Exile." In his 1945 narrative, Hloba makes no mention of either the 102nd or 61st, although he describes the interest among some of the battalion in an American soldier they would meet a few weeks later whose parents were from a village in Volhynia.

69   **what had been a freestanding "brigade" was designated:** Before acquiring its new name as a Waffen-SS Division, the unit of foreign soldiers had been organized in July as the "Schutzmannschaft-Brigade Siegling." Munoz, *Forgotten Legions*, 259–261. Michaelis, *Russians*, 60. Neufeldt, Huck, and Tessin, *Ornungspolizei 1936–1945*, , 63. Carlos Caballero Jurado, *Breaking the Chains: 14 Waffen-Grenadier-Division der SS and Other Ukrainian Volunteer Formation, Eastern Front, 1942–1945* (Halifax, UK: Shelf Books, 1998), 65; French First Army, "Essai sur la 30e Waffen Grenadier Division der SS, depuis sa creation (15 Julliet 1944) jusqu au 15 Novembre 1944," January 23, 1945 (French Army staff monograph on the origins of the 30th Waffen-SS Division), 8; W. Kosyk, "Les Ukrainiens dans la Résistance française," *L'Est Europeen*, Juillet–Septembre 1987, 13; Leonid Rein, "Untermenschen in SS Uniforms: 30th Waffen-Grenadier Division of Waffen SS," *Journal of Slavic Military Studies* 30 (2007): 329–345.

69   **Not all of the units:** Michaelis, *Russians*, 64.

69   **the only item on their uniform:** Rein, "Untermenschen," 338.

69   **Moving the entire 30th Waffen-SS Division:** Michaelis, *Russians*, 69–72.

69   **The arrival in France of a unit of foreigners:** Chris Bishop, *Hitler's Foreign Divisions: Foreign Volunteers in the Waffen-SS 1940–1945* (London: Amber Books, 2005). Many such units used by the Germans throughout Europe were ragtag outfits plagued by desertions. Some functioned passably as support units, and a few groups were effective in combat, such as the SS units of soldiers from Baltic nations who fought hard against the Red Army. In the Balkans, where the reality of the war was a localized everyone-is-the-enemy, there were SS units of Croats and SS units of Serbs. Throughout the war, Croats and Serbs also viciously fought each other. Who fought whom and when they would fight each other depended on how groups were designated and the always changing circumstances of the overall war, not unlike twenty-first-century Syria. Those identified as Royalists fought those identified as Communists and vice versa. Those identified (presumably without assessing individual levels of belief or practice) as Christians fought those identified as Muslims and vice versa. As was the case all across the Continent, common cause was more easily achieved when efforts were directed against two other designated groups, the Jews and the Roma.

69   and have faced the Allies all summer: Three weeks after D-Day there were newspaper reports with estimates that more than two hundred thousand Poles had been forced into what was called Germany's "slave army." According to one account, "The task of determining the nationality and loyalty of the Poles, as well as the Ukrainians, Russians, Croats and others into the German 'slave army' has been complicated, the Polish Telegraph Agency said, by the fact that the foreign soldiers have been forced by the Germans to surrender all their documents," pursuant to a general order published March 7, 1944. "Nazis Force 200,000 Poles Into Army; Try to Picture Them as Eager Volunteers," *New York Times*, June 30, 1944, 2.

69   Even in an outlying area like Haute-Saône: Kosyk, "Les Ukrainians," 14. In early August the Gestapo chief stationed in Doubs, the département to the south of Haute-Saône, gave the go-ahead to a Cossack unit in Rioz (eighteen miles to the south of Vesoul) to burn eight houses and commit one rape. Millar, *Maquis*, 259.

70   One Polish general described: Mark Wyman, *DPs: Europe's Displaced Persons, 1945–1951* (Ithaca, NY: Cornell University Press, 1998, originally published Cranbury, NJ: Associated University Presses, 1989;), 63, quoting Polish general Wladyslaw Anders.

70   Most, if not all, have: Hloba narrative, 1–3. "Mike," conversation with author, January, 2011. Mike (not his real name) wore the feldgrau with another Ukrainian battalion that was in Italy when the war ended. At the age of eighty-six and living in New Jersey, he described being pressed into service for the Germans on threat of death by starvation in a prison camp. Active in Ukrainian circles after coming to America after the war, Mike claimed to know several veterans of Myroslaw's battalion, including a few who had made their way to the United States from Vietnam, where they served the French government in the early 1950s when it was still French Indochina. He described Myroslaw's unit as being formed mainly of deportees, laborers, and prisoners of war who had been sent to a camp in East Prussia, adding in excruciating detail the circumstances of such captures and the grim death sentence that awaited Soviet prisoners held by the Germans. He stated his firm belief that as of 2011 there were no more living veterans of Myroslaw's battalion. He was mistaken or, more likely, intended to make sure that if there were any survivors that they be left alone.

73   I swear to God this sacred oath: Michaelis, *Russians*, 64.

74   Finished with their meeting: Hloba narrative, 4.

74   Seven decades later: Atlanta was the busiest US airport in 2014. "Calendar Year 2014 Passenger Boardings at Commercial Services Airports," US Federal Aviation Administration, last modified September 22, 2015, http://www.faa.gov/airports/planning_capacity/passenger_allcargo_stats/passenger/media/cy14-commercial-service-enplanements.pdf.

76   **In the evenings around dusk:** Betty Cowley, *Stalag Wisconsin: Inside WWII Prisoner-of-war Camps* (Oregon, WI: Badger Books, 2002), 77–80; *Horicon Reporter*, August 10, 1944.

76   **The state government began bringing in foreign workers:** *Horicon Reporter*, August 3, 1944.

76   **The government will pay 15 cents:** Ibid.

77   **Not that he has much choice:** "East's 'Gas' Ration Extended to West," *New York Times*, March 15, 1944.

77   **Julius provides those farmers with custom butchering:** Seventy years later most small meatpackers in America were gone, and more than 80 percent of US beef was processed by plants owned by four corporations. Robert Kunzig, "Carnivore's Dilemma," *National Geographic Magazine*, November 2014.

77   **Recipes are a valuable property, and closely guarded:** They still are. During the 1990s in Dodge County, Wisconsin, one local meat-processing plant was bought out by another, and shortly thereafter the entire operation was closed. Dozens of employees were unexpectedly put out of their jobs as it turned out that the purchase had nothing to do with the business but was all about getting control of a particular summer sausage recipe. Ron Rose, conversation with author, August 11, 2016.

78   **That summer sausage will continue to be available for purchase into the twenty-first century:** When Julius finally left the meat-processing business in the early 1960s, one of his several retirements, he sold his summer sausage recipe to Wayne Hoff of Brownsville, Wisconsin, who was just starting his own custom slaughtering business for small farms, combined with a limited retail operation. Hoff's Quality Meats remains in business, well known in the area for its beef jerky, and bratwurst. And for its summer sausage. Joanne Brown, conversation with author, December 9, 2011; Tim Hoff, conversation with author, August 16, 2016.

79   **Admiral takes you to London:** CBS *World News Today*, August 20, 1944, radio broadcast, audio, Internet Archive, https://archive.org/details/1944RadioNews. Admiral was the brand of Chicago-based Continental Radio and Television Company, which, like many companies during the war, continued advertising their wares despite no longer making any products for consumers.

80   **Billy is a mongoloid:** Billy had Down's syndrome, a description that was not used in his lifetime.

83   **Hanenstein began his lecture with some reminders:** Hloba narrative, 5.

84   **A political refugee who settled in France:** Reuchet, *Le Desarroi*, 262.

84   **Hroza then went on to suggest:** Bertin, *Resistance en Haute-Saône*, 217–219.

84   **Bermont, leader of FFI Groupe V:** Ibid.

84   **Instead, he continued to operate:** Vartier, "Des Russes," 5–6.

84   **Gilbert Decaudin, just days after losing his father, was put in charge:** Reuchet, *Le Desarroi*, 161; Vartier, *Histoires Secrètes*, 220–221.

85   **Doillon broke the ice:** Hloba narrative, 5–7; Bertin, *Resistance en Haute-Saône*, 219.

85   **Wozniak's passion was mainly reserved:** Bertin, *Resistance en Haute-Saône*, 219.

86   **As the conversation began:** Ibid., *Haute-Saône*, 218–220; Hloba narrative, 3.

86   **several specific conditions:** Reuchet, *Le Desarroi*, 263.

87   **Most of them were trumpeting:** "War End Sighted, Montgomery Says," *Milwaukee Journal*, August 21, 1944, 1. "End of War in Sight, Says Montgomery," *Racine Journal-Times*, August 21, 1944, 1. "Nazi Defeat Complete, Decisive — Monty," *Sheboygan Press*, August 21, 1944, 1.

88   **Went straight across Missouri into Kansas:** Boyd, letter to parents, April 23, 1944.

89   **It's probably a good thing:** Boyd, letter to parents, June 7, 1944.

94   **The reality of French resistance:** Jackson, *The Dark Years*, 530–534. "Neat diagrams, however, fail to capture the constantly shifting dynamics of the Resistance." Ibid., 521. Jackson quotes the FFI General Staff as observing on July 14, 1944, "For many regions we are almost totally ignorant of not only the numbers and movements of the enemy, but even the state of our own forces and the operations they have undertaken." Ibid., 549.

94   **In Haute-Saône, the maquisards had a reputation for thuggery:** "Already there had been far too much banditry committed in the name of the F.F.I., particularly in the neighbouring department, the Haute-Saône." Millar, *Maquis*, 194–195. Grandhay, "Les Maquis Haut-Saônois dans leur Environnement Social," 281–289. Former partisan Jean Reuchet submitted, to the same published volume, a brief angry response to the local historian Grandhay's assessment of the situation created by the behavior on the part of some maquisards, although Reuchet did not necessarily contradict what Grandhay described. Jean Reuchet, "Note de Jean Reuchet, President de la Federation des Resistants de Haute-Saône," in *Lutte Armee et Maquis: La Resistance et les Francais*, ed. Francois Marcot (Besançon et Paris: Annales littéraires de l'Université de Franche-Comté, 1996), 495–499. The exchange is a reminder of the complexities of the resistance and of the deep wounds across France that remained unhealed fifty-one years after the war ended.

94   **German reprisals were also effective:** Jackson, *The Dark Years*, 534.

94   **Bermont helped reverse this:** Reuchet, *Le Desarroi*, 156–158.

94   **including with the local version of the FTP:** Despite his acknowledged good relations with the FFI leadership in the area, including Bermont and Doillon, the bitterness of FTP veteran Jean Reuchet over his treatment at the hands of certain other political loyalists was still alive and well fifty years after the war ended. Ibid., 111–113, 130–133.

95   **He knew that the war's long quiet:** Bertin, *Resistance en Haute-Saône*, 219–220; Vartier, *Histoires Secrètes*, 222–223; Vartier, "Des Russes," 9–10.

95   **The BBC was listened to as well:** Millar, *Maquis*, 261; Bertin, *Resistance en Haute-Saône*, 219–220; Vartier, "Des Russes," 9–10.

95   **A few weeks earlier:** Millar, *Maquis*, 301.

95   **Bermont concluded:** Vartier, "Des Russes," 9–10; Bertin, *Resistance en Haute-Saône*, 219–220; Reuchet, *Le Desarroi*, 129, 262.

96   **Geupratte was considered a direct representative:** Vartier, *Histoires Secrètes*, 232.

96   **Each taking a separate route:** Bertin, *Resistance en Haute-Saône*, 219–220; Vartier, "Des Russes," 10.

96   **When the presentation was finished:** Bertin, *Resistance en Haute-Saône*, 219–220; Vartier, *Histoires Secrètes*, 233.

96   **Wozniak dashed off again:** Bertin, *Resistance en Haute-Saône*, 219–220; Hloba narrative, 8.

96   **The next day, Simon:** Vartier, *Histoires Secrètes*, 233; Bertin, *Resistance en Haute-Saône*, 219–220.

97   **Simon returned:** Bertin, *Resistance en Haute-Saône*, 221; Vartier, *Histoires Secrètes*, 233.

97   **On Wednesday, one of the maquis groups:** "Reddition du Bataillon Ukrainien," 1957 (typewritten time line of events involving le BUK), Archives, Département Haute-Saône, Vesoul, France.

97   **The next day a report reached Bermont:** Bertin, *Resistance en Haute-Saône*, 221; Vartier, *Histoires Secrètes*, 233.

98   **On Tuesday came Hanenstein's order:** Hloba narrative, 7–8.

98   **with the same suddenness and lack of explanation:** Hloba narrative, 7–9. Hloba's account suggests the battalion made it to Dijon and no one from the resistance greeted them. Every other account consulted, including Bermont's, indicates that the battalion made it no farther than Gray, southwest of Vesoul and a little more than half the distance to Dijon. Bertin, *Resistance en Haute-Saône*, 219–220.

99   **on late Wednesday afternoon:** Hloba narrative, 9.

99   **they marched four miles to the village of Fresne Saint-Mamès:** The village population in 1936 was 431. Almost seven months to the day before the Ukrainians arrived at Fresne Saint-Mamès, at five o'clock on the afternoon of February 24, one of the residents of the village, fifty-seven-year-old Leon Hildenfinger, was arrested by two village policemen and sent away for his Jewishness. He was one of more than a hundred citizens of Haute-Saône between the ages of eleven and eighty-eight who were arrested that day by local police and slated for transport to the Drancy internment camp outside of Paris, a holding area before deportation to an extermination camp. Jean-Claude Grandhay, *La Haute-Saône Dans La Deuxieme Guerre Mondiale, Sous le Signe de la Francisque, 1940–1944* (Vesoul, France: Imb Imprimeur, 1991), 217–235.

99   **Thus the arrival of the battalion:** Some accounts have the arrival in Fresne Saint-Mamès on a different day, but most, including that of local

historian Jean-Claude Grandhay, indicate the arrival was on Wednesday. The 1957 "Reddition" names the mayor of Fresne Saint-Mamès as "Rollin," although that may be incorrect. Jean-Claude Grandhay, e-mail message to author, April 5, 2013.

100   **the tensions between the Germans and Ukrainians:** Hloba narrative, 9; Bertin, *Resistance en Haute-Saône*, 219–221.

100   **On that Friday evening:** Hloba narrative, 9–10.

100   **the unexpected arrival of yet another pal from the class of 1940:** Johnny Westimayer would stay in the navy after the war, and in 1949 would lose his life during a naval exercise.

101   **As for Don, Camp Pickett had been full of rumors:** Budford Green et al., *Lightning: 78th Infantry Division* (Paducah, KY: Turner Publishing Company, 1996) (cited hereafter as Greene, et al, *78th Infantry Division*), 15. Most believed they would soon be heading to Europe, as training through the summer had been with live ammunition. But there were also some rumors that their division was never going to be sent overseas. Ibid. Whalley Williams, conversation with author, 2010. Williams was a machine gunner who joined Don's outfit after the 1944 Tennessee maneuvers and knew Brownie quite well. At the age of eighty-five, while describing events that took place when he was twenty years old, Williams repeatedly referred to Don as "Sergeant Brown," rather than by his first name, as though a long-dormant reflex had been awakened.

102   **a report that no less than the US Army:** "Army Sees Reich Fall by October," *Milwaukee Journal*, August 25, 1944, 1.

103   **Showing that Friday evening:** *Horicon Reporter*, August 24, 1944, 4.

105   **On Saturday morning, Wozniak:** Hloba narrative, 10; Bertin, *Resistance en Haute-Saône*, 221.

105   **It was early afternoon:** Reuchet, *Le Desarroi*, 262–263.

105   **Informed that Doillon was in the dairy's upper level:** Bertin, *Resistance en Haute-Saône*, 221; Hloba narrative, 10; Reuchet, *Le Desarroi*, 262–263.

106   **Simon told Reuchet:** Reuchet, *Le Desarroi*, 262–263.

106   **halfway to Fresne Saint-Mamès:** Ibid., 262–263, 278.

106   **As they entered Raze:** Ibid.

106   **Questioned by the Germans:** Hloba narrative, 10–12.

107   **Hanenstein placed guards:** Ibid.

107   **Simon then attempted:** Ibid.

108   **The mutiny would take place that evening:** Ibid.

108   **Simon was back at Bermont's command post:** Bertin, *Resistance en Haute-Saône*, 221–222.

110   **But an all-day rain:** "Rain Dampens Old Line Picnic—Not Enthusiasm," *The Milwaukee Magazine*, October 1944, 13, 35, https://milwaukeeroadarchives.com/MilwaukeeRoadMagazine/1944October.pdf.

111   **included a specific mention of how beautiful the day had been:** CBS

World News Today, August 27, 1944, radio broadcast, audio, Internet Archive, https://archive.org/details/1944RadioNews.

112   **He was informed:** Vartier, "Des Russes," 2; Hloba narrative, 12.

112   **Hloba was also told:** Hloba narrative, 12.

113   **Hloba had a chance to reflect on things:** Ibid., 12–13.

114   **When the end of our column:** Ibid. Bermont's recollection was that the location was the one chosen by Hloba and Doillon. Bertin, *Resistance en Haute-Saône*, 222. Some accounts say the flare was red. See, e.g., Vartier, *Histoires Secrètes*, 220.

114   **The others nodded in silence:** Hloba narrative, 13.

114   **A waitress brought over:** Ibid.

114   **A few minutes before the seven o'clock departure:** Ibid., 14.

114   **As Hloba headed toward the rest of the battalion:** Ibid.

115   **Hloba, on horseback:** Vartier, *Histoires Secrètes*, 220; Hloba narrative, 15–16.

115   **On full display:** Hloba narrative, 15–16.

116   **Near the front of the convoy:** Ibid.

116   **As for those few officers in the know:** Ibid.

116   **Hloba had binoculars:** Ibid.

117   **Obersturmführer Bentz:** Ibid., 16–17. Vartier's *Histoires Secrètes* says "Hauptsturmführer Sentz"(p. 234–235) rather than "Bentz," while the 1957 "Reddition" says "Hauptleutnant Sentz."

117   **Hloba steered his horse:** Burke, *Outrageous Good Fortune*, 30; Booth, *Mission Marcel*, 43. Not surprisingly, the Hloba narrative is silent on the fate of Hanenstein. While much of the material about the mutiny in the memoirs of Booth and Burke is questionable, both spoke with Hloba in the weeks following the mutiny and each noted that Hloba was specific with his description of shooting his German commander. Other accounts indicate that Hloba remained on horseback and moved about during the mutiny.

117   **The lone German automobile:** Hloba narrative, 17–18.

118   **Gunfire crackled:** Ibid.; Bertin, *Resistance en Haute-Saône*, 222.

118   **The fighting in that area:** Hloba narrative, 17–18; Bertin, *Resistance en Haute-Saône*, 222.

118   **The battalion doctor:** Hloba narrative 18.

118   **Lieutenant Boiko, who was with the company:** Ibid., 18–19.

119   **Hloba raced over in front of them:** Vartier, *Histoires Secrètes*, 221–222, citing Gilbert Decaudin, who was on the scene within hours of the mutiny.

119   **Half were mowed down:** Hloba narrative, 18.

119   **When the group:** Hloba narrative, 19–20.

119   **littered with German dead:** Bertin, *Resistance en Haute-Saône*, 222; Hloba narrative, 19–20.

119   **The Ukrainians regrouped:** Hloba narrative, 20; Bertin, *Resistance en Haute-Saône*, 224.

120   **Inventory was taken:** These numbers vary from account to account, although all are within the same ballpark.

120   **With impeccable timing:** Hloba narrative, 21; Bertin, *Resistance en Haute-Saône*, 224.

121   **It was half past one on Sunday:** Vartier, *Histoires Secrètes*, 221–222.

121   **The sight was one of horror:** Ibid.

121   **He observed that:** Ibid.

121   **Under Gilbert's direction:** Reuchet, *Le Desarroi*, 161; Vartier, *Histoires Secrètes*, 221–222.

122   **A few days earlier:** Vartier, *Histoires Secrètes*, 221–222, 234–235.

122   **He left, faulting himself:** Ibid., 234–235.

123   **Gilbert would always remember:** Vartier, *Histoires Secrètes,* 223.

126   **A brief but violent afternoon thunderstorm:** Bertin, "Les Comtois de 1944 vus par les Ukrainiens," 13–14; Vartier, "Des Russes," 12.

126   **Simon had caught up:** Vartier, *Histoires Secrètes*, 236; Kosyk, "Les Ukrainiens," 20. Hloba's account describes Doillon connecting with the battalion only when they reached their destination of a particular forest. Hloba narrative, 22. Neither Kosyk nor Vartier mention the mayor's presence.

126   **He remained insistent:** Bertin, *Resistance en Haute-Saône*, 224.

127   **The rainstorm meant:** Vartier, "Des Russes," 12–15; Vartier, *Histoires Secrètes*, 236–237. Bertin, *Resistance en Haute-Saône*, 224–225.

127   **Myroslaw's battalion reached the safety of the Confracourt woods:** Vartier, "Des Russes," 12–15; Vartier, *Histoires Secrètes*, 236–237; Bertin, *Resistance en Haute-Saône*, 224–225; Hloba narrative, 22; Reuchet, *Le Desarroi*, 263.

127   **Bermont wanted it made clear:** Bertin, *Resistance en Haute-Saône*, 228.

127   **The area had already been prepared:** Ibid.

128   **As Sunday's nightfall began to descend:** Bertin, Ibid., 225; Hloba narrative, 22.

128   **Together the handful of young men sang:** The poem was written in 1912 by Galician Bohdan Lepky, and the tune was composed by his brother Lev Lepky.

Чуєш брате мій, товаришу мій,

Відлітають сірим шнурком журавлі у вирій.

Приспів (Refrain):

Кличуть "Кру-кру-кру, в чужині умру,

Заки море перелечу, крилонька зітру крилонька зітру"

Мерехтить в очах безконечний шлях,

Гине-гине в сірій мряці слід по журавлях.

Приспів.

129   **gained notoriety:** After the war some Japanese were prosecuted for torture activities, including "artificial drowning interrogation," also known as "waterboarding." Evan Wallach, "Drop by Drop: Forgetting the History of Water Torture in U.S. Courts," *Columbia Journal of Transnational Law* 45 (2007): 469–493.

129   **theories of "race" and empire:** Richard Toye, *Churchill's Empire: The World That Made Him and the World He Made* (New York: Henry Holt,

2010), 234–235, 315. Given the staggering death toll and the circumstances surrounding the Bengal famine of 1943, its absence from mention or serious examination in so many histories of the Second World War is almost as reprehensible as the British response was to the famine. Churchill's ghastly behavior included telling Roosevelt on one occasion that the famine in India was due to "hoarding." Ibid., 249 (citing September 12, 1944, diary entry of Canadian Prime Minister Mackenzie King). Equally missing from so many chronicles of the war is a description of how India was providing to the Allies the world's largest volunteer army, more than two million men, while at the same time the British were committing more battalions to the internal control of India than they were to fighting the Japanese.

The war historian Sir Max Hastings points out, with a presumably unintended effect of parody, that "Most of [the British] people were warmly sentimental about the contribution of Indian and colonial troops to the war effort, heedless of the fact that their services were purchased for cash and only rarely inspired by loyalty to, or even understanding of, the Allied cause." Max Hastings, *Inferno: The World at War, 1939–1945* (New York: Knopf, 2011), 397. Hastings does not point out that the same could be said about the American troops being "only rarely inspired by loyalty to, or even understanding of, the Allied cause."

Hastings assesses Churchill's response to the Bengal famine as "a brutal insensitivity." Ibid., 407–412. He offers no indication as to what such "brutal insensitivity" toward the Indian people may reflect, but in an earlier volume about the Second World War, he observed that Churchill's "consistent private advocacy of mercy for the German people, once they had been defeated, reflects his greatness of spirit." Max Hastings, *Armageddon: The Battle for Germany, 1944–1945* (New York: Vintage, 2005), 194. As to the matter of Indian services being, as Hastings puts it, "purchased for cash" rather than "inspired by loyalty," some perspective was provided in 1942 by an American Army colonel who explained to a two-time Pulitzer Prize–winning American reporter that he had just visited some Indian coal mines: "Did you know those coal mines are paying about forty per cent dividends to the British shareholders? Well, I saw Indian women down there—some of them pregnant women—carrying baskets of coal on their heads all day. Do you know what they get paid? Four annas a day—just about four American cents a day! Do you think those people are going to be much worried about the Japs taking over India? Well, that's what we're up against." Leland Stowe, *They Shall Not Sleep* (New York: Knopf, 1944), 177.

130 **In the same short span of time:** The Red Army had 811,603 wounded. Hastings, *Armageddon*, 8.

130 **In Belarus:** Rein, "Untermenschen," 330n.

130 **The war's death toll will include more than four million Ukrainian civilians:** Subtelny, *Ukraine*, 479.

130 **Before the month of August was over:** Ferenc Morton Szasz, *The Day the Sun Rose Twice: The Story of the Trinity Site Nuclear Explosion*

(Albuquerque: University of New Mexico Press, 1984), 28; US Department of Energy, National Atomic Museum, "Trinity Site," Trinity Atomic Web Site, http://www.abomb1.org/trinity/trinity1.html.

131   **in a large clearing:** Hloba narrative, 22–23.

131   **Bermont had arrived in the forest wearing his uniform:** Bertin, *Resistance en Haute-Saône*, 224; Vartier, "Des Russes," 15. Bermont's intention that night was to visibly and formally emphasize his taking command of the battalion.

132   **With improvised pomp and formality:** Bertin, *Resistance en Haute-Saône*, 224. The moniker "le BUK" comes from "Bataillon Ukrainien." In 1990, Bertin (Bermont) wrote, "The acronym was simple and sounded good; it is still used."

132   **The day's events in Haute-Saône had no effect:** It appears Churchill was briefed on the incident shortly after it happened. According to Message CX/MSS/T296/99, September 4, 1944: "Another mention of mutiny among RUSSIANS of 30 SS Grenadier Division South East of BESANCON. Note: A battalion of this Division was reported on 28th August as having mutinied." The latter appears to refer to le BUK, and the former to the battalion of Ukrainians forty miles to the south, which had mutinied one day before le BUK. The cover sheet for the day's messages was marked "TOP SECRET" and was hand-initialed with a "C." *Messages of 4 September 1944 for Prime Minister (C/7529).*

133   **Bermont would always believe:** Simon Doillon's original plan was for the soldiers of le BUK to be dispersed and merged into the various maquis units throughout the region, an idea also supported by the FTP's Reuchet. Events in eastern France were moving so fast that it never happened. Bertin, *Resistance en Haute-Saône*, 228–229; Vartier, "Des Russes," 21 (citing a 1970 interview with Bermont). Hloba did, in fact, suggest seizing Vesoul. The idea was quashed by Bermont. He feared the inevitable counterattack by the Germans, given the strategic intersection of roads in Vesoul that was needed for their ongoing retreat. He also knew there would have likely been vicious reprisals, as had taken place in western France, where a day after the Normandy landings, the FTP "liberated" the village of Tulle and held it two days before withdrawing. The Germans then returned and hung ninety-nine local civilians from lampposts, balconies, and trees. The following day was the massacre at Oradour-sur-Glane, where the Germans killed 642, the men of the village machine-gunned and the women and children burned alive in a church. Jackson, *The Dark Years*, 546.

133   **Only two days after the mutiny:** OSS, Report to OSS Headquarters on Operation Cedric, 27 August to 6 October 1944: "At this stage all German traffic was north-east—they were seizing all available transport and reprisals for interference was very severe. As an example, they burnt three villages adjacent to us two days after our arrival."

134   **Around midnight, as the moon was setting:** Bertin, *Resistance en Haute-Saône*, 225; Vartier, *Histoires Secrètes*, 242.

134   **the veteran twenty-three-year-old pilot:** Personnel file, William L. Bales, US Army Air Force, 490th Bomb Group, 857th Bomb Squadron,

http://www.801492.org/Air%20Crew/Bales/Bales%20PPP%20files.pdf; Mission Report 1788, August 27/28, http://www.801492.org/Air%20Crew/Bales/850th-BalesCrew.html. Bales's unit was known as the "Carpetbaggers," based out of Harrington, England, flying missions that provided parachute drop services over France for the OSS. Bales was a few weeks shy of making his 35th mission, which meant a trip home. It was not easy duty. A few weeks before, on August 9, Bales had brought his ship back to Harrington on three engines, along with over a thousand flak and cannon holes. Ibid.

134   They would be back on the ground in England: Harrington Station Operations Log for August 27–28, 1944, http://www.801492.org/Air%20Crew/Station%20179%20Operations%20Log.pdf.

139   By four o'clock the next morning the hunt for the battalion was back on: Vartier, "Des Russes," 16; Bertin, *Resistance en Haute-Saône*, 226.

139   Several hundred *miliciens*: During the Second World War, "voluntary" took on different meanings. The choices for those where the war descended were never as obvious or as simple as sometimes demanded by the perspective and ease of righteousness provided by distance and passage of time. The fascist paramilitary force created by the Vichy regime, known as the Milice, which pursued resisters and rounded up Jews with relish and violence, attracted a thuggish element. But as the war went on many French male youths saw joining the Milice as an escape from the STO. By 1944, in some areas such as Marseilles, a third of the Milice personnel had entered into the service of the fascist force in order to avoid being sent to Germany as forced labor. Jackson, *The Dark Years*, 530.

139   Upon arrival, the French commanders of the unit reported: Bertin, *Resistance en Haute-Saône*, 226. Bertin obtained this information shortly after liberation from one of his resistance-friendly contacts with the *feldgendarme* in Vesoul. Ibid.; Vartier, "Des Russes," 17.

139   Simon decided the battalion should be moved to a new encampment: Hloba narrative, 24.

140   Tents were pitched: Hloba narrative, 24–25.

140   There was discussion that le BUK needed uniforms that looked different: Vartier, *Histoires Secrètes*, 240–241; Hloba narrative, 25.

140   On Tuesday, le BUK went into its first action: 1957 "Reddition"; Kosyk, "Les Ukrainians," 22. Hloba later blamed the failure on the darkness, rain, and insufficient information from the FFI. Hloba narrative, 26.

141   In the early hours of Thursday morning: Hloba narrative, 27; Vartier, *Histoires Secrètes*, 241; Bertin, *Resistance en Haute-Saône*, 196. Bermont cataloged the capture as consisting of ten heavy machine guns, one hundred rifles, two hundred hand grenades, and two binoculars.

142   The return to camp took several hours: "Hloba Narrative," 27–28.

144   Millar's exchange in French: Millar, *Maquis*, 325–326.

144   Millar had been in France: SOE, *Interrogation Report, Real Name Capt. Millar; Nom de Guerre Chancellor (known as Emile)*, December 12, 1944.

144   **Slender but sturdy of frame:** A similar observation was made by the CBS radio newsman Eric Sevareid, who had gotten to know Millar in the very first days of the war, when the latter was a newspaper reporter in Paris. After losing contact with each other, they would have a surprise encounter near Besancon in late September 1944, and share a dinner. Sevareid describes Millar as having "the physique of a guardsman and the rosy face of a beautiful girl," and, regarding the surprise meeting with Millar later in war, referred to "his incredibly beautiful face blooming like that of a young girl in love." Sevareid, *Not So Wild a Dream*, 169, 468.

144   **He arrived in France with two hundred thousand francs:** SOE, *Report of Captain George Reid Millar—Chancellor—Treasurer Circuit; EMILE's REPORT*, (undated), 16.

144   **he directed more than seventy sabotage operations:** SOE, *George Reid Millar, M.C., recommendation for Distinguished Service Order* (undated). Will Irwin, *The Jedburghs: The Secret History of the Allied Special Forces, France 1944* (New York: Perseus, 2005), 195–196.

144   **Consistent with the orders of French general Marie-Pierre Koenig:** Millar, *Maquis*, 197; George Millar, *Road to Resistance: An Autobiography* (Boston: Little, Brown and Company, 1979), 361.

144   **Much of Emile's focus had been on practical improvements:** In his postmission report, Millar wrote that when he reached the Doubs area he delivered an ultimatum: "I would not work in this maquis unless they accepted some of the primary rules of hygiene. Every maquis when it installed itself must first of all dig two holes, just like every section in the British infantry." Millar added that his maquis counterparts "were most loyal to my exaggerated ideas on cleanliness and smells for the rest of my stay in the DOUBS." SOE, *Captain George Reid Millar—Chancellor—Treasurer Circuit; EMILE'S REPORT* (undated, fall 1944), 5.

144   **Since early August:** Millar, *Maquis*, 263.

145   **Two weeks before, he had learned:** Millar, *Maquis*, 300.

145   **He also appointed listeners:** Millar, *Road to Resistance*, 376.

145   **one of eighty-two such groups:** M. R. D. Foot, *SOE in France* (New York: Frank Cass, 2004; first published 1966 by Her Majesty's Stationery Office), 352–353; Jackson, *The Dark Years*, 548.

145   **most of them six months to a year too late:** Bazata was not alone in expressing a view in his postmission report that the team should have been dropped in January. "The Jedburghs, the OGs and other missions, all of whom complained that they were sent in too late, would have had several months with the FFI before they were overrun [i.e., if the planned timetable for American troops advancing after the landing in Southern France had become a reality]." Arthur L. Funk, *Hidden Ally: The French Resistance, Special Operations, and the Landings in Southern France, 1944* (New York: Greenwood Press, 1992), 259.

145   **The other two Jeds arriving:** OSS, Report to OSS Headquarters on Operation Cedric, 27 August to 6 October 1944.

145   **although Bazata claimed otherwise:** According to Emile, Bazata "rattled along in almost comprehensible pigeon-French." Millar, *Road to Resistance*, 384.

145   **enhanced by a glib forcefulness:** In late 1943 the President of the "Jedburgh Board" concluded an assessment of Bazata: "This officer was much too anxious to impress and creates a bad impression by his glibness and plausibility. But he has real drive and initiative and when in control of a situation sheds most of his superficial defects and shows genuine powers of leadership." OSS personnel records for Douglas Dewitt Bazata, Jedburgh Board Report, December 30, 1943.

145   **that at various moments annoyed, charmed, and frightened Emile:** While making his parachute jump, Bazata had been severely cut in the legs by the steel ribbon static line. In his postmission report to SOE authorities, Millar describes Bazata as "an admirable officer under difficulties," adding that "when the doctor finally saw him, he ordered him to bed, and told me revoltingly that the American was 'a hero.' When the Americans got near he endangered my life repeatedly with his own disregard of danger." SOE, *Report of Captain George Reid Millar—Chancellor—Treasurer Circuit; EMILE's REPORT*, (undated, fall 1944), 15–16. In his second wartime memoir, written thirty-four years later, Millar noted that "the mercurial and, to be truthful, showy Bazata would not be left at home. I was mainly with him. He was a handful and a responsibility. Although his leg was still painful he got about quickly on foot, and if a restful moment materialised he was likely to spoil it by saying, unslinging his carbine, 'For Pete's sake, Emile, let's get down to that road and bag us a couple of Krauts.' 'Bagging' Germans was not to my taste." Millar, *Road to Resistance*, 386–387.

145   **shared for similar reasons by many French:** Throughout his career of chronicling SOE activities during the Second World War, British historian M. R. D. Foot tended to call things as he saw them, without automatically conflating the undeniable dash and verve of such operations with achievement and effectiveness of performance. His writing avoids the adoring tendencies that have taken hold in the twenty-first century within a certain radius around Washington, DC, with regard to military and paramilitary "special operations." Foot makes clear that the wartime reality for the SOE, as it also was for the OSS, consisted of the usual human basket of individual tragedies and achievements thoroughly mixed with bonehead maneuvers and dreadful failures. Many operatives were brave and clever, but no more so than airmen and infantry soldiers whose units often paid a far higher price for a far greater period of time, with a result of greater consequence. In the Churchillian terms so loved by many in the idolatrous sect that has grown around the OSS, never in the field of human conflict has so much adoration been given to so few who accomplished no more and most likely less than others in the same overall battlefield.

Foot's writings occasionally assume a proper British posture, such as when commenting about French concerns over the presence of the Jedburghs. Foot stoops to an unfortunate cartoonish strawman to allow dismissal without exploration, as though the French concerns did not signify: "Xenophobe or at least Anglophobe French authors have suggested that the JEDBURGHS' role was to restrict resistance operations to what suited the secret plans for world domination of the British intelligence service, an unconvincing account of the purpose of teams many of which had only French members and all of which worked on SHAEF's directions." Foot, *SOE in France*, 352.

Notably, while Foot complained that the French misunderstood the British, a CIA review of his book undertaken for internal agency consumption complained that the author did not recognize how the merger of certain elements of the SOE and OSS to support French resistance during the war involved "some considerable self-abnegation on the part of the Americans." John A. Bross, "The Nurture of Resistance," review of *SOE in France*, by M. R. D. Foot, and *Inside SOE*, by E.H. Cookridge, Central Intelligence Agency (internal publication), 1966, https://www.cia.gov/library/center-for-the-study-of-intelligence/kent-csi/vol11n02/pdf/v11i2a11p.pdf.

The Bross review carries a certain linguistic significance, perhaps even historically so, given that the phrase "considerable self-abnegation" is not normally associated with either the OSS or its successor organization.

145 **Beyond Emile's natural dislike of large organizations:** Millar, *Road to Resistance*, 380–382.

146 **He was uncomfortable with having to change his operations:** Ibid., 379–380.

146 **Bazata and his team were in wireless contact:** Ibid., 381.

146 **While the storm was raging:** Millar, *Maquis*, 325.

146 **operating his own FFI Groupe 22:** Reuchet, *Le Desarroi*, 161.

146 **Menigoz also requested a drop of antitank weapons:** Millar, *Maquis*, 326. According to Emile's official description of the incident, "With the Jeds I saw it was now our duty to begin to supply the HAUTE SAONE. We got off to a flying start when a group leader MENIGOZ (who had a particular band called the "GROUPE LORRAINE", which operated West of Vesoul, but whom I always respected) came flying in to tell me that he and his friend Captaine SIMON had 650 Russians in the FORET de CHERLIEU, denying West-East traffic on the important road running into VESOUL. We asked London for material for these men. They were Ukrainians (all traitors to me) but we reckoned that they were really 1,300 (650 lost to the Boche and 650 gained to us). The funny thing was that their Russian C.O. put across all the old German propaganda about the Russian menace, and pled that Britain, America, France, must fight together against the Soviet. I believe the Russians fought well and with heavy casualties to the end, but I was pulled out before I could get full news of them." SOE, *Report of Captain George Reid Millar—Chancellor—Treasurer Circuit; EMILE's REPORT*, (undated), 11.

146 **the usual European style of stiff-backed formal handshakes:** Millar, *Maquis*, 326–327. In his second wartime memoir, Millar says that Menigoz spent the night and that the following morning he would take one of the Jeds, Chapelle ("Chapel," according to Bazata's postmission report), along to inspect "the

Ukrainians in situ." Millar, *Road to Resistance*, 385. Chapelle's real name was Louis Lesne. Irwin, *The Jedburghs*, 193. It is more likely that Millar's published 1946 version of events regarding Menigoz is correct, although his official report hints of some contact, perhaps by Lesne at Millar's direction, with the "Russian C.O." Hloba. SOE, *Report of Captain George Reid Millar — Chancellor — Treasurer Circuit; EMILE's REPORT*, (undated), 11.

146   **Satisfied, Menigoz went off:** Millar, *Maquis*, 326–327.

147   **From Cedric C-3564/34:** OSS Report, Operations, Team Cedric, Summary of W/T Messages Exchanged, September 1–9, 1944.

148   **The German retreat from the west had filled the main roads:** I Iloba narrative, 29; Millar, *Road to Resistance*, 381, 387.

148   **The group was led by Captain Polichtchuk:** Vartier, *Histoires Secrètes*, 238–239; Vartier, "Des Russes," 17.

149   **At ten o'clock the Ukrainians attacked:** Hloba narrative, 29–31; Bertin, *Resistance en Haute-Saône*, 196.

149   **Two thousand years later:** In October 2015 it was reported that Colombian mercenaries, wearing Saudi uniforms and under UAE military command, were involved in fighting in Yemen. Jineth Bedoya, "Los Colombianos que Pelearán otra Guerra en el Golfo," *El Tiempo*, October 18, 2015, http://www.eltiempo.com/mundo/medio-oriente/soldados-colombianos-que-irana-yemen/16406208; Emily B. Hager and Mark Mazzetti, "Emirates Secretly Send Colombian Mercenaries to Yemen Fight," *New York Times*, November 26, 2015. In addition to selling weaponry to the Saudis, the American support consisted of, at least, the active searching of vessels and providing targeting information. Maria Abi-Habib and Adam Entous, "U.S. Widens Role in Saudi-led Campaign Against Houthi Rebels in Yemen," *Wall Street Journal*, April 12, 2015.

150   ***Bellum omnium contra omnes:*** "The war of all against all." Thomas Hobbes, preface to *Elementa philosophica de cive* (Lausanne: 1782, originally published Paris: 1642, digitized 2014). https://books.google.com/books?id=5P1eA AAAcAAJ

153   **From Cedric C-3717/48:** OSS Report, Operations, Team Cedric, Summary of W/T Messages Exchanged, September 3–9, 1944.

153   **Too busy to change from civies:** Presumably the last line is Bazata covering for himself because he was not following the bizarre requirement that Jed teams be in uniform during their mission on the ground. In his official history, M. R. D. Foot attempts to defend the requirement with some interesting logic: "That the JEDBURGHS' security was not seriously compromised by their uniforms is illustrated by the interesting fact that none of them was captured; their casualties were all sustained in gun battles with the enemy, or incurred at the very start of their missions by parachuting accidents." Foot, *SOE in France*, 353. Bazata noted in his postmission report that his instructions had been to "give no cover story if taken in uniform but try to pass as soldiers performing ordinary duties. If taken in civilian clothes, try to pass as airmen," parenthetically adding, "We found it utterly impossible to wear uniforms at any time." OSS, Report to OSS Headquarters on Operation Cedric, 27 August to 6 October 1944, 2.

153 **Hoping to serve Onion:** "Onion" was a parachute drop field, next to the Ognon River. Bazata and his team had arrived on another nearby drop field given the name "Turnip."

154 **They will cover all your area and work to Emile and Boulayas instructions:** Boulaya was an irrepressible FFI chieftain named Joseph Bartholet, originally from Besancon, who was working closely with Emile.

154 **However mission had strong approval:** Koenig had personally denied the original request by Booth in July, and London's suggestion of his "strong approval" is a stretch of truth, perhaps already well practiced in the newly established American spymaster circles and an interesting piling on to force acceptance by Emile and Bazata of the drop of the American colonel and eight other officers into an area overrun by Germans to undertake a vaguely defined mission.

155 **Propose sending large night operation:** For presentational purposes the following Cedric-SFHQ message traffic between September 6 and 8, 1944, was not included in the text of the chapter:

6 September From Cedric C-4009/83

Aseb Trof road cut. Confused Boche using all small roads. Ambushing road Besancon wherever possible but low ammunition. Example killed 70 lost 1 retired, ammunition gone. This is common. Villages burned. Solid convoy autos, trucks, tans north on Rioz Villersexel roads. Same Marchaux Villersexel road. Released prisoners Aseb. Killed Gestapo second command there with our Welrod. Our Russians doing well north surviving 2 serious attacks. Bridge at Port sur Saône important air target. Heavy convoy passing. Guarded by 3 Boch companies 1288 millimeters. Emile and I having great sport with Boche but drop Onion.

7 September From SFHQ to Cedric C-418

Please keep a lookout for Jed Rupert alias Maniere of team Dodge who has been taken by Gestapo from Lyon to Belfort on 21st August. Rupert is a U.S. major.

7 September From Cedric C-4097/80

Following from Mesure–contacted agent from Roderick. Reports liaison Americans Chateau Faine, Beure. Contact Ligne, Boulaya, Francois. Will go Aseb Thursday with Corjet. From Cedric–All traffic ended. Saved one road for Allies. Will get liaison to Americans. Again thank you and Air Force for containers. Need more however.

155 **12-man mission on Iris:** "Iris" was a drop field six miles due south of Vesoul, outside the village of Filain, a few miles northeast of Paul Guepratte's command post.

155   **Important do not drop bodies tonight:** In his postmission report, Bazata wrote that after the September 8 SFHQ message about new drops "we immediately sent London an emergency asking that all operations stop until further word from us. However, on the night of September 10, London dropped half of the Col. Booth mission on field AQUARELLE, where they were immediately surrounded by Germans and held in check for a week. (AQUARELLE is a field unaccepted for personnel)." Bazata also described his unsuccessful attempt, along with Emile, to reach Booth. OSS, Report to OSS Headquarters on Operation Cedric, 27 August to 6 October 1944.

156   **The phrases came over the BBC:** Bertin, *Resistance en Haute-Saône,* 143. Booth's memoir says that only a cargo drop had been expected on the ground, and that he and the others were unexpected, suggesting the BBC code phrase was "the fox will run," meaning that only a supply drop was scheduled. Booth, *Mission Marcel,* 27. The description by Bermont and the communications between London and Bazata/Emile both suggest otherwise, although there is agreement that the air field had been approved only for cargo drops. According to Bermont "nine friends" meant nine bodies could be expected, which would have been the case if the second plane had found the drop zone. Bertin, *Resistance en Haute-Saône,* 143.

156   **a drop near Vesoul:** There would be a dozen drops in Haute-Saône during the first half of September 1944. Bertin, *Resistance en Haute-Saône,* 155.

156   **The "Russian speaking parachutist" touted by London:** Booth, *Mission Marcel,* 21.

156   **During the car trip he met the commander:** Fabrizio Calvi, *OSS: La Guerre Secrète en France* (Paris: Hachette, 1990), 496 (Calvi interviewed Kuzmuk October 8, 1988); Booth, *Mission Marcel,* 21–22.

157   **When he and Kuzmuk arrived at Harrington:** "I believed, for the first time in weeks, that MARCEL was really going to get away." Booth, *Mission Marcel,* 21–22.

157   **He was also a Princeton man:** Nelson A. Denis, *War Against All Puerto Ricans: Revolution and Terror in America's Colony* (New York: Perseus, 2015), 147–148; "Princeton Shows 'The Scarlet Coat,'" *New York Times,* December 24, 1924, 11. One of Booth's first assignments with the OSS was to provide ears and eyes on the island of Puerto Rico, using the cover of running a bottling and import firm and operating a popular seedy bar. Denis, *War Against All Puerto Ricans,* 150–151.

157   **In mid-1942, Booth was sent to Spain:** *Smith Alumnae Quarterly,* August 1942 (letter from a 1927 Smith graduate describes the "American Colony" in Puerto Rico, and notes Waller Booth's absence after being stationed in Spain).

157   **in early 1944 the OSS chief for Iberia:** Booth, *Mission Marcel,* 5–6. Booth had been part of the OSS intelligence operation Medusa, targeting France from Spain.

157   **Booth was welcomed by OSS operations in the United Kingdom:** Ibid. The Proust Project, not to be confused with Booth's later creation, Mission

Marcel Proust, was a program aimed at creating a pool of auxiliary agents for operations that could not be covered by the larger Sussex Plan and its fifty-four teams of agents (118 men and 2 women) that were trained and then dropped into France between January and September 1944. "History of Sussex and Proust," (undated), http://www.plan-sussex-1944.net/anglais/proust_plan.htm.

157   **his proposed mission was then personally rejected by French general Marie-Pierre Koenig:** A. Manuel, Bureau Central de Renseignements et d'Action (BCRA), to Col. John Haskell, chief, SI (Secret Intelligence) branch, OSS, August 24, 1944. The Manuel letter was in response to an August 21, 1944, letter from Haskell directly to General Koenig proposing a mission to Haute-Savoie, which was already liberated.

157   **Undeterred, Booth made numerous trips:** Booth's drafts of his postmission memorandum indicate that memos went back and forth between Haskell and Booth about the mission, starting on July 12, 1944. The authorization from Koenig came on August 28, followed by OSS authorization on September 1, even though a location for the barely described operation had not yet been determined. Booth even tried to place the mission in northern Italy, but it was rejected by those in the OSS already on the ground in Italy. Booth, *Mission Marcel*, 14–20.

157   **Marseille fell on August 28:** Jackson, *The Dark Years*, 555.

157   **his self-styled mission:** Booth would call it Mission Marcel Proust. Others joked that it was an appropriate name because it was a mission "in search of lost time." Calvi, *OSS: La Guerre Secrète en France*, 495.

158   **Just a few days into his new position:** In the 1988 interview with author Calvi, Kuzmuk said the conversation took place the day before the parachute drop. Calvi, *OSS: La Guerre Secrète en France*, 496. The records in the National Archives and Records Administration (NARA), including Kuzmuk's OSS personnel file, suggest it was probably a few days before that.

158   **Also on board:** The Frenchmen were Second Lieutenant Paul Marchadier, known to Booth at that time only as Chamard, and Captain Andre Cornut, who had not heard from his wife and infant son in Paris since the June 1940 German occupation. Booth, *Mission Marcel*, 3–5; Air Transport Operation Report 20721, Operation Messenger 40, 9/10 September 1944, www.801492.org /Air%20Crew/B24MRs/2072-Gilpin-10Sep44.jpg; "788th/859th BS, Gilpin Crew," The Wartime Experiences of The Carpetbaggers in Still Photos, http://www.801492.org/Air%20Crew/Gilpin/Gilpin%20Crew.html.

158   **As the plane reached its cruising altitude of eight thousand feet:** Booth, *Mission Marcel*, 3–5; Burke, *Outrageous Good Fortune*, 21–22.

158   **German soldiers were now pouring into Haute-Saône:** Millar, *Maquis*, 347.

158   **Four days before, Bermont had met with the famous Emile:** Bertin, *Resistance en Haute-Saône*, 229.

158   **Bermont decided that le BUK should move:** Hloba narrative, 31; Bertin, *Resistance en Haute-Saône*, 145. Contrary to the Hloba account, Kosyk suggests that the move to Confracourt was by "mutual agreement" of Simon Doillon and

Hloba. Kosyk, "Les Ukrainians," 23–24. It is difficult to imagine Doillon having done so except with authorization and, more likely, orders by Bermont.

159 **After the first few days of participating in ambushes:** Some French chronicles hint of some sort of an incident a day or two after Melin involving Hloba going against a Doillon directive, possibly by pulling le BUK out of an engagement against a retreating German force. Vartier, *Histoires Secrètes*, 241.

159 **While Bermont saw the Ukrainians as disciplined and brave:** Ibid., 239.

159 **Years later he would wonder:** Bertin, *Resistance en Haute-Saône*, 229.

159 **Simon and Hloba used one of the cars:** Hloba narrative, 33.

160 **The drop area had no radio-transmitting station:** Bertin, *Resistance en Haute-Saône*, 143.

160 **a double ring of protection:** As for the inner ring of defense, protection was provided by members of a local maquis group, D'arc, who were the first to have greeted the arrivals. Bertin, *Resistance en Haute-Saône*, 144–145; 1957 "Reddition." In the memoirs of Booth and Burke there are continuing references to a person they identify as either a "Major Darc" or a "Captain Darc." There was no such person. The FFI Bataillon D'arc was headed by Captain Roch and operated under the direction of FFI Groupe Haute-Saône leader Bermont. The Bataillon D'arc included several smaller groups, including Maquis de Combeaufontaine based in the Bois de Confracourt. Bertin, *Resistance en Haute-Saône*, 137; Reuchet, *Le Desarroi*, 157. It remains a mystery to whom Booth and Burke were referring when they used the name "Darc." Booth suggested that "Major Darc" was educated at Saint Cyr, and Burke refers to Simon and Claude as "Darc's lieutenants," while in fact they were Bermont's lieutenants. Booth used the same moniker in his postmission memorandum, which never mentions Bermont (or Bertin) by name. It is possible their "Darc" was Bermont, or Geupratte, Captain Roch, Menigoz, or someone else in Maquis de Combeaufontaine. During the German retreat it was not unusual for locals to take credit in front of passing American troops for someone else's resistance activities and accomplishments. The memoir of Bermont unequivocally gives all credit for effecting the mutiny of the Ukrainians to his lieutenant Simon Doillon. Booth and Burke's "Darc" does not. Their descriptions suggest a level of swagger and boasting by the person they call "Darc" that does not square with the measured voice of Pierre Bertin that comes through in his writings and those of others who knew him.

160 **Everyone was in place:** Bertin, *Resistance en Haute-Saône*, 144–145.

160 **Hours before, the plane had entered French airspace:** Gilpin was nine months on the job and well on his way toward completing fifty-eight missions during his service in England. Air Transport Operation Report 20721, Operation Messenger 40, 9/10 September 1944, http://www.801492.org/Air%20Crew/B24MRs/2072-Gilpin-10Sep44.jpg; "788th/859th BS, Gilpin Crew," The Wartime Experiences of The Carpetbaggers in Still Photos, http://www.801492.org/Air%20Crew/Gilpin/Gilpin%20Crew.html.

160 **Standing with those waiting for the arrival:** Bertin, *Resistance en Haute-Saône*, 144–145; Air Transport Operation Report 20721, Operation Messenger 40,

9/10 September 1944, http://www.801492.org/Air%20Crew/B24MRs/2072-Gilpin-10Sep44.jpg.

161   **Bermont would always believe:** Bertin, *Resistance en Haute-Saône*, 145.

161   **As the low groan from the departing B-24 tailed off:** Bertin, *Resistance en Haute-Saône*, 145, 147.

162   **As he looked at the deep shadows cast against the moonlit stone walls:** Booth, *Mission Marcel*, 27.

162   **It was a little after noon:** Booth, *Mission Marcel*, 48–50; Burke, *Outrageous Good Fortune*, 27–28.

162   **Simon Doillon brought over Hloba:** Hloba narrative, 35; Burke, *Outrageous Good Fortune*, 28.

162   **The Americans took note of Hloba's slight build:** Calvi, *OSS: La Guerre Secrète en France*, 496.

163   **As they neared a Ukrainian kitchen crew:** Booth, *Mission Marcel*, 50.

163   **Booth turned to Hloba and explained:** Hloba narrative, 35–36; Calvi, *OSS: La Guerre Secrète en France*, 496–497.

163   **At two o'clock, Booth conducted another makeshift ceremonial inspection:** Hloba narrative, 36.

163   **News arrived in the forest by messenger:** Burke, *Outrageous Good Fortune*, 32; Hloba narrative, 36.

163   **A thunderstorm passed through that evening:** Burke, *Outrageous Good Fortune*, 32.

164   **They started the day with a barrage:** Ibid; Hloba narrative, 38.

164   **With Simon and Claude in command:** In his postmission report, Booth included a summary of what transpired: "During the days of 12 and 13 September 1944, the Germans attacked the Ukrainian-Maquis forces three times. The enemy committed between 800 and 900 infantrymen, a battery of 88mm guns and several 57mm guns to the attack. The Ukrainian-Maquis forces threw back each attempt and inflicted heavy losses on the enemy forces. During the battle the Ukrainian forces looked to Captain Doillon and Lt. Vougnon for guidance and not to their own major who was lacking in military ability." OSS, Lt. Col. W. B. Booth Jr., Field Report, Annex IV, Mission Marcel Proust, January 12, 1945.

164   **An hour and a half after the initial exchange:** Hloba narrative, 38; Burke, *Outrageous Good Fortune*, 32–33.

164   **Several times the German companies advanced:** Burke, *Outrageous Good Fortune*, 32–33.

164   **At dawn the following day:** Hloba narrative, 38–39; Burke, *Outrageous Good Fortune*, 33.

165   **In the forest, things had turned bleak:** Burke, *Outrageous Good Fortune*, 33–34.

165   **The next morning the German guns were silent:** Burke, Ibid. Hloba describes the date as September 11, but more likely it was September 12. Hloba narrative, 39. From other accounts it is also likely that by that point Hloba's involvement, at least from a leadership standpoint, may have been minimal.

165 **A villager soon appeared in the distance:** Hloba narrative, 39; Burke, *Outrageous Good Fortune*, 35. Hloba wrote it was a young boy, while Burke stated that it was an old man with legs stiff from shrapnel wounds in World War I.

165 **The German fear of being captured alive:** Burke, *Outrageous Good Fortune*, 35–36; E. Michael Burke to the chief of the SI, memorandum, Paris OSS Headquarters, October 24, 1944.

166 **a descent from a slight rise in the road:** Burke, *Outrageous Good Fortune*, 35–37.

166 **One name would be added for the Second World War:** Booth, *Mission Marcel*, 63–64; Burke *Outrageous Good Fortune*, 32, 38. "Morts pour la France," http://www.memorialgenweb.org/mobile/fr/com_mplf.php?insee1=70169&nom_commune=Confracourt&; http://www.memorialgenweb.org/mobile/fr/resultcommune.php?insee=70169&dpt=70&idsource=42461&table=bp07.

167 **Soon it was an actual crowd:** Burke, *Outrageous Good Fortune*, 37.

167 **Burke sent someone from the village:** Burke, *Outrageous Good Fortune*, 36–39.

167 **Burke spotted Bazeau's wife:** Twenty years later, Waller Booth wrote in a newspaper column: "Mme. Bazeau has not remarried. She still lives in Confracourt and supplements her meager pension by dress-making. At the end of each day, when the household chores are done, she makes her way to the churchyard to care for her husband's grave. Often the flowers she brings are augmented by those of citizens of that district of the Haute-Saône, and sometimes by tokens of grateful pilgrims like me who have occasionally been able to return to the shrine." Waller B. Booth, *The Charleston News and Courier*, June 14, 1964, 16.

167 **Burke sat and took all of it:** Burke, *Outrageous Good Fortune*, 38; Bertin, *Resistance en Haute-Saône*, 218–219.

167 **By the afternoon flags were being unfurled:** Hloba narrative, 40.

168 **Paris had nothing on the celebration in Confracourt:** Ibid.; Booth, *Mission Marcel*, 62–64.

168 **Missing from the celebration in Confracourt:** Hloba narrative, 42; Bertin, *Resistance en Haute-Saône*, 231; Reuchet, *Le Desarroi*, 264.

169 **Silent, Brooding, Everlasting Fate:** "The Olympian gods were cruel, jealous, capricious, malignant; but beyond and above the Olympian gods lay the silent, brooding, everlasting fate of which victim and tyrant were alike the instruments. . . . Full as it may be of contradictions and perplexities, this obscure belief lies at the very core of our spiritual nature, and it is called fate or it is called predestination according as it is regarded pantheistically as a necessary condition of the universe, or as the decree of a self-conscious being." James Anthony Frounde, *Calvinism: An Address Delivered at St. Andrew's* (London: Longmans Green, 1871), 11, https://archive.org/details/calvinismaddressoofrouuoft.

169 **It had taken less than a week:** Bertin, *Resistance en Haute-Saône*, 274.

169   **as Allied soldiers entered the area:** Booth, *Mission Marcel*, 65–66; Burke, *Outrageous Good Fortune*, 39–40; Vartier, "Des Russes," 21. With the arrival of the US Seventh Army, the story of le BUK was picked up by American reporters: "WITH THE SEVENTH ARMY IN SOUTHERN FRANCE, Sept. 14 (AP)—A unit of Ukrainians pressed into service by the under-powered German Army was disclosed today to have killed its Nazi officers and gone over to the Allied side. Some of the troops were prisoners captured as they served in the Russian Army and others were impressed Ukrainians. They were sent to France to combat the underground groups, it was announced." "Ukrainians Go Over to Allies," *New York Times*, September 15, 1944, 5.

169   **On a Saturday morning:** Kosyk, "Les Ukrainians," 26.

169   **took their wounded to Vesoul:** Hloba narrative, 41.

170   **To the Russians:** In early 1944, SHAEF had made inquiry to Moscow representatives about the preferred disposition of Russian nationals captured in post-D-Day combat. They received a dismissive response that such a question was unanswerable because there were no Russians serving in the German military. A different message emerged from Moscow in the initial weeks after D-Day, when the first Russian and other non-German fighters were captured and were treated by Americans as German prisoners of war. SHAEF message to US military mission to Moscow, Russian Nationals Is Subject, S-65786, 7 November 1944. The British practice was different, segregating their "Russian" prisoners and shipping them to the UK. By early September, meetings by the Russian, Americans, and British on repatriation had begun. As outlined by Russian major general Vasilieve during a September 19, 1944, meeting with British general Venables and Firebrace, and American major general Barker, Moscow sought Russian and other Soviet non-Germans in German uniform to be brought under Russian control and organized for shipment back to their homes. Minutes of meeting, SHAEF G-1 Division, GAP 383.6–20, 20 September 1944.

170   **To the British:** Memorandum by Major General, IC Administration, 21st Army Group, "Disposal of Non-German Nationals," July 6, 1945, 21 Agp/41381/A(Wehr), 1. As late as July of 1945, instructions from London to British missions also stated that among non-Germans held as prisoners of war or disarmed personnel, "persons styling themselves as Ukrainians" and identified by Soviet representatives as Soviet citizens "would be repatriated to the USSR without regard to their personal wishes."

170   **To others, at least some of the soldiers in le BUK were Poles:** In the early fall of 1944, SHAEF estimated that more than twenty thousand prisoners of war held by the Allies in France were Russians, Cossacks, or other non-Germans. There was no coherent policy among the Allies as to how they should be treated. The situation was further complicated by SHAEF's interest in not getting in the way of a nascent French government beginning to assert its jurisdiction over matters taking place on its soil. The complexities only grew during the subsequent months as the military conflict advanced eastward across the Continent, where upward of 5 percent of prisoners were discovered to be Russians and other non-Germans, each with their own individual story. Added to the mix were civilian refugees (including Germans) that had begun pouring toward the west, fleeing the Red Army. Numerous SHAEF meetings with the Russians, multiple pleas for political guidance from the Joint Chiefs of Staff, and a Yalta "decision" of sorts all brought no resolution. The British and Americans continued to take different approaches to repatriation.

It was a complicated brew among the Allies. On the one hand, as is often celebrated, London was not shy during those days about lecturing the Americans on the geopolitics of the Continent and the coming descent of an iron curtain. Considerably less attention has been given to how, in those same days, the British were so miserably late in coming to grips with the fundamental human rights issues presented by the large numbers of non-German prisoners and refugees who were so resistant to being sent to an existence under the authority of Moscow, more than a few to the point of suicide. See, e.g., Nicholas Bethell, *The Last Secret: Forcible Repatriation to Russia 1944–1947* (London: Andre Deutsch Limited, 1974); Nikolai Tolstoy, *The Secret Betrayal 1944–1947* (New York: Scribner, 1977).

The communications in British and American archives pertaining to repatriation, dating from late 1944 into mid-1945, are fascinating to read, so much so they deserve something close to an "as is" publication. The materials show an unsurprising mix of naïveté and imperial hubris, on the part of both parties. More significant, though, the raw files reveal a striking fussiness in the Western view of the ongoing war that could not have been more distant from the feral reality of the Ostfront and the resulting atavistic orientation toward a Great Patriotic War. Most histories of the Second World War provide little acknowledgement and even less meaningful analysis of the simultaneous existence of two such fundamentally different perspectives by Allies regarding the same ongoing conflict, and what it meant to the war and its aftermath.

170   the correct side of a boundary line: The August 1919 description of George Curzon, then British secretary of state and architect of the proposed and rejected "Curzon Line" as the boundary of the Polish eastern frontier, was written by then British chief of general staff Sir William Robertson. Philip Warner, *Passchendaele* (South Yorkshire, UK: Pen and Sword, 2005), 63.

170   Assigning group identity: After the end of the First World War, a solution to the nationalist foment was thought to be in the drawing of new boundaries on the Continent. It was a failure. At the end of the Second World War, instead of boundaries being shifted, people were moved. This required, or perhaps reflected, the Western Allies' fixation on assigning millions of displaced and destitute people to a particular national sovereignty or "ethnonationality." The undertaking was more than just a bungling of the first degree. Gregor Dallas writes that after the First World War "the idea of 'national sovereignty' did not go away. Among the Western Allies, the Second World War even reinforced it. They attempted to impose it on the rest of Europe by transferring 'ethnic groups' to national blocs; not only was this inhumane, it had no basis in law, for there was never an international peace settlement. So a terrible legal ambiguity hung over millions of people in Europe. It took more than five years to sort the problem out. Some of the sorting out was brutal in the extreme. The Jews, in the immediate aftermath of the war as throughout the war, suffered the worst; they belonged to no 'nation' and neither the Western Allies nor, in particular, the Soviet Union made much effort to solve the problem." Gregor Dallas, *1945: The War That Never Ended* (New Haven: Yale University Press, 2005), 481.

The triumphant Western Allies sought a tidier European geography and they achieved it. The effects of moving people lasted longer than the post–World War I solution of moving boundaries. Unconfronted, though, was the core of the matter: the obsessions with tribal identity and ethno-national sovereignty. In the twenty-first century the same cauldron is once more astir, heated with newly stoked fears over demographics and the otherness of certain unwanted groups. There can be little doubt where it will lead, on European soil and elsewhere.

170   **Kuzmuk was ordered by Booth to remain with le BUK:** Booth, *Mission Marcel*, 67; OSS, *Booth Mission Report*, 3.

170   **He would spend most of his days:** Calvi, *OSS: La Guerre Secrète en France*, 503.

170   **The time at the abbey:** Hloba narrative, 41.

170   **But the days were also draped in a gray shroud:** Vartier, "Das Russes," 22.

170   **Kuzmuk became very fond of the Ukrainians:** Calvi, *OSS: La Guerre Secrète en France*, 503.

171   **A few days into their encampment:** Hloba narrative, 41. Despite regular meetings between the Western Allies and their Red Army counterparts and assurances to the contrary, in late September and early October there were repeated reports from Lyons and other locations about Russian officers roaming the French countryside without SHAEF authorization, looking for what they considered "escapers and evaders" and attempting to set up facilities for assembly and evacuation. Six Army Group message for SHAEF, BX-16673, 25 September 1944.

171   **On September 19, Kuzmuk was visited:** Calvi, *OSS: La Guerre Secrète en France*, 503–504.

172   **Bermont learned what was going on:** Andre-Paul Comor, *L'Épopée de la 13e demi-brigade de Légion étrangère, 1940–1945* (Paris: Nouvelles Editions Latines, 1988), 285.

173   **Booth was summoned to Vesoul for a meeting:** Booth, *Mission Marcel*, 94–97.

173   **Within days, by at least September 22:** SOE, Report of September 1944, No. 4 Special Force Unit, W. G. Bartlett, Col. & ESN Head, Lt. Col.

174   **The 13th DBLE (13e Demi-Brigade de Légion Étrangère) had fought in Norway in 1940:** Comor, *13e demi-brigade de Légion étrangère*, 284–285. With regard to the arrangement with General de Lattre, Comor cites de Lattre's book,

Histoire De La Première Armée Française. Rhin et Danube (Paris: Plon, 1949), 179–180.

174   the promised period of rest: Calvi, *OSS: La Guerre Secrète en France*, 504.

174   Booth also used the meeting to achieve informal agreement: Booth, *Mission Marcel*, 103–104; Burke, *Outrageous Good Fortune*, 41.

174   Hloba, along with a few of his officers and Kuzmuk: Booth, *Mission Marcel*, 75.

174   Booth had arranged for them to join his small team: OSS, Lt. Col. W. B. Booth Jr., Field Report, Annex IV, Mission Marcel Proust, January 12, 1945. Both Doillon and Vougnon were awarded US military decorations.

174   In less than a month, Simon would be dead: Death came to the twenty-nine-year-old Simon Doillon on October 7, 1944. Burke, *Outrageous Good Fortune*, 46; Booth, *Mission Marcel*, 152–153, 156–158.

174   Claude Vougnon would weep for two days: On Christmas Eve 1944, Simon's brother, a pilot with the RAF, was shot down over the skies of Germany. As for Booth, he would be recalled to OSS HQ before the end of the month. Claude would go on to serve in combat with the French First Army. There is a stone memorial to both Doillon boys in Haute-Saône.

175   Of the twenty or so from le BUK: "Le BUK, bataillon ukrainien de la Haute-Saône," *Le Blog de Betty Faivre* (of Confracourt), August 18, 2009, http://bettyfaivre.over-blog.com/article-34294189.html. By contrast, hundreds from the other mutineer Ukrainian battalion, stationed to the south of Haute-Saône, were repatriated by force, turned over to the control of a Soviet Army colonel. They were taken by train to Marseilles, where the Russians had set up an assembly area, and then by boat to Odessa. According to a French officer who participated in the transport to Marseilles, there were riots and bloody fights, along with suicides and murders. It is likely most were executed once they arrived at Odessa. Vartier, "Das Russes," 39.

175   As for the hundreds who joined the French Foreign Legion: Calvi, *OSS: La Guerre Secrète en France*, 504. The personal intervention by Kuzmuk on behalf of the Ukrainians was likely one of a number of incidents that resulted in Booth's unhappiness with Kuzmuk's performance during the mission. In his postmission report, Booth wrote, "All American personnel performed their duties creditably except Lt. Kuzmuk, whose case has been dealt with separately." OSS, Lt. Col. W. B. Booth Jr., Field Report, Marcel Proust Mission, January 12, 1945, 4. In his own post-mission report, Mike Burke wrote, "Prior to the arrival of Marcel, the battalion had been willing and anxious to carry out the orders of Simon and Claude, despite any attendant danger. Unfortunately, however, Lt. Kuzmuk's attitude created a situation that threated to nullify any control Simon and Claude had over the Ukrainians. Lt. Kuzmuk was about to be withdrawn as liaison officer with the battalion, when the area was overrun by our forces." E. Michael Burke to the chief of the SI, memorandum, Paris OSS Headquarters, October 24, 1944.

175   The Ukrainians were then scattered throughout various units: Comor,

13e demi-brigade de Légion étrangère, 285–286. Hloba did not join the French Foreign Legion. The following spring he noted his unhappiness with the scattering of the soldiers after the first battle, characterizing the dispersal as having been done because of political circumstances. Hloba narrative, 41.

175   **On November 9, *Pravda* reported:** UMILMIS Moscow Russia From Deane to SHAEF Main for General Smith, REF No M-21658, SHAEF 154/10, November 9, 1944. Later reporting revealed that the reference in the *Pravda* account to Marseilles was a mistake in identity, that those particular Ukrainians (not from le BUK but from the mutineer battalion of Ukrainians to the south) were not being recruited but were by then in Italy, on their way to Odessa.

175   **In December, the Russians would up the ante:** Comor, *13e demi-brigade de Légion étrangère,* 285–286. Those who commanded the Ukrainians were unanimous in extolling the bravery of the Ukrainian soldiers. Lieutenant Colonel (later General) Bernard Saint-Hillier, who was with the 13th DBLE most of the war and became its overall commander in March 1945, also added an opinion about certain propensities of the Ukrainians pertaining to alcohol and women ("qu'ils sont un peu pillards et portes sur la fille"). Ibid.

176   **continued in the next decade to serve in postwar French Indochina:** Comor, *13e demi-brigade de Légion étrangère,* 285–286 (citing French intelligence officer Henri Jacquin, who served in the French Indochina war); Calvi, *OSS: La Guerre Secrète en France,* 504.

176   **The faded and deliberately obscured record suggests that a very small number:** Years later, Jean Reuchet observed that it was a small minority of le BUK that found refuge in the region. Such a haven was not within the reach of the rest, who had no alternative other than repatriation into the hands of the Russians or joining the 13th DBLE. The latter would enter the hard fighting that took place in the Vosges and Alsace, where losses were significant. Reuchet, *Le Desarroi,* 264. Some of le BUK reportedly made their way to Argentina, where they formed a settlement of farmers. Vartier, "Das Russes," 39.

176   **Another was Myroslaw:** While there are a few undated photographs suggesting that Myroslaw spent the winter of 1944-1945 in France, it is also possible that he fled from the Russian officers then roaming the French countryside by heading east. Among the possessions found after his death was a work permit issued by a locksmith in Saar for a brief period ending in February 1945. In areas controlled by the Germans a work permit had particular significance because it was needed to obtain food. Saar fell to the Allies in March.

177   **He marveled at how it rained late each afternoon:** Boyd, letter to parents, September 19, 1944.

177   **Got a letter from Brownie:** Boyd, letter to parents, September 26, 1944.

178   **In the early afternoon it began to rain:** "The Weather in the Nation," *New York Times,* October 14, 1944, 25.

178   **he stepped outside the barracks at Camp Kilmer:** US Army Division Historical Association, *Lightning, The History of the 78th Infantry Division*

(Nashville, TN: The Battery Press, 2000; originally published by Infantry Journal Press, 1947) (cited hereafter as *Lightning*), 16.

178   **When Brownie had returned to Camp Pickett from Wisconsin:** Ibid., 15–16.

179   **Brownie made a mental note:** Don, letter to parents, January 16, 1945.

179   **As for the small area of Haute-Saône not yet freed of occupiers:** The rest of Haute-Saône would not be liberated until November 25. "Chronologie de la Liberation," Archives, Département Haute-Saône, Vesoul, France.

179   **Many explanations have been offered:** The relevant volume of the official series, "United States Army in World War II," provides the usual inventory of potential explanations for the sudden cessation of Allied momentum, but also notes, albeit in a most careful roundabout wording, that a "torpor" existed during those days at the highest command levels. Charles B. MacDonald, *The Siegfried Line Campaign* (Washington, DC: US Army Center of Military History, 1993; first published 1963 by Office of the Chief of Military History), 618–619.

179   **the unusually heavy fall rains:** The rains in France during the autumn of 1944 were the heaviest of the century. Russell Weigley, *Eisenhower's Lieutenants* (Bloomington, IN: Indiana University Press, 1981), 366.

180   **He learned that day:** Boyd, letter to parents, October 15, 1944.

181   **It just seems since I had that wonderful furlough it put a spark in me:** Ibid.

181   **For Don, Friday had a late finish:** Three ships were needed to transport Don's division: the *Carnarvon Castle*, the *John Ericsson*, and the *George O. Squier*. *Lightning*, 16–17; *Combat Journal: The Story of the Timberwolf Regiment of the 78th Lightning Division in World War II, 1944-1945* (Fulda, Germany: Parzeller, September 1, 1945) (cited hereafter as *311th Combat Journal*), 13. Edwin P. Parker, *Memoirs of Edwin P. Parker* (Durham, NC: 78th Division Veterans Association, 1976), 20–21; Green et al., *78th Infantry Division*, 15–16. "William H. Hess," Heroes Forever, http://www.heroesforever.nl/William%20H%20Hess. htm (Hess was with Company B of the 311th Regiment); US Army, *The Story of the 310th Infantry Regiment, 78th Infantry Division, in the War against Germany, 1942-1945* (Berlin: Druckhaus Templhof, 1946) (hereafter cited as *Story of the 310th*), 21. Lloyd Chauvin, conversation with author, January 2010. Chauvin was in a machine gun platoon in Company M, 311th Regiment, 78th Division. He knew Don well, going back to the first days in 1943 at Camp Butner and, in 1944, Camp Pickett.

181   **At the top was the entrance to a ship:** In peacetime, the *Carnarvon Castle* had been a British luxury cruise liner with accommodations for 659 passengers in three classes. The upcoming trip was its first since being refitted as a troop ship. The remainder of Don's division was carried by two other ships. Originally built in 1926 in Belfast, and rebuilt in 1938, the *Carnarvon Castle* saw action at the start of the war as an armed merchant cruiser, with a top speed of eighteen to twenty knots. "Royal Mail Steam Packet Company Kylsant Empire

Part 7," Ships Nostalgia, Interactive Shipping Encyclopedia, last modified February 2, 2009, http://.shipsnostalgia.com/guides/Royal_Mail_Steam_Packet _Company_Kylsant_Empire_Part_7; "The Royal Navy in South Atlantic," Sixtant, World War II in the Atlantic, http://www.sixtant.net/2011 /artigos.php?cat=the-royal-navy-in-south-atlantic&sub=royal-navy-ships-%281 33-pages--150-images%29&tag=16%29amc-carnarvon-castle-f-25.

181 **Those that would be in their convoy:** "Convoy CU.43," CU Convoy Series, Arnold Hague Convoy Database, http://www.convoyweb.org.uk/cu /index.html?cu.php?convoy=43!~cumain. Had Boyd not entered the Army Air Corps in the fall of 1943, he would have been in the same convoy as Don, which included four troopships carrying his old outfit, the US 14th Armored Division. On the first page of the small address book he carried throughout the war, Boyd would write down, presumably in mid-1945, two German place names. Only many years later was it determined that they were the places where Don's 78th Infantry Division and Boyd's old 14th Armored Division were positioned on V-E Day. How he was able to determine those positions, or why he did so, or whether it meant he had a chance to attempt a visit with his old outfit or to make contact with Don's Company M during the days following the end of the war in Europe is unknown.

182 **They had not yet been told their destination:** *Lightning*, 18; *311th Combat Journal*, 14.

185 **fewer people were listening:** The resulting reduction in the national radio-listening audience, attributed to wartime shortages of new radios and radio parts, was estimated to be as much as 15 percent. Richard K. Bellamy, "Riding the Airwaves," *Milwaukee Journal Green Sheet*, August 21, 1944, 2.

186 **Nurtured initially in the great remove:** Author Paul Fussell, a combat veteran in the European war, wrote at length about publicity hound antics by American high-level command and described a wartime industrial complex devoted to "morale culture" that lived on after the war. As to the temperament of the troops in the field, Fussell noted that "among those fighting there was an unromantic and demoralizing sense that it had all been gone through before. . . . What is missing from all the high-minded wartime moments is any awareness of the mind of the troops in the field. They were neither high- nor particularly low-minded. They were not -minded at all." Paul Fussell, *Wartime: Understanding Behavior in the Second World War* (New York: Oxford University Press, 1989), 132, 143–178, 179.

186 **devoted to a grand cause:** Another example of the perspective carried by many of the boys: "Despite recruiting posters to the contrary, I realized that our bunch of GIs was not fighting for mother, country, and apple pie. Bullshit. We wanted to live. Our ties were to those unfortunates fighting next to us, sharing the same fate, and beating the same odds." John B. Babcock, *Taught to Kill* (Dulles, VA: Potomac Books, 2007), 54. Babcock was in Don's division, part of Company L in the 310th infantry Regiment.

186 **the digestive systems of thousands of boys:** Al Zdon, "Laying Wire

Across Europe: The story of John Finnegan," *Minnesota Legionnaire Magazine*, early 2000s (no longer available online). Finnegan was with Don's regiment, part of the Second Battalion's HQ Company and later an editor of the *311th Combat Journal*.

187   **as the last of his regiment disembarked:** Three thousand two hundred soldiers made up Don's regiment. The 311th was one of four regiments in the 78th Infantry Division, and was itself made up of three battalions. Don was in the regiment's Third Battalion which had four companies, along with a headquarters company. His unit, Company M, arrived at the front with 150 soldiers and 8 officers. Brownie was a mortar squad leader, part of a heavy weapons platoon that consisted of three machine gun squads and three mortar squads.

187   **sometimes up to ten in a room, in what had once been hotels and private homes:** *Lightning*, 18–19.

187   **Except for the initial unsettling sight of barbed wire:** *311th Combat Journal*, 14–15; Babcock, *Taught to Kill*, 20–22. In addition to the published accounts and official records cited, the chronicle of Don's time at the front is also drawn from conversations and correspondence with several members of Don's company: Lloyd Chauvin, Red Garcia, and Whalley Williams, as well as a medic attached to the company, Robert Reed. Where appropriate, their comments are cited.

187   **New orders came:** *311th Combat Journal*, 15; US Army, Company M, 311th Regiment, Morning Report, November 19, 1944; *Lightning*, 18–20.

187   **Weighted down by a full field pack:** *311th Combat Journal*, 15–17; Babcock, *Taught to Kill*, 20–22; Green et al, *78th Infantry Division*, 16.

187   **"Really beat up":** Don, letter to parents, January 16, 1945. When Boyd departed Europe in late 1945, he sailed out of Le Havre. By then he had seen much of the war's devastation and should not have been surprised by anything. Nonetheless, he was shocked at the abject ruin of Le Havre, and the memory of the sight would always stay with him.

188   **It was their first look:** *Lightning*, 18–19; *311th Combat Journal*, 15–17; Babcock, *Taught to Kill*, 20–22; Green et al, *78th Infantry Division*, 16; "William H. Hess," Heroes Forever; Chauvin, conversation; Fred DeMien, "The Military Service of Frederick G. DeMien," *Flash*, April 1999, 88, 90–91. DeMien was with Company K of the 311th Regiment in Don's Division. *Flash* was the periodical published by the 78th Infantry Division Veterans Association.

188   **The rain kept coming:** *311th Combat Journal*, 17; *Lightning*, 20; Chauvin, conversation.

188   **Two days later, Brownie and his mortar squad left camp:** US Army, Company M, 311th Regiment, Morning Reports, November 1–30, 1944; *311th Combat Journal*, 17; *Lightning*, 20.

190   **At least until the US First Army became even more desperate:** Weigley, *Eisenhower's Lieutenants*, 569–570. Things would change two months hence, the hands of the great being forced by the overwhelming need for infantrymen. Upon the personal insistence of Eisenhower, black soldiers were to be trained separately in black units, notwithstanding the US Army Ground Forces Reinforcement System having been set up to train soldiers as individuals, not as groups. Ibid., 660–663.

In mid-March, some black riflemen would enter combat with a battalion that was attached to Don's regiment and positioned alongside Don's battalion. According to the 1946 history of the 310th Regiment, 78th Division, "A volunteer platoon of first-class Negro troops had joined Company A, two days previously [March 14, 1945], and were seeing their first engagement. Under the immediate command of Technical Sergeant John A. Staggers, the Negro troops carried the fight to the Germans with unusual ferocity and valor. We were proud of them." *Story of the 310th*, 105.

Four years after the war, a soldier who had been a platoon sergeant in the same battalion wrote, "Company A was actually a reinforced rifle company, having received on 12 March [1945] a 'Sunday Punch' in the form of a fourth rifle platoon. This platoon was composed of all-volunteer Negro soldiers who, a few weeks previously, had taken a condensed form of infantry training in France and were sent at once to the First Battalion, 310th Infantry. This platoon soon proved to be an excellent fighting force and a welcome addition to a sorely depleted rifle company." The author of the monograph footnoted that particular paragraph with the citation, "Personal Knowledge." Edwin Freakley, "Operations of the 1st Battalion, 310th Infantry (78th Division) in the Crossing of the Ludendorff Bridge at Remagen, Germany, and the Expansion of the Bridgehead, 7–17 March 1945" (Rhineland Campaign) (personal experience of a platoon sergeant), monograph for Advanced Infantry Officers Course, Fort Benning, GA, 1948–1949, 23.

190   **settled by Celts:** The oldest buildings where Don grew up were barely a hundred years old, built during the mid-1850s, including the three-story old stone shop, considered ancient, where Julius had his meat locker business.

190   **once the home of Charlemagne:** Karl Baedeker, *Germany: A Handbook for Railway Travellers and Motorists* (Leipzig: Karl Baedeker, 1936), 269–270.

191   **Never in his life, Don would later say:** Don, letter to parents, January 16, 1945. Aachen was actually considerably larger than the combined 1940 population of Green Bay (46,235) and Wausau (27,268). *The Federal Writers' Project Guide to 1930s Wisconsin*, 591. Aachen had "163,000 inhabitants" according to Baedeker's 1936 *Germany*.

191   **Moving at a deliberate, slow pace:** US Army, 311th Regiment, After Action Report, December 1–31, 1944.

191   **One of the planes:** DeMien, "Military Service," 98.

192   **Once inside, the absence of daylight:** *Lightning*, 35; DeMien, "Military Service," 92; US Army, *Blue Infantrymen: The Combat History of the Third Battalion, 310th Infantry Regiment, Seventy-Eighth "Lightning" Division* (np, 1946), 1.

192   **Artillery was no longer a distant thunder:** Writing in a secretly kept journal about two weeks before, another infantryman who had just arrived in the Hürtgen Forest attempted to describe what it felt like during a heavy barrage: "The concussion is so great that our internal organs quiver and dance. It's hard to describe

the exact sensation. It's as though heart and lungs, stomach and liver and lights, were suspended in Jell-O and the bowl being shaken violently. It's not too unpleasant after you get used to it, but sleep is frequently difficult." Raymond Gantter, *Roll Me Over: An Infantryman's World War II* (New York: Presidio, 1997), 37. Gantter was an enlisted man with the US First Infantry Division, 16th Regiment, Company G, arriving at the front in the Hürtgen Forest on November 21, 1944.

192 **The war's noise would always be beyond replication:** According to one of the newly arrived boys in Don's division, "We instantly realized that war sounds like nothing else. . . Screaming exploding 88's, silent approaching muffled exploding mortars, the cacophonous chatter of machine guns, the crack of rifles, all mixing sounds that punctuate the knowledge that war is hell." "World War II Remembered by Harry C. Foster," *Flash*, April 1999, 18. Foster was with the 310th Regiment, Company M, 78th Infantry Division. Writing at the age of seventy-five about things that transpired when he was twenty, Foster thought it necessary to add that not everything he carried from those years was available for sharing with others: "I do not intend a narration on all my experiences in combat nor do I intend to touch upon the wounded, the fatalities, the frightened, the shell shocked, the pains and thoughts that race through one's head or the peace of mind when the firing ceases." Ibid.

192 **The boys had been ordered to dig in:** DeMien, "Military Service," 92.

193 **There had been no training for the absolute aloneness:** "The state of mind that action induces primarily and superficially is fear, with peaks of almost hysterical tension. Fear becomes commonplace—like death, an accepted everyday, ever-present condition. War is no longer entirely freakish and uniquely barbaric. It becomes normal and real with the deep reality of a nightmare." John Ellis, *The Sharp End: The Fighting Man in World War II* (London: Aurum Press, 1990), 100, quoting Neil McCallum, author of *Journey with a Pistol* (London: Victor Gollancz, 1959).

193 **The first night in Germany:** DeMien, "Military Service," 98; Babcock, *Taught to Kill*, 24; *Lightning*, 22, 32–34. Responding to a questionnaire in August 1944, 65 percent of a US Division in northwest Europe admitted that "on at least one occasion they had been unable to perform adequately because of extreme fear." Almost half, 42 percent, said that this happened on more than one occasion. In another survey of a US Division, 20 percent of the boys admitted to shitting their pants in combat because of fear. Ellis, *The Sharp End*, 102–103. One soldier in a division positioned near Don described his first frigid night in a foxhole at the front: "Words cannot convey the awfulness of this ordeal to the reader. My buddies and I agreed it would be impossible to exaggerate how hopeless, miserable, and depressed we felt." George W. Neill, *Infantry Soldier: Holding the Line at the Battle of the Bulge* (Norman, OK: University of Oklahoma Press, 2000), 97. A longtime journalist, Neill served during the war as an infantry rifleman with the 99th US Infantry Division.

193 **out of a Bill Mauldin drawing:** *311th Combat Journal*, 23; *Lightning*, 33; Al

Zdon, "Laying Wire Across Europe." The units being relieved by the 311th regiment included the 13th Regiment from the ill-fated 28th Infantry Division, one of five US Divisions (along with the First, Second, Fourth, and Ninth) that were almost completely destroyed during the previous months of repeatedly futile attacks made in the area known as the Hürtgen Forest. "After months of fighting, the forest floor had taken on an aspect reminiscent of the ravaged 'no-man's-land' of World War I. Wasted machines and shattered equipment were strewn throughout the forest and the stench, from bodies left in the open, was almost unbearable." Ted Ballard, *Rhineland 15 September 1944–21 March 1945*, US Army Center of Military History (2003) http://www.history.army.mil/brochures/rhineland/rhineland.htm.

193 **Each of those badly aged souls:** William F. Meller, *Bloody Roads to Germany* (New York: Berkley, 2012), 56; Edward G. Miller, *A Dark and Bloody Ground* (College Station, TX: Texas A&M University Press, 2003), 53; Howard Apter, "The Terrible Victory," *Saga Magazine*, October 1962, reprinted in *Rhine Journey*, a collection of articles published by 78th Division Veterans Association, undated (c. 1970), 1–10.

194 **The corpses of American boys:** Mack Morriss, "The Huertgen Forest," *Yank Magazine*, January 5, 1945, 1–2; Cecil B. Currey, *Follow Me and Die: The Destruction of an American Division in World War II* (New York: Berkley/Jove, 1991), 296.

194 **a place known as the Ardennes:** Charles B. MacDonald, *A Time for Trumpets* (New York: HarperCollins/Perennial, 2002), 83–84.

194 **They were near the village of Germeter:** US Army, Company M, 311th Regiment, Morning Reports, December 9–15, 1944.

194 **East of Aachen:** *Biennial Reports of the Chief of Staff of the United States Army to the Secretary of War*, 1 July 1939–30 June 1945 (Washington, DC: US Army Center of Military History, reprinted 1996), 144.

194 **There has never existed:** The next sentence of the official report states, "The dams of the Roer were seriously inhibiting General Eisenhower's progress." Ibid. The latter is a dishonorable mischaracterization. While there is some disagreement as to the exact date, there is no dispute that it was no earlier than the very last days of November 1944 when the dams beyond the Hürtgen Forest were even recognized as a critical objective (unlike the forest) for achieving further advancement into Germany. The main element "seriously inhibiting General Eisenhower's progress" was the insistence over the course of the autumn of 1944 that the Hürtgen Forest was a military objective, attributable only to Eisenhower and his leadership team of generals and, in particular, Lieutenant General Courtney H. Hodges, commander of the US First Army, who was allowed by his superiors to lead thousands of American boys into slaughter.

194 **The word "splendidly":** No doubt such a use of the word "splendidly" is akin to the more modern invocation of the word "synergy," similarly aimed at providing a happy but factually empty characterization to a functionally useless joinder of business or government organizations.

195   remains inexplicable as a military objective: Charles MacDonald, the former Deputy Chief Historian of the Army, could not have been more gentle and vague when writing about the Hürtgen Forest in the official US Army history of the war: "The basic truth was that the fight for the Huertgen Forest was predicated on the purely negative reason of denying the Germans use of the forest as a base for thwarting an American drive to the Rhine. In the process the fight thus far had failed to carry the only really critical objective the forest shielded—the Roer River Dams." MacDonald, *The Siegfried Line*, 493. In another written history that was not an official publication of the government, MacDonald provided more clarity: "The real tragedy in battle is when men suffer and die for objectives that are not commensurate with the cost. Those in the Huertgen Forest fought a misconceived and basically fruitless battle that could have, and should have, been avoided." Charles B. MacDonald, *The Battle of the Huertgen Forest* (New York: J. B. Lippincott Company, 1963; Reprinted by University of Pennsylvania Press, 2003), 205. German generals could not understand the American fixation with the Hürtgen Forest, nor did they have much respect for the military planning and execution under the leadership of the US First Army. Currey, *Follow Me and Die*, 304–305. A capsule summary of the horror of the combat in the forest was provided after the war by the German Generalmajor (equivalent to a US brigadier general) Rudolf Freiherr von Gersdorff, who stated, "I have engaged in the long campaigns in Russia as well as other fronts . . . and I believe the fighting west of the Roer, especially in the Hurtgen, was the heaviest I have ever witnessed." Miller, *A Dark and Bloody Ground*, 203; Currey, *Follow Me and Die*, 51–52. "The forest could have been bypassed to the south, with the dams as the objective. The forest without the dams was worthless; the dams without the forest were priceless. But the generals got it backward, and went for the forest. Thus did the Battle of Hürtgen get started on the basis of a plan that was grossly, even criminally stupid." Stephen Ambrose, *Citizen Soldiers* (New York: Simon and Schuster, 1997), 167.

195   Cota: In November 1944, Major General Norman D. Cota was the commander of the US Army 28th Infantry Division. Considered a hero for his actions during the Normandy invasion, his performance at Hürtgen was so dreadful that, for at least a period in the early years of the twenty-first century, it was included as a case study of leadership at the US Army Command and General Staff College at Fort Leavenworth, Kansas. Lt. Col. (ret) Thomas G. Bradbeer, "Major General Cota and the Battle of the Huertgen Forest: A Failure of Battle Command?" (undated monograph), http://usacac.army.mil/cac2/cgsc /repository/dcl_MGCota.pdf.

One author summarized Cota's failures: "Whatever Cota may have done before, whatever he became afterward, his mistakes in this battle are legion. He tried to present a successful front to his superiors while he knew full well that the battle was a disaster, that victory was an illusion, that his men were being massacred. His G-3 periodic reports portrayed such an unrealistic picture of the combat they can only have reflected three possible motives: the effort of a staff that wanted to hide from Cota what was occurring; or they reported what Cota thought was happening; or what he wanted Generals Gerow and Hodges to think was happening." Currey, *Follow Me and Die*, 301.

195   **Hodges, Bradley:** Lieutenant General Courtney H. Hodges was commander of the US First Army, reporting to Lieutenant General Omar Bradley, who commanded the US 12th Army Group. Throughout the fall, Hodges was obsessed with the forest as a military objective, ordering four separate assaults that were doomed before they began. All of them failed, American boys needlessly sacrificing themselves. What transpired would have been easily foreseeable with only the most basic awareness of the situation at the front, as one would think would be the responsibility of leadership. The appalling episode is not welcome among the touchstones within the accepted narrative of the war. With very few exceptions, historians of the Second World War have been prone to give an oddly genteel treatment to the abominable detachment and failures that were the hallmarks of the Allied leadership performance in the fall of 1944 that led to the repeated unnecessary massacre of American boys.

A number of such accounts read as though the authors are reluctant to pursue such behavior among good friends or, perhaps, those with whom they feel a great affinity. In his volume on the final nine months of the war in Europe, Sir Max Hastings observes that "a fatal combination of *unimaginative command decisions* by Bradley and Hodges and *undistinguished combat performance* by some of the units committed enabled the Germans to inflict greater pain than they suffered in the Hurtgen" (italics added). Hastings, *Armageddon*, 193. In a later volume on the Second World War, Hastings characterizes Hodges as the "*least impressive* commander of a US Army," and suggests that the "autumn operations were conducted with *notable clumsiness*" (italics added). Hastings, *Inferno*, 563. In a more recent offering, historian Antony Beevor describes the performance of Hodges in early November as one of "obstinacy and a failure to listen," carefully chosen dual-purpose words that in many present-day circles within Western capitals would be considered simple excesses of tough-minded leadership. Antony Beevor, *Ardennes 1944: Hitler's Last Gamble* (New York: Viking, 2015), 64. The description is a very strange way to describe the performance of an American general who repeatedly sent boys off to die in vain, attempting to achieve a militarily unnecessary objective under a plan that, as Beevor also observes, "was just about as inept as it could be."

On the other hand, terms like "panic" and "laziness" appear to be reserved for lieutenants, sergeants, and privates, written with an almost audible sniff. One recent example of this phenomenon: "General Patch's Seventh Army was heavily outnumbered, and it fought well, with just a few exceptions due to panic in the rear or laziness at the front." Beevor, *Ardennes 1944*, 327. No similar descriptions are used for those whose decisions placed the Seventh Army in a position to fight while "heavily outnumbered." It remains unclear what on earth would constitute "laziness at the front" by those boys thrust into such conditions made worse by dithering leadership and awful logistical support during those days in November and December 1944.

195 **Eisenhower:** The behavior of Cota and Hodges combined with what passed for involvement by Bradley and Eisenhower, along with the enabling sycophancy in the rear-echelon ranks that stood between them and the boys at the front, all make for sickening reading. What happened in the Hürtgen Forest deserves to be far more familiar among the general public, and not only because it is an important part of the American Second World War experience. The episode also deserves wider understanding as a more broadly applicable cautionary tale about the unique peril always lying in wait within outsized organizations due to the inevitably catastrophic sweep of second- and third-order consequences when dysfunction takes place among a detached few at the highest levels. Recent examples in American society are plentiful, where the effects of a twitch from a certain insulated level within inordinately swollen institutions have roiled across the everyday life experiences of millions of Americans—whether it involves basic banking activities, flying from one part of the country to another, maintaining an insurance policy, relying upon an electrical power or communication network, or using a social media service.

195 **As did the political leaders of the day:** In 1975, combat veteran and novelist James Jones wrote, "One can perhaps honestly say that history is in fact written by the upper classes for the upper classes. And if that is so, then the whole history of my generation's World War II has been written, not wrongly so much, but in a way that gave precedence to the viewpoints of strategists, tacticians and theorists, but gave little more than lip service to the viewpoint of the hairy, swiftly aging, fighting lower class soldier." James Jones, *WWII: A Chronicle of Soldiering* (Chicago: University of Chicago Press, 2014; originally published by Grosset & Dunlap, 1975, as the text for a volume of illustrations), 61. Jones, whose novels set during the war included *From Here To Eternity* and *The Thin Red Line*, served in the Pacific, including at Guadalcanal.

195 **familiar top-heavy, smoothed-out vision of the Second World War:** Commenting on a wartime debacle in Sicily where Allied soldiers were killed by their own guns, combat veteran Paul Fussell writes, "Popular histories of the war emphasizing the moral, administrative, and engineering distinction of the Allies easily ignore [the particular Sicilian debacle].... This is typical of popular histories of the war written on the adventure-story model: they like to ascribe clear, and usually noble, cause and purpose to accidental or demeaning events. Such histories thus convey to the optimistic and the credulous a satisfying, orderly, and even optimistic and wholesome view of catastrophic occurrences—a fine way to encourage a moralistic, nationalistic, and bellicose politics." Fussell, *Wartime*, 21–22.

196 **a sprinkling of flavor:** A succinct articulation of the formula for delivering a properly unrevealing high-church narrative of the Second World War was provided by British war historian Sir Max Hastings in an early 2016 survey of new books about the war. Presumably intended as the highest praise, Hastings notes that the work of a particular author "combines in his usual masterly fashion the big picture with shellhole-level anecdote." Max Hastings, "What's New About the War?" *New York Review of Books*, March 10, 2016.

196   the cloister of the high-level command post: In a diary entry for Thursday, January 25, 1945, command-post denizen and army combat historian Forrest Pogue writes, "In virtually every section (ours included) 2/3 of the time is wasted. It is particularly horrible to see the wastage when you see people of talent assigned as clerks, and then not doing anything. Every headquarters company has a large staff which waits on the headquarters people. In [every] Army, Corps, Division, Regiment I have seen carpenters who nothing but make knick knacks for the officers; here we have a sign painter who spends nearly all his time making cute signs like 'Close the door softly'; 'No loitering'; 'Pick up your laundry,' etc. — all done with special lettering and pictures. Nearly every after action report we got has much extra art work on the covers. We work about 2 days out of 7 in our section.... Down in regiment where they cry for men I saw two men spend all their time taking care of the Colonel (while it may be true that they help to save valuable time which he would spend in taking care of his stuff, there is much time that he doesn't do anything either). The COMZ [Communications Zone, which included Services of Supply Headquarters] set-up is shocking. 150 hotels in Paris; working on a schedule of 8:30–5:30 (more nearly 4:30); off one afternoon a week; frequently other afternoons off. They have no conception of front line life. It is nearly as bad here at Corps and in many cases clear up to Regiment. Only in battalions and companies do the headquarters people show most of the discomforts of the men in the line." Forrest Pogue, *Pogue's War: Diaries of a WWII Combat Historian* (Lexington, KY: University Press of Kentucky, 2006), 333–334. Pogue served as a combat historian with the US Army V Corps from Normandy through the Rhineland campaign.

196   As Don's regiment had taken its position: *Lightning*, 33–34; Chauvin conversation. A mortar platoon in the company normally had six 81 mm mortars, organized into three sections, each composed of two squads. A squad was led by a sergeant, such as Don, while the gunner was a corporal with one assistant and five ammunition bearers. US War Department, "Infantry Battalion," Table of Organization and Equipment, No. 7–15, Washington, DC, 26 February 1944, http://www.militaryresearch.org/7-15%2026Feb44.pdf4.

196   moving Don's squad on foot: Babcock, *Taught to Kill*, 46; Williams, conversation.

197   Orders had gone out: DeMien, "Military Service," 93; *Lightning*, 28, 33–35; Parker, *Memoirs*, 22.

197   You are about to enter your first combat: Parker, *Memoirs*, 22.

198   Twice in the previous twelve months: In April of 1944, Don's division lost all of its privates, sent overseas to participate in the Normandy invasion. Many of the replacements came from the release of more than a hundred thousand from the Army Specialized Training Program, which had been set up to provide some college education to inductees identified as intelligent. "We joked that the ASTP replacements raised the IQ of the unit." Chauvin, conversation. More than twenty thousand boys were also released to ground forces in early 1944 from the aviation cadet program, which Boyd wanted so badly to join but had been turned away from in January 1944 because the program for future pilots was full. Weigley, *Eisenhower's Lieutenants*, 374–375, 436; *Story of the 310th*, 16.

198   **Their replacements were arriving:** *Story of the 310th*, 16–17.

198   **there had been little time:** With an openness not to be found concerning US military personnel matters in the twenty-first century, the 1946 army-published history of another regiment in Don's division described the situation in the 78th: "Contrary to common belief, 65% of the enlisted men of this regiment were not seasoned infantry trainees, but rather had come to the organization from other branches within three or four months before departure from the States. While there may be some question as to the real training value of maneuvers, there can be no doubt that hunger, loss of sleep, exposure to the elements and actual physical hardships for long periods was to be a new experience for these people." *Story of the 310th*, 19. A survey during the war found that "out of 1,000 infantry and artillerymen interviewed as they came out of the line at Cassino [early in the 1944 Italian campaign] fully two-thirds of them averred that training in such things as finding and handling mines and booby-traps, the nature of enemy weapons, enemy tactics, enemy defenses, and what to do for trench foot had been completely inadequate." Ellis, *The Sharp End*, 19, 304–307.

198   **Hardly an American infantry division in Europe:** MacDonald, *Time for Trumpets*, 116; Weigley, *Eisenhower's Lieutenants*, 570. Weigley is not alone in his conclusion that "the American army in Europe fought on too narrow a margin of physical superiority for the favored American broad-front strategy to be anything but a risky gamble." Ibid., 464. However, Weigley also goes on to make a curious defense of Eisenhower's strategy by declaring that it was not that the broad-front strategy was wrong, but that Ike had not been given enough troops to carry it out "safely." The assertion is much like saying someone is too short for their weight. It was the unwavering adherence to a broad-front strategy that generated the dangerous logistics and personnel situation and reflected a strategic planning that managed to be both faith-based and cautious at the same time.

198   **As for how the boys:** Harold E. Cahill, "Operations of the 310th Infantry (78th Infantry Division) in the Attack on Rollesbroich, North of Malmedy, 13–16 December 1944" (Rhineland Campaign) (personal experiences of antitank company commander), monograph for Advanced Infantry Officers Course, Fort Benning, GA, 1949–1950, 10, 19–21.

198   **American tanks were no match for German tanks:** Miller, *A Dark and Bloody Ground*, 207; Hastings, *Armageddon*, 81–86. The tanks were undergunned and carried only light armor. They had been designed for speed and mobility, one of many incompatibilities with the undertaking of a "broad-front strategy."

198 At the front there was a shocking reliance on runners for communication: Warren Fagerland, "As I Recall the War," Black Hills Veterans Writing Group, http://www.battlestory.org/index.php?p=1_76_WARREN-FAGERLAND-ARMY (Fagerland was with Company F, 310th Regiment, 78th Division); Miller, *A Dark and Bloody Ground*, 207–208; Robert Reed, conversations with author, February and March 2007.

199 Coming from a nation with a 1944 economic output: Mark Harrison, *The Economics of World War II: Six Great Powers in International Comparison* (Cambridge: Cambridge University Press, 1998), 27 (economic output as measured in terms of gross domestic product, in international dollars and 1990 prices). The 1944 comparison: US $1499 b; UK $346 b; Germany $437 b; Japan $189 b.

199 rags that they could find: Ed Cunningham, "Winter War," *Yank Magazine*, March 2, 1945, 3–5.

199 When Don's division arrived: Green et al, *78th Infantry Division*, 26.

199 Don was able to secure: Don, letter to parents, January 16, 1945.

199 The boots Don wore: Cahill monograph, 10, 20–21; Edward G. Miller, *Nothing Less Than Full Victory* (Annapolis: Naval Institute Press, 2007), 187; Ellis, *The Sharp End*, 186–187; Cunningham, "Winter War," 3–4; John H. Barner, "Operations of the 2nd Battalion, 311th Infantry (78th Infantry Division) in the Attack on Kesternich, Germany, 30 January–1 February 1945" (Rhineland Campaign) (personal experience of a company commander, cannon company which supported this action), monograph for Advanced Infantry Officers Course, Fort Benning, GA, 1949–1950, 7–8.

199 There were no white camouflage suits: Barner monograph, 7–8.

199 rattled like a bunch of tin cans: Cunningham, "Winter War," 3–5; Gantter, *Roll Me Over*, 109–110.

200 The clothing situation was so severe: Cahill monograph, 19–21. General Parker, commander of Don's division, personally raised the matter of clothing with General Hodges and also pressed the issue with General William Simpson, who commanded the US Ninth Army. Ibid.; Miller, *A Dark and Bloody Ground*, 207–209.

200 It is difficult to overstate: Cunningham, "Winter War," 3–4; Neill, *Infantry Soldier*, 107–108, 324–332. On December 29, 1944, a US rifleman who was positioned not too far away from Don and did not have any winter gear, wrote in his diary, "I wish the smug people at home could see this 'best-equipped army in the world,' particularly in our present dress. We read about us in rare magazines and hometown papers, and we look at ourselves in stark amazement. No matter what the papers say, we *look* like Czech guerrilla forces." Gantter, *Roll Me Over*, 112. Gantter's outfit received their winter gear at the end of January 1945. Ibid., 141.

Latter-day narratives of the war present things differently. According to the epilogue in the final volume of a recent award-winning trilogy about the Second World War in Western Europe: "From D-Day to V-E Day, GIs fired 500 million machine gun bullets and 23 million artillery rounds. 'I'm letting the American taxpayer take this hill,' one prodigal gunner declared, and no one disagreed. By 1945 the United States had built two-thirds of all ships afloat and was making half of all manufactured goods in the world, including nearly half of all armaments. The enemy was crushed by logistical brilliance, firepower, mobility, mechanical aptitude, and an economic juggernaut that produced much, much more of nearly everything than Germany could—bombers, bombs, fighters, transport planes, mortars, machine guns, trucks—yet the war absorbed barely one-third of the American gross national product, a smaller proportion than any other belligerent. A German prisoner complained, 'Warfare like yours is easy.' There was nothing easy about it, of course." Rick Atkinson, *The Guns At Last Light* (New York: Picador, 2014), 633.

One can easily imagine the dogface scowl and foul-mouthed sardonic comment from Don and the others in his squad in response to such rapture so detached from the war's reality. Don and most of the other boys already knew that such a notion of what supposedly "crushed" Germany would be difficult to explain to the 4.9 million German soldiers who were meeting their death on the Ostfront (versus 580,000 German military deaths in Africa, Italy, and northwest Europe combined). Ellis, *The Sharp End*, 322. The swoon over the American economic performance when compared to other belligerent nations experiencing the war's kinetic activities within their borders is beneath comment.

200   **To the extent such a temporary change in higher-level command:** Writing not only as a military historian but as someone who fought in the Ardennes, Charles MacDonald later reflected on how little information a frontline soldier had: "Did it really matter to the American soldier, fighting for his life in the harsh cold and snow of the Ardennes, who commanded him at the top? Who was this Montgomery? Who was Bradley? Who, even, was Hodges or Gerow, Collins, or Ridgway? (Patton was another matter.) A frontline soldier was immensely well informed if he knew the name of his company commander, who had just arrived the day before to replace that other one who had lasted only a week." MacDonald, *Time for Trumpets*, 614.

200   **The toilet paper was of high importance:** Chauvin, conversation; Babcock, *Taught to Kill*, 56; Gantter, *Roll Me Over*, 98.

200   **The morning of Don's fourth full day:** Douglas E. Nash, *Victory Was Beyond Their Grasp: With the 272nd Volks-Grenadier Division from the Hürtgen Forest to the Heart of the Reich* (Bedford, PA: Aberjona Press, 2008), 109, 124; *Blue Infantrymen*, 1; *311th Combat Journal*, 20.

201   **After half an hour:** Chauvin, conversation; Nash, *Victory Was Beyond*, 118; *Lightning*, 34–36.

201   **Some of them saw an officer killed:** US Army, 311th Regiment, After Action Report, December 13, 1944.

202   **One company in Don's battalion:** Ibid.

202   **Some of the boys:** DeMien, "Military Service," 92–93; *Lightning*, 33–36; Bill   Roose,   "Turner's   Ultimate   Sacrifice,"   November   8,   2012,

https://www.nhl.com/redwings/news/turners-ultimate-sacrifice/c-645248.
Lieutenant Joseph Turner, formerly a goalie with the Detroit Redwings, participated in the combat that day as part of K Company, 311th Infantry, 78th Division. Initially declared missing in action as of December 13, 1944, his status was changed to killed in action after his body was recovered on January 12, 1945.

202   **Two other companies never advanced:** US Army, 311th Regiment, After Action Report, December 13, 1944.

202   **In the early afternoon:** Ibid.

202   **Only three among their wounded:** US Army, Company M, 311th Regiment, Morning Reports, December 1944.

202   **Another nearby company:** DeMien, "Military Service," 92–93. Sixty-eight years later, another member of Company K of the 311th Regiment, Dr. William B. Gaynor, recalled that first day of combat with bitterness toward those who insisted on engaging the Germans in such a setting. "We lost 98 percent of our platoon that day. I wasn't a happy warrior. I didn't like the Army. I didn't like what you call the chickenshit leadership, and whatnot." Roose, "Turner's Ultimate Sacrifice."

202   **Later that day the commander of the same company:** DeMien, "Military Service," 92–93.

202   **The next day brought:** Miller, *A Dark and Bloody Ground*, 182.

202   **the Germans went silent:** Reed, conversation; MacDonald, *Time for Trumpets*, 95–96.

203   **The bombardment came from thousands of German guns:** MacDonald, *Battle of the Huertgen Forest*, 194; Nash, *Victory Was Beyond*, 139; MacDonald, *Time for Trumpets*, 117–121.

203   **killed during the shelling:** US Army, Company M, 311th Regiment, Morning Reports, December 1944.

203   **a few rubbers of bridge:** MacDonald, *Time for Trumpets*, 185–186.

203   **Only once during the autumn:** MacDonald, *Battle of the Huertgen Forest*, 24.

203   **The noise of the planes:** *Lightning*, 57–58.

203   **In most historical accounts:** See, e.g., MacDonald, *Time for Trumpets*, 75–79.

203   **The information about the counterattack existed and had been gathered:** Hugh M. Cole, *The Ardennes: Battle of the Bulge* (Washington, DC: US Army Center of Military History, 1993; first published 1965 by Office of Chief of Military History), 56–63. Beevor, *Ardennes 1944*, 102–105.

204   **It would not be the last time:** "Intelligence failure" explains nothing. The repeated invocation over the years is the necessary predicate in the unhumble grammar used by historians of the war to give a pass to the highest levels of leadership for what happened at Ardennes. Those who lead and command any organization are the ones who set the overall frame of mind by which everyone is to provide their particular service. In the months before Ardennes, the atmosphere established and nurtured by SHAEF not only ensured but de facto demanded information and analysis that was strictly in accord with certain notions about the direction of the war, which, as it turns out, were quite detached from the war's reality. While this organizational scenario is well known to the American scene, military and otherwise, when it comes to assessing the run-up to the Ardennes, most war histories still seem to say otherwise. For example, one biographer of Eisenhower notes that the intelligence had been "tuned" to justify Ike's policies in an atmosphere requiring reassurances that the end of the war was near. But he then attributes such an environment not to top Allied leadership but to lesser beings in SHAEF G-2. Carlo D'este, *Eisenhower: A Soldier's Life* (New York: Holt, 2002), 640–641.

In another recent chronicle describing Ardennes, one war historian wrote, "To be sure, there were clues, omens, auguries. Just as surely, they were missed, ignored, explained away. For decades after the death struggle called the Battle of the Bulge, generals, scholars, and foot soldiers alike would ponder the worst US intelligence failure since Pearl Harbor and the deadliest of the war. Only from the high ground of history could perfect clarity obtain, and even then the simplest, truest answer remained the least satisfying: mistakes were made and many men died. What might have been known was not known. What could have been done was not done." Atkinson, *The Guns At Last Light*, 412. Thus does "intelligence failure" become a sort of least untruthful answer capable of explaining away virtually any fiasco, whether in 1944, 2003, or various points in between and beyond, while also delivering an absolution as a privilege held by an unaccountable few, something not available to those who bleed.

204   **Equally notable was the amount of time:** Hastings, *Armageddon*, 204–207; D'este, *Eisenhower: A Soldier's Life*, 646. General Courtney Hodges went into an almost complete paralytic emotional collapse during those first days of the attack. See, e.g., Beevor, *Ardennes 1944*, 203–204; Jean Edward Smith, *Eisenhower in War and Peace* (New York: Random House, 2012), 408–410.

204   *die Hölle im Hürtgenwald*: "the hell in Hürtgen Forest"

206   **A serene pink onto the same blanket of snow:** Martha Gellhorn, "Battle of the Bulge," in *Reporting World War II, Part Two, American Journalism 1944–1946*, ed. Samuel Hynes, Roger Spiller, Nancy Sorel, and Anne Matthews (New York: Library of America, 1995), 599–606.

205   **Dull gray clouds hung low:** Nash, *Victory Was Beyond*, 147.

206   **Don and thousands of other American boys were positioned in a meteorological area:** Marvin D. Kays, *Weather Effects During the Battle of the Bulge and the Normandy Invasion* (White Sands Missile Range, NM: Atmospheric Science Laboratory, 1982), 7–14, 19–21. The forested terrain of highlands, ridges, and ravines also contributed to wide variances in weather within the region. The average yearly number of days of freezing temperatures in one point (Stavelot) versus another (Bastogne) less than forty miles away differed by more than thirty days. Ibid., 9.

206   Off to his left and off to his right: *Lightning*, 58–63; Nash, *Victory Was Beyond*, 146; US Army, 311th Regiment, After Action Report, December 1944.

206   Fortune had placed: *Lightning*, 57–58; MacDonald, *Time for Trumpets*, 599; Nash,.*Victory Was Beyond*, 151.

206   a forbidding arctic murk: MacDonald, *Time for Trumpets*, 252.

206   Don's division completed a gradual shift: Barner monograph, 6–7; *311th Combat Journal*, 23.

207   Nearby were a few villages: Nash, *Victory Was Beyond*, 127; Reed, conversation.

207   Someone in the proper boots and warm outerwear that Don did not have: "Blue-Star Commando" was the derisive nickname given by the doggies to rear-echelon troops, those stationed in command posts and with supply outfits. "There's much talk and laughter about 'Blue-Star Commandos,' SOS [Services of Supply] and rear area troops wearing all the combat and paratrooper boots and combat jackets." Cunningham, "Winter War," 3–5.

207   an official written report reflecting that "a strict non-fraternization policy was put into effect": US Army, 311th Regiment, After Action Report, December 1944.

207   Where usable bomb craters could not be found: Babcock, *Taught to Kill*, 37; Reed, conversation.

207   The holes we sleep in: Don, letter to parents, January 16, 1945.

207   The favored technique: Chauvin, conversation; Cunningham, "Winter War," 3–5.

208   Don and one of his buddies: It was a common practice throughout the Ardennes area for the boys to build their own stoves. Cunningham, "Winter War," 3–5.

208   You should see that baby heat: Don, letter to parents, January 16, 1945.

208   What Don really wanted: Ibid.

208   A bitterly cold Christmas came and went: *Lightning*, 62–64, 68–70; US Army, 311th Regiment, After Action Report, December 1944; *Story of the 310th*, 50; Chauvin, conversation.

208   Allied leadership effortlessly spread its own fears: On December 20, 1944, Sergeant Forrest Pogue wrote in his diary, "Remarkable how little we know of the situation; how much the high-ranking officers deal in rumor-mongering. . . . Much complaint about our failure to go to the Rhine in September. It seems remarkable that few expected counterattack." Pogue, *Pogue's War*, 295. The jitters at SHAEF approached a level of panic, yet it is rarely called out by historians. Eisenhower pressed Marshall to get some sort of help from Stalin, an undertaking not without cost and of little or no benefit. Ike also sought a transfer of divisions from Italy, or, in the alternative, having one hundred thousand marines sent to him from some unnamed place he may or may not have had in mind. Perhaps the most lasting achievement of the surprise German counterattack was in the motivation it provided for Ike to set his staff to work on a plan for raising volunteers from the Negro "race" to join the American infantry. MacDonald, *Time for Trumpets*, 604–605.

208   gas masks were handed out: US Army, 311th Regiment, After Action Report, December 1945. Thousands of miles away, still in Mississippi, Boyd wrote to his parents: "Boy they sure had us ready to go across in a hurry down at Gulfport when the Germans broke thru in Belgium. Guess it threw a scare into them." Boyd, letter to parents, January 7, 1945.

209   Conversations were brief: Reed, conversation; Chauvin, conversation.

210   Most of the boys knew that it was never a matter of weakness or strength: Reed, conversation; Chauvin, conversation. As noted by historian Gerald Linderman, "To the men on the line, neuropsychiatric collapse was no phantom. They took issue both with those commanders who denied its reality and with those psychiatrists who, while granting its existence, attributed it to the 'accumulation of experience' beginning at birth and thus held that soldiers who faltered in battle were those who had entered the service already impaired. Combat soldiers thought otherwise; they had watched the collapse of men they knew to be weak and strong, deceitful and straightforward, doubting and devout. They at first associated psychological damage with weapons injuries, notably blows to the brain, but soon decided that long exposure to deprivation, danger, and the deaths of friends was ample cause. They found no way to determine why some broke down and others went on, why some recovered and others stayed disordered; but with time in combat every man, they became convinced, would arrive at his breaking point." Gerald F. Linderman, *The World Within War* (Cambridge, MA: Harvard University Press, 1997), 355. Linderman notes that one of the most-celebrated American battles, on Okinawa, yielded one of the least-celebrated statistics: not only were 7,613 American boys killed or missing and 31,807 wounded, but there were also 26,211 psychiatric casualties. Ibid., 356. Unfortunately for those boys who made it through the war and came home, if they lived long enough into the twenty-first century they were made to endure being in the vicinity of those habitually given to breaking wind with their vacuous and ultimately dismissive "thank you for your service."

210   The weather alone was a punishing enemy: Eisenhower's war memoir includes a rather daft discussion of the shortages on the European front. Focusing only on gasoline and cigarettes, he does not mention the dire clothing and weapons situation. Ike assures the reader that, about the gasoline and cigarettes, he "was thoroughly angry." Apparently blind to irony and to the outrage it triggered at the front (which lingered after the war), he pridefully describes how those found guilty of black-market activities were offered a chance of an alternative to a severe prison sentence—in the form of joining other infantrymen like Don at the front. As for the trench foot that ripped through the infantry in the fall and winter of 1944–1945, Ike's perspective was that "effective prevention was merely a matter of discipline; making sure no one neglected the prescribed procedure," and he even includes a brief if bizarre primer on proper foot-care technique. For anyone who knew some of those dogfaces and what they went through because of the well-dressed failure in performance throughout rear-echelon areas, the entire section makes for strange and vile reading, even for those with an otherwise generally high regard for Ike. Dwight D. Eisenhower, *Crusade in Europe* (New York: Doubleday and Company, 1948), 315–316.

210   **As December turned into January:** US Army, Company M, 311th Regiment, Morning Reports, December 1944–January 1945; Barner monograph, 36; Babcock, *Taught to Kill*, 58–59.

210   **Cleanliness was rapidly becoming:** *Lightning*, 68; *Story of the 310th*, 49–50; DeMien, "Military Service," 96.

211   **On the fourth day:** Nash, *Victory Was Beyond*, 184, 189; US Army, 311th Regiment, After Action Report, January 1945.

212   **After a few hours they would freeze solid:** DeMien, "Military Service," 97; Miller, *A Dark and Bloody Ground*, 208.

212   **only with the bottoms of the coats rolled up:** *311th Combat Journal*, 23–24.

213   **For each of the first twenty days:** US Army, Company M, 311th Regiment, Morning Reports, January 1945.

213   **The Germans were accomplished at:** Reed, conversation; Chauvin, conversation; Babcock, *Taught to Kill*, 72.

213   **"usual" combat duties included going on hunts for sewing machines:** Cahill monograph, 20–21; *Lightning*, 75; Babcock, *Taught to Kill*, 71.

213   **Excess white rags and tape:** DeMien, "Military Service," 95.

213   **taunts flew back from American loudspeakers:** Babcock, *Taught to Kill*, 74–75.

213   **Patrols were often sent out with the specific mission:** US Army, 311th Regiment, After Action Report, December 1944 and January 1945.

214   **Well, be good and don't worry:** The letter was edited, no doubt at least for some grammar and to remove the plus signs that both Don and Boyd habitually used as shorthand for the word "and." It was then taken down to the town newspaper and appeared in the March 1, 1945, edition, under the headline "48 Hour Pass Intrigues Soldier."

214   **On the day Brownie returned:** US Army, 311th Regiment, After Action Report, January 1945.

214   **And so it continued:** Ibid.

214   **It was around that time:** Ibid.

214   **the largest land battle in American history:** Miller, *Nothing Less Than Full Victory*, 186.

215   **An episode such as the Ardennes:** In the twenty-first century it is most unsettling to compare writings and remarks of combat veterans during the first three decades after the war with the more recent historical output that has evolved into a stream of adventure-story encomiums on the Second World War experience, suggesting something approaching a time of national enchantment and individual human growth. The depth of the bow to the spirit of Oliver Wendell Holmes and his grand assignations about youthful hearts "touched with fire" during war appears to be directly proportional to the level of pomposity and name-dropping in the acknowledgements section of such volumes.

Thirty years had not yet passed after V-J Day when philosopher and World War II veteran J. Glenn Gray confronted the ghost of Holmes and wrote, "Who of us today would adhere to the doctrine [Holmes] wrote as a mature man of fifty-four: *War when you are at it is horrible and dull, it is only when time has passed that you see that its message was divine.* Who today would experience anything but disbelief when [Holmes] continues: *I do not know what is true. I do not know the meaning of the universe. But in the midst of doubt, in the collapse of creeds, there is one thing I do not doubt, that no man who lives in the same world with most of us can doubt, and that is that the faith is true and adorable which leads a soldier to throw away his life in obedience to a blindly accepted duty, in a cause which he little understands, in a plan of campaign of which he has no notion, under tactics of which he does not see the use.*" (italics added to set apart quote of Holmes described by Gray).

Gray underscored how things were different in the wake of the Second World War: "There may well be those who still subscribe to such a faith; in fact, almost certainly some exist in every nation. But it is a safe guess that fewer exist in our decade than formerly, and perhaps a reasonable prophecy that their numbers will steadily decline, despite the fact that more men are under arms than ever before." J. Glenn Gray, *The Warriors: Reflections on Men in Battle* (Lincoln, NE: First Bison Books, 1998; first published 1959 by Brace, Harcourt), 223. No doubt Gray would be surprised and dismayed at how his prophecy has not proved "reasonable" in a later American society that docilely accepts the notion of perpetual war urged forward by those who have no personal stake in its prosecution.

215   Precious little of the Ardennes victory can be attributed to Allied leadership: Readers of recent histories of the Ardennes could be forgiven if they were to conclude that the battle turned on the patter between generals as recorded by a multitude of dutiful attendants. Historians of the war continue to show a bewildering confusion between accessibility to command-post accounts and a grasp of frontline realities large and small. Patton always provided good copy, and few things are more overblown in all the majestic chronicles of the Second World War than the accounts of him leading a rush to relieve the defenders of Bastogne. The achievement had almost nothing to do with the success or failure of the German offensive. According to Forrest Pogue, "Several commanders, including General Eisenhower, have given high praise to the units on the north flank of the Bulge for their role in blunting the first drives of the great offensive in the north, but their contribution has been dimmed by the memory of the great defense put up at Bastogne and the brilliant Third Army march northward. But had units to the east and north of Bastogne not slowed the enemy, the Germans would have been west of that objective and perhaps at the Meuse before the airborne divisions could have arrived from Reims." Pogue, *Pogue's War*, 325–326. Relevant to Brownie's unit, it does not appear that much analysis has ever been done on an intriguing question of whether the ill-fated mid-December attack at Kesternich by two regiments from the 78th Division (undertaken while Don's regiment provided a diversion farther to the north) may have unwittingly thrown one of the biggest wrenches into the entire works of the German offensive—given the place of the encounter and its residual effects on the movement on German supplies and troops a few days later when the Ardennes counterattack got under way.

Success of the Ardennes counterattack was completely dependent on how far the Germans could manage to advance in the first twenty-four to forty-eight hours. Decades of accounts that all but scoff at the desperation in the German move has led to ignorance about just how achievable those early objectives were, the result of the indefensible positioning of the thin American lines without any reserve. The latter is rarely given deep examination, usually referenced only in the context of high-level pearl-clutching such as Bradley's petulance during those days toward Eisenhower and Montgomery, and his open fretting over a potential Congressional investigation. See, e.g., Beevor, *Ardennes 1944*, 328.

The skewed narrative of the Ardennes was locked in early. Historians have done little to move the story outside the high-strung orbit of Eisenhower, Patton, Bradley, and Montgomery, who were all quite walled off from what was unfolding at the front lines in the opening days of the battle, and even beyond. They each generated many well-recorded dramatic personal exchanges but lent very little to the shape of circumstances of the battle on the ground, other than arranging for its awful beginning and ensuring an orderly German retreat. The American victory at Ardennes did not turn on their performance.

215   **In the first days of the German offensive, there was much high-level bravado:** Writing to another general on December 17, Eisenhower said, "If things go well we should not only stop the thrust but should be able to profit from it." Weigley, *Eisenhower's Lieutenants*, 496. In his order of the day for December 22, Eisenhower said, "By rushing out from his fixed defenses the enemy may give us the chance to turn his great gamble into his worst defeat." MacDonald, *Time for Trumpets*, 604.

It is doubtful any other series of military communications and meetings during the entirety of the Second World War was more heavily documented or commented upon by participants and observers than what transpired in those first days after the German counterattack—even though (or perhaps because) such exchanges had so little consequence or connection to what was happening at the front. But the episode makes obvious the strange and, at times, all too conspicuous vicarious association on the part of war historians toward those at an elevated level, an overdone attachment to the oh-so-exquisite swagger, cleverness, and ribald humor. For example, virtually every recent history of the Ardennes includes the same quote, attributed to Patton, about having "the guts" to let the Germans go all the way to Paris, and "then we'll really cut 'em off and chew 'em up." See, e.g., Weigley, *Eisenhower's Lieutenants*, 500; D'este, *Eisenhower: A Soldier's Life*, 644; MacDonald, *Time for Trumpets*, 420; Smith, *Eisenhower*, 411; Michael Korda, *Ike, An American Hero* (New York: Harper 2008), 537; Beevor, *Ardennes 1944*, 189. Few things demonstrate more readily the complacency resulting from war historians all sitting too close to the same campfire and smelling their own smoke than the repeated inclusion of the same insignificant loud-mouthed bluster at a staff meeting. Far less attention is given to the failure of Allied leadership to undertake an initiative to encircle the "bulge," allowing a measured retreat that merely flattened the front to where it was in mid-December. At least one celebrated biographer of Eisenhower apparently saw no irony in calling the Ardennes "his finest hour as a military commander." Smith, *Eisenhower*, 410.

216   brazenly small behavior: In volume after volume written on the Ardennes battle, each one more formulaic than the next, the behavior of the generals is rendered into a modern version of Greek hymns celebrating individual gods, verses of titillation over Bradley's perpetually hurt feelings, Patton's relentless bombast, Montgomery's buffoonish arrogance, and Eisenhower's struggles dealing with it all after having set the battlefront stage for the German counterattack. In his voluminous chronicle on the Ardennes, Charles MacDonald succumbs like others and deploys an eye-glazing amount of words to dissect the vainglorious back-and-forth that went on between Bradley and Montgomery. He concludes his volume with the commonly expressed and fully deserved salute to the dogfaces. Unlike many others, MacDonald attaches, however gently, the otherwise hackneyed phrase "intelligence failure" where it belongs: "The Victory in the Ardennes belonged to the American soldier, for he provided time to enable his commanders—for all their intelligence failure — to bring their mobility and their airpower into play." *Time for Trumpets*, 618–619.

216   As the end of the month approached: US Army, 311th Regiment, After Action Report, January 1945; "Ernest William Little," Heroes Forever, http://www.heroesforever.nl/Ernest%20W%20Little.htm. Jack Jolly and Ernie Little were in Company M, 311th Regiment, 78th Division. Jolly was with Little in the days leading up to the latter's death in combat action, and provided an account of the events to Little's family. The information was included as part of an online tribute by a Dutch citizen caring for Ernie Little's grave, located in the Netherlands American Cemetery and Memorial, Limburg, Netherlands.

216   His outfit then moved into the ruins: "Ernest William Little," Heroes Forever; Chauvin, conversation.

216   Nearby was an intersection: *311th Combat Journal*, 24.

216   With little talk: "Ernest William Little," Heroes Forever; *311th Combat Journal*, 25.

216   The boots were too heavy: "Ernest William Little," Heroes Forever.

216   They were told their objective: Ibid.

216 **Most of the latter would be tossed aside a few steps into the battle:** James L. Cooper, "Huppenbroich, Germany," extract from "My Father's War" (unpublished, 2011) http://freepages.history.rootsweb.ancestry.com/~eightysecondohio/Battle%20of%20Huppenbroich,%20Germany%201945/huppenbroich%20extract.pdf.. The author's father, Charles W. Cooper, was a member of Company K, part of Don's Third Battalion in the 311th Regiment of the 78th Infantry Division. Williams, conversation.

217 **Don checked over his squad:** "Ernest William Little," Heroes Forever; *311th Combat Journal*, 25.

217 **As the final minutes drew down:** Ibid.

217 **At five in the morning:** Ibid.

217 **It came at half past five:** "Ernest William Little," Heroes Forever.

217 **First they had to cross:** Vernon Greene, "As I Saw It: The Eyewitness Report of a Soldier Who Fought During World War II and Survived," *Special Warfare Magazine*, September 2002, 58. Greene was in Company M, 311th Regiment. He served as a platoon leader, in charge of four machine gun squads. He later received a battlefield promotion. Greene retired from the Army in 1974, holding the rank of colonel.

217 **Waiting for them:** US Army, Operations of the 78th Division, Combat Interviews, 30 January to 4 February, 1945, 14–15.

217 **six of the dozers were lost:** *Lightning*, 79.

217 **The road into Huppenbroich remained unplowed:** Frank Camm Jr., "Seizing the Roer River Dam," The Personal Memoirs of Frank Camm Jr., http://www.62vgd.de/78th/Frank_Camm/. Frank Camm commanded a combat engineer company in the 303rd Engineer Battalion in the 78th Infantry Division. He retired from the Army in 1981, holding the rank of lieutenant general. During the war, his father was also with Don's division, an artillery colonel who later retired from the Army as a brigadier general. Ibid.

217 **The cold air chewed:** Ibid.; Barner monograph, 21; *Lightning*, 85.

217 **When the boys had advanced:** US Army, Operations of the 78th Division, Combat Interviews, 30 January to 4 February, 1945, 15.

218 **Lightening-like flashes shattered:** *311th Combat Journal*, 26–27; Camm, "Seizing the Roer River Dam."

218 **brought some quick improvisation:** Camm, "Seizing the Roer River Dam"; Barner monograph, 24.

218 **During an interview a few weeks later:** US Army, Operations of the 78th Division, Combat Interviews, 30 January to 4 February, 1945, 45 (quoting Third Battalion commander Lieutenant Colonel Andy Lipscomb).

218 **It was left to two more companies:** Ibid., 15.

218 **First light showed itself:** Barner monograph, 14; *311th Combat Journal*, 25–27; US Army, Operations of the 78th Division, Combat Interviews, 30 January to 4 February, 1945, 16; Nash, *Victory Was Beyond*, 213–214; Williams, conversation.

219   **Past the ravine:** US Army, Operations of the 78th Division, Combat Interviews, 30 January to 4 February, 1945, 16 (quoting the observations of Lipscomb).

219   **The final approach was done in single file:** Cooper, "Huppenbroich, Germany."

219   **Behind them, on top of the hill:** "Ernest William Little," Heroes Forever.

219   **Around ten o'clock:** Ibid. Jack Jolly, who related the story to Ernie's family, was one of the few who survived the shelling, having just stepped out of the mineshaft as part of the scout patrol. Ibid.

219   **Inside Huppenbroich:** US Army, Operations of the 78th Division, 30 January to 4 February, 1945, 16; US Army, 311th Regiment, After Action Report, January 1945; Cooper, "Huppenbroich, Germany."

219   **The following morning:** US Army, Company M, 311th Regiment, Morning Report, January 31, 1945. Another company in Don's battalion, Company K, would lose almost a third of its soldiers during that first day and the following day. Cooper, "Huppenbroich, Germany." Don's battalion as a whole suffered 125 casualties that day. DeMien, "Military Service," 98; Miller, *A Dark and Bloody Ground*, 191; US Army, Operations of the 78th Division, 30 January to 4 February, 1945, 16.

221   **Well over a foot of snow:** "Past Wisconsin Climate," Wisconsin State Climatology Office, last modified July 2, 2014, http://www.aos.wisc.edu/~sco/clim-history/acis_stn_meta_wi_index.htm.

221   **The 1945 version would offer only four clear and sunny days:** "Summary of February 1945 weather," *Milwaukee Journal*, March 1, 1945.

222   **scenes from the popular book, *Mr. Lincoln's Wife*:** Anne Colver's novel was published in 1943.

223   **The German-language worship:** Both services would be handled as usual by Reverend Schwertfeger, as he had been doing since arriving in town shortly after Marie was born. The English-language service had been introduced only after the end of the Great War, an event deemed worthy of coverage by the Milwaukee newspapers: "The German Lutheran Church of 1500 members, the largest in Dodge County, will introduce English into the services Sunday. A complete English sermon will mark the event. This is an important occurrence in the history of the community in getting Americanism started." "English To Be Used in German Church," *Milwaukee Journal*, January 12, 1919.

223   **1932's Surprise Selling Sensation:** Advertising insert, *Horicon Reporter*, October 1932.

223   **Ernst paid his nephew $31.50:** According to his ledger, in August 1944 Ernst paid $63.98 to the Bodden Brothers for a load of coal, which, unlike some years, did not need a later topping up.

225   **He awoke that Sunday morning to a nasty mix of rain, snow, sleet, and ice:** Pogue, *Pogue's War*, 338.

225   **When the offensive began:** Miller, *Nothing Less Than Full Victory*, 205.

225   **On the previous Sunday:** US Army, 311th Regiment, After Action Report, February 1945.

225   **On Monday they were on the move again before daylight:** US Army, 311th Regiment, After Action Report, February 1945; *Lightning*, 97. Don's battalion spent the day clearing Germans out of an area just northeast of Kesternich, the small town in ruins after months of close-up fighting so vicious and destructive the boys had dubbed it "little Aachen." US Army, 311th Regiment, After Action Report, February 1945; *Lightning*, 104. The official regimental report for February 5 stated that Don's battalion "continued to mop up enemy elements." The term "mopped up" rankled boys at the front, perceiving it to be a dismissive characterization by someone in a pressed uniform who had no clue of what was actually entailed in such an operation, which was no less deadly than anything else. The term is frequently seen in such reports, part of the jargon of savviness used in a detached command post and, unsurprisingly, taken up by even more detached historians in later years.

In 1963, A. J. Liebling, whose war reporting from Europe for *New Yorker* magazine remains fresh and clear-eyed seven decades after it was written, offered some commentary on postwar books and their relationship with reality: "A sentence like *Middleton's VIII Corps finally secured La Haye-du-Puits on July 8* evokes, for me, a Chinese-American pfc in a company command post in an abandoned *estaminet*, drunk on a bottle of eau-de-vie he had salvaged intact from the broken majority behind the bar. The brandy and the fragile walls gave him the illusion of security while the town burned all around. A hundred yards away, a dead S.S. officer sat in a wicker garden chair on the terrace in front of a small chateau, his field glasses in his lap. He had been looking down the road for American tanks that were nearer than he thought. The men pronounced the place Hooey da Pooey. Or, *Although St.-Lo was taken, it was by no means safe* brings back the sensation of lying on cobblestones, face down, and looking up to steal a glance at the man lying in front of you, noticing that his eyes were closed, like those of a girl waiting to be kissed. Yet he was a brave man, always pushing to get out in front. And a sequin of red-hot metal, too tiny to do harm, floating down before your eyes and lodging on the cloth of his trouser leg, where it made a hole like a very small cigarette burn." A. J. Liebling, "The Beginning of the End," *New Yorker*, October 19, 1963, 216; also in Pete Hamill, ed., *A.J. Liebling: World War II Writings* (New York: Library of America, 2008), 790–791.

225   **On Tuesday, at a half hour before midnight:** *Lightning*, 106; Camm, "Seizing the Roer River Dam."

226   **The town they were to take was spread:** Charles MacDonald, *Victory in Europe, 1945: The Last Offensive of World War II* (New York: Dover, 2007, unabridged reprint; originally published by the US Army Center of Military History and US GPO, 1973), 73–74.

226   **A platoon of tanks:** Camm, "Seizing the Roer River Dam."

226   **The shelling continued through the night:** Ibid.; *Lightning*, 106–107.

226   **The German barrage was so loud:** *Lightning,* 106–107; Camm, "Seizing the Roer River Dam"; DeMien, "Military Service," 100.

226   **It took until Wednesday morning:** Greene, "As I Saw It," 58–59; MacDonald, *The Last Offensive,* 79–80; DeMien, "Military Service," 99–100.

227   **They reached the top of the hill:** The crest was called "Hill 493"; Weigley, *Eisenhower's Lieutenants,* 601.

227   **The lead tank was two hundred yards:** Greene, "As I Saw It," 58–59; Miller, *A Dark and Bloody Ground,* 197–198; Miller, *Nothing Less Than Full Victory,* 200–201; MacDonald, *The Last Offensive,* 79–80; *311th Combat Journal,* 31; *Lightning,* 109–110. The latter says the tank was hit twice.

227   **In the chaos:** Ibid.

227   **The platoons and squads were reassembled:** US Army, 311th Regiment, After Action Report, February 1945; Chauvin, conversation.

227   **Somehow, through the fatigue:** Greene, "As I Saw It," 58–59; DeMien, "Military Service," 101; Chauvin, conversation; MacDonald, *The Last Offensive,* 80; *Lightning,* 109–110; Camm, "Seizing the Roer River Dam."

227   **Those who made it into the town:** Miller, *Nothing Less Than Full Victory,* 200–201; Camm, "Seizing the Roer River Dam"; DeMien, "Military Service," 101; Chauvin, conversation; MacDonald, *The Last Offensive,* 80; *Lightning,* 109–110.

228   **sporadic fighting continued:** MacDonald, *The Last Offensive,* 80; *Lightning,* 109–110.

228   **At around the same time:** Miller, *Nothing Less Than Full Victory,* 202; Miller, *A Dark and Bloody Ground,* 198.

228   **On Monday, one general had overruled:** Miller, *Nothing Less Than Full Victory,* 200. A little later the same day, the commanders in Don's division were also surprised by a sudden higher-level order to engage the enemy that evening. *Story of the 310th,* 66–67.

229   **New orders came that night:** MacDonald, *The Last Offensive,* 77–78.

229   **overturning an order issued by the commanding general of Don's division:** Miller, *Nothing Less Than Full Victory,* 198–199; Nash, *Victory Was Beyond,* 238–239, 242–243. Major General Clarence Ralph Huebner, inserted into the situation by General Courtney Hodges, was commanding general of V Corps of the US Army, having previously commanded the US First Infantry Division.

229   **inserted into the situation by the commander of the US First Army:** Weigley, *Eisenhower's Lieutenants,* 434.

229   **Several times during the week:** Weigley, *Eisenhower's Lieutenants,* 601–603; Miller, *A Dark and Bloody Ground,* 195–198.

229   **the commander of a different infantry division who just happened to walk into headquarters:** During a routine visit to V Corps headquarters, General Louis A. Craig (commander of the Ninth US Infantry Division) encountered General Huebner after the latter had just finished a midday telephone conversation with General Hodges, who was again expressing his dissatisfaction with the situation. MacDonald, *The Last Offensive*, 81. By Friday, the commander of Don's division and his staff were effectively eliminated from a direct role in the ongoing battle. Miller, *Nothing Less Than Full Victory*, 202.

229 **to be in charge of the attack on Schmidt and onward to take the dams:** In his memoirs published three decades after the war, General James Gavin wrote, without using names, about witnessing an encounter between two individuals that can only be Huebner and Craig. According to Gavin, who during those days was commanding general of the 82nd Airborne Division, what he observed took place sometime between the taking of Schmidt and the seizure of the dams: "In the meantime I noticed that the Corps Commander and the Division Commander were bent over a map. The Corps Commander occasionally drew a short line, a quarter to a half of an inch, with a blue grease pencil. It represented an infantry battalion, and he was suggesting to the Division Commander a tactical scheme by moving battalions about. I had the strangest feeling when I realized how remote they were from the realities, from what it was like up where the battalions were. The thought crossed my mind that the disaster that had befallen the 28th Division in the Kall River valley [i.e., in the Hürtgen Forest] might have had some relationship to the lack of understanding in higher headquarters of what the actual situation on the ground was. It turned out to be true, as I learned later." James M. Gavin, *On to Berlin* (New York: Viking Press, 1978; reprinted Bantam Trade Edition, 1985), 265–266.

Gavin also describes with disgust the sight of corpses of American boys still scattered throughout the Hürtgen Forest terrain, killed months before and just emerging in the snowmelt of February 1945: "A catastrophe must have occurred there in the fall of 1944. I could not understand why the bodies had not been removed and buried. Neither Corps nor Army headquarters must have been aware of the conditions in the canyon. Otherwise, the bodies would have been buried and the disabled tanks recovered." Ibid., 264.

229 **the Germans abandoned the area:** The wide chasm between the world of the high-level command post and the actuality of the war has often been carried onward by historians of the war, with cringe-worthy offerings in the breezy overdone voice of the savvy, along with a painful blindness to cold irony. One unfortunate example attempts to sum up the taking of Schmidt and the dams: "Too many cooks had appeared from time to time to meddle in the tactical broth, but once the pressure was off and the division's role could be assessed with some perspective, General Huebner could remark to General Hodges that he had 'made him another good division.'" MacDonald, *The Last Offensive*, 83.

229 **Before leaving, they released:** Nash, *Victory Was Beyond*, 246; Wiegley, *Eisenhower's Lieutenants*, 603.

229 **The front line on Sunday:** Wiegley, *Eisenhower's Lieutenants*, 603; *311th Combat Journal*, 35.

229 **As Sunday morning's snow and frozen rain:** US Army, Company M,

311th Regiment, Morning Reports, December 1944–February 1945. The casualty rate of other companies in Don's battalion was greater.

229 **Hilmer Hobbs:** "Staff Sergeant Hilmer W. Hobbs," 1947 obituary, in Saint Ansgar [Iowan] Museum Obituary collection, last modified June 27, 2009, http://iagenweb.org/boards/mitchell/obituaries/index.cgi?review=239313. Additional background information on Hobbs and the others in Don's company killed during those twelve days and cited in the following notes was obtained through Company M's morning reports, US Army enlistment and draft records, www.findagrave.com, and the 1940 Federal Census records.

230 **Sergeant Hobbs left behind a widow:** Sometime in 1945, after Hilmer's death, his parents learned that his brother, Merle, had survived the sinking of the USS *Houston*. Merle returned home after enduring more than three and a half years as a prisoner of the Japanese, performing slave labor in disease-infested conditions in Burma and Thailand, including on the bridge over the River Kwai. In February 1946, Merle married Marilyn, Hilmer's widow. Merle passed away one year after they celebrated their golden wedding anniversary. "Merle Hobbs" [obituary], *Mason City Globe-Gazette*, March 17, 1997. "St. Ansgar Man Survived USS Houston Sinking, Burma Captivity," *Mason City Globe-Gazette*, August 23, 2014.

230 **known back home in Myrtle, Missouri:** "Pfc. Sherman Clark Killed in Action," *South Missourian Democrat*, February 15, 1945, www.facebook.com /permalink.php?story_fbid=10171996749667780&id=111413672212056. Twelve streets at Camp Grohn, a US military base near Bremen, Germany, from 1945 to 1954, were named for boys from the 311th Regiment killed in the war, including one in honor of Ray Clark. "Camp Grohn Streets Get Names from Valiant Heroes of 311th Regiment," *Timberwolf*, 311th Regimental newspaper, March 1, 1946.

230 **Ernie Little:** Little's remains are in the World War II Netherlands American Cemetery in Margraten, Netherlands, where a local citizen, Hans van Toer, adopted the grave for caretaking. In 2007, with the assistance of a resident of Huppenbroich, Germany, van Toer placed a plaque near the mineshaft in commemoration of the twenty-two American boys who were killed on January 30, 1945. "Ernest William Little," Heroes Forever.

232 **Boyd spent the night:** Boyd, letter to parents, January 11, 1945. The crew was transporting a brand-new B-17, along with one passenger, a second lieutenant who was a P-51 pilot and, according to Boyd, "a swell guy from Alabama."

232 **Their journey took them along the North Atlantic Route:** John D. Carter, "The North Atlantic Route," in *The Army Air Forces in World War II*, ed. Wesley Frank Craven and James Lea Cate, ch. 4, vol. 7, *Services Around the World* (Washington, DC: Office of Air Force History, 1983), 92–113.

232 **not a single plane:** "Weather Was ATC's Big Foe," *Stars and Stripes*, March 12, 1945, 8.

233 **The tense final minutes of the flight were beyond anything Boyd had ever known:** After the war the crew's navigator, William "Mickey" Burke, earned a PhD from the University of Rochester and was a researcher at several medical schools in addition to teaching biochemistry. In 2003, a colleague of Burke's wrote a brief note to inform the 306th Bomb Group veteran's association of the navigator's passing. "Bill and I were co-workers and friends for some thirty-plus years. He did not speak often about his experiences in WWII but I will never forget his 'difficulties' in 'finding' Iceland on his flight to England." "William T. Burke," Correspondence files, 306th Bomb Group Historical Association, http://www.306bg.us/CORRESPONDENCE/b/burke_william_t.pdf.

234 **Only afterward came the understanding:** Boyd sent home a *Stars and Stripes* clipping with a note to his parents to remind him to tell a story about it, underlining certain sentences: "Radio jamming by Nazi submarines occasionally sent some planes off their course to crash against the mountains of Greenland." "The most treacherous route was from Labrador to the British Isles via Iceland or Greenland." "Weather Was ATC's Big Foe," *Stars and Stripes*, March 12, 1945, 8.

237 **and a church that had seen:** A clock dial was added to Saint Peter's of Thurleigh in 1897, in honor of Queen Victoria's Diamond Jubilee. "Thurleigh Welcome Pack," Thurleigh, Bedfordshire, www.thurleigh.net/welcome.php.

237 **The base at Thurleigh was home to what was officially called a "bombardment group":** Boyd and the crew were part of the 367th squadron, which, along with the 368th, 369th, and 423rd, made up the 306th Bomb Group. According to lore the bomb group at Thurleigh was the basis for the fictional 918th (306 x 3) Bomb Group in the 1949 movie *Twelve O'Clock High*.

237 **the Clay Pigeon Air Force, complete with its own logo and a reputation:** Russell A. Strong, *First Over Germany: A History of the 306th Bombardment Group* (Winston-Salem, NC: Hunter Publishing Company, 1982), 303.

237 **On the previous mission to Berlin:** Robert F. Dorr, *Mission to Berlin: The American Airmen Who Struck the Heart of Hitler's Reich* (Minneapolis: Zenith Press, 2011), 295; Strong, *First Over Germany*, 303–305; Roger A. Freeman, *The Mighty Eighth War Diary* (London: Jane's Publishing, 1980; reprinted by Motorbooks International, 1990), 432–433.

237 **the crew was dispersed:** US 306th Bomb Group, Mission Report, February 26, 1945.

238 **nothing short of miraculous:** Years after Boyd's death, found among his boxed-up wartime possessions was a folded small sheet of paper, undated and blank except for what he had handwritten at some point during the war: "The air, like the sea, is not unsafe but terribly unforgiving of carelessness & neglect."

238 **Getting into formation took time.** US 306th Bomb Group, Mission Report, February 26, 1945.

239 **Boyd was one of more than twelve thousand:** On the day's raid to Berlin were 1,207 bombers, with a minimum of nine in a crew, plus seven accompanying fighter planes. Freeman, *The Mighty Eighth War Diary*, 450.

240 **He would later try to explain:** Boyd, letter to parents, March 20, 1945. He overestimated; the size of the stream of bombers more closely aligned to the distance between Chicago and Saint Louis.

241 **He recorded in his own personal notebook that it was "intense":** As to Boyd's assessment of the flak, the official 306th Bomb Group mission report for the day assessed the level of German antiaircraft activity by approvingly quoting the mission leader, who "with nine trips over Berlin, says today was the easiest of lot."

242 **Seems funny to go out on a raid:** Boyd, letter to parents, February 27, 1945.

243 **Their ship was named "Weber's Wagon":** The pilot was twenty-one-year-old John Pinchback, from Georgia. The copilot was Eugene Hartman, from South Bend, Indiana. The navigator was William Burke, from Rochester, New York. The bombardier was Donald Wilson, from Cincinnati, Ohio. Engineer was Robert Stout, from Jackson, Michigan, who did all the artwork on the plane. The radio man was Joe Stehle, from Annapolis, Maryland. William Dooley, from Lynchburg, Virginia, was the ball turret gunner. On some missions they were joined by an add-on, usually a gunner.

244 **Weber's Wagon and thirty-eight other ships:** US 306th Bombardment Group, Intelligence Narrative, March 8, 1945.

244 **Only Berlin, Cologne, and Hamburg:** Richard Overy, *The Bombing War* (London: Penguin Books, 2014), 471, citing Olaf Groehler, *Bombenkrieg gegen Deutschland* (Berlin: Akademie Verlag, 1999). Berlin: 68,285; Cologne: 48,014; Hamburg, 38,319; Essen 36,852. A caution from an American reader: at the time of this writing the US-published version of Overy's book had been given a different title and was missing hundreds of pages of material that was in the UK-published version of the book.

244 **Three days after Boyd's mission:** Overy, *The Bombing War*, 397.

244 **By the time Boyd arrived:** From January to April 1945, American bombers alone delivered a bomb tonnage onto German cities that was four times what was dropped by the Luftwaffe during the ten months of the Blitz on England. Ibid., 390–391.

244 **contrary to war-planning expectations:** Ibid., 462–467. From the days of B-17s over Germany, through the years of B-52s over Vietnam, extending into the twenty-first-century age of drones, there has continued to be a wishful perception of "precision" or "surgical" bombing actions as a sanitary way of conducting warfare, a delusion that nourishes, as it did in World War II and every campaign that has followed, a hubris and absurd alternate reality often possessed by high-level command.

244 **March would be a busy month:** Donald L. Miller, *Masters of the Air: America's Bomber Boys Who Fought the Air War Against Nazi Germany* (New York: Simon and Schuster, 2006), 445. The last confirmed kill by a B-17 gunner from Thurleigh was on March 18, 1945. Strong, *First Over Germany*, 310.

During the first half of March Boyd may have shot down a German fighter. Or he may not have. He never spoke of it after the war. Almost ten years after his passing, a conversation with one of Boyd's fellow crewmen included an unexpected question as to whether Boyd ever talked about his shooting down a

German fighter. Indicating he was not surprised to learn that Boyd had not mentioned it, the radio operator from Weber's Wagon went on to say that it happened very fast and that other planes had been shooting at the German plane as well. He described how the rest of the crew on Weber's Wagon was convinced that the kill was Boyd's but that Boyd himself was not sure, and no claim was made for official credit. Joe Stehle, conversation with author, 2005.

The Stehle account may be a better explanation for the lone skull and crossbones, painted alongside other references to Boyd below his tail-gunner window, than Boyd's dismissal of a question about it years later, when he would only comment that the plane had all sorts of decorative art on it. If it is true that he shot down a German plane, it is very easy to understand Boyd not wanting to have to deal with anyone else about it. Quite a few combat veterans came home to live in that town, but in the war's aftermath of several decades there was no open talk, no celebration, and no displays of admiration about who killed "Krauts" or "Nips," even though it is certain that some did. Those boys saw themselves and were seen by others as citizens who had returned home after doing a job, not warriors. They also did not have to contend with the twenty-first century's shrunken sense of holding segments of the human experience as private.

245   **He learned early on how difficult it was to keep functioning:** After the war, Boyd would not speak about the nature of the terror (other than it was unavoidable) but would describe having to adjust his mind, as though it were a matter of getting on with the day while wearing shoes that pinched or having to sit too close to someone with very bad breath. To a much younger listener, his description was baffling in its clinical and offhand account of how he just had to teach himself that the presence of fear did not matter to what was at hand. Another veteran's description was similar: "Handling his fear was another problem [for a newcomer to battle]. Learning to live with it, and to go ahead in spite of it, took practice and a certain overlay of bitter panache that took time to acquire. There were damned few fearless men." Jones, *WWII*, 56.

245   **The skies on Thursday were overcast all the way to Essen:** US 306th Bombardment Group, Intelligence Narrative, March 8, 1945.

246   **During those weeks:** Reed, conversation; Chauvin, conversation.

246   **Far beyond the wide plain was a small cluster of dark bumps:** "Final Battle for the Dam," *Flash*, May 1957, in *Rhine Journey*, 78th Division Veterans Association, undated (c. 1970), 26–27.

246   **After Don's battalion jumped off:** *Lightning*, 141; Pogue, *Pogue's War*, 344.

246   **They took one town after another, places like Obergartzem:** *311th Combat Journal*, 38.

247   **Don's regiment secured towns they would know:** *Lightning*, 141.

247   **Many German soldiers were captured while hiding in barns and woods from the SS:** *Lightning*, 150; Camm, "Drive to the Rhine," http://www.62vgd.de/78th/Frank_Camm/.

247   **Some of the male civilians waving to the column:** Emmet J. Burrows,

"The Operations of Company A, 27th Armored Infantry Battalion (9th Armored Division) in the Seizure of the Remagen Bridgehead, 7–8 March 1945" (Rhineland Campaign) (personal experience of a rifle platoon leader), monograph for Advanced Infantry Officers Course, Fort Benning, GA, 1950, 14.

247   **The pace was exhausting:** Reed, conversation; Freakley monograph, 8–9, 22.

247   **About the only good thing during that first week of March:** Green et al, *78th Infantry Division*, 33.

248   **Rain was falling:** Ken Hechler, *The Bridge at Remagen* (New York: Ballantine Books, 1957; reprinted by Presidio Press, 2005), 171; Reed, conversation.

248   **A few from the greeting party:** Reed, conversation.

248   **Someone in Don's outfit shouted at the truck driver:** Ibid.

248   **Thursday's first light:** Hechler, *Bridge at Remagen*, 189.

248   **They soon entered a traffic jam:** *Lightning*, 169; Freakley monograph, 10–14.

249   **A little more than twice the size of Don's hometown:** A few years before the war the population of Remagen was 5,800. Baedeker, *Germany*, 288.

249   **Nineteen hundred and forty-five years before:** Twelve miles to the south of Remagen, Julius Caesar made his first crossing of the Rhine, in 55 BCE, the same year he also led soldiers across the English Channel into Britain. Lt. Col. John H. Montgomery, "The Remagen Bridgehead," *Military Review*, July 1949, 7; Henry Tozer, *A History of Ancient Geography* (Cambridge: Cambridge University Press, 1897), 296.

249   **Their truck slowly maneuvered:** Greene, "As I Saw It," 59.

249   **By the time the boys arrived in Remagen that morning:** Andrew Rawson, *Remagen Bridge* (South Yorkshire, UK: Pen & Sword Books, 2004), 102.

249   **The screams and whistles of shells:** Hechler, *Bridge at Remagen*, 195.

249   **The first three Stukas:** Steven Zaloga, *Remagen 1945: Endgame Against the Third Reich* (Oxford, UK: Osprey, 2006), 56; Williams, conversation.

249   **The Germans would send ten planes:** MacDonald, *The Last Offensive*, 228; Hechler, *Bridge at Remagen*, 189.

250   **The spray of hot metal over the river:** Camm, "Remagen Bridgehead," http://www.62vgd.de/78th/Frank_Camm/remagen_bridgehead.htm. Camm was on the west side of the river at the time. His account of the incident includes his speculation that the death of the division's head of G-4 (Logistics), who was killed as he was crossing the bridge, may have been the result of the abundant flak being hurled at the descending German pilot harnessed in his parachute.

250   **Instead, after inching down:** Rawson, *Remagen Bridge*, 102.

250   **The delay due to not only traffic:** *311th Combat Journal*, 42–43. In Remagen, General William Hoge, commander of Combat Command B, Ninth US Armored Division, ordered the 311th Regiment to detruck on the west side before crossing. At the same time, Hoge's staff ordered the regiment to cross the bridge on trucks, instructing the battalion commanders in the regiment to that effect as they passed by.

250   **A little after high noon:** *311th Combat Journal*, 42–43; Hechler, *Bridge at Remagen*, 172. The order in which the regiment's units crossed was the First Battalion, then Don's Third Battalion, then the Second. The 311th was the first full military regiment to cross the Rhine since the time of Julius Caesar. Camm, "Remagen Bridgehead."

250   **Their crossing would be on foot:** US Army, Combat Interview, Remagen Bridgehead (8–20 March, 1945), 1, based on interviews of two company commanders (Gero and Ferry) and two other officers from the 311th's Third Battalion (cited hereafter as Combat Interview, Remagen Bridgehead, Gero and Ferry).

250   **They were told to leave their mortar gear:** Greene, "As I Saw It," 59–60.

251   **As Don and the others approached:** Hechler, *Bridge at Remagen*, 195.

251   **Their orders were to run like hell:** Reed, conversation.

251   **But few boys crossing that day:** Hechler, *Bridge at Remagen*, 175; David Pergrin, *First Across the Rhine: The 291st Engineer Combat Battalion in France, Belgium, and Germany* (Saint Paul, MN: Zenith, 2006), 229–230.

251   **Each time a shell ricocheted off:** Freakley monograph, 14–15; Reed, conversation; Chauvin, conversation (he recalled the final dive into the gutter on the west side); DeMien, "Military Service," 102; Williams, conversation. Whalley Williams described how, for reasons unremembered, he was one of the last in Don's unit to cross the bridge that day. The oncoming darkness in the late afternoon of March 8 made it impossible for him to see the river below the bridge during his sprint, both a hazard and a blessing.

251   **The area abutting the river:** *Lightning*, 170; Freakley monograph, 18.

251   **There were no white sheets:** US Army, 311th Regiment, After Action Report, March 1945.

252   **they all sat down at the table and ate a hot meal:** Chauvin, conversation.

252   **The orders were given directly to their regimental commander:** *311th Combat Journal*, 42. "General Hoge directed that the Regiment be marched in a column of battalions four and one half miles north, where they were to seize and secure the town of Honnef and extend their position to the east by securing the high ground near Himberg, a little more than two miles distant (some two and one half miles distant). The Regimental commander was assured that it was nothing more than a march." Ibid.; US Army, Combat Interview, Remagen Bridgehead (8–20 March, 1945), 15, based on interviews of the commander of the 311th Regiment (Col. Chester M. Willingham) and the Assistant S-3 (Operations and Training) (Capt. R. T. Holister) (cited hereafter as Combat Interview, Remagen Bridgehead, Willingham).

252   **The three battalions assembled and started out:** Combat Interview, Remagen Bridgehead, Willingham, 3; US Army, 311th Regiment, After Action Report, March 1945, 4; DeMien, "Military Service," 103.

252   **Don's unit came under attack:** *Lightning*, 170.

252   **one of the last sights presented:** Rawson, *Remagen Bridge*, 103–104, quoting the commander of Don's battalion. During the incident, ten German soldiers fled and were fired upon under orders of their German commander. At least five were killed.

252 **The fight to secure Unkel continued:** Rawson, *Remagen Bridge*, 105.

253 **The same general who had provided assurances:** As of that evening, the 311th was officially under command of General Hoge of Combat Command B, Ninth Armored Division. Combat Interview, Remagen Bridgehead, Willingham, 4.

253 **At ten o'clock that evening:** Ibid.

253 **A platoon from each company was sent out into the blindness:** Ibid.; *Lightning*, 171; Combat Interview, Remagen Bridgehead, Gero and Ferry, 2; *Lightning*, 175.

253 **It was almost dawn and the advance platoons were still missing:** Combat Interview, Remagen Bridgehead, Gero and Ferry, 2–3; *Lightning*, 171–173, 175–176.

253 **From there, it was a matter of using grenades, mortars, and rifles:** DeMien, "Military Service," 103.

253 **The German resistance was intense, fighting over every room in every house:** US Army, 311th Regiment, After Action Report, March 1945; Rawson, *Remagen Bridge*, 110.

253 **By darkness Rheinbreitbach was secured:** *Lightning*, 177.

254 **The first nights on the east side:** *Story of the 310th*, 99; *311th Combat Journal*, 44; Hechler, *Bridge at Remagen*, 176; Rawson, *Remagen Bridge*, 107–110.

254 **News of what happened at Remagen:** Sportswriter turned *New York Times* war correspondent Drew Middleton soared with his front-page account: "The forcing of the Rhine should be a heavy blow to German morale. Hundreds of stories and legends of German folklore are set in the Rhine valley, and the great river was an impassable defensive barrier in the minds of Germans. Not since 1805, when Napoleon swept across Europe from the English Channel coast to rout the Austrian at Ulm, has the Rhine been crossed by an invading army. To the Germans of the Second and Third Reichs it was an invasion stronger than any Hindenburg or Siegfried Line." Drew Middleton, "First Army Across Rhine South of Cologne; Bridgehead Is Firm; Most of Bonn Seized; Foe Reports Fierce Battle West of Oder," *New York Times*, March 9, 1945, 1.

254 **The next day an order from Ike was delivered by General Bradley:** MacDonald, *The Last Offensive*, 220; Weigley, *Eisenhower's Lieutenants*, 620–629. The bridgehead at that point was only half a mile from the river. Weigley, *Eisenhower's Lieutenants*, 631. Weigley seems to suggest that for Ike to give more support toward taking advantage of the crossing at Remagen would have been a "favoring" of that crossing over the planned Montgomery crossing to the north, an odd choice of a word, although he does also note that "SHAEF regarded an approved plan as equivalent to inscriptions on tablets of stone." Ibid., 629.

254 **Regardless of any orders, expanding the bridgehead was not a simple matter:** Neither the restraints ordered by Bradley nor the challenge at the front line would alter the "leadership" practices of General Hodges, who would continuously complain about the lack of progress toward a breakout. As was his style, he soon became fixated on General John Milliken, commander of the III Corps, who one month before had been moved from being under Patton to the position under command of Hodges. Within a week of the Remagen crossing, Hodges would tell Bradley, "Mind you, I have only the greatest admiration and respect for the GIs doing the fighting out there, but I think they have had bad leadership in this bridgehead battle." Bradley agreed with Hodges, both no doubt confident in their shared expertise and familiarity with bad leadership. Hodges removed Milliken from command on March 17, 1945, the same day the railroad bridge collapsed. For his performance at Remagen, Milliken had the twin rewards of being forced out by Hodges and receiving a Silver Star, the third highest military recognition for valor. Weigley, *Eisenhower's Lieutenants*, 629–630; MacDonald, *The Last Offensive*, 229.

255 **Not Anywhere a Thing More Dismal:** "As he watched the mourning horses the son of Kronos pitied them, and stirred his head and spoke to his own spirit: 'Poor wretches, why then did we ever give you to the lord Peleus, a mortal man, and you yourselves are immortal and ageless? Only so that among unhappy men you also might be grieved? Since among all creatures that breathe on earth and crawl on it there is not anywhere a thing more dismal than man is.'" Richmond Lattimore, trans., *The Iliad of Homer* (Chicago: University of Chicago Press, 1962), 366.

255 **Before the day was over:** One week before, on Iwo Jima, death came to another boy, nineteen-year-old Sam Bennett, who had married a local girl, Vivian Schessow. With another marine he had crawled forward under heavy mortar and sniper fire to help what they thought were some wounded fellow marines lying in a trench. They were, in fact, bodies of dead Japanese soldiers dressed in American uniforms, a discovery Bennett made shortly before he too was killed by Japanese sniper fire. "Marine Sam K. Bennett Killed in Action," *Horicon Reporter*, March 29, 1945.

255 **The previous two days had been the first time since late February:** Combat Interview, Remagen Bridgehead, Willingham, 4.

255 **The day would be a bloody one for Don's regiment:** Overall, Don's regiment would take 145 casualties on that day. US Army, 311th Regiment, After Action Report, March 1945. It would also be the same day that General Eisenhower would issue an order that there would be no initiative undertaken to take advantage of the Remagen crossing. Following up on his order the previous week, which limited advances to a thousand yards a day, on March 13 he ordered Bradley to forbid a breakout from the bridgehead, and to limit any overall advance to no more than ten miles east of the Rhine. The decision went against what several of Ike's generals had been urging, reflecting SHAEF staff aims to quell any interference with the future Montgomery-led assault across the Rhine then being meticulously planned within an inch of its existence, involving more than a million men. John Toland, *The Last 100 Days: The Tumultuous and Controversial Story of the Final Days of World War II in Europe* (New York:

Random House, 1966), 225. In blunt language for histories of the day, Toland noted that "to a field commander such an order was ridiculous," and that "it was an ironically cautious ending to such a bold beginning." Ibid.

As a historian, Toland was not without controversy, but like most of the war histories of that era, his account reads as though the Second World War was fought vigorously if not single-handedly by no more than twenty or thirty officers of high rank on each side. In his volume on a period of the war that included Remagen and the Hürtgen Forest (the latter vaguely referenced but unsurprisingly not mentioned by name), he notes that the book is "based primarily on interviews" of ten generals, seven colonels, a handful of lower ranked officers, and two sergeants. Ibid., 600. Thus were written the histories that established what has become the received narrative of the Second World War, with little variance from that framework and its perspective on the war. It is worth considering that in 1966 the veterans association of Don's division was still two years away from holding its first postwar reunion. For the veterans of Boyd's 306th Bombardment Group it would be another twelve years before they would do the same. Those men were living their lives, many still trying to chase the time that had been taken away from them during the war years. The stories some of them carried would emerge in postwar histories, but as "shellhole-level anecdotes," set piece decorations within the established "big picture" narrative of the Second World War, rather than being used to give shape to the narrative.

255   **He would send the article home for his mother to save:** The account in the *Stars and Stripes* noted that "plans for the attack were laid after photo reconnaissance three days ago showed the one-time seaside resort on the Oder estuary teeming with activity." "Heavies Hit Near Rhine, Along Baltic," *Stars and Stripes*, London edition, Tuesday, March 13, 1945, 1.

256   **At the Tuesday morning briefing:** The teletype was sent by General William E. Kepner, commander of the Second Air Division of the Eighth Air Force. "12 March 1945; Mission #257; Target: Swinemunde," 392nd Bomb Group, http://b24.net/missions/MM031245.htm. Boyd's 306th Bombardment Group was part of the First Air Division of the Eighth Air Force, both divisions having participated in the previous day's raid.

256   **It would be fifty-eight years before George's letter to Don would be opened:** The letter George had written would be returned to him several weeks later, the envelope unopened and marked "Deceased." He gave the letter, still sealed, to Don's daughter in 2003.

257   **a good intent of heart:** The historian Gerald Linderman recounts that, in letters between the war front and the home front, any mention of the war's essence and its reality was studiously avoided, instead focusing on "the casual and the cosmetic." He notes that "the Please-don't-worry of soldier letters was the liturgical complement of the Please-be-careful of family letters. In any practical sense, they were idiot phrases." Gerald Linderman, *The World Within War*, 322.

Linderman's description of "idiot phrases" also captures many of the communications from the supposed high ground of history regarding the air war over Europe. Much of what has been written over the years repeatedly conflates the valor of the American and British boys in the air with a rightness applicable to the conduct and effectiveness of the overall bombing campaign. With few exceptions, most notably Richard Overy's *The Bombing War*, the historiography of the air war over Europe has had an unmistakable lean toward a triumphant endorsement of punitive bombing—that it was the millions of German people who voted Hitler into power and supported him, and therefore that "in doing so they put themselves, their cities and their children at terrible risk." Miller, *Masters of the Air*, 441. Many chronicles of the war have told the tale, with emotional relish, of the destruction and horrible civilian losses due to the German bombing of Warsaw, Rotterdam, and Coventry and many other parts of England. All true, but few of those volumes have gone near the absence of war crimes prosecution for those same terrible German bombings, for obvious reasons. And for similar reasons the postwar trials held in Nuremburg (a city with 90 percent of its building destroyed by Allied bombing) also did not take up prosecutions over war crimes regarding the acts of dissolving Poland or invading Finland.

The war historian Miller hardly sets out a radical position when he writes of the top two American architects of the air war: "It would be wrong, however, to criminalize the behavior of Carl Spaatz and Frederick Anderson. If these commanders are guilty of anything it is of misjudging the depths of Nazi unreason." Miller, *Masters of the Air*, 480.

Such words about the "unreason" of those being bombed are relevant in the twenty-first century for those living in a society that allows its elected officials over the course of more than fifteen years to conduct multiple air wars shrouded in an unprecedented level of obfuscation and secrecy aimed at precluding broader public discussion and debate of either the effectiveness of drone strikes, their legality, their consistency with how American society should be projecting leadership into the world, or what such actions may themselves be unleashing.

257   For those on the receiving end, there was no difference: A fairly typical muddling of the issue presented by the bombing of civilians is provided by British historian Sir Max Hastings, perhaps with more sparkling circumlocution than most: "The USAAF, doctrinally and morally committed to precision attack, never publicly admitted that its operations, and especially radar-guided blind bombing, inflicted almost as much injury upon civilian life and property as did the area attacks of the RAF. Moreover, it was asking much to invite the Allied peoples, who had themselves suffered so much from German aggression, to be overly troubled about German civilian casualties."

After Hastings dismisses US moral intentions about "precision bombing" as irrelevant because such bombing caused as much civilian damage as British "area bombing," he then nimbly pivots to suggest that intentions do matter when considering the Anglo-American bombing campaign as a whole: "More than a few Germans, and even some Anglo-American critics, see a moral equivalence between Nazi wickedness in massacring innocents, especially Jews, and Allied wickedness in burning cities. This seems mistaken. The bomber offensive was designed to achieve the defeat of the Axis and the liberation of Europe. The Nazis' mass murders not only killed far more people, but lacked the justification of pursuing a strategic purpose." It is a curious suggestion by Hastings that the German mass murders had no strategic purpose when they most certainly did, however depraved. Hastings cites nothing to support a conclusion that critics of the Allied bombing campaign "see a moral equivalence," an overused strawman suggesting that any Allied conduct above the rather low bar of Axis behavior is off-limits to examination or criticism.

The hagiographic treatment of the Allies' conduct during the European air war by so many historians of the Second World War has done no favors for a latter-day American society ensnared in a state of ignorance about the realities and the consequences of an ongoing "surgical" bombing campaign in at least seven different nations by its own masters of the air. Echoing historian Donald Miller, Hastings finishes his case for deflecting criticism of the Allied bombing of civilians by stating that "the destruction of cities and the deaths of significant numbers of their inhabitants seems a price they had to pay for the horrors they unleashed upon Western Civilisation." Hastings, *Inferno*, 477–479. As for such pronouncements about a price civilians "had to pay" for horrors unleashed by those who would invade nations and use air power to remove governing regimes, the inhabitants of twenty-first-century Western countries can only hope that Sir Max Hastings is just another historian, and not an unwitting prophet.

258   A staggering volume of desertions plagued the US infantry: In terms of "official" numbers there were 40,000 American deserters, of whom 2,854 were court-martialed and 49 sentenced to death, all but one such sentence overturned by higher authorities. Ellis, *The Sharp End*, 211–212; Hastings, *Armageddon*, 185. Another estimate suggests that 150,000 American and British soldiers deserted the ranks during the war, a full 10 percent of those who saw combat at the front. Charles Glass, introduction to *The Deserters: A Hidden History of World War II* (New York: Penguin, 2013), xi, xiii.

The "official" desertion count is grossly understated, as it does not include the numbers covered by the army's preferred designation of such wandering boys as "absent without leave" (AWOL). On the other hand, each individual situation was often fluid; some would return to fighting units. Ellis, *The Sharp End*, 211–212; Martin van Creveld, *Fighting Power: German and U.S. Army Performance, 1939–1945* (Westport, CT: Greenwood Press, 1982), 117–119. Van Creveld describes US Army desertion rates in 1944 of 45.2 per thousand and 63 per thousand in 1945 (citing R. A. Gabriel and P. L. Savage's 1978 *Crisis in Command: Mismanagement in the Army*), but also writes that "absolute figures on desertion are unavailable." The lone American soldier of World War II executed for desertion, Private Eddie Slovik, was a member of the 28th Infantry Division. His death sentence was approved by division commander General Cota in mid-November 1944, during the 28th's disastrous attack into the "death factory" of the Hürtgen Forest. Slovik's personal request for clemency from General Eisenhower was turned down. Ike approved the execution on December 23, 1944, seven days after the Germans had unleashed their surprise attack in the Ardennes.

258 **the previous day's mission had been to Swinemünde:** As of 2016, Swinemünde is part of Poland, known as Swinoujscie.

258 **He parenthetically added that it was a naval and military installation:** A request for the bombing had come a few days before from the Russians, who cited a large concentration of German shipping in the port and described Soviet aviation as being occupied with supporting the approaching ground troops. Helmut Schnatz, *Der Luftengriff auf Swinemünde* (Munich: Herbig Verlagsbuchhandlung, 2004), 51–55.

258 **His ship had been one of thirty-seven:** There were four hundred five other B-17s and two hundred twenty B-24s. Out of the hundreds of planes, one B-17 was lost, as were four of the fighter plane escorts. Four German aircraft were shot down. Freeman, *The Mighty Eighth War Diary*, 461–462; "Missions by Date: March 12, 1945," Eighth Air Force Historical Society, http://www.8thafhs.com/old/missions_by_date.php.

258 **At one in the afternoon:** US 306th Bombardment Group, Intelligence Narrative, March 12, 1945.

258 **Boyd reported that from his tail-gunner position he had observed an unusual amount of black smoke:** Ibid.

259 **Before the war it was known mainly as a resort town:** Karl Baedeker, *Northern Germany* (Leipzig: Karl Baedeker, 1925), 323–324.

259 **Its prewar population.** In 1939 the population of the city was 26,593. Michael Rademacher, "German Administrative History, District of Pomerania," http://www.verwaltungsgeschichte.de/usedom.html.

259 **The mouth of the river Swina:** Jozef Plucinski, "12 marca 1945 r.—wprowadzenie" ("March 12, 1945—Introduction"), March 10, 2010, http://www.iswinoujscie.pl/artykuly/13257. Plucinski was a local historian of Swinemünde.

259 **The streets were filled:** A. Kruger and M. Zuber, "Die Toten auf dem Golm: Die Bombardierung Swinemündes und der Friedhof auf dem Golm" ("The Dead on the Golm: The Bombing of Swinemünde and the Cemetery on the Golm"), *Deutschlandradio Kultur*, neunzehn fünfundvierzig/Archiv, April 25, 2005, http://www.deutschlandradiokultur.de/die-toten-auf-dem-golm.1134.de.html?dram:article_id=177116.

259 **sitting around everywhere:** Wolfgang Bayer, "Das geplante Inferno" ("The Intended Inferno") in Spiegel Spezial: Der Bombenkrieg gegen die Deutschen (Spiegel Special: The Bombing Campaign against the Germans), *Der Spiegel*, April 1, 2003, 50–53.

259 **Some of the arriving women:** Jörg Friedrich, *The Fire: The Bombing of*

Germany, 1940–1945, trans. Allison Brown (New York: Columbia University Press, 2006; originally published as *Der Brand* by Propylaen, 2002), 147.

259   Carts and carriages: Herbert Weber, "Swinemünde 12th March 1945—A Witness from the Ground," March 22, 2006, 467th Bombardment Group Online Archive, http://www.the467tharchive.org/swinemunde.html. Weber was a fourteen-year-old eyewitness to the bombing of Swinemünde. He submitted an account of his experience to the 467th Bomb Group veterans association after a chance meeting at a 2006 airshow in Florida with an American airman who had been on the raid.

259   now seemed to fill every available space: Plucinski, "The Day the Bombs Fell."

259   Shelter was being provided: Bayer, "The Intended Inferno"; Friedrich, *The Fire*, 14.

259   Behind the beach areas there were public gardens: Weber, "Swinemünde 12th March 1945."

259   The harbor was crowded that morning: Friedrich, *The Fire*, 14; Plucinski, "The Day the Bombs Fell."

260   The Kriegsmarine deployed everything: Friedrich, *The Fire*, 146.

260   The refugees in Swinemünde included survivors of the worst sea disaster in history: On the night of the sinking of the *Gustloff*, survivors were dropped off at Swinemünde by a minesweeper craft that had rescued them. Wilhelm Gustloff, "Helga Knickerbocker's Experience on the Wilhelm Gustloff," http://www.wilhelmgustloff.com/stories_sinking_HKnickerbocker.htm. "Marine Disaster—Rose's Story," http://www.wilhelmgustloff.com/stories_sinking_RPetrus.htm. Friedrich, *The Fire*, 146–147.

260   Bodies were washing up every day along the Baltic coast: A description of those days along the Baltic coast was included in an American intelligence report: "Special authorization had been granted the Informant to use the Wehrmacht transport facilities from Danzig to Schlawe. Authorization was however, cancelled at the last moment as a local Gauleiter had requisitioned all the available cars for the evacuation of his and other Nazi officials families. The informant saw several hundred German soldiers and uniformed Party men collecting corpses on the coast between Zoppot and Gdynia. There were corpses piled on a side road which had been closed to civilians. The informant talked with a German soldier who stated that the bodies had been washed ashore from two large refugee ships from East Prussia which had been torpedoed or had struck mines. Some 5,000 persons were estimated to have been drowned. From Schlawe to Stettin, the journey took six days. A stream of refugees was passed by the informant. Frequently, he saw people digging graves for relatives who had died on the road. Women shouting hysterically and children crying for food were heard by this man. Also he saw old men sitting resignedly by the roadside, refusing to continue.... There was utmost confusion further west, where streams of refugees from the east and the north east had collided with the refugees from Berlin streaming south." US Seventh Army, G-2 Intelligence Reports, Germany, February 23, 1945.

261   There was no panic: Bayer, "The Intended Inferno."

261   At the outer reaches of the harbor: Ibid.; Account of Fritz von Pilgrim, 467th Bombardment Group Online Archive, www.the467tharchive.org /swinemunde.html. Sixteen years old at the time of the Swinemünde raid, Fritz von Pilgrim manned one of the antiaircraft guns. In 1949 he immigrated to the United States, and two years later entered the US Air Force, serving as a gunner and refueling operator.

261   They came down at a rate of almost fifty per minute: The bombing raid's total tonnage of sixteen hundred was three times the amount that fell on Coventry during the famous Luftwaffe bombing in November of 1940, where 533 tons were dropped and 568 civilians were killed. Ward Thomas, *The Ethics of Destruction: Norms and Force in International Relations* (Ithaca, NY: Cornell University Press, 2001), 169.

261   One of the first bombs landed near the railroad station: Beyer, "The Intended Inferno."

261   During the bombing raid, Martin was hit in the neck: Friedrich, *The Fire*, 150.

261   The refugee encampments in the park near the beach: Account of Fritz von Pilgrim; Bayer, "The Intended Inferno." Author Jörg Friedrich appears to suggest that the bombing of the encampments near the beach and the use of contact fuses that would detonate in the trees were purposeful. Friedrich, *The Fire*, 148. Conversely, the Swinemünde historian Jozef Plucinski seems to suggest that the bombing of the wooded park areas was done purposefully as a targeted dumping area for those planes looking to avoid civilian casualties when they could not find military targets, a humanitarian effort gone tragically wrong. Plucinski, "The Day the Bombs Fell." Both claims are contradicted by consistent mission reports by the crews on the mission that targets were successfully hit and by the normal practices with regard to targeting and operation.

261   The bombs detonated upon contact with the trees: Bayer, "The Intended Inferno."

262   The second bomb set fire to the vessel: Ibid.; Friedrich, *The Fire*, 150; Plucinski, "The Day the Bombs Fell."

262   When the bombs stopped falling: Bayer, "The Intended Inferno"; Friedrich, *The Fire*, 149. In recent years, after the publication of Friedrich's *The Fire*, some have responded that no strafing by American planes took place at Swinemünde, insisting that each of the four hundred fifty-two P-51 fighter pilots would never have defied a high-command order to drop down and do some strafing. It is also suggested that there was confusion on the part of eyewitnesses, as to whether strafing took place or, in the alternative, that such strafing must have been done by Russian planes. Helmut Schnatz, *Der Luftangriff auf Swinemünde: Dokumentation einer Tragodie* (Munich: Herbig, 2004), 88–93. The dismissal of eyewitness reports is generally more wishful than persuasive.

Some of the overall postwar amnesia concerning the American massacre of thousands of civilians at Swinemünde was the byproduct of the postwar geopolitical divisions on the Continent, including the forced removal of local ethnic Germans and the transfer of the territory from Germany to Poland. Christian Schutz, "Speaking the Unspeakable," *The Guardian*, August 27, 2003. But the main reason the Swinemünde story is not well known is because it is incompatible with the scriptural narrative established in the decades following the Second World War, untouched by war historians perhaps also fearful that even outlining such an event would draw accusations, however wearisome, of being tantamount to suggesting a moral equivalence of the incident with Nazi wickedness.

262 **Dazed survivors began to walk about:** Kruger and Zuber, "The Bombing of Swinemünde"; Axel Büssem, "Inferno am Ostseestrand" ("Inferno on the Baltic Beach"), *Stern*, March 11, 2005, http://www.stern.de/politik /geschichte/swinemuende-inferno-am-ostseestrand-3543394.html.

262 **Strewn about were heads, limbs, torsos, and other pieces of human anatomy:** Bayer, "The Intended Inferno"; Plucinski, "The Day the Bombs Fell."

262 **Women were running around and screaming:** Kruger and Zuber, "The Bombing of Swinemünde," quoting an eyewitness.

262 **The injured were calling out for help:** Friedrich, *The Fire*, 150.

262 **In the harbor area there were noticeably fewer ships:** Friedrich, *The Fire*, 150; "The Inferno," Swinemünde: Town History, http://swinemuende.name /das_inferno.htm.

262 **Eight-year-old Isa was found alive:** Bayer, "The Intended Inferno."

262 **Legs, arms, severed heads, and other remains of humans and animals:** Kruger and Zuber, "The Bombing of Swinemünde."

262 **After the raid the cleanup began:** Plucinski, "The Day the Bombs Fell."

263 **Dead babies and the bodies of children were sorted by size:** Büssem, "Inferno on the Baltic Beach," quoting an eyewitness who was nineteen at the time.

263 **One of the cadets found the body of a woman who had apparently been killed while giving birth:** Bayer, "The Intended Inferno."

263 **The exact toll of Monday's raid:** Debate continues over the final death toll. Estimates of twenty-three thousand dead which emerged in the 1950s and 1960s are dismissed by some, including by Friedrich in *The Fire*, who suggests that such a figure is "hard to fathom" and wonders whether it might be half or a third of that. Friedrich, *The Fire*, 151. Another historian, Helmut Schnatz, attempts in his book to dispel five-figure estimates, most notably by developing a proper ratio of civilian deaths per ton of explosives through a formula based on the death tolls during raids in larger German urban areas. Schnatz, *Der Luftangriff auf Swinemünde*, 95–105. Such a calculation ignores Swinemünde's small area and that it had been overrun with tens of thousands of refugees who had no shelter. The arithmetic would also seem to fall apart given the deaths in sunken transport ships, almost six hundred people on the *Andros* killed with a mere 1.5 tons of explosives. Definitive answers about the massacre's toll and the use of strafing will no doubt have to wait, perhaps for centuries until something akin to the 2012 discovery and exhumation of the remains of Richard III under a parking lot. Only an archeological dig that includes an examination of the civilian bodies buried in the mass graves would likely put such questions to rest, including those about American strafing.

263   the port of Swinemünde suffered little damage: Plucinski, "The Day the Bombs Fell."

263   Soviet reconnaissance photographs showed the existence of hundreds: "12 March 1945; Mission #257; Target: Swinemunde," 392nd Bomb Group, http://b24.net/missions/MM031245.htm.

264   One month after the bombing of Swinemünde, General Kepner sent another teletype: Ibid. Kepner sent the teletype on April 7, 1945. Eighth Air Force Commander General James Doolittle, often cited for his initial objection to the early February bombing raid on Berlin because it targeted the city center, added to Spaatz's message: "I am pleased and gratified to forward to you this splendid commendation contained in basic communication from Lieutenant General Spaatz. Please convey to all air commanders and crews my sincere appreciation for the outstanding effort which they displayed in the execution of the operation against military objectives in the town of Swinemunde. Signed DOOLITTLE." Ibid.

264   oining a thousand other planes: Freeman, *Eighth Air Force Diary*, 487–488. On April 14, 1945, eight hundred thirty-one B-17s dropped 2,300 tons of explosives, and three hundred thirty-six B-24s dropped another 1,000 tons onto French soil. On April 15, 2,100 tons were dropped by almost a thousand B-17s and 700 tons were dropped by three hundred fifty-nine B-24s. The bombloads dropped by the Second and Third Air Divisions of the Eighth Air Force (Boyd's bomb group was in the First Air Division) included five 100-pound tanks filled with napalm. Ibid.

264   The second day of those missions: News reports reflected an excitement about the introduction of napalm: "Using a new type of fire bomb for the first time, as well as thousands of tons of high explosives, 8th Air Force Fortresses and Liberators flew more than 2,450 sorties Saturday and Sunday to wipe out German pockets of resistance in the Gironde area and free the big French port of Bordeaux. Many of the 1,300 bombers taking part in yesterday's clear weather assault were loaded with tanks which explode on impact, ignite incendiary material and splash the flaming contents over an area of approximately 60 square yards. Tanks containing more than 460,000 gallons of this liquid were showered on the target areas in the vicinity of Royan on the east side of the Gironde estuary in an assault co-ordinated with movements of French ground forces." "Heavies Throw Fire to Free Bordeaux," *Stars and Stripes*, April 16, 1945, 1.

265   During the war and afterward: Boyd was not alone in his lifelong disquiet. One B-17 top-turret gunner turned author later wrote, "Nevertheless, I was bothered by my part, as insignificant as it was, in the impersonal fury of destruction poured down on Europe from above. And I think that most of the men who manned the bomber crews were uneasy whether they admitted it or not." John Comer, *Combat Crew: The True Story of One Man's Part in World War II's Allied Bomber Offensive* (London: Little, Brown and Company, 1988), 102.

265 **the shameless use by the top brass of the phrase "precision bombing":** In 1944 the Ninth US Air Force was often referred to by GIs as the "American Luftwaffe" because of its reputation for repeatedly bombing US troops by mistake. The 30th US Infantry Division experienced attacks from American bombers at least thirteen times. Ellis, *The Sharp End*, 71–72.

266 **To be kept tightly clenched inside for the rest of his days:** "Instead of talking about it, most men didn't talk about it. It was not that they didn't want to talk about it, it was that when they did, nobody understood it. It was such a different way of living, and of looking at life even, that there was no common ground for communication in it." Jones, *WWII*, 202.

266 **As for accuracy of military portrayal:** According to Pacific War veteran James Jones, "No fight I know about personally (and perhaps, by extension, all battles—if they follow the same reason and rules) was ever written up historically as it really happened, but rather was written as filtered through the ideals-systems of the historians and the officers who fought it wished that it might have been, and in fact believed that it was." Ibid., 60.

267 **The most imposing of these was the Drachenfels:** Its summit provided German forces with a clear sight to the bridge area. Two days of fighting would be needed to secure the Drachenfels, and during that time, Don's regiment would find the cave where according to legend Siegfried's dragon lived. They came upon no dragon, only an aircraft parts factory and a thousand slave laborers. *311th Combat Journal*, 46–47; Camm, "Remagen Bridgehead."

267 **Don had entered an infantryman's nightmare:** The last two words are taken from a sergeant positioned not far from Don, who wrote that the terrain of the Siebengebirge was "beautiful to behold" and "an infantryman's nightmare." Freakley monograph, 22–23.

267 **Five days after the crossing it was still impossible for Don's battalion to stay together:** Camm, "Remagen Bridgehead"; Combat Interview, Remagen Bridgehead, Gero and Ferry, 1–3.

267 **German antitank weapons easily blocked progress:** Camm, "Remagen Bridgehead."

267 **Where the woods thinned out and the slopes became more gentle:** Freakley monograph, 23.

267 **Everywhere were sharp angles:** Combat Interview, Remagen Bridgehead, Gero and Ferry, 3–4.

267 **Vehicles for crew-based weaponry could not be used:** *Lightning*, 175.

267 **At the higher elevations the ground was so steep:** Combat Interview, Remagen Bridgehead, Gero and Ferry, 5–6.

268 **Göring offered up pilots flying suicide missions:** Zaloga, *Remagen 1945*, 57.

268   Explosions of every sort: Pergrin, *First Across the Rhine*, 279–282.

268   Engineers working on the bridges and those who crossed the river: Hechler, *Bridge at Remagen*, 192.

269   More than a hundred heavy German guns and howitzers: MacDonald, *The Last Offensive*, 225. During the first two days of the crossing, the bridge was hit twenty-four times. Zaloga, *Remagen 1945*, 56–57; Pergrin, *First Across the Rhine*, 236–237.

269   Joining the barrage from miles away were huge German railroad guns: MacDonald, *The Last Offensive*, 228; Camm, "Remagen Bridgehead."

269   On the east side of the river the dreaded Nebelwerfer had entered the scene: Freakley monograph, 24.

269   Long snakelike barriers were floated out onto the water: Pergrin, *First Across the Rhine*, 283.

269   Landing craft cruised constantly: Hechler, *Bridge at Remagen*, 191–192. German frogmen were dispatched from Vienna on March 11, and after several postponements, set out the night of March 17 with plastic explosives to blow the temporary bridges (the Luddendorf bridge had already collapsed that day). They were stopped by the blinding searchlights. Ibid.

269   At night, boys on the heights of the east side could see an eerie glow: Rock DiLisio, *Firings from the Fox Hole: A World War II American Infantryman Writes Home* (Lincoln, NE: iUniverse, 2006), 62. The author's father, Angelo DiLisio, was with the 309th Regiment in Don's division.

269   The bridge was kept brightly lit: Hechler, *Bridge at Remagen*, 191; Camm, "Remagen Bridgehead"; Pergrin, *First Across the Rhine*, 283.

269   the same frightening sensation: Pergrin, *First Across the Rhine*, 249, 252.

270   Each one would hit the surface of the earth at more than three thousand miles per hour: Ibid., 279–282; MacDonald, *The Last Offensive*, 223, 228; Hechler, *Bridge at Remagen*, 198; Zaloga, *Remagen 1945*, 59.

270   On the first day after the crossing: *Lightning*, 177.

270   The P-38 could be seen chasing something smaller and twice as fast: DiLisio, *Firings from the Fox Hole*, 63; Reed, conversation; Chauvin, conversation; Zaloga, *Remagen 1945*, 57; Camm, "Remagen Bridgehead."

270   Almost 150 German airplanes of various types, including jets: The numbers of attacks and kills vary from source to source, but all are in the same ballpark. According to one estimate, over the course of nine days, 367 German planes attacked the bridge and 109 were shot down with a further 36 unconfirmed kills. Rawson, *Remagen Bridge*, 145; Pergrin, *First Across the Rhine*, 279.

270   Each one was destroyed: Rawson, *Remagen Bridge*, 133.

271   The overcast and cold drizzle: MacDonald, *The Last Offensive*, 227; Freakley monograph, 22.

271   There were now almost seven hundred antiaircraft weapons placed around the bridgehead: Zaloga, *Remagen 1945*, 56–59.

271   Some of the planes were not just shot down: Reed, conversation.

271   no thoughts that the war had somehow changed: Chauvin, conversation; Reed, conversation.

271   the days approaching the ides of March 1945 were a numbing blur: Chauvin, conversation; Reed, conversation. A participant in a unit attached to Don's regiment during that week and positioned at times alongside Don's battalion described his outfit as "depleted in manpower, low in spirits, physically exhausted, and with morale at a low ebb." Freakley monograph, 24–26.

272   Capture of Honnef Gives American Firm Anchor: *Milwaukee Journal,* March 13, 1945, 1.

272   It was like nothing Marie or anyone else around town could remember: "The month of March, just past, set a new 26 year record high for temperature, the average recording for the several days of the month being 46.3 degrees above zero. . . . The previous high was 40.8 of 1938, closely followed by 40.76 of March, 1921. The mercury reached a high of 78 on March 27th while the low reading was 11 on March 7th." *Beaver Dam Daily Citizen,* April 2, 1945, 5. The temperature record set in March 1945 would not be broken until 2012.

274   Spring had emerged the day before: "The weather here suddenly cleared and the sky is blue and the sun real warm." "15 March 1945," WWII Letters to Wilma, March 15, 2012, http://wwii-letters-to-wilma.blogspot.com/2012/03/15-march-1945.html. "Spring, boring from within, has taken possession." "Another spring day, lucent and pale gold." Gantter, *Roll Me Over,* 221–222 (diary entries, March 15 and 16); *Blue Infantrymen,* 42.

274   Don had spent the night in the basement of an abandoned house: Reed, conversation.

274   The gaps of silence that morning: Pergrin, *First Across the Rhine,* 282–284.

274   Up ahead were SS troops who that day would be maniacal: Freakley monograph, 24–27.

276   And then he died: Reed, conversation. For decades after the day Marie got the telegram, what happened to Don was an unresolved family mystery. The question was one that never went away, as always is the case for the families of those killed in war. In the late 1990s, a document was finally tracked down that listed an official determination that Don's death was due to a shrapnel wound in the chest. Some research a few years later led to another soldier in Don's company, Red Gonzalez, who suggested placing an inquiry in the 78th Division's Association newsletter, seeking information on Don and what happened that day. The response came in the form of a brief telephone message, consisting of a name, a telephone number, and then a few more words: "I was the last person to speak with Don."

Robert Reed was the medic who held Don when he died. After Reed completed his account of what happened on March 16, 1945, there was a long silence on both ends of the telephone conversation. And then he added, "You know, that was the first time I've spoken aloud about that since the day it happened." There were subsequent communications, Reed speaking in measured and eloquent terms about what those days were like. It was evident that, like so many, much stayed deep within him during the decades following the war. He was memorably if not hauntingly articulate on what it was like to carry around the most profound and unanswerable mystery for so many of the boys who came home from the war: why did it happen to others, and not to him.

When American boys died at the front during World War II, one of the saddest aspects was the revelation of just how pitifully few possessions they had, living for months in the worst conditions with barely a few totems of their humanity that could be looked at and touched. Don was no different. When he died, his personal effects consisted of some photographs in two billfolds (which held no money), a pencil, a broken fountain pen, and a prayer book.

Three days after Don was killed his remains were buried at the Henri-Chapelle cemetery in Belgium, probably by German POWs, which was the practice at the cemetery at that time. Placed next to him, on his left side, was the body of another boy from the 78th Division, Charles Mallernee of Canton, Ohio, also killed on March 16. Dead at the age of twenty-one, Mallernee had been a construction worker before the war. His remains were later disinterred, moved to lie near his home in Ohio. "Charles L. Mallernee: Army Enlistment Record from World War II," World War II Enlistment Archive, http://www.ww2enlistment.org/index.php?page=directory&rec=5701921; "PFC Charles L. Mallernee," Find A Grave, November 17, 2008, http://www.findagrave.com/cgi-bin/fg.cgi?page=gr&GRid=31486868&ref=acom.

On Don's right-hand side were placed, on the same day, the remains of Private George Winkowitsch, also killed near Honnef on March 16. He had just turned twenty-four and had married Helen only eleven months before. Winkowitsch had grown up on a farm, and before entering the service had worked at a gas station in Wall, South Dakota. Less than a month before his death he had written his parents: "May the dear lord end this war soon, so all of us can go home again. . . . Oh, if this awful war would only end." The remains of George are still at the Henri-Chapelle American Cemetery in Belgium, plot D, row 3, Grave 12. "In Memory of Private in the Armed Forces George William Winkowitsch," South Dakota Department of Veterans Affairs, World War Two Memorial, May 9, 2002, http://vetaffairs.sd.gov/sdwwiimemorial/SubPages/profiles/Display.asp?P=2091.

In the fall of 1947, Don's body was disinterred and shipped back to Wisconsin. Those who exhumed his remains discovered twenty Belgian francs and two hundred Belgian "old issue" francs hidden in his uniform, the rotted and awful-smelling currency likely the winnings from the gambling he loved to do with the other boys. Also found were three souvenir coins, which at Marie's request were shipped back to Julius. Don's remains arrived at the town's railroad station a little after seven o'clock on the frozen Monday evening of December 15, 1947. His remains were the first of the local boys killed in action to return home. The American Legion held a well-attended ceremony and marched behind the coffin as it went from the train depot to the funeral home, one block off Main Street near the bank.

278   **A Numberless Sorrow:** "As it is, there must be on your heart a numberless sorrow for your son's death, since you can never again receive him won home again to his country." Lattimore, *Iliad*, 377.

278   **another weirdly warm day in the ongoing stretch:** Three days before it had been eighty degrees, during a week when it was normal for snow to be on the ground.

278   **At least one person from town:** *Beaver Dam Daily Citizen*, March 30, 1945, 5.

279   **After putting her twelve-year-old brother, Billy:** From that day forward, Billy reverted to calling her "Rie," and never again called her "Brownie."

279   **the crew's radio operator:** Stehle, conversation.

280   **Just a few days after the great firebombing:** Norman Davies, *No Simple Victory: World War II in Europe, 1939–1945* (New York: Penguin, 2006), 125.

280   **Three B-17s collided with each other:** US 306th Bombardment Group, Intelligence Narrative, April 17, 1945.

280   **Boyd had witnessed a similar collision:** Boyd made a reference to seeing the collision in his personal combat mission notes about an April 8, 1945, mission to Halberstadt.

280   **Five hundred civilians were killed:** Overy, *The Bombing War*, 483. The next day's edition of the *Stars and Stripes* noted that the mission had been "to pound three railway centers in Dresden." "8th Fighters Add 200 to Bag of Nazi Planes," *Stars and Stripes*, April 18, 1945, 1.

281   **Ten days after his final combat mission:** A few days before, Boyd and the whole Weber's Wagon crew had gone into London together. It was his first visit to the city. Perhaps reflecting his overall mood at the time, he wrote, "London's very old, and dirty, and war has made it repulsive to me and it's so very crowded." Boyd, letter to parents, April 27, 1945.

285   **Boyd spent some of V-E Day in the air:** Arthur P. Bove, *First Over Germany* (College Station, TX: Newsphoto Publishing, 1946), 48–50. Includes an account of the Weber's Wagon V-E Day tour.

286   **On V-E Day everyone was restricted to the base:** Boyd, letter to parents, May 12, 1945; Strong, *First Over Germany*, 315.

287   **raucous if not ready to hold their own:** "There had been great fear for the conduct of the Yanks, but the spectacle of the staid and reserved English letting their hair down as it had never been down before so startled the Yanks that they were left without a leg to stand on. For once the British 'out-hollered' and 'outdrank' the Americans." Strong, *First Over Germany*, 315, quoting the 367th squadron diary.

288   **Boyd wandered around:** Boyd, letter to parents, May 12, 1945.

290   **Blossom moved back home for a few months:** She would teach in Lombard, Illinois, and would be paid $1,700 in eighteen equal installments by the DuPage County School District beginning September 15, 1945.

291   **The boys took some last pictures with their ship:** On May 24, Weber's Wagon was transferred to another air base, at Ridgewell, England, and two weeks later the ship was flown back to the United States by a crew from another bomb group, a three-day trip. Richard Bettencourt, "Ridgewell England, 1945," 381st Bombardment Group Association, Unit History Stories, October 2, 2005, http://www.381st.org/Unit-History/Stories/Authors-A-D/Ridgewell-1945.

291   **His bomb group was one of two:** The other was the 305th bomb group, based in Chelveston, about fifteen miles away from Thurleigh. Robert J. Boyd, *Project "Casey Jones," Post-Hostilities Aerial Mapping: Iceland, Europe, and North Africa, June 1945–December 1946* (Offutt, NE: Headquarters Strategic Air Command, 1988). Ian D. White, 305th Bomb Group and the Postwar Project Casey Jones, 2006, http://www.armyairforces.com/Project-CASEY-JONES-the-photomapping-of-postwar-Europe-Northern-reaches-and-N-Africa-m161738.aspx.

291   **As such things tend to be:** Boyd wrote his parents, "Awhile ago I told you our work is classed top secret. I can't & never could see just why, except maybe for one small reason which I won't go into. At first tho we were told we could write home about it & later not to. At any rate I don't think there are many people who do not know what we are doing. Bill Dooley's friend in the Pacific wrote him about it." Boyd, letter to parents, July 2, 1945.

292   **Now, in the first place, we who are doing this work:** In the decades after the war, Boyd showed few inhibitions in describing his days with the Casey Jones Project, compared to the restraint he exhibited in talking about his combat missions. He told stories about the secrecy demanded by distant high-level authorities and the deep frustration among the boys in Thurleigh because of the resulting problems some had with their families back home. But Boyd never mentioned the letter to the *Stars and Stripes*, which he undoubtedly signed and may have even helped write, given some of the phrases. The existence of the letter was not discovered until well after his passing.

292   **Signed by 84 Air corps officers and EMs:** "'Top Secret' Job?" *Stars and Stripes*, July 3, 1945, 3. Those boys who signed the letter are no longer with us. Regrettably, they did not leave behind their brand of gumption and the once very American readiness, if one would see chickenshit, to say chickenshit. It is easy to imagine the guffaws if those boys had been confronted by an official pronouncement like the one made in 2013 by the US Department of Defense to all of its millions of employees and contractors—that not only was classified information *in the public domain* still to be treated as classified information until declassified by an "appropriate U.S. government authority," but that those "who seek out classified information *in the public domain*, acknowledge its accuracy or existence, or proliferate the information in any way will be subject to sanctions." Office of the US Under Secretary of Defense, Memorandum for Department of Defense Security Directors, June 7, 2013 (italics added). It does not speak well of a latter-day

American society where such odious self-protective grandiosity (and just plain chickenshit) is taken seriously as a matter of "security."

293 **It turned out to be a lucrative venture:** After the war, Boyd did not speak of the money, other than to Marie.

294 **Inevitably, one of the boys would lean back:** To witness radioman Joe Stehle's animated description of the ceremonies of the evening snack, sixty years after they took place, was an experience that approached successful time travel.

294 **On those long trips we really live in the sky:** Boyd, letter to parents, July 15, 1945. About England in the summer he wrote, "The skys here are as beautiful as the land cause there's always so many cloud formations, it being an island."

294 **Best of all, as he put it to Blossom:** Boyd, letter to Blossom, July 9, 1945.

295 **near Reims, was an American quartermaster base:** In early 1945 ten "Labor Supervision Units" were formed by the US Army, comprised of over a thousand small cells of US Army officers and NCOs, under whom prisoner-of-war labor service companies were to be attached. There were 1,160 cells making up ten labor supervision units. George Lewis, Lt. Col., *History of Prisoner of War Utilization by the United States Army 1776–1945* (Washington, DC: US Department of the Army, June 1955), 211–222, 226–228, 232–234.

295 **An emphasis had been placed:** Ibid., 217, 222. Service labor consisting of German prisoners of war began to be used in the rear areas, which, in turn, allowed for even more service troops to be released for infantry duty in the combat zones. During the spring, as the end of the war in Europe approached, there were fears that the labor shortage would become even worse when troops were redeployed to the Pacific. Ibid., 232.

295 **They were given some training:** By December 1944, the 175th Labor Supervisory Center command near Reims was administering 7,677 German prisoners guarded by 262 Polish Guards organized into fourteen companies. US Army, US Forces European Theater, Report from Headquarters 175th Labor Supervision Center: Western Base Section to Commanding General, Western Base Section, January and February 1945. The numbers of prisoners and guards were constantly changing. In January, the 175th HQ administered twenty-seven Labor Supervision Companies, twenty-two Labor Service Companies, and thirteen Polish Guard Companies—Myroslaw and 167 other "Polish Guards" employed to guard 6,836 German POWs. Ibid.

295 **Hloba was another who stayed:** While Hloba was in Paris he was certified as a Polish translator. In late 1944 both Hloba and Myroslaw were reporting to the same US Army lieutenant, according to signatures of respective passes they carried.

296 **When he was an ocean away from the war:** The same was true for Lev Hloba. After his death in 2012, in Canada, Hloba's family discovered Hloba's wartime papers in a lockbox, including a citation awarding him the Croix de Guerre. It was their introduction to the mutiny and le BUK. Daniel Nolan, "PASSAGES: Spec Photographer Had Major Role in Little Known Second World War Mutiny;

Leon Hloba: April 24, 1924 to Dec. 31, 2012," *Hamilton Spectator*, January 14, 2013. Hloba had immigrated to Canada in 1951 and, as Leon Hloba, worked as a photographer with the *Hamilton Spectator* between 1955 and 1989. Ibid.

Included among the items were several letters from Waller Booth, whom Hloba had written in early 1948 from one of the displaced persons camps in Aschaffenburg, Germany, seeking assistance. By then Booth was back in Puerto Rico, having opened a bar in late 1947 while working under cover for the CIA. The club was unmarked and had no name, but was wildly popular, with a floor show and nightly screenings of *Casablanca* on the second floor that played continuously until four o'clock in the morning. Denis, *War Against All Puerto Ricans*, 151–154.

In the spring of 1948, Booth wrote to Hloba: "I have just received your letter and am pleased to learn that you are well though I regret you have lost all your family [Hloba had learned that the Soviets had shot his father, brother, and sister-in-law]. I do not know where Kuzmuk is and I do not know what I can do to help you but I would like very much to do something for you if I can; I will never forget the magnificent job that you and your battalion did for the Allied Cause. Unfortunately, things move slowly and it may be months before I can do accomplish anything, but I won't forget you and you will hear from me again. With very best wishes I am . . ." Waller Booth Jr., letter to Lev Hloba, April 9, 1948.

During the following autumn, Booth wrote a thank-you note, which made its way to Hloba: "Dear Sir or Madam, I am somewhat baffled, though exceedingly grateful, upon receipt of a very beautiful wooden handkerchief box and I wish to extend to you my sincere thanks. Since your address is the same as that of Major Hloba, I assume that you were a member of the Ukrainian battalion, than which I have never seen a finer fighting unit and to each one I am deeply indebted. Please give my regards to Maj. Hloba and, if you care to tell me, I should be pleased to know why you wanted to send me the lovely case." Waller Booth Jr., thank-you note addressed to S. Skuja, October 19, 1948.

On August 5, 1949, Booth forwarded some papers for Hloba to fill out, and handwrote a cover note that "we will see what we can do about getting you a job."

In October of 1949, Waller Booth Sr. wrote from Louisville: "Dear Sir: I sent a package to you this morning which I trust will reach you in due time and in good shape. I am doing this at the request of my son, W. B. Booth, Jr., whom, of course, you know very well. It is with a great deal of pleasure that we send you these things and I trust that you can use them. However, I do not know whether my size will fit you or not. After receiving them I would appreciate it if you would drop me a line telling me whether or not they are usable. Mrs. Booth and I wish to express our deep appreciation for the help that you rendered our son while he was in France. From the account he gave us it is very doubtful whether or not he would have returned to us unscathed except for the very great help that you gave him. With all good wishes I am yours sincerely . . ." Waller Booth Sr., letter to Lev Hloba, October 19, 1949.

298   **Later that same day:** "Schedule of the Arrival of the Troops," *New York Times*, January 4, 1946, 3.

298   **On the day before:** "30,837 Due Today on 11 Troopships; Greatest Number of Servicemen since V-J Day Is Scheduled to Arrive," *New York Times*, January 3, 1945, 1.

298   **demonstrations as well as riots:**

In Manila: Lindesay Parrott, "Pacific Veterans Press for Return; Slogan, 'No Boats, No Votes,' Is Being Stamped on the Mail for the United States," *New York Times*, December 5, 1945. "There is also a general cry—which this correspondent does not think well founded—that the 'brass hats' do not want to see the size of their forces cut down and are therefore trying to keep as many men as possible here." Ibid., 6; "GI Protests Win Pledge of Return; Manila Chief Promises Earliest Release Following Two-Day Demonstrations," *New York Times*, January 7, 1946, 1.

In Germany: Kathleen McLaughlin, "Bayonets Disperse GI's in Frankfort; Armed Guards Break Up March on McNarney's Headquarters to Speed Return Home," *New York Times*, January 10, 1946, 4.

In Japan: "Caution on Morale Given Eighth Army; General Hall Warns That Our Enemies Are Watching Signs of Troop Discontent," *New York Times*, January 10, 1946, 4. "Gen. Charles P. Hall acting commander of the Eighth Army said today that GI demonstrations against the War Department redeployment policy had given 'the first indication that a general breakdown in morale and discipline is beginning to show up in the occupation troops.' He warned that the enemies of the Allies would be quick to take advantage of the situation." Ibid. It was not made apparent by General Hall which "enemies of the Allies" would be quick to take advantage of the situation four months after the Second World War ended.

In Paris: Placed between the articles about the troops protesting in Japan and Germany was a picture of American soldiers marching with flares across the Champs-Élysées in Paris, under the caption "Our Soldiers in Paris Protest Demobilization Delays," *New York Times*, January 10, 1946, 4.

298   **American boys would confront Eleanor Roosevelt:** R. Alton Lee, "The Army 'Mutiny' of 1946," *Journal of American History* (December 1966): 563. Lee observed, from the vantage point of 1966, "That such flouting of military authority was permitted without reprisal is illustrative of the essentially democratic and civilian army that has evolved in the United States." Ibid., 570.

The same point was made in 1988 by historian and author Gerald Linderman in a published lecture while a visiting professor of history at the US Army Command and General Staff College. Delivered two years before the first US invasion of Iraq and entitled, "Military Leadership and the American Experience," Linderman's lecture offered some historical context for his overall conclusion that "The U.S. has never possessed an unquestioning soldier and has never even approached the idea of legions, those willing or compelled to expend themselves in the name of remote and ill-understood policy, as were the formations of Rome or of nineteenth-century Britain in defense of the outposts of empire." He added, "We still have no legions, nor shall we ever."

Linderman also flatly stated ,"We have had no experience of a military culture, no military island within our own society on which values other than those on which those of the society at large pertain." Gerald Linderman, "Military Leadership and the American Experience," *The John F. Morrison Lecture in Military History*, US Army Command and General Staff College, Fort Leavenworth, KS, October 4, 1988, 3, 4, 17.

No doubt what Linderman described was true in 1988, as it was in 1946 and 1966, and as it was during the First World War.

Twenty-five years later the thesis no longer stands. With little acknowledgement within broader American society and even less self-examination or debate, what Lee and Linderman described as the "peculiarities of the American citizen-soldier" has given way to an unprecedented and previously unknown American "warrior" culture—one that is separated out from American culture. For the first time in its national history, America in the twenty-first century has evolved a military culture based on values other than those on which American society at large pertain. The American military force now going to war in many lands at the same time exists as its own island. For those who serve in battle as part of its force, there is no easy return from that island, a vicious price for a dramatic change that has yet to be confronted by the American republic.

As for "the idea of legions," scoffed at by Linderman in 1988, as of early 2016, the United States had 9,800 troops in Afghanistan and 30,000 mercenaries (known in the twenty-first century as "contractors"). During the first decade of the twenty-first century the CIA's rendition and detention paramilitary force was made up of more than 75 percent contractors. US Defense Department, "Contractor Support for US Operations in the USCentcom Area of Responsibility," First Quarter, FY 2016, www.acq.osd.mil/log/ps/.CENTCOM_reports.html/5A_January_2016_Final.pdf. At least one in five (and likely more) of America's intelligence force now consists of contractors, not American government officials. Wilson Andrews and Todd Lindeman, "Funding the Intelligence Program," *Washington Post*, August 29, 2013, http://www.washingtonpost.com/wp-srv/special/national/black-budget/. As for those mercenaries who go into harm's way on behalf of an American policy, one writer on foreign policy who follows the issue has observed that the US military tracks more closely the fate of the dogs it uses than the number of contractor personnel wounded or killed. Micah Zenko, "The New Unknown Soldiers of Afghanistan and Iraq," *Foreign Policy Magazine*, May 29, 2015, http://foreignpolicy.com/2015/05/29/the-new-unknown-soldiers-of-afghanistan-and-iraq/.

The explosive growth in the use of employees of for-profit enterprises as an American force of war is a byproduct of an all-volunteer military combined with a steady increase in the undertaking of kinetic actions in multiple foreign lands at the same time. Whether, in the phrasing of Linderman, such profit-seeking formations are being expended "in the name of remote and ill-understood policy" in defense of the outposts of empire remains a matter of debate that has yet to be held. The unprecedented situation is also made possible by an equally unprecedented growth in governmental secrecy during those same years, stoked by farcical oversight on the part of American elected legislators and a firm yielding by a cowed American judiciary branch.

America either has a citizen-soldier military force or it does not. While those who govern have studiously avoided facing this question, the institutional cracks within the current American military (and a broadly privatized intelligence community) are increasingly becoming visible and are revealing yawning gaps of unsustainability.

The continuing lack of societal acceptance of a draft toward an American military force that is drawn from all elements of society will have to be faced for what it is: a restraint on how and when American military action is projected. Even draft-era presidents from Franklin Roosevelt through Harry Truman and Dwight Eisenhower knew this to be true, and Lyndon Johnson had to learn it the hard way. Neither national security nor foreign policy is a dogma without choice. A reckoning over the nature of the US military and paramilitary forces is inevitable, and American society will be better for it.

298   Whatever the desires of military leadership and the organizational problems: On January 10, 1946, Under Secretary of War Kenneth Royall declared that a "hysteria to get the boys back home" was endangering American occupation policy. *New York Times*, January 11, 1946, 4. The newspaper's account of Royall's speech to the Rotary Club in Roanoke, Virginia, was surrounded by a display of other articles describing protests and near-riots by American soldiers in Calcutta, Tokyo, Honolulu, and Frankfurt.

Included on the same page among those articles was a small news item noting that months of fighting between Polish militiamen and bands of Ukrainians was continuing in southeast Poland, with almost a thousand killed. Ibid.

299   Some voices in Washington: The counsel for the US House Committee on Un-American Activities claimed evidence of "a well-laid Communist plot to stir up the soldiers." *New York Times*, January 21, 1946, 3. Alton Lee's analysis twenty years later says otherwise: "These protest meetings were not Communist-inspired but were instinctive demonstrations sparked by real and imaginary grievances. But since they had the result of promoting a reduction of American power vis-a-vis the Soviet Union, the Communists naturally took advantage of the situation and endorsed the demonstrations. The riots, however, had no ideological bases." Lee, "The Army 'Mutiny' of 1946," 570.

299   On the Sunday after his first full week: *Horicon Reporter*, January 17, 1946, 5.

300   In 1945 there were seventeen million displaced persons: These numbers are conservative, according to Keith Lowe, *Savage Continent* (New York: St. Martin's, 2012), 27–28.

300   **During those days millions were searching:** Wyman, *DPs: Europe's Displaced Persons,* 55–57.

301   **On a September day:** The address no longer exists. The entire neighborhood was bulldozed in the 1960s and then left fallow for forty years. The Duke House was the last building in LeBreton Flats to fall, demolished on October 27, 1965. "LeBreton Expropriation Remembered, Heritage Ottawa Lecture Marks the Capital's Victim of Urban Renewal," *Ottawa Community News,* April 26, 2012, http://www.ottawacommunitynews.com/news-story/3955192-lebreton-expropriation-remembered-heritage-ottawa-lecture-marks-the-capital-s-victim-of-urban-renew/.

301   **In late February he wrote to one of his crewmates:** Boyd's letter of February 1945 was to radio man Joe Stehle, who was eighty-five years old when he shared it with Boyd's youngest son. Stehle handed it over with some obvious hesitation, an observable demonstration of the protectiveness toward others with whom he was in battle, something always noticeably present in the way surviving combat veterans shaped their conversations, even many years later. Some of the words in Boyd's handwriting suggested an explanation for Stehle's reluctance. They also provided an answer to a longtime mystery.

During the decades after the war, Boyd was never heard by his children to say the f-word. Not once did it cross his lips in front of them, through hammered fingers, arguments with baseball umpires, or a dumbass move by another highway driver. His repertoire for such occasions included plenty of other well-known choice words, but not once was the f-bomb dropped. As years went on, when Boyd's children faced struggles with self-discipline involving the use of certain words around their own children, doubts began to grow whether Boyd even had any working familiarity with the word, much like "Ethernet" or "snarky" never entered his vocabulary.

The letter shared by Joe Stehle proved otherwise. Twenty-three-year-old Boyd was a master with the f-word, skillful enough to use it as an adjective, adverb, noun, verb, and even as some sort of floating punctuation mark.

302   **He would work hard and not say much to anyone:** After Boyd had passed away, a cousin who was fifteen during that summer said that when his own younger brother came home two decades later from combat in Vietnam, he was immediately reminded of what Boyd was like in 1946.

302   **Just before Labor Day:** According to Blossom's contract with the Monroe Wisconsin School District, she would be paid $2,000 in twelve equal payments on the last day of each month. One of the general terms of the contract stated that "the marriage of a woman teacher" during the term of the contract would terminate the contract, except at the option of the Board of Education.

303   **Initially feeling some discomfort in her chest:** One year earlier, in October 1945, Boyd and Blossom's cousin Eunice had been fatally stricken with polio at the age of thirty-one, leaving two small young children.

303   **It was gone within a matter of weeks:** Only after Boyd's money was gone

did Herb and Lylle approach the March of Dimes, who would pay all of the bills for Blossom during the next several years (the cost of her illness during the first two years alone came to $23,000). She would face years of almost barbaric physical therapy just to regain the ability to sit upright and to learn how to breathe voluntarily. She did so while being adamant for the rest of her life that she never be photographed without a smile on her face. By the mid-1950s, with Herb and Lylle carrying her every day from her bed to an easy chair, she was able to start giving piano lessons, even though she could never physically demonstrate with her hands. Many boys and girls in that town, including her youngest nephew, learned music from her while gaining an inestimable education about life. Blossom would pass away in 1968, at the age of 48.

304   He would not have occasion: Another crewmember, Joe Stehle, the radio operator on Weber's Wagon, did not get on an airplane after the war until 1992, when he flew over to England for a reunion at Thurleigh. Stehle, conversation.

305   It was all over by morning: Julius would remarry and outlive two more wives, his third bride being the former chief telephone operator in town from 1932 until dial service was established in 1949, when she was transferred to Mayville (where she retired in 1965 as one of the last two manual board operators in Wisconsin). "Mayville Woman Starts Retirement," *Fond du Lac Commonwealth Reporter*, December 21, 1965

306   The loss of Don was always just under the surface: Joanne Brown, conversation.

309   Insignificant Mortals: Apollo to Poseidon: "Shaker of the earth, you would have me be as one without prudence if I am to fight even you for the sake of insignificant mortals, who are as leaves are, and now flourish and grow warm with life, and feed on what the ground gives, but then fade away and are dead. Therefore let us with all speed give up this quarrel and let the mortals fight their own battles." Lattimore, *Iliad*, 430.

310   He was a citizen who had served, never a soldier who was a citizen: Boyd paid dues every year to the American Legion but did not participate. At first his stance on the Legion was mainly due to his sense that the organization was dominated by those from the era of the Great War. In later years, he continued to stay away, while still paying his annual dues, because the national organization seemed to go out of its way to reflect a notion that its members were soldiers first and citizens second. He was not alone in holding such views. Bill Mauldin, "Poppa Knows Best," *Atlantic Monthly*, April 1947, 29–36.

311   Left unsaid was the discomfort: The barriers and occasional surly impatience showed by Boyd when being probed about his war experiences were commonplace, a trait that has become ill-suited for a later confessional age. One author describes well a similar experience with his grandfather, also a World War II veteran: "I should add that in the years when I knew him, my grandfather rarely discussed the war in my presence. No doubt he had other things on his mind or perhaps I was too young, but I gathered that another reason was the intensity of his feelings on the subject. My grandfather looked back on the war with great pride. . . . But somewhere along the line, I learned that nothing aroused Granddad's impatience—even anger—more readily than casual or ill-informed talk about the war. Perhaps it was impossible for anyone to grasp the true meaning of that event entirely to my grandfather's satisfaction, or perhaps Granddad was simply determined not to dwell on the past." David Eisenhower, introduction to *Eisenhower: At War, 1943–1945* (New York: Random House, 1986), xvi.

FURTHER READINGS

Many homes have a bookshelf devoted to the Second World War, often laden with the usual suspects of doorstop girth and similar suitability. The following six books, perhaps less well known, are offered for a general reader as delivering a good story with the fresh tang of having been written contemporary with the war. All six books are blessedly uncontaminated by someone else's latter-day "big picture" effluent, and reveal an American wartime temperament not always found in more recent histories.

Alistair Cooke. *The American Home Front: 1941–1942*
(New York: Atlantic Monthly Press, 2006)

Starting in February 1942, Cooke made several journeys from Washington, DC, to each of the four corners of the forty-eight states, traveling first by car and then by bus and rail. The result is an eloquent yet unvarnished contemporary depiction of a very complicated American wartime character. Cooke finished the manuscript in 1945 but then put it away, to be found at the bottom of a closet weeks before his death in 2005 at the age of ninety-seven.

Raymond Gantter. *Roll Me Over*
(New York: Presidio Press, 2007)

Gantter's book belongs alongside the more well-known Pacific War's *With the Old Breed*, by Eugene Sledge. Both should be kept in the literary medicine chest of American households as an antidote to casual bloviation about being "at war." Arriving in Belgium in November 1944, Gantter was a college-educated infantryman who jotted down notes at the front on any available scrap of paper. He finished the manuscript in 1949, but it was not published until 1997, twelve years after his death. The account captures, as few do, the altered state of being needed at the front, and stands on its own as a full-bodied narrative of a conflict quite apart from the familiar well-styled command-post framework so fully embraced by better known historians.

Bill Mauldin. *Up Front*
(New York: Norton, 2000. Originally published by Holt and Company, 1945)

Mauldin's drawings of Willie and Joe are an enduring and well-known signpost of the war. But it is the prose of this book that startles, an almost viscous bitterness throughout about command-post conduct and its total disconnect with the war of the American dogface, the war as it actually was. The bite in the words of a twenty-three-year-old cartoonist cannot but give pause to a twenty-first-century American reader, forcing reflection on scant mainstream writing about an insular and top-heavy military community that careens from mission to mission without accountability by elected representatives crazed by the catnip of fear.

George Millar. *Maquis*
(London: Cassell, 2003. Originally published by William Heinemann, 1945. American edition first published by Doubleday, 1946, as *Waiting in the Night: A Story of the Maquis, Told by One of Its Leaders*)

Millar's account of being a secret agent in France during the summer of 1944 is rich with humanity and filled with humor based on an appreciation of life's foibles and contradictions. According to archived SOE files, Millar finished a complete book manuscript within a month of his return to England, and by December 1944 had submitted it for internal review before its publication shortly thereafter. The book is remarkable for having no intrusion of postwar hindsight, giving it an unmatched freshness among wartime memoirs.

Eleanor Perényi. *More Was Lost*
(New York: New York Review Books, 2016. Originally published by Little, Brown and Company, 1946)

Eleanor Stone was a nineteen-year-old American girl when, in 1937, she married a Hungarian baron with a large estate but little money, taking up a new life near the Carpathian Mountains in what was then "Ruthenia" under Czech control. Her book shimmers all the way through, with its close-range American-eye descriptions of the human entanglements in Central Europe as the war approached. The brief, almost watercolor passages about her observations of Paris during the first weekend of September 1939 are part of what makes the book a rare jewel among all historical writing about the run-up to the war.

Eric Sevareid. *Not So Wild a Dream*
(Columbia, MO: University of Missouri Press, 1995. Originally published by Knopf, 1946. Republished with new introduction by Atheneum, 1976)

Sevareid was not the only journalist to write about his coming of age in a restive prewar America and working as a news reporter in wartime Europe. Separating the book from other such memoirs is his self-awareness and openness about wrestling with it. His writing voice is as pure American Midwest as ever existed. The 1976 republished version of the book is worthy if only because of Sevareid's new introduction and its tale about his father's final days.

SELECTED BIBLIOGRAPHY

Alexander, Caroline. *The War That Killed Achilles*. New York: Viking, 2009.

Apter, Howard. "The Terrible Victory." *Saga*, October 1962.

Babcock, John. *Taught to Kill*. Dulles, VA: Potomac Books, 2007.

Baedeker, Karl. *Austria-Hungary: Handbook for Travellers*. Leipzig: Karl Baedeker, 1911.

———. *Germany: A Handbook for Railway Travellers and Motorists*. Leipzig: Karl Baedeker, 1936.

———. *Northern Germany*. Leipzig: Karl Baedeker, 1925.

Beevor, Antony. *Ardennes 1944: Hitler's Last Gamble*. New York: Viking, 2015.

Bertin, Pierre. "Les Comtois de 1944 vus par les Ukrainiens." *Le Jura Francais*, Juillet–Septembre 1984.

———. *Resistance en Haute-Saône*. France: D. Gueniot, 1990.

Bishop, Chris. *Hitler's Foreign Divisions: Foreign Volunteers in the Waffen-SS 1940–1945*. London: Amber Books, 2005.

Booth, Waller. *Mission Marcel Proust*. Philadelphia: Dorrance, 1972.

Boshyk, Yury, ed. *Ukraine during World War II: History and Its Aftermath*. Edmonton: Canadian Institute of Ukrainian Studies, University of Alberta, 1986.

Bove, Arthur. *First Over Germany*. College Station, Texas: Newsphoto Publishing, 1946.

Brandon, Ray, and Wendy Lower, eds. *The Shoah in Ukraine*. Bloomington, IN: Indiana University Press, 2008.

Bross, John. "The Nurture of Resistance." Review of *SOE in France*, by M. R. D. Foot, and *Inside SOE*, by E. H. Cookridge. Central Intelligence Agency (internal publication), 1966, https://www.cia.gov/library/center-for-the-study-of-intelligence/kent-csi/vol11no2/pdf/v11i2a11p.pdf.

Budurowycz, Bohdan. "The Greek Catholic Church in Galicia, 1914–1944." *Harvard Ukrainian Studies* 26 (2002–2003): 291–375.

Burke, Michael. *Outrageous Good Fortune*. New York: Little, Brown and Company, 1984.

Bussewitz, Walter R., and Allie B. Freeman. *History of Horicon*. Horicon, WI: Horicon Rotary Club and Chamber of Commerce, 1948.

Calvi, Fabrizio. *OSS: La Guerre Secrète en France*. Paris: Hachette, 1990.

Carter, John D. "The North Atlantic Route." In *Services Around the World*. Vol. 7 of *The Army Air Forces in World War II*, edited by Wesley Frank Craven and James Lea Cate. Washington, DC: Office of Air Force History, 1983.

Cole, Hugh M. *The Ardennes: Battle of the Bulge*. Washington, DC: Office of Chief of Military History, 1965. Reprinted by US Army Center of Military History, 1993.

Comer, John. *Combat Crew: The True Story of One Man's Part in World War II's Allied Bomber Offensive*. London: Little, Brown and Company, 1988.

Comor, Andre-Paul. *L'Épopée de la 13e demi-brigade de Légion étrangère, 1940–1945*. Paris: Nouvelles Editions Latines, 1988.

Cooke, Alistair. *The American Home Front: 1941–1942*. New York: Atlantic Monthly Press, 2006.

Cowley, Betty. *Stalag Wisconsin: Inside WWII Prisoner-of-War Camps*. Oregon, WI: Badger Books, 2002.

Creveld, Martin van. *Fighting Power: German and U.S. Army Performance, 1939–1945*. Westport, CT: Greenwood Press, 1982.

Cunningham, Ed. "Winter War." *Yank Magazine*, March 2, 1945.

Currey, Cecil. *Follow Me and Die: The Destruction of an American Division in World War II*. New York: Berkley/Jove, 1991.

Dallas, Gregor. *1945: The War That Never Ended*. New Haven: Yale University Press, 2005.

Davies, Norman. *No Simple Victory: World War II in Europe, 1939–1945*. New York: Penguin, 2006.

———. *Vanished Kingdoms*. New York: Viking, 2011.

Dean, Martin. *Collaboration in the Holocaust: Crimes of the Local Police in Belorussia and Ukraine, 1941–44*. New York: St. Martin's Press, 2000.

Denis, Nelson. *War Against All Puerto Ricans: Revolution and Terror in America's Colony*. New York: Perseus, 2015.

D'este, Carlo. *Eisenhower: A Soldier's Life*. New York: Holt, 2002.

DiLisio, Rock. *Firings from the Fox Hole: A World War II American Infantryman Writes Home*. Lincoln, NE: iUniverse, 2006.

Dorr, Robert. *Mission to Berlin: The American Airmen Who Struck the Heart of Hitler's Reich*. Minneapolis: Zenith Press, 2011.

Eisenhower, David. *Eisenhower: At War, 1943–1945*. New York: Random House, 1986.

Eisenhower, Dwight. *Crusade in Europe*. New York: Doubleday and Company, 1948.

Fagles, Robert, trans. *The Iliad*. New York: Penguin, 1998.

The Federal Writers' Project Guide to 1930s Wisconsin. Saint Paul: Minnesota Historical Society Press, 2006. Originally published by Duell, Sloan, and Pearce, 1941.

Foot, M. R. D. *SOE in France*. New York: Frank Cass, 2004. First published in 1966 by Her Majesty's Stationery Office in London.

Freeman, Roger A. *The Mighty Eighth War Diary*. London: Jane's Publishing, 1981. Reprinted by Motorbooks International, 1990.

Friedrich, Jörg. *The Fire: The Bombing of Germany, 1940–1945*. Translated by Allison Brown. New York: Columbia University Press, 2006. Originally published as *Der Brand* by Propylaen, 2002.

Funk, Arthur. *Hidden Ally: The French Resistance, Special Operations, and the Landings in Southern France, 1944*. New York: Greenwood Press, 1992.

Fussell, Paul. *Doing Battle: The Making of a Skeptic*. New York: Little, Brown and Company, 1996.

———. *Wartime: Understanding Behavior in the Second World War*. New York: Oxford University Press, 1989.

Gantter, Raymond. *Roll Me Over: An Infantryman's World War II*. New York: Presidio, 1997.

Gavin, James M. *On to Berlin*. New York: Viking Press, 1978. Reprinted by Bantam Trade Edition, 1985.

Glass, Charles. *The Deserters: A Hidden History of World War II*. New York: Penguin, 2013.

Grandhay, Jean-Claude. *La Haute-Saône dans la Deuxieme Guerre mondiale, Sous le Signe de la Francisque, 1940–1944*. Vesoul, France: Imb Imprimeur, 1991.

———. "Les Maquis Haut-Saônois dans leur Environnement Social." In *Lutte Armee et Maquis: La Resistance et les Francais*, edited by Francois Marcot, 279–289. Besançon et Paris: Annales littéraires de l'Université de Franche-Comté, 1996.

———. *Vesoul: 12 Septembre 1944*. Vesoul, France: Imprimerie Marcel Bon, 1994.

Green, Budford, Walter Morse, Lewis Guidry, and Gardner Hatch. *Lightning: 78th Infantry Division*. Paducah, KY: Turner Publishing Company, 1996.

Greene, Vernon. "As I Saw It: The Eyewitness Report of a Soldier Who Fought During World War II and Survived." *Special Warfare Magazine*, September 2002.

Hamill, Pete, ed. *A.J. Liebling: World War II Writings*. New York: Library of America, 2008.

Harrison, Mark. *The Economics of World War II: Six Great Powers in International Comparison*. Cambridge: Cambridge University Press, 1998.

Hastings, Max. *Armageddon: The Battle for Germany, 1944–1945*. New York: Vintage, 2005.

———. *Inferno: The World at War, 1939–1945*. New York: Knopf, 2011.

———. "What's New About the War?" *New York Review of Books*, March 10, 2016.

Hechler, Ken. *The Bridge at Remagen*. New York: Ballantine Books, 1957. Reprinted by Presidio Press, 2005.

Hobbes, Thomas. *Leviathan*. Reprint of the original 1651 edition, Project Gutenberg, 2009. https://www.gutenberg.org/files/3207/3207-h/3207-h.htm

Hynes, Samuel, Roger Spiller, Nancy Sorel, and Anne Matthews, eds. *Reporting World War II, Part One, American Journalism 1938–1944*. New York: Library of America, 1995.

———, eds. *Reporting World War II, Part Two, American Journalism 1944–1946*. New York: Library of America, 1995.

Irwin, Will. *The Jedburghs: The Secret History of the Allied Special Forces, France 1944*. New York: Perseus, 2005.

Jackson, Julian. *France: The Dark Years*. New York: Oxford University Press, 2001.

Jones, James. *WWII: A Chronicle of Soldiering*. Chicago: University of Chicago Press, 2014.

Jurado, Carlos Caballero. *Breaking the Chains: 14 Waffen-Grenadier-Division der SS and Other Ukrainian Volunteer Formation, Eastern Front, 1942–1945*. Halifax, UK: Shelf Books, 1998.

Karnad, Raghu. *Farthest Field: An Indian Story of the Second World War*. New York: Norton, 2015.

Keegan, John. *The Battle for History: Re-fighting World War Two*. New York: Vintage Books, 1996.

———. *The Second World War.* New York: Penguin, 1989.

Kershaw, Ian. *The End: The Defiance and Destruction of Hitler's Germany, 1944–45.* New York: Penguin, 2011.

Korda, Michael. *Ike: An American Hero.* New York: Harper, 2008.

Kosyk, Volodymyr. "Les Ukrainiens dans la Résistance française." *L'est Europeen,* Juillet–Septembre 1987.

Kubijovyc, Volodymyr. *Memoranda of the Sevcenko Scientific Society; Ethnic Groups of the South-Western Ukraine: Halycyna–Galicia Vol 1 1939.* London: Association of Ukrainian Former Combatants in Great Britain, 1953.

Lattimore, Richmond, trans. *The Iliad of Homer.* Chicago: University of Chicago Press, 1962.

Lewis, George. *History of Prisoner of War Utilization by the United States Army, 1776–1945.* Washington, DC: US Department of the Army, 1955.

Lewis, Norman. *Naples '44: A World War II Diary of Occupied Italy.* New York: Carroll & Graf, 2005.

Linderman, Gerald. *The World Within War.* Cambridge, MA: Harvard University Press, 1997.

Lowe, Keith. *Savage Continent.* New York: St. Martin's, 2012.

Lukacs, John. *The Last European War.* Garden City, NY: Anchor Press, 1976. Reprinted by Yale University Press, 2001.

MacDonald, Charles. *The Battle of the Huertgen Forest.* New York: J. B. Lippincott Company, 1963. Reprinted by University of Pennsylvania Press, 2003.

———. *The Siegfried Line Campaign.* Washington, DC: Office of the Chief of Military History, 1963. Reprinted by the US Army Center of Military History, 1993.

———. *A Time for Trumpets.* New York: HarperCollins/Perennial, 2002.

———. *Victory in Europe, 1945: The Last Offensive of World War II.* Unabridged reprint. New York: Dover, 2007. First published 1973 by the US Army Center of Military History.

MacMillan, Margaret. *Paris 1919: Six Months That Changed the World.* New York: Random House, 2002.

Magocsi, Paul Robert, and Christopher Hann, eds. *Galicia: A Multicultured Land.* Toronto: University of Toronto Press, 2005.

Mauldin, Bill. *Back Home.* New York: William Sloane Associates, 1947.

———. *Up Front.* New York: Holt and Company, 1945.

Meller, William. *Bloody Roads to Germany.* New York: Berkley, 2012.

Meyer, Faith. *The History of the John Deere Horicon Works, 1861–1986.* Fond du Lac, WI: Action Printing, 1986.

Michaelis, Rolf. *Russians in the Waffen-SS.* Atglen, PA: Schiffer, 2009.

———. *Ukrainians in the Waffen-SS.* Atglen, PA: Schiffer, 2009.

Millar, George. *Maquis: The French Resistance at War.* London: William Heinemann, 1945. Reprinted by Cassell, 2003.

———. *Road to Resistance: An Autobiography.* Boston: Little, Brown and Company, 1979.

Miller, Donald. *Masters of the Air: America's Bomber Boys Who Fought the Air War Against Nazi Germany.* New York: Simon and Schuster, 2006.

Miller, Edward. *A Dark and Bloody Ground*. College Station, TX: Texas A&M University Press, 2003.

———. *Nothing Less Than Full Victory*. Annapolis: Naval Institute Press, 2007.

Morriss, Mack. "The Huertgen Forest." *Yank Magazine*, January 5, 1945.

Munoz, Antonio. *Forgotten Legions: Obscure Combat Formations of the Waffen-SS*. New York: Axis Europa, 1991.

Nash, Douglas. *Victory Was Beyond Their Grasp: With the 272nd Volks-Grenadier Division from the Hürtgen Forest to the Heart of the Reich*. Bedford, PA: Aberjona Press, 2008.

Neill, George. *Infantry Soldier: Holding the Line at the Battle of the Bulge*. Norman, OK: University of Oklahoma Press, 2000.

Neufeldt, Hans-Joachim, Jurgen Huck, and Georg Tessin. *Zur Geschichte der Ornungspolizei, 1936–1945*. Koblenz, Germany: 1957.

Novick, Peter. *The Holocaust in American Life*. New York: Houghton Mifflin, 2000.

Orden, David, Robert Paarlberg, and Terry Roe. *Policy Reform in American Agriculture: Analysis and Prognosis*. Chicago: The University of Chicago Press, 1999.

Overy, Richard. *The Bombing War*. London: Penguin Books, 2014.

Paillat, Claude. *Le Monde Sans la France, 1944–1945: Le Prix de la Liberté*. Paris: Robert Laffont, 1991.

Parker, Edwin. *Memoirs of Edwin P. Parker*. Durham, NC: 78th Division Veterans Association, 1976.

Perényi, Eleanor. *More Was Lost*. New York: New York Review Books, 2016. Originally published by Little, Brown and Company, 1946.

Pergrin, David. *First Across the Rhine: The 291st Engineer Combat Battalion in France, Belgium, and Germany*. Saint Paul, MN: Zenith, 2006.

Pogue, Forrest. *Pogue's War: Diaries of a WWII Combat Historian*. Lexington, KY: University Press of Kentucky, 2006.

Pyle, Ernie. *Brave Men*. New York: Grosset & Dunlap, 1944.

Rawson, Andrew. *Remagen Bridge*. South Yorkshire, UK: Pen & Sword Books, 2004.

Rein, Leonid. "Untermenschen in SS Uniforms: 30th Waffen-Grenadier Division of Waffen SS." *Journal of Slavic Military Studies* 30 (2007): 329–345.

Reuchet, Jean. *Le Desarroi, Le Souffrance, L'espoir "vecu" par les Combattants de la Resistance de Haute-Saône*. Paris: Edition Crimee, 1996.

———. "Note de Jean Reuchet, President de la Federation des Resistants de Haute-Saône." In *Lutte Armee et Maquis: La Resistance et les Francais*, edited by Francois Marcot, 495–499. Besançon et Paris: Annales littéraires de l'Université de Franche-Comté, 1996.

Rothschild, Joseph. *East Central Europe Between the Two World Wars*. Seattle: University of Washington Press, 1974.

Schnatz, Helmut. *Der Luftengriff auf Swinemünde*. Munich: Herbig Verlagsbuchhandlung, 2004.

Sevareid, Eric. *Not So Wild a Dream*. New York: Knopf, 1946. Republished by Atheneum, 1976. Reprinted by University of Missouri Press, 1995.

Sharp, Samuel. *Poland: White Eagle on a Red Field*. Cambridge, MA: Harvard University Press, 1953.

Sledge, Eugene. *With the Old Breed.* New York: Random House, 1981.

Smith, Jean Edward. *Eisenhower in War and Peace.* New York: Random House, 2012.

Snyder, Timothy. *Bloodlands: Europe Between Hitler and Stalin.* New York: Basic Books, 2010.

———. *The Reconstruction of Nations.* New Haven: Yale University Press, 2003.

Sorokowski, Andrew Dennis. "The Greek Catholic Parish Clergy in Galicia, 1900–1939." PhD diss., School of Slavonic and East European Studies, University of London, 1991.

Stauter-Halsted, Keely. *The Nation in the Village: The Genesis of Peasant National Identity in Austrian Poland, 1848–1914.* Ithaca, NY: Cornell University Press, 2004.

Stowe, Leland. *They Shall Not Sleep.* New York: Knopf, 1944.

Strong, Russell. *First Over Germany: A History of the 306th Bombardment Group.* Winston-Salem, NC: Hunter Publishing Company, 1982.

Subtelny, Orest. *Ukraine: A History.* 3rd ed. Toronto: University of Toronto Press, 2005.

Sword, Keith, ed. *The Soviet Takeover of the Polish Eastern Provinces, 1939–1941.* London: Macmillan, 1991.

Szasz, Ferenc Morton. *The Day the Sun Rose Twice: The Story of the Trinity Site Nuclear Explosion.* Albuquerque: University of New Mexico Press, 1984.

Thomas, Ward. *The Ethics of Destruction: Norms and Force in International Relations.* Ithaca, NY: Cornell University Press, 2001.

Toland, John. *The Last 100 Days; The Tumultuous and Controversial Story of the Final Days of World War II in Europe.* New York: Random House, 1966.

Toye, Richard. *Churchill's Empire: The World That Made Him and the World He Made.* New York: Henry Holt, 2010.

Tozer, Henry. *A History of Ancient Geography.* Cambridge: Cambridge University Press, 1897.

US Army Division Historical Association. *Lightning, The History of the 78th Infantry Division.* Nashville, TN: The Battery Press, 2000. Originally published by Infantry Journal Press, 1947.

US Army. *Biennial Reports of the Chief of Staff of the United States Army to the Secretary of War.* July 1939–30 June 1945. Washington, DC: US Army Center of Military History, 1996.

———. *Blue Infantrymen: The Combat History of the Third Battalion, 310th Infantry Regiment, Seventy-Eighth "Lightning" Division.* Np, 1946.

———. *Combat Journal: The Story of the Timberwolf Regiment of the 78th Lightning Division in World War II, 1944–1945.* Fulda, Germany: Printed by Parzeller, 1945.

———. *The Story of the 310th Infantry Regiment, 78th Infantry Division, in the War Against Germany, 1942–1945.* Berlin: Druckhaus Templhof, 1946.

Vartier, Jean. "Des Russes Dans Le Maquis Francais." *Les Ecrivains Contemporains,* Octobre–Novembre 1973.

———. *Histoires Secrètes de l'occupation en Zone Interdite (1940–1944).* Paris: Hachette, 1972.

Wallach, Evan. "Drop by Drop: Forgetting the History of Water Torture in U.S. Courts." *Columbia Journal of Transnational Law* 45 (2007): 468–506.

Warner, Philip. *Passchendaele*. South Yorkshire, UK: Pen and Sword, 2005.

Weigley, Russell. *Eisenhower's Lieutenants*. Bloomington, IN: Indiana University Press, 1981.

Wilson, Andrew. *The Ukrainians: Unexpected Nation*. New Haven: Yale University Press, 2009.

Wyman, Mark. *DPs: Europe's Displaced Persons, 1945–1951*. Cranbury, NJ: Associated University Presses, 1989.

Zaloga, Steven. *Remagen 1945: Endgame Against the Third Reich*. Oxford, UK: Osprey, 2006.

INDEX

Page numbers in *italics* indicate illustrations.
The letter "n" after a page number indicates a note.

ABOUT THE AUTHOR

Matt Rohde was raised in Horicon, Wisconsin. Each summer during his college years he returned home to a paid internship as a school janitor, where most of his post-secondary education took place. His first job after graduation was as a daytime bartender in a Milwaukee hotel, followed by several stints when he drove truck and loaded boxes at a cheese factory. He later completed a three-decade career with the federal government as the senior-most US official responsible for multilateral trade policy coordination, including negotiations at the World Trade Organization, serving in the Executive Office of the President through several administrations. Throughout his government tenure as an attorney, analyst, trade negotiator, and advisor to cabinet officials, he was often called upon to give presentations at the State Department's Foreign Service Institute, the FBI Academy, the National Security Agency, and the Central Intelligence Agency. He holds a juris doctor degree and a bachelor of music, and is an accomplished classical pianist.

CPSIA information can be obtained
at www.ICGtesting.com
Printed in the USA
LVOW08s1843040118

561821LV00006B/940/P